ABOUT THE AUTHORS

Patrick Massey has been a member of the Competition Authority since its establishment on 1 October 1991. He graduated from Trinity College Dublin with an honours degree in economics, and subsequently completed a masters degree in economics in 1984. He taught at the National Institute for Higher Education in Limerick from 1980 to 1982 before joining DKM Economic Consultants. From 1989 to 1990 he worked for the New Zealand Treasury as a senior economic analyst. In November 1990 he was appointed to the Fair Trade Commission. He has represented the Authority on the OECD Committee on Competition Law and Policy and the EU Advisory Committee to DG-IV on Restrictive Practices and Dominant Positions. He has written a number of papers on economic policy generally and on competition policy in particular. He is also author *of New Zealand: Market Liberalisation in a Developed Economy*.

Paula O'Hare is a graduate of Trinity College Dublin and Kings Inns. From 1987 to 1993 she practised as a barrister on the Eastern Circuit. She is a co-author of *Company Law in Ireland* (BPP, 1991). Since 1993 she has been the legal adviser to the Competition Authority and has represented it on the OECD Committee on Competition Law and Policy and the EU Advisory Committee to DG-IV.

COMPETITION LAW AND POLICY IN IRELAND

Patrick Massey
Paula O'Hare

Oak Tree Press
Dublin

Oak Tree Press
Merrion Building
Lower Merrion Street
Dublin 2, Ireland

© 1996 Patrick Massey and Paula O'Hare

A catalogue record of this book is
available from the British Library.

ISBN 1-86076-021-X (pb)
ISBN 1-86076-033-3 (hb)

Printed in Ireland by Colour Books Ltd.

FOREWORD

Competition policy in Ireland has traditionally not had the political support it deserves. Yet, a system of effective competition is arguably what Ireland needs most to develop microeconomic performance and thus to reap the potential benefits of the European Single Market and the rapid liberalisation of global trading arrangements. For in order to be truly competitive in international markets, indigenous firms must begin by being competitive at home.

Restrictions on competition, be they the result of anti-competitive behaviour by firms or induced by state controls or monopolistic practices, are inimical to true competitiveness. The harm they do to our economic life is significant. Indeed, competition is to the market economy system what democracy is to the political system. It can be regarded as the concomitant to freedom in political democracy. Under a system of effective competition, consumers and producers can exercise freely their choices in the market without hindrance from inefficient and costly centralised planning or unnecessary state controls.

A system of effective competition is a spur to efficiency and productivity. It ensures that enterprises remain in touch with the needs of consumers. It stimulates innovation, technological development and quality improvements in products and services. It automatically secures structural adjustments through incremental steps and thereby safeguards jobs and welfare over the medium to long term.

In recent years in Ireland, we have become more aware of the importance of competition policy. A Competition Act has reached the statute book supplementing the competition provisions of the Treaty of Rome. In political discourse, it has become more fashionable to recognise the role that competition policy can play. However, if we are to pay more than lip service to competition policy, much more is necessary. More effective enforcement of competition policy is the best guarantee that competition law will be taken seriously by economic operators.

However, the area identified in the book where most improvement is needed is the state-controlled sector. Too many unjustified monopolistic restrictions remain, which inhibit the emergence of genuine competition in energy, transport, telecommunications and health insurance. As a result, the economy generally, and consumers and tax-payers in particular, pay dearly for the inefficiencies, subsidies and excessive prices that result. Not only have successive governments delayed the introduction of meaningful competition in these public-utility areas, but they have often added insult to injury by seeking derogation from highly desirable European laws which would promote liberalisation. Sham arguments are advanced to suggest that these economic areas are not suitable for competition. A protectionist mentality seems to persist in the public service that is at sharp variance with the overall national interest and ultimately is very damaging, even to the state companies that are the object of protection.

The work by Patrick Massey and Paula O'Hare is a most valuable contribution to thinking on competition law and policy in Ireland. It traces some of the most important recent developments in a fast-moving area. It correctly identifies the serious problems of absence of competition in the state-controlled sector.

Greater public awareness of the issues is always the important first stage in achieving meaningful change. Patrick Massey and Paula O'Hare's book admirably informs the reader and increases knowledge of often complex issues in a highly readable text. Competition policy is always at the juncture between economics and law and in this respect too the authors fulfil an important public service by explaining clearly the concepts at issue.

Peter D. Sutherland S.C.

PREFACE

The passing of the Competition Act, 1991 signalled a major re-appraisal of the role of competition policy in Ireland. It indicated a degree of political recognition of the important role that an effective competition policy could play in the promotion of economic welfare. The Competition (Amendment) Act, 1996, which provides for civil and criminal enforcement of the 1991 Act, represents a further step in this process. This reflects a wider re-assessment that has been taking place throughout the world which has seen radical changes in the means by which governments intervene in economic life. The Competition Acts represent an attempt to implement economic policy by legal means. Our aim in writing this book is to provide the reader with an insight into the issues that arise as a consequence. The interaction between law and economics has a long tradition in the US. It is hoped that this book will succeed in promoting an exchange of ideas between the two disciplines in Ireland.

The Competition Acts are to a greater or lesser extent based on two very highly developed systems of competition law. The long title to the Act describes it as being "by analogy with" Articles 85 and 86 of the Treaty of Rome — the EU competition rules — which in turn have their origins in the much older US Sherman Act which dates back to the last century. There are numerous works which describe in great detail the long history of competition law in the US and EU. The present text does not attempt to provide a comprehensive guide to the jurisprudence of either of these regimes. Rather, it seeks to analyse the economic principles underlying competition law. It also recognises that competition law does not work in a vacuum. Government interventions frequently have considerable effects on competition. Thus an analysis of competition policy must also take account of such measures which frequently have been made by way of statute.

The authors would like to express their thanks to Judge John Cooke of the Court of First Instance, Patrick Lyons, Gerard Hogan BL, Frances Ruane, Joseph Durkan, Nuala Butler BL, John Fingleton and Denis Cagney who read drafts of various chapters in the book. Each of them provided us with some useful insights but responsibility for the final content is ours alone. Any views expressed in the book are the responsibility of the authors and do not purport to represent those of the Competition Authority. We would also like to express our thanks to David Givens of Oak Tree Press for his decision to publish the book and for all his help and assistance along the way.

Patrick Massey
Paula O'Hare

CONTENTS

TABLE OF CASES

**Decisions of the Court of Justice and Court of First
Instance**

Commission Decisions

United States Cases

Federal Trade Commission Decisions

British Cases

Australian Cases

New Zealand Cases

COMPETITION AUTHORITY DECISIONS

TABLE OF STATUTES

Statutory Instruments

European Legislation

Foreign Legislation

1

INTRODUCTION

The view that competition is desirable has long been a central tenet of mainstream economic thinking. Over 200 years ago, Adam Smith, generally regarded as the founder of modern economics, wrote in his famous work *The Wealth of Nations* that:

> When the stocks of many rich merchants are turned into the same trade, their natural competition tends to lower its profits; and when there is a like increase of stock in all the different trades carried on in the same society the same competition must produce the same effect in them all (Smith, 1776: 190).

It is true that economists are not the sole advocates of competition. There are also important political arguments for competition, which are outlined below. Nevertheless, the view that competition is beneficial is based, to a considerable extent, on economic theory. Thus any analysis of competition law and policy must begin by considering the basic economic thinking which regards competition as a desirable state of affairs. A basic understanding of economic thinking on competition is also desirable because competition law, in a very real sense, represents an attempt to effect economic policy by legal means. Competition policy has traditionally been neglected in Ireland, but in recent years there has been a growing realisation of its importance, reflected not only in major changes in Irish competition legislation but in calls for a re-examination of the role of State monopolies and various regulatory restrictions on competition. Competition is a positive force for creating jobs and promoting economic growth. Policies that effectively promote competition, including competition law, have a major role to play in generating continued improvements in living standards and overall economic welfare.

The Benefits of Competition

The basic reason for economists being strong advocates of competition is that economic theory indicates that competition will result in higher levels of output and lower prices than would otherwise be the case. Competition also increases consumer welfare by providing consumers with greater choice. It is true that economists' views as to how competition works in practice have changed considerably since 1776 when Adam Smith wrote his book. The study of business firms' behaviour and the effects of competition, or the lack of it, has long been a focus of attention in the United States, where it is known as Industrial Organisation Theory. In Europe it is more commonly referred to as Industrial Economics. It is a branch of economics that has seen, and continues to see, much research and debate, and it has not lacked controversy. Until quite recently, however, it has received relatively little attention in Ireland. This is, perhaps, surprising, given that one of Ireland's most famous economists, Francis Edgeworth, made a major contribution to the theory of how firms behave.

Economists generally regard competition as desirable because it puts pressure on firms to operate at their most efficient level. To lay people the concept of efficiency, with which economists appear possessed, is often seen as entailing a cold ruthless approach with little heed given to the human consequences. This view is, in fact, highly mistaken. To economists the quest for efficiency is about avoiding or reducing waste. In simple terms, in a world in which not all human wants are currently satisfied and the resources available to us are both scarce and finite, even in Ireland it is clear that a significant proportion of the population is not materially well-off, a failure to make the best possible use of resources and avoid waste is unacceptable. Inefficiencies involve costs in the form of lower output and hence fewer employment opportunities and reduced standards of living for the community. As Blinder (1987: 16) observed, "economists have failed to articulate their reasons for worshipping at the shrine of efficiency, in which case we ought to do more missionary work". In a similar vein, Krugman (1994: 76) pointed out that concern about anti-competitive behaviour:

... is not simply a matter of fairness: the efforts of monopolies and cartels to keep prices high distort economic incentives, imposing efficiency losses very similar to those produced by taxation.

In the case of a small open economy such as Ireland's, monopolies in the domestic market impose significant costs on the rest of the community. In a small open economy increased exports are essential to increase output, employment and incomes. A lack of competition in the sheltered sector of the economy can result in increased costs to the traded sector by increasing the cost of the inputs that producers of traded goods purchase from the sheltered sector.[1] Firms in the traded sector, which includes, for example, many types of manufacturing, are exposed to international competition in both domestic and export markets. If such firms must pay higher prices for inputs purchased from the non-traded sector, such as electricity, than their foreign competitors, this puts them at a disadvantage relative to their overseas rivals, thus undermining their ability to compete in export markets and with imported goods in the domestic market. A competitive sheltered sector will result in lower costs to firms in the traded sector, making them more competitive internationally and resulting in greater employment within the economy.

Economic analysis also indicates that firms which are exposed to competitive market forces respond more quickly to changes in economic conditions. If this is the case, it follows that a more competitive economy will adjust faster and better in response to macroeconomic shocks. The argument that competition forces firms to increase efficiency has been restated in more recent work by Porter (1990) who argues that competitive domestic markets are necessary to prepare firms for international competition. For all of these reasons economists would argue that increased competition in the domestic economy will improve prospects for

---

[1] Economists tend to distinguish between business sectors which compete with foreign firms in either the domestic or export markets and those sectors that are not exposed to competition from foreign rivals. Those activities that are not exposed to foreign competition are defined as sheltered or non-traded sectors. Those sectors in which Irish firms compete with foreign-based rivals are referred to as traded or unsheltered sectors.

growth in output and employment, while there is a considerable amount of evidence to support the view that restrictions on competition ultimately harm employment prospects. Thus, far from posing a threat to jobs, competition can have a positive impact on employment.

One does not need to have a blind faith in economists to accept that competition is likely to be beneficial while restrictions on competition will prove to be harmful, since it is easy to identify real-life examples which illustrate this point. Take the case of airline routes considered in Chapter 12. Ten years ago there was virtually no competition on airline services to and from Ireland. Instead, airlines agreed with one another on prices, the number of seats that they would make available on various routes, and a number of other factors. In the mid-1980s competition was introduced on the Dublin–London route. The effect was to lower prices and, not surprisingly, the amount of journeys being made has increased quite considerably, in sharp contrast on both counts to the experience of the years before deregulation. At one time, effectively only building societies provided mortgage loans to individuals wishing to buy a house. The result was a system where loans were rationed leading to waiting lists. Consumers were obliged to keep minimum sums on deposit with the society for some period, to pay the society's legal fees as well as their own, and they were often required to purchase insurance for their house through the society providing them with a loan. That situation has also changed radically in the past 10 years. Now there are far more financial institutions in the market for mortgage loans. The result is that waiting lists are a thing of the past as lenders now have to fight to gain customers. There is a greater range of mortgage services available and tying restrictions for insurance are gone. Employment in building societies has not fallen as a result of this increased competition — it has risen.

Technically, it is illegal for anyone to operate bus services in competition with the subsidiaries of the State-owned CIE. In fact, many private bus operators do operate regular services between Dublin and various other parts of the country. The large numbers of people availing of such services is a clear indication that such operators are providing services for which there is a demand, in many cases at a lower price than the one provided by the State-owned firms. The taxi industry in Ireland is a clear example of the problems posed by lack of competition caused by restrictions on entry. Such restrictions mean that taxi services are inadequate, particularly in Dublin as most inhabitants of the capital are aware. Taxi licences in the city were reportedly changing hands for as much as £70,000 in 1995, a clear indication that there are monopoly rents[2] being earned in the industry.[3]

It is possible to think of numerous other examples of benefits accruing from competition in particular business sectors. At a macroeconomic level, research suggests that the aggregate benefits of increased competition in the economy could be considerable. Empirical research for the US and UK suggests that the cost of anti-competitive behaviour could represent between 1 and 2 per cent of total national income, which in Ireland's case would amount to at least £300 million. If anything, the costs of such restrictions in Ireland could well be even higher given the existence of State monopolies in many sectors and the fact that, in the past, competition law has not been forcefully applied in many areas of the economy.

Political Arguments for Competition

While competition is frequently favoured on economic grounds, there are also strong political arguments in its favour. Competition is considered to be desirable because it decentralises and disperses power. In addition, in a competitive system the question of the allocation of resources is decided by market forces and not by the whim of politicians and bureaucrats. A competitive system is also believed to provide greater freedom of opportunity as, in such a system, restrictions on entry to occupations or trades are regarded as unacceptable. Scherer and Ross (1990) argue that limiting the power of government and private individuals and firms to

---

[2]   Economists use the term "rents" to describe income accruing to suppliers which is in excess of what would accrue in a competitive market.

[3]   In Chapter 12 we argue for the abolition of such restrictions. In early 1996, Dublin Corporation announced proposals to issue 200 new taxi licences. Following protests by taxi drivers, the number of new licences was reduced to 100.

exercise control over people's lives was a fundamental objective of those who drafted the US Constitution. Such views are reflected in the judgments of the US courts in competition cases.

> Antitrust laws in general, and the Sherman Act, in particular, are the Magna Carta of free enterprise. They are as important to the preservation of economic freedom and our free-enterprise system as the Bill of Rights is to the protection of our fundamental personal freedoms. And the freedom guaranteed each and every business, no matter how small, is the freedom to compete — to assert with vigour, imagination, devotion, and ingenuity whatever economic muscle it can muster.[4]

Economic concentration enables large firms to wield significant political power. As Adams and Brock (1994: 262) observe:

> In the real world, corporate giants are able to mobilize the vast political resources at their command — executives and union leaders, suppliers and subcontractors, governors and mayors, senators and representatives, Republicans and Democrats — in order to capture public policy and to subvert it for their own antisocial ends.

Thus competition policy is necessary not only to prevent undue concentration of economic power, but also to guard against excessive concentration of political power. As Adam Smith pointed out long ago:

> . . . the cruellest of our revenue laws, I will venture to affirm, are mild and gentle, in comparison to some of those which the clamour of our merchants and manufacturers have extorted from the legislature for the support of their own absurd and oppressive monopolies (Smith, 1776: 612).

In an Irish context, the Beef Tribunal raised some questions as to the extent to which large firms may exert influence over Government policy.

Clarke (1985: 259) has argued that policy in the UK has never reflected the same pro-competitive approach as that found in the US.

---

[4]   *United States* v. *Topco Associates Inc.*, 405 US 596 (1972).

In terms of philosophy, the UK approach stops short of the view that a competitive economy is desirable *per se*: either because it produces socially desirable economic conduct and performance, or, *a fortiori*, because it is desirable as an end in itself. The view that a competitive economy might be an end in itself is an important idea in some areas of US policy but has never figured strongly in the UK.

Competition policy in Ireland traditionally has been more akin to that of the UK than the US. It may be that politicians and bureaucrats, unlike the US founding fathers, prefer to exercise more direct control over how resources should be allocated, at least in some cases. More fundamentally, it may reflect the fact that politicians in Ireland, while frequently paying lip service to the idea of promoting competition, simply do not believe that competitive markets will have beneficial results.

Political distrust of competition is evidenced by the fact that, in a very large number of sectors of the Irish economy, State intervention has restricted competition to a very considerable extent, to the benefit of both public and private-sector firms, but to the serious detriment of consumers. Protecting many State companies against competition resulted, according to the National Planning Board (1984: 113), in a situation in which "consumers are dissatisfied but have no alternative source of supply and no effective redress if the service provided is unsatisfactory". The reluctance to embrace competitive markets can also be seen in the fact that successive Governments have tended to adopt a very cautious approach to competition legislation. This has occurred in spite of the fact that over the years successive official reports have highlighted the need for an effective competition policy. Thus, in 1953, when competition law was first introduced, its application was confined to goods and their distribution. Subsequent amendments added various categories of services but it was not until 1987 that virtually all sectors of the economy could be said, at least theoretically, to be subject to the legislation. Over the years numerous reports[5] pointed to the inadequacies of the legislation and a more effective prohibition-based system of competition law, first recommended in 1977, was not

---

5 See Chapter 5.

introduced until 1991. Even then it was decided that enforcement of the legislation would be left to the private sector. The shortcomings of this approach were subsequently recognised and this has led to the introduction of amending legislation which has given the Competition Authority responsibility for enforcement.

While favouring competition in principle, politicians are often opposed to it in specific cases because competition is often wrongly perceived to threaten jobs. Such ideas are not new. In 1829, for example, Martin Van Buren, then Governor of New York, wrote to US President Andrew Jackson calling for the canals to be protected against competition from the railways.

> If canal boats are supplanted by railroads, serious unemployment will result. Captains, cooks, drivers, innkeepers, repairmen and lock tenders will be left without means of livelihood, not to mention the numerous farmers now employed in growing hay for horses (*Business and Finance*, 17 June 1993).

The reality, as already stated, is that competition increases employment in the economy as a whole, although it may lead to some job losses in inefficient firms which have in the past been protected against competition. The view that competition will harm employment has been advanced with respect to the ESB and Telecom. In OECD countries with the longest experience of telecom liberalisation, jobs in new entrants have offset those lost in incumbent firms (OECD, 1995). Fitzgerald and Johnston (1995) report that simulations using the ESRI medium-term model suggest that the initial impact of competition in the energy utilities would be to reduce employment by about 3,000 in the first year but that the loss of employment in utilities would be offset by increased employment in other sectors in future years. Fingleton (1995) argues that a more effective competition policy would reduce unemployment in Ireland.

Politicians may also hold the view that competition will have other undesirable consequences. In particular, opposition to competition may reflect concerns about the distributional consequences of market forces. There is no doubt that market forces will produce a highly unequal distribution of income. Adopting market-oriented economic policies ought not, and indeed should not, involve an acceptance of the personal income distribution which the market is likely to throw up. The way to tackle such problems is to have a rational and efficient tax/welfare system. A discussion of the essential elements of such a system is outside the scope of the present text.[6] For the moment, however, it is important to recognise that restrictions on competition represent a highly inefficient means of securing a fairer distribution of income.

Non-Economic Views of Competition

Non-economists' views on competition frequently differ considerably from those of economists. Scherer and Ross (1990), for example, point out how business people are apt to view competition as a conscious striving for patronage on the basis of price and, perhaps, non-price factors. They describe this latter sort of behaviour as rivalry, the essence of which is a striving for potentially incompatible positions, combined with a recognition by the parties involved of the incompatibility of their positions. Such a view is reflected, for example, in the majority judgment of the Australian High Court in *Queensland Wire*:

> Competition by its nature is deliberate and ruthless. Competitors jockey for sales, the more effective competitors injuring the less effective by taking sales away. Competitors almost always try to "injure" each other in this way . . . these injuries are the inevitable result of the competition section 46 [of the Australian Trade Practices Act] is designed to foster.[7]

Such behaviour is not equivalent to the economist's definition of pure competition, where there are so many producers that no individual seller's decision can have any perceptible effect on the market. This is not to say that economists totally discount the concept of rivalry. Adam Smith essentially saw competition as a rivalrous process and Ellig (1992) points out that market rivalry theories were widely held up to the 1920s. Even today market rivalry theories are espoused by some exponents of both

---

[6] Guiomard (1995) contains a useful discussion, readily accessible to non-economists, on combining competition with policies to reduce inequity.

[7] *Queensland Wire Industries Pty. Ltd.* v. *The Broken Hill Proprietary Company Limited,* (1989) ATPR 20-925.

the Austrian and Chicago schools of economic thought.

Similarly, while economists support competition as a means of enhancing efficiency, others, including lawyers and politicians, see competition as a means of promoting "fairness". The concept of "fair competition" can be quite different from that favoured by economists. The concept of fairness is an extremely subjective one meaning different things to different people. Should small firms, for example, be helped to compete against larger ones, even though they may be less efficient at producing what consumers want? After all, as Korah (1990a) points out, small firms that are efficient should not need special treatment. Aid to those that are not imposes costs and encourages the growth of inefficient firms. Inefficiencies involve the waste of scarce resources, which would not appear to be desirable from society's point of view. To take another example, a firm that has undertaken a substantial investment to develop or promote a particular new product may thereby establish a monopoly position for itself. Korah (1990a) has argued that the European Commission, which is responsible for the enforcement of EU competition law, has, on occasion, taken a hostile approach to firms in such circumstances. If the firm is not allowed to enjoy some benefit for having undertaken the risky investment, this might simply deter the development of new products, a result that would not appear to be in society's interests.

In many instances where businesses and their employees complain about "unfair competition" they are really objecting to legitimate competitive behaviour. Almost anything that gives a competitor an advantage can be regarded as unfair. The ban on below-cost selling in the Groceries Order reflects judgments about fairness rather than competition considerations. (This point is returned to in Chapter 5). In certain circumstances it may be considered that, although they impose a cost on society, measures designed to promote greater fairness are justified. This is an issue on which economists, as such, can offer limited guidance. Certainly they can attempt to highlight the costs and trade-offs implicit in such measures. It is very rare, however, that the actual trade-off involved is considered. In a small open economy like Ireland the additional cost of inefficiencies imposed on the traded sector simply serves to undermine jobs in that sector. Measures designed to be "fair" to one group may have some extremely unfair effects on others. For example, protecting jobs in one firm may lead to job losses elsewhere.

While this book argues that competition is generally beneficial, the authors would accept that, on occasion, competition can produce undesirable outcomes. Bailey (1986), for example, describes how, during the latter part of the last century, unrestricted access to the town gas industry in UK cities was sometimes characterised by firms connecting their pipes to those of their rivals, effectively selling gas which they were stealing from their competitors. In a small number of cases attempts to link in to gas pipes owned by competitors resulted in fatal accidents. Such episodes prompted the Government of the day to intervene to prevent such no-holds-barred competition. In general, however, it remains true that competition is beneficial while restrictions on competition, for which all sorts of plausible justifications are frequently advanced, are likely to prove harmful.

The Plan of the Book

The text may be divided into three broad parts. The first of these outlines the theoretical and factual background for competition law and policy in Ireland. Thus in Chapter 2 economic thinking on competition is outlined briefly. Chapter 3 then provides a brief overview picture of the Irish economy and its component parts. This is followed in Chapter 4 by a description of competition law as it operates in the United States and the EU.[8] The historic development of competition law in Ireland is outlined in Chapter 5 which marks the transition to the second part of the book, which deals with current competition legislation in Ireland. Although the Competition Act, 1991 represented a radical departure in Irish competition law, some elements of the former legislation remain in place and thus the discussion in Chapter 5 deals with matters which are still of practical interest.

Chapter 6 describes the main elements of the 1991 Act and the 1996 amending Act. The two key features of the 1991 Act — the

---

[8] The US is generally recognised as the home of modern competition law. US law influenced the basic EU competition rules on which the Irish Competition Act, 1991 is based.

prohibition on anti-competitive arrangements contained in Section 4 and the prohibition on abuse of a dominant position in Section 5 — are discussed at length in Chapters 7 and 8. An analysis of the legislation and its impact is offered in Chapter 9. This part of the book concludes with an analysis of the treatment of mergers under Irish law in Chapter 10.

The third part of the book considers some wider policy issues, particularly the interaction between competition legislation and other legislative provisions. Chapter 11 looks at intellectual property and its treatment under competition law. In Chapter 12 the interaction between regulation and competition in various sectors of the economy is considered, while Chapter 13 deals with the difficult issues involved in public-utility industries. Some conclusions are offered in Chapter 14.

2

THE CASE FOR COMPETITION

Chapter 1 noted that the view that competition is beneficial is based, to a considerable extent, on economic theory. The present chapter sets out the economic arguments in favour of competition. The basic starting model is the concept of pure competition which is the yardstick against which the performance of other types of market structure are measured. The chapter describes how economic theory regarding competition has evolved over the past 50 years and notes that there are some disagreements among economists as to what exactly constitutes anti-competitive behaviour. The main types of behaviour which are of interest from a competition perspective are then considered.

Pure Competition — The Basic Model

Orthodox economic thinking on competition takes as its starting point the model of pure competition. For a market[1] to be purely competitive it must have a large number of buyers and sellers of a homogenous product, with free entry and exit.[2] Homogenous products are products which consumers regard as identical or perfect substitutes for one another so that they have no preference for one producer's product over that of another. Because it is assumed

---

[1] The concept of a market lies at the heart of economic thinking about competition. The question of identifying the appropriate market is also fundamental in evaluating whether or not competition has been impaired by a particular practice and is therefore vital in many competition law cases. The famous neo-classical economist Alfred Marshall defined a market as "a specific physical or geographic location in which trade takes place, and in which at any point in time there is only one price at which any commodity is exchanged". The question of market definition is considered in Chapter 8.

[2] Pure competition is not the same as perfect competition since the latter also requires that all market participants have perfect knowledge of all market circumstances.

that there are large numbers of buyers and sellers, no individual buyer or seller can hope to influence market price, since the effect of any variation in the amount they buy or sell on the market price will be minuscule. Any attempt by an individual producer to raise the price of its product will cause consumers to switch to other suppliers' products, so there is no scope for anyone to charge more than the competitive price. The Dublin Corporation Fruit and Vegetable market is probably a good example of a market that approximates closely to the purely competitive model. It has large numbers of buyers and sellers and there are various categories of homogenous products since, for example, consumers generally will not prefer one seller's potatoes to those of any other. In the absence of collusion among sellers, no individual buyer or seller can affect the market price.

Orthodox theory assumes that firms strive to maximise profits. In a purely competitive market, firms will earn only normal profits — that is, a return equivalent to what they might earn by investing their capital elsewhere. Such normal profit, therefore, represents the minimum return necessary to keep a producer in the market, and economists regard it as an essential cost of production. If at a particular price supernormal or economic profits were generated for producers, such profits would attract new firms into the market. The extra output being supplied would drive down the price, since otherwise this additional output would remain unsold, until all the firms in the industry were again earning only normal profits. In such a market, competitive pressures would also force all firms to maximise operational efficiency in order to reduce costs to a minimum.

Economic theory suggests three possible ways in which competition will lead to increased efficiency:

• Technical or productive efficiency arises because competition forces firms to produce at the least possible cost the goods and services that they sell to consumers.

• Allocative efficiency arises where the resources used to produce goods and services are allocated to their most productive use as firms which can use resources more productively bid them away from others. Combined with the pressure on firms to produce at the lowest possible cost, this will result in prices being set in closer relation to their cost of production so that, from society's point of view, resources will be channelled to their most productive use.

- Dynamic efficiency arises because competition encourages firms to adapt in response to changing circumstances, constantly to improve their products and to strive for technological improvements and other means of reducing costs.

The Cost of Monopolies

The opposite extreme to a purely competitive market is one having a single producer, a monopoly. While the competitive firm can have no effect on price by varying output, the same is not true of the monopolist. If the monopolist increases output, the additional output can only be sold if the price of the product falls. It is not just the price of the extra output that will be lower, all of the monopolist's output must be sold at the new lower price, unless the market is segmented in such a way that the monopolist is able to discriminate between customers. If even a modest increase in sales would require a significant fall in price (i.e., demand is relatively inelastic), then increasing output would not be attractive because the gain from selling some additional output at the lower price would be more than offset by the loss of revenue arising from having to reduce the price of the existing output. Looked at another way, if demand is relatively inelastic, a substantial rise in price would result in only a relatively small drop in sales. It would be attractive for the monopolist to produce less and sell at a higher price as such a strategy would result in higher (supernormal) profits. Consequently, orthodox economic theory predicts that under monopoly price will always be higher, and output lower, than under competition.[3]

The fact that monopolists earn supernormal profits may not be a major problem. After all, the owners and shareholders of monopoly

---

[3] Such a conclusion assumes that the costs of production are the same under both competition and monopoly — that is, there are no economies of scale or scope. This may not be the case, a point that is considered below.

firms which, in a modern economy, include life insurance and
pension funds, would share in the monopoly profits, so that such
profits may be widely distributed and not necessarily confined to
a small élite. If the existence of monopolies simply means that income is redistributed from one group in society to another, then
the issue is largely one of the appropriateness or otherwise of
such a redistribution, which is a political choice. The real problem
with monopolies is their effect on overall economic welfare. Consumers will frequently be prepared to pay more for a particular
product than its current price. The difference between what they
would be prepared to pay and what they actually pay is referred
to as the consumer surplus. Even though prices under a monopoly
will be higher than in a competitive market, many consumers will
still buy the product at the higher monopoly price. The monopolist
has managed to capture some of the surplus that those consumers
previously enjoyed at the competitive price. There has been a redistribution from consumers to the monopolist. However, some
consumers will not be prepared to pay the monopoly price. All
those consumers who would pay more than the competitive price,
but not as much as the monopoly price, also experience a loss of
consumer surplus which does not go to the monopolist — since
these consumers choose not to buy the product — but instead is lost
to society. Economists refer to this loss as a dead-weight loss and it
measures the loss in allocative efficiency caused by the monopoly.

A second difficulty with a monopoly is that, unlike a firm in a
competitive market, it will not be forced out of business if it does
not operate at its most efficient level. As Hicks (1935: 8) so aptly
put it: "The best of all monopoly profits is a quiet life." This has
caused some economists to argue that there is less incentive for
monopolists to operate efficiently. This efficiency loss is known as
X-inefficiency. The concept of X-inefficiency was first identified by
Leibenstein (1966). It is seen by many economists as constituting
a further cost of a monopoly, as it implies that the monopolist's
costs will be higher than those of the firm operating under pure
competition.

Posner (1975) argues that, because a monopolist can expect to
enjoy monopoly profits, there is an incentive for firms to secure
and maintain a monopoly by persuading the government to pass

legislation preventing entry to the market by other firms. Experience in many countries indicates that legislation is one of the principal ways of creating and sustaining a monopoly, a point that is considered further in Chapter 12. Monopoly profits make it attractive for the firm to hire economists, lawyers, accountants and lobbyists to persuade government to pass such legislation or to retain it where it already exists, a process known as "rent seeking". It entails a further cost to society, since the resources engaged in such activity could have been more productively used elsewhere. The extent of this cost is the value of the output that such resources could have produced in such alternative employment. The Culliton Report on industrial policy found that "rent-seeking" behaviour was prevalent in the Irish economy (Culliton, 1992).

In sum, economists believe that monopolies involve substantial losses to society in the form of reduced efficiency and other costs. Such costs lead to lower levels of output and employment in the economy overall. It is for this reason that economists have traditionally taken a hostile approach to monopolies. The point was made forcefully by the great classical economist John Stuart Mill, who was particularly critical of advocates of monopolies, observing that:

> They forget that whatever competition is not, monopoly is; and that monopoly in all its forms, is the taxation of the industrious for the support of indolence, if not of plunder (Mill, 1848: 141).

Other Common Forms of Market Structure

It is clear that many markets do not satisfy the requirements of pure competition so that the contrast between the two polar extreme cases of pure competition and pure monopoly is somewhat artificial. Alternative models of industrial structure exist in economics, such as the oligopoly model devised by Cournot (1838) and developed by Bertrand (1883) and Edgeworth (1897). Oligopoly models of industrial structure and behaviour are generally regarded as the closest approximation to conditions in many real-world markets. An oligopolistic market is characterised as having a relatively small number of producers. Firms in such circumstances recognise that any action by them will have an impact on market price and provoke a response by the other firms in the market.

The recognition by firms of their interdependence provides them with an incentive to come together and agree not to compete, in effect to form a cartel. Even where firms in oligopolistic markets act independently, their behaviour will still be heavily influenced by expectations concerning the behaviour of other firms in the market. Chamberlin (1933) argued that if firms recognised their mutual interdependence and their interests in high prices, then price would tend to be set at the monopoly level, since this would maximise industry profits. In effect, monopoly pricing could occur without explicit collusion if the industry structure were conducive to such developments. The smaller the number of firms in an industry, the greater the recognition by them of their mutual interdependence and the greater the likelihood of the industry price being set at the monopoly level without any formal collusion. The UK Monopolies and Mergers Commission (MMC) report on Parallel Pricing, for example, stressed that it was very difficult to get oligopolistic firms that are set on a co-ordinated course of action to compete if they do not want to (MMC, 1973). According to Rees (1993), the only feasible requirement for "competitive" behaviour in oligopoly markets is that it be non-co-operative.

The behaviour of firms in oligopolistic markets will depend on their expectations regarding the behaviour of their rivals. Clearly, firms can hold widely differing views as to how their rivals will behave so that oligopolistic markets can produce a wide range of outcomes. Outcomes consistent with both extremes of pure competition or monopoly and various intermediate points along this spectrum are possible, depending upon the level of co-operatio 1 between firms and their expectations concerning the behaviour of their rivals. It is recognised, therefore, that intense competition may exist in a market with only a small number of firms. Nevertheless, collusive behaviour is a constant threat in oligopolistic markets. As Cable (1994) observed, oligopoly theory remains a cornerstone in modern analyses of market behaviour despite major theoretical developments over the past 20 years.

A further development in economic theory concerning industry structure and performance was Chamberlin's theory of monopolistic or imperfect competition. Essentially, this refers to a situation where there is a large number of producers of differentiated products — that is, products which are not regarded by consumers as close substitutes for one another although they are substitutable to some degree. The differentiated nature of the products means that monopolistic competitors enjoy a degree of market power. In such markets competition occurs not only in respect of price but on quality, labelling, advertising and sales promotion. Intensive advertising campaigns by individual producers, designed to create a distinctive image for their product in an attempt to differentiate it from those of their competitors, are a characteristic feature of such markets. One need only think of television advertising for what are essentially commodity goods — for example, washing powder or sliced white bread — which stresses that the product being promoted is, in some sense, superior to the alternatives. Non-price competition is important in such markets. It has been argued that such non-price competition may involve excessive product diversification and advertising which is wasteful. Others argue that greater product diversification benefits consumers by providing a greater choice and variety of goods.

There has been considerable research into developing models capable of forecasting firms' behaviour under oligopolistic market conditions. Recent developments in this area have involved models based on game theory. According to Cable (1994: 2), "the application of game theory has made industrial economics one of the most exciting and vigorous areas of economics since the mid-1970s". Such models emphasise the importance of conduct in contrast to the traditional approach which focused more on structure. Game theory views firms in oligopolistic markets as effectively being in a position similar to that of players in a game. The individual firm will attempt to choose a strategy which maximises its payoff or profit from the game. At the same time, the firm is aware that its profits will depend on the strategies adopted by its rivals. The stable solution to such games arises when neither of the players (assuming there are two) has an incentive to alter its strategy. Such a solution is called a Nash equilibrium. Many of the models used in game theory are highly complex and encompass variable sum payoffs — that is, total industry profits vary depending on the strategies of the individual firms. The strategic options available to the firms in such models may be quite limited or may be infinite in number.[4]

Criticism of the Orthodox Model

It has been argued that since the assumption that firms are profit maximisers is an essential element underlying economists' perceptions about how firms behave, if this is invalid then it may undermine the entire argument about the effects of competition and monopoly. Firms may have a variety of other objectives such as maximising revenue or market share or achieving some target market share. While recognising that there are many valid grounds for questioning the assumption that firms are profit maximisers, Scherer and Ross (1990) argue that empirical results indicate that it provides a close enough approximation to the way firms behave in practice for its predictions to be valid. A second criticism advanced is based on the fact that, in some industries, economies of scale are such that the most efficient (lowest cost) level of output is achieved by a single firm — a monopoly. Such industries are said to be natural monopolies. The electricity grid is a prime example of a natural monopoly. It is therefore argued that, in such circumstances, the monopolist's lower costs of production mean that the monopoly price would be lower than the competitive

---

[4]   An example of game theory is the so-called prisoners' dilemma. This relates to the position faced by two suspects arrested by the police for a particular crime, say armed robbery, and being questioned separately. Each knows that if they both do not confess the police will only be able to make a lesser charge, of possession of stolen goods, stick, carrying a relatively light sentence of, say, one year. Each individual knows that if they confess, turn State's evidence and their accomplice does not, they can avoid a custodial sentence, while the accomplice will receive a sentence of, say, 10 years. If they do not confess and their accomplice does, they face the prospect of a lengthy prison sentence themselves. If both confess and the authorities, therefore, do not need them to give evidence against their accomplice, they will both receive a sentence of, say, six years. The optimal strategy for each of the individuals acting alone is to confess, even though this leaves them worse off than if both remained silent. Such a paradoxical outcome frequently arises in many oligopoly game models. If the game is played repeatedly, however, the players are likely to adapt their behaviour and act in a collusive fashion. Rees (1993) employs game theory to show that the MMC conclusion, that duopolists in the UK salt market had "seriously restrained price competition", was correct.

one. It is certainly true that some industries do constitute genuine natural monopolies. Experience, however, shows that only a relatively small number of industries come into this category.[5]

The fact that it is impossible or undesirable to satisfy all the requirements of the purely competitive model in the real world, whether because of economies of scale or other factors, raises questions about the appropriate objective of policy in such circumstances. This has given rise to what has become known as the theory of second best, which states that when competition does not exist in all areas, encouraging the maximum possible conformity to the rules of competition may not be the best solution. Scherer and Ross (1990: 37) conclude that:

> Because it indicates that maintaining competitive pricing whenever possible is not necessarily optimal, but offers little clear guidance toward improved policies in the absence of information seldom if ever attainable, the theory of second best is a counsel of despair.

Consequently, they argue that a third best approach might be to adopt the policy that yields the most favourable result in terms of resource allocation and eliminating avoidable monopoly power is about as likely to achieve this as is encouraging monopoly where it did not previously exist, so that promoting competition remains the most desirable option.

Doubts concerning the pure competition model's usefulness as a policy guide led to the development in the 1930s of the concept of "workable competition" pioneered by Clarke (1940). Clarke argued that some departures from the pure competition norm were not as harmful as commonly presumed and sought instead to formulate certain minimal criteria for judging the workability of competition. Clarke's work gave rise to a multitude of articles which essentially identified a series of criteria which could be used to assess the degree of competition in particular markets. Such criteria may be divided into three broad categories — structure, conduct, performance. The concentration on structure, conduct and performance reflected previous work

---

[5] The issues involved in dealing with natural monopolies such as exist in electricity and telecommunications are considered in Chapter 13.

by Mason (1939) which gave rise to the Structure-Conduct-Performance model associated with the so-called "Harvard School" of economists. According to this model, an industry's performance depends on the conduct of the firms in the industry and this in turn depends on its structure, as characterised by the number and size of buyers and sellers, the degree of product differentiation, the presence or absence of entry barriers, the degree of vertical integration and the firm's product diversification. The traditional view was that if policy ensured that market structures were competitive, conduct and performance could largely be left to take care of themselves. Correspondingly, if an industry did not have a competitive structure, competition was likely to be impaired. Stigler, who was later to adopt a rather different view, wrote in the early 1950s that:

> An industry which does not have a competitive structure will not have a competitive behaviour (Stigler, 1952: 167).

Views on competition evolved during the 1960s and 1970s and concern shifted away from purely structural questions. If, as empirical research appeared to suggest, firms in concentrated markets enjoyed above normal profits, why did these not lead to new entry which would force prices and profits down, as predicted by orthodox theory? The evidence that supernormal profits seemed to persist in some sectors clearly ran contrary to expectations. The most plausible explanation advanced for the failure of firms to enter the market was that there were barriers which prevented such entry.

Entry Barriers

Much of the pioneering work on identifying entry barriers was undertaken by Bain (1956). Entry barriers are no longer considered to be as pervasive as they once were, and indeed features which were in the past considered to constitute a barrier to entry are no longer regarded in this light. Literally defined, a barrier to entry would amount to anything that prevented immediate entry. Such a definition is regarded as inappropriate since it would mean that the cost of recruiting staff or building a plant could be regarded as an entry barrier. In considering barriers to entry, economists are concerned purely with factors that enable firms to enjoy supernormal profits in the long-run without attracting new entrants — that is, long-run barriers to entry. Geroski (1994: 136) defines barriers to entry as "any structural, durable feature of a market or its infrastructure that inhibits the ability of outsiders to enter and compete with established insiders". Entry barriers allow incumbents to earn persistently high profits, even in the long run, and, as Geroski observes, the size of such profits is an indication of the height of entry barriers.

The existence of large capital requirements, of itself, does not constitute an entry barrier, as long as there are well-developed capital markets which ensure that viable projects can be financed. It is recognised, however, that if the threat of retaliation by incumbent firms, and the risk of not being able to recover the capital outlay in the event that entry is unsuccessful, are both high, then the need for large-scale investment may deter new entrants. Similarly, economies of scale are no longer seen as problematic. The main concern is with practices that are seen to create "artificial" entry barriers. In some instances, the first firm to launch a new product may gain some advantage, called the first-mover advantage. The first mover may face lower marketing costs because it faced no rivals, whereas subsequent entrants must compete with the first. If the presence of the incumbent raises the costs of other would-be entrants, then the first firm will enjoy a permanent advantage, which may create a permanent long-run barrier to entry. Schmalensee (1982) cites the example of the first firm which gains familiarity among customers who are then reluctant to switch. For example, its brand name may become the generic name by which consumers identify the product. (Vaseline is a case in point). It is argued that it would be very difficult for a new entrant to enter the market when consumers use the brand name of the other product when asking for it in their local shop.[6] Burke et al. (1991) report that there are numerous examples in the literature of advertising expenditure as a form of entry barrier.

---

[6] This may in fact cut both ways since, if the first mover's brand name becomes the generic name for the product, consumers may in fact accept the rival product on the basis that they are homogenous products.

Alternative Economic Views of Competition

The Chicago School

An alternative to the traditional structure-conduct-performance viewpoint is the price theory approach which focuses more on the economic incentives facing individuals and firms in order to explain business behaviour. Such models, which rely heavily on micro-economic theory to help explain structure, conduct and performance within a particular industry, are associated with the work of authors such as Director, Bowman, Bork, McGee, Posner and Stigler. Proponents of this approach have come to be known as the "Chicago school". Chicagoans tend to consider allocative efficiency as the most important goal of competition policy. In contrast, the Harvard school continues to adopt a more broadly based view of the objectives of competition policy so that, although they regard allocative efficiency as important, they also consider income distribution and the dispersion of aggregate concentration as valid goals (see, for example, Scherer and Ross, 1990; Shepherd, 1994; and Adams and Brock, 1994).

Over 50 years ago, Nobel laureate Ronald Coase (1937) argued that a firm and a market are alternative means of organising economic activity. In other words, firms can choose between integrating vertically and handling all aspects of production and distribution of their products internally or they can concentrate on one stage in the process and conclude agreements with other firms to handle other stages. A firm can choose to manufacture its own raw materials, operate its own transport fleet and own a chain of retail outlets for selling its products, or it can simply manufacture the products and purchase materials from others and contract with others to arrange distribution. The option chosen will depend on the relative costs of the two alternatives.

The Chicago approach criticised the theoretical shortcomings of the traditional Harvard approach. Posner (1979), for example, claimed that the traditionalists had discarded the basic tools of economic theory. Proponents of the Chicago approach tend to take a more benign view of industry structure and vertical restraints than do those associated with the Harvard or structuralist school, emphasising the benefits of economies of scale and superior efficiency accruing to larger firms in concluding that highly concentrated market power is not necessarily a problem:

> I doubt that there is any significant output restriction prob-
> lem arising from the concentration of any industry (Bork,
> 1978: 178).

Bork argued that even if there were some persistent correlation
between concentration and profitability, as many studies have
shown, such a correlation could be explained by harmless factors.
Similarly, Chicagoans regard many vertical restraints as efficiency-
enhancing measures designed to reduce transaction costs. According to the Chicago viewpoint, monopoly profits cannot be sustained as new entry would force prices down. It questions the very
existence of artificial entry barriers and is only concerned with
barriers that serve to keep out firms which are equally as efficient
as the incumbents.

The Chicago view was originally regarded "as little more than
a lunatic fringe" (Posner, 1979). It has certainly altered the way
many economists and lawyers think about economic policy and
the appointment of many prominent Chicagoans to the bench by
the Reagan and Bush administrations means that this viewpoint has had a significant impact on antitrust practice in the
United States. Ellig (1992), however, highlights some serious
shortcomings in the theoretical foundations of the Chicago
approach:

> Since the Chicago view tries to blend contradictory notions of
> competition, it should come as no surprise that it has failed to
> produce a logically consistent theory of economic efficiency.
> Shepherd performed the task of identifying the logical inconsis-
> tencies, but he did not explicitly examine the underlying rea-
> sons for their existence. The inconsistencies result from Chi-
> cago theorists' attempts to mix two incompatible notions of
> competition, both of which have a long lineage in the history of
> economic thought (p. 877).

In some areas the views of the Harvard and Chicago schools have
certainly converged. Nevertheless, significant differences remain.
Audretsch (1988: 135) notes that "within the literature of any one
view there is often little or only minimal acknowledgement of the
existence and claims of the other". The development of game theory

has tended to cast doubt on some of the main Chicago tenets and has led to something of a resurgence of the traditional approach, albeit in a considerably modified form.

The "Austrians"

An alternative viewpoint, associated with authors such as Schumpeter and Hayek, so that it has come to be known as the "Austrian school", sees the economy as being in a continuous state of flux. Opportunities and incentives for gain are constantly emerging. Entrepreneurs who are alert to the opportunities that are being thrown up by the market are central to the competitive process. Inherent in models of entrepreneurship is the concept of arbitrage, whereby individuals take advantage of price differentials between markets to buy cheap and sell dear. Such behaviour may be commonly observed in financial markets. An alternative example is provided by owners of second-hand shops which specialise in buying old furniture and reselling it for a profit. An individual who sets up a business to produce a particular commodity does so based on a view that a combination of raw materials and labour can be obtained for less than the price which can be obtained for the finished goods produced by them.

The Austrian view of competition is very different from that of the traditional model. Indeed, according to Hayek (1957) the definition of perfect competition in fact means the absence of competitive behaviour by firms. Entrepreneurs who spot opportunities will enjoy temporary monopoly profits. It is argued that such profits are essential to encourage entrepreneurs to undertake the risk of developing new products.[7] In contrast to the pure competition model, new entrants will not enter the market selling homogenous products but will try and develop a new alternative to attract consumers to switch from existing products. Thus, instead of producing crisps, a firm that wants to enter the snack-food market will develop an alternative such as turkey rings for example.[8]

---

[7]   Such arguments may be relevant, for example, to intellectual property.

[8]   It is interesting to note, for example, that a very high number of new grocery products regularly appear only to disappear within a relatively short space of time.

> [I]t is not that kind of competition which counts (competition in respect of existing products using existing technology) but the competition from the new commodity, the new technology, the new source of supply, the new type of organisation . . . competition which commands a decisive cost or quality advantage and which strikes not at the margins of the profits and the outputs of existing firms but at their foundations and their very lives (Schumpeter, 1942: 84).

In contrast to the traditional view, Schumpeter argued that firms will only take on the significant costs entailed in developing new technology if they are protected from competition. Further, as a higher level of technological innovation is seen to increase the economy's long-term growth rate, an economy with monopoly producers will, in the long term, enjoy higher living standards than one with competitive industries. According to the Austrian view, without the possibility of a temporary monopoly, many (perhaps most) products might never exist as it would be in no one's interest to invent them. Critics of the Austrian approach regard the sort of product differentiation which is central to it as specious if not exploitative. Austrians question the need to regulate or control monopolies or prevent mergers which would create monopolies. In their view, very few firms can hope to dominate markets indefinitely. Where powerful monopolies have existed for a length of time, it is argued that this has been because they enjoy some form of state protection.

Contestability

Proponents of contestability theory argue that, provided that it is easy for firms to enter and exit a market, the only way for existing firms in an industry to deter new entrants is to operate at the level of price and output which would arise in a perfectly competitive market structure. Contestability theory stresses that potential competitors can effectively constrain market power so that antitrust and regulatory attention may be unnecessary (see Baumol et al., 1982). Schwartz (1986) points out that contestability theory shifts attention away from structural measures of market power (such as concentration ratios[9]), and from the nature of

---

[9] Such ratios attempt to measure the extent to which market share is concentrated in the hands of a small number of firms.

oligopoly interactions, towards variables that affect the ease of entry and exit. Its underlying premise is that a monopolist or oligopolist will behave efficiently and competitively where there is a threat of losing some or all of its markets to a new entrant. Baumol and Willig (1986) claimed that perfect competition is a special case of perfect contestability. According to contestability theory high fixed costs need not deter new entrants. Rather, the issue is whether the firm will be able to recoup such costs if it is subsequently forced to withdraw. If it cannot, then such costs are said to be sunk costs. If costs are not sunk, it is possible for new entrants to hit and run — that is, enter and then withdraw in the face of retaliation by the dominant incumbent. Essentially, the only entry barrier in a contestable market is the fear of price reactions by incumbent firms and this fear is removed if exit is costless.

Armstrong et al. (1994) have criticised contestability theory for its assumption that firms can enter the market faster than the incumbent can respond by cutting prices. In fact, as Schwartz (1986) points out, the proponents of contestability theory acknowledge the importance of rapid price response by incumbents but this caveat is frequently overlooked. He notes that structural conditions that make entry and exit easy, such as low sunk costs, "are incorrectly taken as sufficient to insure contestability" (ibid.: 55). Research has indicated that even minor departures from the conditions required for perfect contestability results in very different outcomes, while some markets which were thought to be "contestable" are not so in fact. In the early 1980s, for example, it was argued by many economists that airline routes constituted a contestable market. Bailey and Baumol (1984), however, argue that airline behaviour has resembled that expected of rival oligopolists in standard analysis, not from players in a contestable market. New entrants have, for example, had difficulty gaining access to take-off and landing slots, preventing "hit and run entry" in many cases. Shepherd (1990) goes somewhat further, arguing that the theory rests on two contradictory assumptions and probably does not fit any important real-world markets. The main advocates of "contestability theory" have themselves indicated its limits:

> Contestability theory does not, and was not intended to, lend support to those who believe (or almost seem to believe) that the unrestrained market automatically solves all economic problems and that virtually all regulation and antitrust activity constitutes a pointless and costly source of economic inefficiency. . . . For before anyone can legitimately use the analysis to infer that virtue reigns in some economic sector and that interference is therefore unwarranted, that person must first provide evidence that the arena in question is, in fact, highly contestable (Baumol and Willig, 1986: 9).

The absence of past entry is not conclusive proof of the existence of barriers to entry, as this could be equally well explained by the fact that the industry was declining or prices were at a competitive level. Similarly, if incumbent firms perceive that new entry is unlikely and act with disregard for potential competitors, it is not to the point that new entry is feasible. It follows that if the threat of potential entry is sufficiently strong to deter anti-competitive behaviour by undertakings in a particular market, the existence of restrictive practices such as price fixing or market sharing is, *a priori*, an indication that the threat of entry is unlikely or perceived to be unlikely by existing firms, and that the market is therefore not a contestable one. As discussed in Chapter 8, the European Commission has taken into account the contestability of markets in considering dominance.

Cartels and Their Effects
As already noted, the oligopolistic structure of most real-world markets means that collusion is a constant threat. Firms face a clear incentive to form cartels since such behaviour will enhance their profitability. As with other forms of legislation, to be effective restrictions on anti-competitive behaviour must constitute an adequate deterrent. The level of deterrent will depend both on the penalties involved for breaches of the law and the likelihood of being apprehended. Cartels are more likely when the expected punishment for forming a cartel is low relative to the expected gains. This point has considerable implications for competition law and is considered at length in Chapter 9.

A cartel is an arrangement involving interdependent firms,

supposedly in competition with each other, whereby they agree not to compete. Cartel arrangements may involve agreements to raise prices, restrict output, divide markets, or some other form of co-operation. As Langenfeld and Morris (1991: 651) noted:

> [C]ollusive behaviour is not limited to prices, market division, and boycotts. Competitors may employ horizontal agreements to raise their rivals' costs by disadvantaging firms outside the agreement or preventing innovative practices of non-participating firms.

Where all the firms in an industry participate in a cartel the outcome is, in many respects, the same as if there were a single monopoly producer. Where some firms remain outside the cartel, the outcome is similar to that of a large firm in a dominant position facing competition from several smaller competitors. The threat of sanctions by the cartel may greatly limit the ability of non-members to compete with its members. There is widespread agreement among economists regarding the harmful effects of cartels:

> Economists are almost unanimous in their condemnation of cartels, especially those engaged in price fixing, because no expert has satisfactorily established that consumers will benefit from price fixing. On the contrary, economic analysis can show that cartels are inefficient and lessen consumer welfare. It is, therefore, not surprising that antitrusters have the closest meeting of minds on the baleful influence of cartels (Breit and Elzinga, 1989: 12).

Chicagoans regard price-fixing and market division arrangements among competitors as one of the few legitimate targets of competition law.

The ultimate objective of cartels is to raise prices whether directly or indirectly. Price fixing is likely to lead to prices being set at the level which allows the most inefficient cartel member to operate profitably.[10] Cartels reduce the incentive for firms to cut costs. A cartel may be undermined by the entry of new firms which do not join the cartel. Cartel arrangements suffer from an inherent

---

[10] As Baumol (1992) notes, a cartel may entail greater costs than a pure monopoly which at least will allocate output to its most efficient plants.

weakness in that each member of the cartel has an incentive to "cheat". In order to raise the market price of the product in question, the members of the cartel must agree to reduce production. If they succeed in pushing up the price, however, it is in each individual member's interest to increase production at the higher price. As a result, many cartels self-destruct without any government intervention. These shortcomings of cartel arrangements can be illustrated by reference to a real-world example. In the early 1970s, the major non-communist oil producing countries came together under the banner of OPEC, the Organisation of Petroleum Exporting Countries, to establish a cartel. In the short term, they succeeded in raising oil prices substantially. Over time, however, the increase in oil prices resulted in increased energy efficiency and a switch to alternative sources of energy (substitution). At the same time, it also led to greater efforts to identify and develop other sources of supply (new entry). Thus, over time, the price of oil fell again. In addition, OPEC's efforts to push up prices have been repeatedly undermined by cheating by some of its members who produced above their quota because of the higher price and the scope to do so undetected.

Four factors can aid the detection of cheating by cartel members:

- There are only a few firms in the industry.

- Prices do not fluctuate independently.

- Prices are widely known.

- All members sell identical products at the same point in the distribution chain.

The smaller the number of firms involved, the easier it is to organise. If the products are homogeneous and prices are widely known, it is easy to establish whether a member is cheating. To deter cheating, cartels must also be able to impose sanctions to punish members who cheat. Such sanctions may take many forms. An extreme example was provided by a Mafia-organised cartel in the concrete and construction industries in New York City. A former member of the Genovese family, who ran this cartel, told senators that it was "a very disciplined organisation" with strict rules and capital punishment "for serious violations" (Carlton and Perloff, 1990: 225). Similarly, the Iraqi invasion of Kuwait in August 1989 was, in part at least, a response to Kuwait's failure to adhere to OPEC production ceilings designed to push up crude-oil prices.[11]

Clearly, some cartels are more successful than others. As Carlton and Perloff (1990) point out, we know a lot about the cartels that have been caught but, by definition, very little is known about those that have managed to avoid detection. Empirical research supports the view that cartels are more likely in concentrated industries and that they are likely to involve relatively few firms. Trade associations, by lowering the costs of meeting and enforcing arrangements between firms, facilitate the establishment and enforcement of cartels. Many detected cartels, particularly in the United States, have involved trade associations (Carlton and Perloff, 1990). While economists normally argue that cartels are only feasible when there are relatively few firms in an industry, anti-competitive arrangements have frequently been detected in professions involving large numbers of individuals. There is a series of US cases involving cartels among real estate agents. In *Goldfarb* v. *Virginia State Bar*,[12] an association representing lawyers was found to have infringed the provisions of the Sherman Act by enforcing a system of minimum fee schedules for certain legal services. In *Mass. Board*,[13] it was found that restrictions on advertising by optometrists were anti-competitive. While advertising restrictions are common in many professions, studies have consistently shown that they result in higher prices (Langenfeld and Morris, 1991). In a series of reports on various professional groups in Ireland, the former Fair Trade Commission (FTC) concluded that certain of their practices were anti-competitive (see, for example, Restrictive Practices Commission (RPC), 1987a, 1987b; and FTC, 1990).[14] George Bernard Shaw's

---

[11] Policing costs may also mean that cartels generate higher costs than pure monopolies.

[12] *Goldfarb et ux.* v. *Virginia State Bar et al.* 421 US 733 (1975).

[13] Massachusetts Board of Registration in Optometry, 110 FTC [Federal Trade Commission] 549 1988.

[14] This point is returned to in Chapter 12.

claim that "All professions are a conspiracy against the laity" may contain more than a grain of truth.

Vertical Restraints

Firms engaged at different levels in the production and distribution process may also enter into restrictive arrangements of various kinds — for example, manufacturers may have exclusive distribution agreements with retailers whereby the retailer does not handle products which compete with those of the manufacturer. Arrangements involving firms at different stages in the production/ distribution process are known as vertical agreements. Common forms of vertical restraints include exclusive distribution, exclusive purchasing, franchising and resale price maintenance (RPM). The latter practice involves manufacturers seeking to fix the price at which retailers sell their products. There is considerable disagreement among economists regarding the desirability or otherwise of vertical restraints. There is also a tendency to distinguish between non-price restraints, such as exclusive distribution, and resale price maintenance, although some would argue that there is no logical basis for making such distinctions.

Non-price Vertical Restraints[15]

Exclusive distribution agreements are agreements between the manufacturer/supplier of a product and resellers at either wholesale or retail level, whereby the manufacturer appoints that reseller as its sole distributor for a specific territory and, in many instances, the reseller may agree not to sell competing products. The reseller may also agree to promote the product in various ways. Such agreements appear *prima facie* anti-competitive as they clearly prevent other resellers within the territory from selling the supplier's products and may also deny producers of competing products access to the most able distributors within the territory. The case usually made for exclusive distribution is that it may be essential to provide the reseller with an incentive to devote greater efforts to selling the manufacturer's goods

---

[15] The discussion here focuses primarily on exclusive distribution, although similar arguments apply to arrangements such as exclusive purchasing and franchising.

through promotional efforts and/or increased service in the form of information about the product, instruction in its use, the holding of larger stocks and the like. It is argued that retailers would not provide such services in the absence of the exclusive arrangements, since consumers would avail of such free services provided and then purchase the goods in question from lower-cost outlets which would effectively "free ride" on the services provided by others. This in turn would cause retailers providing such services to discontinue them, thereby reducing sales of the product. As against this, it is argued that relatively few products are susceptible to "free riding" of this kind. Many consumers know what they want and do not need pre-sales service. Similarly, consumers will only go to lower-priced outlets, having availed of the free pre-sales service provided in the more expensive outlet, in the case of goods that are expensive and where the cost saving is significant. "Free riding" is only possible in the case of pre-sale services.

Exclusive distribution is seen to limit intra-brand competition since it prevents competition between retailers in respect of individual suppliers' products. However, those who regard such restrictions as beneficial argue that reduced intra-brand competition resulting from such arrangements is more than offset by increased inter-brand competition — that is, competition between retailers to promote the brands for which they have exclusive rights. Steiner (1991) argues that there is no *a priori* basis to support the view that sacrificing intra-brand competition to invigorate inter-brand competition is a welfare enhancing trade-off. He concludes that the:

> ... intuitively appealing theory that interbrand competition by itself effectively limits retailers' power to mark-up, is simply wrong. It is horizontal intrabrand competition that is primarily responsible for reducing costs and moderating markups in distribution (*ibid.*: 194).

Similarly, Chard (1980: 407) argues that "any restriction on intra-brand competition is likely to result in higher prices at the distribution level".

Economists are more divided on the merits or harm of vertical restraints, such as exclusive distribution, than in the case of horizontal restraints where there is considerable agreement. The traditional "Harvard school" approach tended to regard many forms of vertical restraints as anti-competitive but this view is not shared by proponents of the "Chicago school". In their view, many of these practices confer no obvious anti-competitive benefits upon firms, so that, by implication, the rationale for them is that they are efficiency-enhancing. In effect, economists' views regarding non-price vertical restraints range across a broad spectrum. At one extreme, there are those who would argue that all vertical restraints should be automatically deemed to be anti-competitive. At the other, there is a minority within the "Chicago School" who consider that all vertical restrictions should be deemed legal *per se*. Most economists are somewhere in between and agree that such restrictions should be subject to a rule of reason test. Such an approach requires that each and every vertical restraint be assessed on the basis of its economic effects in the relevant market. Adherents of the Harvard approach tend to be more interventionist, requiring a weaker burden of proof that such restraints are anti-competitive, while Chicagoans are less interventionist. Whether exclusive distribution arrangements will prove beneficial depends to a large extent on the characteristics of the goods in question and various other market conditions. At the very least, exclusive distribution involves some trade-off between inter- and intra-brand competition. The outcome of such a trade-off again will vary depending on the circumstances in each individual case. Thus, from a competition point of view, exclusive distribution agreements with retailers for PCs are quite different from exclusive distribution agreements with retailers for breakfast cereal. Tirole (1988) notes that vertical restraints may be privately desirable and at the same time socially undesirable. and concludes that:

> One should be cautious when assessing the effects of such restraints, but unqualified hostility toward vertical restraints is inappropriate (*ibid.*: 181)

Resale Price Maintenance

Resale Price Maintenance (RPM) describes a practice whereby a supplier agrees to supply retailers on condition that they sell the

goods at a price specified by the supplier. Such arrangements restrict the ability of retailers to determine their own prices. They
also eliminate price competition between retailers for the suppliers' products. Where one manufacturer seeks to fix the price at
which retailers sell its products is known as individual RPM.
Collective RPM arises where all the manufacturers of competing
products adopt such an approach. As with non-price vertical restraints there is some disagreement among economists as to
whether or not RPM is an undesirable practice. "Chicago school"
economists have challenged traditional economic thinking concerning RPM. Essentially, their argument is that manufacturers
will not impose RPM unless it leads to increased output and
profits and the justifications for RPM are similar to those for non-
price vertical restraints — that is, it causes the retailer to devote
greater efforts to selling the manufacturer's goods by preventing
"free riding" and this benefits consumers so that sales are increased, resulting in greater output of the goods in question. Consequently, RPM should not be seen as anti-competitive, but as a
mechanism for increasing distribution efficiency to the benefit of
consumers, retailers and suppliers.

In response, opponents would argue that a lot of products are
not susceptible to free riding and that free-rider arguments can
only apply in respect of pre-sale services. In addition, other methods are available to induce greater efforts by retailers to sell the
manufacturers' products. RPM may be operated as part of a cartel
arrangement, whether between suppliers or retailers. In the case
of a supplier cartel, RPM may be used as a means of preventing
cheating by cartel members. By preventing discounting among
retailers, it reduces the incentives for suppliers to renege on the
cartel arrangement as there is no point in suppliers cutting their
price to retailers if retailers cannot pass on such price cuts.[16] A
retail cartel may also put pressure on suppliers to operate a system of RPM as a means of ensuring compliance by all retailers.
Scherer and Ross (1990) show that RPM may also inhibit competition by preventing the entry of discount outlets, and thus it can

---

[16] This point is considered in Chapter 7 in the context of the Competition
Authority decision on the Net Book Agreement.

obstruct retailing innovations. Manufacturers who have relied on RPM to encourage product promotion by retailers and increase sales may be unwilling to dispense with such arrangements long after the need to promote new products has ended. Where many manufacturers engage in RPM, it may be difficult for one to end the practice, since retailers may simply cease stocking the firm's products. They conclude that, on balance, the evidence suggests that RPM is likely to restrict competition and result in prices being higher and output lower than would otherwise be the case.

RPM is prohibited under the competition laws of most developed countries. Legislation which permitted RPM was repealed in the United States in 1976 and the Supreme Court has regarded RPM as a *per se* violation of the antitrust rules. Legislation prohibiting RPM was enacted in Canada in 1951, in France in 1953 and in the UK in 1964. While UK legislation allows for exemption from this prohibition, there have only been four requests for such exemption, and exemptions have only been granted in respect of books and over-the-counter medicines. The Hilmer review of competition policy in Australia concluded that:

> The Committee has not been presented with convincing evidence that efficiency-enhancing RPM occurs with such frequency that the *per se* prohibition should be relaxed (Hilmer, 1993: 57).

Since 1990, both Canada and New Zealand have reviewed their competition laws and in both countries it was decided that RPM should continue to be subject to a *per se* prohibition.

Abuse of Market Power

Many real-world markets are characterised by having one very large firm which accounts for a large share of the relevant market, with a number of much smaller competitors which may be unable to compete very strongly with the larger firm. In such a situation, the large firm may effectively be able to ignore the actions of its competitors and influence market prices by varying its output. A firm in such circumstances is said to have market power or be in a dominant position in the relevant market. It is not the absolute size of a firm that determines whether it has market power, but its size relative to the market. Although a dominant firm may not enjoy a monopoly in a particular market, it can, by exercising its market power, harm consumers and competitors. Competition policy is therefore concerned with abuses of market power by dominant firms in addition to restrictive agreements between firms. A firm may be dominant because it may be more efficient than rival firms; it may have grown larger as a result of economies of scale; or its products may be regarded as superior to those of its competitors. Alternatively, it may be that its dominant position has arisen because it was given a position of privilege by licensing or some other form of Government regulation.

Essentially, to be regarded as dominant, a firm or group of firms must have sufficient power to enable it to raise prices or act in some other way independently of its rivals. This requires not just that the firm have a large market share, but that the prospect of entry by new stronger competitors also be limited to some degree. In the absence of entry barriers, any attempt by a firm with market power to raise prices, for example, would attract new firms into the market, thus driving prices down:

> An attempt to exercise market power in an industry without entry barriers would cause new competitors to enter the market. This additional supply would drive prices back to the competitive level. Indeed, the threat of new entry can be as potent a pro competitive force as its realisation. As the Supreme Court has recognised, the presence of potential entrants on the fringe of a market can prevent the exercise of market power by the incumbent firms even if the potential entrants never actually enter the market.[17]

The Australian High Court took a similar view in *Queensland Wire* where the majority held that:

> It is only when for some reason it is not rational or possible for new entrants to participate in the market that a firm can have market power.[18]

---

[17] Federal Trade Commission, Final Order: In the Matter of the Echlin Manufacturing Company, and Borg-Warner Corporation, Docket No. 9157, Washington, DC, 28.6.85.

[18] *Queensland Wire Industries Pty. Ltd.* v. *The Broken Hill Proprietary Company Limited*, (1989) ATPR 20-925.

Barriers to entry need not be absolute. Over a prolonged period of time a firm's position of dominance in the market might well be eroded. Indeed, the gradual erosion of a dominant firm's position is a common occurrence which is well documented in the economics literature. Such erosion, however, proceeds very slowly and Shepherd (1990) reports that there are numerous major cases of dominance lasting more than five decades. Such a gradual decline in its market power will not serve to prevent the dominant firm from pushing up prices or exercising market power in any other way for some considerable period of time. Similarly, a dominant firm may engage in behaviour such as predatory pricing designed to prevent or impede entry by new firms. Such strategies can prove quite successful in preventing the emergence of effective competition for a considerable period of time. A dominant firm may be capable of eliminating any small rival if it so chooses, at any given point in time, or may even be capable of eliminating all of its rivals. The dominant firm is able to employ competitive weapons which are not available to its smaller rivals. There are admittedly strong incentives for smaller firms to compete aggressively since they could achieve large increases in profitability by doing so, and indeed this does happen on occasion. As against this, however, smaller firms face the threat of overwhelming reactions by the dominant firm, which can act as a significant deterrent. Thus, rather than challenging the dominant firm across the board, smaller firms are likely to confine their activities to specialist niches, thereby not posing a major threat to the dominant firm. As pointed out, Chicagoans are highly sceptical of the existence of artificial entry barriers. Consequently, they tend to be dismissive of the possibility of dominant firms abusing their market power and see the existence of market concentration as an indication that a firm has increased its market share by being more efficient than its rivals.

A firm with market power may engage in practices that are designed to, and have the effect of, restricting or distorting competition. In practice, anti-competitive behaviour by firms with market power can take many other forms. As Clarke (1985: 250) observed: "The scope for single-firm anti-competitive practices is limited only by human ingenuity."

Rather than purport to provide a comprehensive list of all possible forms of abusive behaviour, we simply confine ourselves to the more interesting and/or commonly observed types of abusive behaviour.

Predatory Pricing

Claims that dominant firms have sought to eliminate their rivals by slashing prices are not uncommon. In economic terms, however, predatory pricing has a precise definition. It is a policy of price cutting by a firm in a dominant market position designed to reduce or eliminate the competition it faces, so as to enable the firm to reap higher profits at a later stage following the diminution in competition which has occurred as a result of predation. There are therefore several features that are necessary for pricing to be regarded as predatory. Firstly, it involves deliberately reducing profits (or even incurring a loss) for a period of time in the hope of enjoying supernormal profits later on. Secondly, to establish predation it is necessary to show that the objective of price cutting is to reduce the number of competitors by eliminating one or more of them, or to weaken them to a degree that they can no longer offer strong competition. Thirdly, in order for a firm to benefit from predatory pricing, it is essential that it be able to earn supernormal profits in the future. Such a possibility is reduced in markets where there are low barriers to entry or in contestable markets. In such circumstances any attempt by the predator to raise prices above their competitive level following the elimination of competitors as a result of predatory pricing will only serve to attract new firms into the market, thereby forcing prices back to their original level.

As recently as the early 1980s, detailed economic analysis on the issue of predatory pricing argued that it was not a rational profit-maximising strategy for firms to engage in, and that instances of actual predatory pricing were rare. Since then, however, research has suggested that predatory pricing may be a rational strategy for a firm to adopt. Thus, by accepting the losses necessary to eliminate a particular rival, a firm may establish a reputation for toughness which discourages would-be entrants, even though there may be no actual barriers to entry. Alternatively, successfully eliminating one firm may cause other remaining competitors not to respond aggressively to moves by the predator to raise prices above the competitive level. Other situations where predatory pricing has been found to be a rational strategy are where firms cut prices in an attempt to convince rivals that fundamental market conditions are bad or that in fact the predator firm's costs are actually quite low, thereby encouraging them to leave the market or not to enter at all. Predatory pricing may also be used as part of a strategy to soften up a rival firm for takeover.

It is important to distinguish between predatory pricing and aggressive price competition. Cutting prices as part of a short-term strategy to improve market share would not be considered predatory in economic terms. Predatory pricing is considered anti-competitive since its objective is to eliminate competitors or deter them from competing aggressively, thereby reducing the degree and intensity of competition in the marketplace to the benefit of the predator. While over the past 15 years it has been recognised that the scope for predatory pricing is wider than previously thought, it remains the case that actual cases of predatory pricing have been relatively rare.

As already stated, it is not essential for losses to be incurred in order for prices to be deemed predatory. Clearly, however, it becomes much harder to establish predation where in fact a firm does not incur actual losses. Equally, it can be perfectly rational for a discriminating monopolist (or cartel) to charge a price below average total cost in some markets, since such a strategy is effectively profit maximising. The object of the firm in those circumstances is not the elimination of its competitors, but the maximisation of its own profits. More commonly, when firms launch new products they may frequently sell them at a loss, initially as part of a promotional campaign. Changes in demand may also force firms to cut prices simply to dispose of unsold stocks.

On the other hand, for a firm to sell in any market at below the marginal cost of production involves unnecessary reductions in its overall profits. Based on this thinking, Areeda and Turner (1975) argued in a highly influential article that predation only arises when prices are held below marginal cost.[19] The authors recognised that in practice measuring marginal cost may be extremely difficult and they argued that courts could infer that pricing was predatory in nature where prices were set below average variable costs,[20] which can be more easily identified than marginal costs but are still difficult to measure. The Areeda-Turner article prompted a considerable debate in the economics literature, some of it critical of their suggested approach, and some suggesting alternative approaches. The Areeda-Turner rule is designed to restrain firms as little as possible, reflecting in part the authors' view that predation is a rare phenomenon. It also suffers from the problem that the launch of new products will frequently involve promotions which result in selling at below average variable cost. Similarly, in an industry where there is learning by doing, firms may initially find themselves selling below short-run marginal costs, since it is only over time that they learn the most efficient way to produce, thereby reducing their marginal costs. Both of these instances would be classed as predatory behaviour on the basis of the Areeda-Turner approach, although they are not in fact predatory. Simple price-cost rules cannot establish conclusively whether or not behaviour is predatory, although they can certainly offer useful guidelines. Thus, except in certain limited circumstances, there would appear to be few rational explanations for a firm to sell below its short-run marginal costs. Such behaviour may therefore be taken as indicating a strong probability that the action is predatory. Nevertheless, it will also be necessary to consider factors such as market structure, the presence or absence of barriers to entry and other factors in order to come to a view as to whether a firm could hope to recoup the losses entailed in a predatory campaign in the future.

---

[19] Marginal cost is the cost of producing the last unit of output.

[20] Variable costs, as the name implies, vary with the level of production. They include costs such as the cost of raw materials and labour. Fixed costs, on the other hand, do not vary with output and must be met even if zero output is produced — for example, the costs of premises and machinery. In the short run, it is rational for a firm to produce once it covers its variable costs.

Price Discrimination

Price discrimination involves the sale of different units of a good or service at different prices where the differential is not equivalent to differences in the cost of supply. As Scherer and Ross (1990) note, however, there is no simple all-inclusive definition of price discrimination. Three conditions are necessary for price discrimination. Firstly, the firm must have some degree of market power giving it some control over price. Secondly, it must be able to segregate its customers into groups with differing price elasticities of demand. Thirdly, there must be no scope for arbitrage — i.e., customers paying the lower price must not be able to sell to those being charged the higher price.

First-degree price discrimination involves charging each individual customer the maximum price that that individual would be prepared to pay. It is normally difficult for a firm to engage in first-degree price discrimination because, for example, it is difficult to prevent arbitrage. In the case of scarce goods, sealed bid auctions represent a means of engaging in first-degree price discrimination. Second-degree price discrimination is a common phenomenon in many consumer goods markets and involves giving volume discounts. Thus, for example, a soft drinks supplier may decide to sell six packs of cola at a lower unit price than the individual cans. The rationale behind this is simple. Some consumers will only want an individual can and will pay a higher price for that can, while others would be prepared to buy more than one can if the price was lower, and others may buy none at all at the high price charged for an individual can. Such consumers may well be attracted by the lower unit price to purchase six packs. The firm thus has the benefit of the high price paid by those consumers wishing to purchase individual cans along with the benefit of sales to those consumers who are prepared to purchase more than one can, but only at a lower price. Two-tier tariffs, where consumers pay a fixed charge for access plus a separate charge for each unit of the product consumed, as in the case of telephone services, represent another form of second-degree price discrimination. Third-degree price discrimination arises where different prices are charged to different groups of consumers. Airline tickets are a good example where discounted tickets are offered to consumers subject to certain conditions. Another everyday example of third-degree price discrimination can be found in the case of cinemas which charge lower prices for afternoon shows than for evening shows. The market is segmented because many people work in the afternoon and cannot go to the lower-price show. In the absence of such discrimination, a higher price for afternoon shows would reduce the numbers attending them, and the cut in overall revenue might force cinemas to charge even higher prices for evening shows. In this case, price discrimination is arguably beneficial to everyone concerned. It is thus necessary to judge instances of discrimination on a case-by-case basis.

Price discrimination may take many forms, with diverse consequences. Some forms of discrimination may increase the efficiency of resource allocation compared to simple monopoly pricing. In the case of natural monopolies, theory suggests that regulators should apply pricing rules embodying a degree of price discrimination.[21] Other types of discrimination may have a neutral impact on efficiency while others may lead to serious inefficiencies. Price discrimination is practised not only by dominant or monopoly firms. As Tirole (1988) observes, most price discrimination takes place in oligopolistic markets and indeed the examples we have listed — airline services, soft drinks and cinemas — all involve a multiplicity of firms.

Tying

Tying describes the practice of tying the sale of one or more goods to the sale of another good. For example, a firm with market power in the case of good A may supply it on condition that customers also buy good B from it. In such circumstances, good A is described as the tying good, while good B is the tied good. In the past, for example, photocopier manufacturers used to require customers to purchase paper and other supplies from them. The traditional argument against tying is the leverage argument. According to this view, tying is a means of extending market power into other markets. If the market for B is competitive, it is argued that

---

[21] See Chapter 13 on this point.

tying sales of A to those of B allows the firm to secure additional monopoly profits from sales of B. Here again, Chicagoans have been somewhat sceptical, arguing that a tie-in may not provide any leverage at all for the firm. It is argued, for example, that if A and B have to be used in fixed proportions, there is no incentive for firms to tie sales of B to A, since it can fully extract monopoly profits from sales of A alone. Firms have sought to justify tying arrangements as being necessary to ensure that the quality of the tied product is adequate, although the apparently obvious answer to such claims is that specifying quality standards for product B, when it is used in conjunction with A, would appear sufficient.

Essential Facilities

A dominant firm may control a resource which is essential to engage in a particular line of business but which potential rivals could not hope to duplicate. Denying a competitor access to essential facilities, defined as facilities vital to a competitor's survival, has been attacked under competition law in many countries. Under the essential facilities doctrine, the owner of such an essential facility must make it available to competitors. Clearly, the owner ought not to be obliged to grant access to the facility free and the question of the appropriate charge to be levied for such access is itself an interesting one. The essential facilities doctrine was first expounded more than 80 years ago in the US in the *Terminal Railroad* case.[22] This involved a situation in which all of the railroad bridges in St Louis were owned by a group of railroad companies. The court ruled that the owners had to provide access to competitors on reasonable terms. Under US law to establish that a facility is essential a plaintiff has to show:

> (1) control of the essential facility by a monopolist; (2) a competitor's inability practically or reasonably to duplicate the facility; (3) the denial of the use of the essential facility to a competitor; and (4) the feasibility of providing the facility.[23]

---

[22] *United States* v. *Terminal Railroad Association of St Louis*, 224 US 383 (1912).

[23] *MCI Communications Corp.* v. *American Telephone & Telegraph Co.*, 708 F.2d 1081, 1132-33 (7th Cir.), 464 US 891 (1983).

A clear example of the type of situation where the doctrine might arise occurs in the case of natural monopolies such as the national electricity grid. A firm wishing to compete in the electricity generation industry must have access to the grid in order to sell to customers.[24] In recent years, there have been several EU cases where the essential facilities doctrine was applied.

Exclusionary Behaviour

Dominant firms may engage in various other practices besides predatory pricing designed to prevent entry to the market by new firms. As already noted, in the absence of entry barriers, if a dominant firm set its price above the competitive level, this would provide an incentive for new firms to enter the market, which would cause it to lose market share and force prices down. If the dominant firm enjoys economies of scale, so that its unit costs of production would be lower than those of a new entrant, assuming that entry can only occur on a small scale, the dominant firm may decide not to charge the highest possible price for its products. It may instead set prices at a level that would be low enough to make it unattractive for new firms, with their higher unit costs, to enter the market, while still maintaining price above the competitive level. The firm clearly forgoes some supernormal profits in the short-run but the pay-off is that, by deterring new entry, it enjoys higher profits over time. Such a pricing strategy is referred to in the economics literature as limit pricing. Of course, new firms may be able to enter at a sufficient scale to achieve the same level of economies as the incumbent. New entrants may believe that their entry to the market will cause prices to fall to such a degree that entry would be unprofitable because of the increase in supply. Of course, such an outcome is, to some extent, dependent on the incumbent firm not reducing its output in response to new entry — an unlikely outcome. Carlton and Perloff (1990) point out, however, that if the incumbent can in some way commit itself to maintaining its existing level of output, then entry will be deterred, and the incumbent has successfully practised limit pricing. A detailed analysis of limit pricing is contained in Milgrom

---

[24]   See Chapter 13.

and Roberts (1982). As Tirole (1988) notes, with some small changes, the limit-pricing model can be reinterpreted as one of predatory pricing.

Dominant firms may also seek to deter entry by raising rivals' costs, if it can do so without significantly raising its own. Firms may try and increase the cost of information to would-be entrants. For example, an incumbent could respond to test marketing by a new entrant in a particular area by running a rival promotion campaign in that area, making it harder for the entrant to judge consumer response to its product. High levels of advertising designed to build brand loyalty may also represent a form of entry barrier although Carlton and Perloff (1990) report that the evidence on this point is mixed. Dominant firms may seek to deter customers from switching to new suppliers by offering to reimburse them for any difference between their current price and the lowest price that may be offered in the future. Dominant firms may also try and deter entry through plant location strategies. In the case of products where transport costs are high, new entrants could enter a market at a niche level by locating their plant closer to a significant group of customers than the incumbent. The incumbent may seek to pre-empt such moves by setting up several plants located in a way that is designed to exclude scope for entry. Dominant firms may also apply vertical restraints to block entry, a point considered elsewhere in the text.

Conclusions

Economists' thinking about how competition works in practice has evolved considerably since its virtues were first expounded by Adam Smith over 200 years ago. It has been argued that the assumptions underlying theoretical models which show that competition is beneficial are unrealistic, raising some doubts as to the validity of such models' predictions. Nevertheless, there is widespread evidence that in competitive markets prices are lower than under monopolies. On some issues, considerable disagreements exist among economists as to what does and does not constitute anti-competitive behaviour, although such disagreements occur more at a theoretical than a practical level. There is fairly widespread agreement within the profession regarding the undesirability of cartels. There is much less agreement regarding vertical restraints, although it is possible to conclude that the mainstream viewpoint would favour assessing non-price vertical restraints on a case-by-case basis, in the light of the market circumstances in which they operate. The mainstream viewpoint is also concerned with abuses of market power, although the Chicago school has tended to be largely dismissive of such concerns.

3

THE STRUCTURE OF IRISH INDUSTRY

The traditional economics approach to competition, based on the structure-conduct-performance paradigm, viewed highly concentrated market structures as problematic, since the smaller the number of firms in a market, the greater the risk of collusion. According to this viewpoint market power is also viewed as undesirable since firms which can exercise market power may do so to the detriment of consumers and rivals. Such claims tend to be dismissed by proponents of the Chicago school who argue that highly concentrated market structures are not problematic, while contestability theory stresses that, regardless of the existing market structure, provided that there is ease of entry and exit, a market will behave competitively. Aggregate concentration looks at the overall level of concentration in the economy — that is, the extent to which total economic activity is concentrated in the hands of a few large firms. Market concentration is concerned with the degree of concentration in individual product markets. The present chapter attempts to provide an overview of the structure of the Irish economy. Such an exercise must necessarily be a rather limited one given the serious inadequacies of the data available,[1] in particular the absence of any official published data on the level of either aggregate or market concentration.[2] In the case of financial services there is a greater amount of published statistical data available which, although still somewhat incomplete,

---

[1]   The point is that not only does the CSO not publish such data, but it is extremely difficult to estimate even rough measures of concentration from official statistics.

[2]   In several sectors of the economy such as electricity, gas, telecommunications and postal services the State has effectively established statutory monopolies. In a number of other sectors Government regulation restricts entry thereby limiting the number of suppliers. These sectors are considered in Chapters 12 and 13 respectively.

permits a more detailed analysis of that sector.

The fundamental feature of the Irish economy is that it is a small open economy and many sectors are exposed to competition from overseas producers. The sheltered sector is nevertheless significant and, as noted in Chapter 2, restrictions on competition in that sector can undermine the competitive position of firms which are exposed to international competition. Fingleton (1995) has argued that competition is lacking in many sheltered sectors.

Major Companies in the Irish Economy

The Irish economy is relatively small and this is reflected in the fact that most Irish companies are relatively small by international standards. As can be seen from Table 3.1, only five Irish non-financial companies were estimated to have a turnover in excess of £1 billion in 1994. A further 12 had a turnover of more than £500 million, while in total only 106 non-financial business firms had turnovers in excess of £100 million. These firms are, however, quite large by domestic standards. Of course, many large and even not so large Irish firms generate a sizeable proportion of their turnover from exports and overseas subsidiaries. Thus a high overall turnover need not necessarily translate into market power in any particular domestic market.

TABLE 3.1: NON-FINANCIAL IRISH COMPANIES BY SIZE IN 1994

Turnover Range	Number of Firms
>£1bn	5
£500m–£1bn	14
£200m–£500m	29
£100m–£200m	58
Total >£100m	106

Source: *Business and Finance,* The Top 1,000 Companies, 1994.

There have been considerable changes in the structure of Irish companies over a relatively short period of time. *Business and Finance*, for example, reported that from its listing of the Top 300 companies published in January 1982, 67 had gone out of business, been taken over, floated, privatised or restructured (*Business and Finance*, 26 January 1995). It also reported that of the top

300 companies in the January 1995 list, only 127 or 42 per cent were in the 1982 listing, and concluded that "there is no getting away from the fact that corporate Ireland has undergone a profound restructuring over the past 13 years" (ibid.). The picture that emerges is one of considerable fluidity, with firms expanding and contracting, new ones entering and others forced to close or being taken over.

The Manufacturing Sector

Some information on the structure of manufacturing industry is provided by the Central Statistics Office (CSO) annual *Census of Industrial Production* (CIP). The data published in the CIP are limited in a number of respects. An enterprise is defined as the smallest legally autonomous unit engaged wholly or primarily in industrial production and in practice is equivalent to a company or firm. In the past, the information on enterprises related only to those with 20 or more persons engaged, so that many smaller firms were excluded. The 1991 CIP includes all enterprises with three or more employees. According to the 1991 CIP, there were 4,126 manufacturing enterprises in the State, This compares with a figure of 1,683 in the 1990 CIP, which covered only firms with more than 20 employees. Another deficiency with the data in the past was that the various industry categories used in the CIP included firms producing a wide range of products, many of which would not be in competition with one another. Thus an industry classification is not synonymous with a market.[3] Because the 1991 CIP includes a far higher number of firms, it includes, for the first time, information on the number of firms at a much more disaggregated level than previously. The 1991 CIP identifies 130 separate manufacturing sectors, compared with only 29 categories in the 1990 CIP. This certainly provides considerable new information on various sectors and greatly increases its usefulness for analysing

---

[3] Take, for example, the Timber and Wooden Furniture category. This included firms producing such diverse items as wooden pallets, painters' and decorators' brushes, upholstered furniture, church furniture, coffins and mattresses. The reason it included such a wide range is partly the high level of aggregation of the published data. It would still not, however, be possible to equate the data at even the three-digit level with a specific market.

markets. The CSO does not produce any meaningful data on industrial concentration. For example, one method of measuring concentration would be to focus on the proportion of total output in an industry sector accounted for by the four or five largest firms, referred to as the four- or five-firm concentration ratio. Where there are very few firms in a sector, with one or two very large firms, arguably the four-firm concentration ratio could allow firms to obtain information on the business operations of their rivals. An alternative measure of market concentration is provided by the Herfindahl Hirschman Index (HHI). The HHI is calculated by squaring each firm's market share and adding up the squares. It avoids the risk of providing confidential information to competitors in a particular sector and it would appear to be relatively straightforward for the CSO to include such data in the CIP. In the absence of such data, it is only possible to obtain a very incomplete picture of the structure of Irish manufacturing industry.

TABLE 3.2: NUMBER OF MANUFACTURING ENTERPRISES

Year	Number of Enterprises
1981	1,733
1982	1,717
1983	1,660
1984	1,636
1985	1,621
1986	1,619
1987	1,586
1988	1,593
1989	1,667
1990	1,683
1991	4,126

Note: The 1991 figures are not comparable with those in previous years.
Source: CSO, Census of Industrial Production.

Table 3.2 looks at trends in the total number of manufacturing enterprises in the State over time. Between 1981 and 1987 the total number of manufacturing enterprises declined by 147, or just over 8 per cent, before increasing by 97 over the next three years. The figures do not suggest any significant long-term decline in the number of manufacturing companies, but rather are consistent with a decline in the number of firms during economic downturns and an increase as economic activity picked up. It is not possible to establish from the data whether or not concentration has increased.

Table 3.3 looks at the distribution of manufacturing enterprises ranked by turnover. According to the CIP, only 91 manufacturing enterprises had a turnover in excess of £50 million. Yet these firms, which represented just over 5 per cent of all manufacturing enterprises, accounted for over 50 per cent of the turnover of all manufacturing enterprises. Over 63 per cent of manufacturing enterprises had a turnover of less than £5 million, but these accounted for less than 10 per cent of total manufacturing turnover. At an aggregate level, therefore, manufacturing industry is relatively highly concentrated.

TABLE 3.3: DISTRIBUTION OF MANUFACTURING ENTERPRISES BY TURNOVER IN 1990

Turnover Category	% of Enterprises	% of Total Manufacturing Turnover
>£50m	5.3	52.6
£15m–£50m	11.1	24.2
£5m–£15m	20.1	13.4
£1.5m–£5m	33.8	7.7
> £1.5m	29.6	2.1

Source: CSO, Census of Industrial Production.

Table 3.4 looks at the number of enterprises in individual manufacturing sectors. Of the 29 manufacturing sectors identified in the 1990 CIP, only two had fewer than 10 firms. At the other end of the scale, four industries had more than 100 firms while a further nine had over 50 firms. It would appear, therefore, that in a significant number of industries, there is a large number of producers. Of course, as already noted, these firms are not necessarily competing in the same market. There may be 156 firms producing metal articles but clearly the goods they produce are not substitutes for one another. The real problem with the figures is that they relate to very broad industry groups. (As already noted, the 1991 CIP included information at a far more disaggregated level, and details are given in Appendix 3.1. The level of information included is far more detailed than in Table 3.4.) Of the 29 sectors, 19 recorded a decline in the total number of enterprises between 1981 and 1990, while the remaining 10 recorded an increase. A decline in the number of enterprises in a particular sector could

TABLE 3.4: NUMBER OF ENTERPRISES IN EACH INDUSTRIAL SECTOR

	1981	*1990*	*Change*
Non-metallic minerals	90	84	-6
Chemicals incl. man-made fibres	90	110	+20
Production and processing of metals	25	17	-8
Manufacture of metal articles	183	156	-27
Mechanical engineering	73	84	+11
Office and data processing machinery	23	34	+11
Electrical engineering	98	148	+50
Motor vehicle assembly incl. parts	29	19	-10
Manufacture, other means of transport	15	12	-3
Instrument engineering	35	44	+9
Meat processing	78	86	+8
Manufacture of dairy products	62	55	-7
Grain milling and animal feeding stuffs	47	35	-12
Bread, biscuits and flour confectionery	81	52	-29
Sugar and sugar confectionery	19	17	-2
Other food	50	65	+15
Drink and tobacco	35	30	-5
Wool industry	29	18	-11
Knitting industry	40	36	-4
Other textiles	51	38	-13
Leather and leather goods	12	9	-3
Footwear	21	9	-12
Clothing	184	133	-51
Timber and wooden furniture	107	97	-10
Paper and paper products	38	36	-2
Printing and publishing	107	118	+11
Manufacture of rubber products(a)	14	17	+3
Processing of plastics	63	95	+32
Other manufacturing industries	34	29	-5
Manufacturing total	1,733	1,683	-50

(a) includes retreading of tyres.

Source: CSO; Census of Industrial Production.

reflect an increase in concentration, at least in terms of domestic production, but as the majority of manufacturing sectors face competition from imports, a decline in the number of domestic producers may be caused by increased competition from imports.

It is generally considered that competition is strong in most manufacturing industries because they face competition from imports. This presumption, while broadly true, must be subject to two significant caveats. Firstly, Irish firms may collude with overseas rivals. In 1995, for example, Irish Cement was fined by the European Commission for participating in a European-wide cartel, the essential feature of which was that the members agreed not to sell into each others' home markets. Secondly, one must also take account of the importance of distribution channels. A lack of competition at the distribution level could reduce the impact on domestic manufacturers of competition from abroad.

Building and Construction

Details on the number of firms engaged in various segments of the building and construction industry are given in Table 3.5.

TABLE 3.5: DETAILS OF BUILDING AND CONSTRUCTION ENTERPRISES

Description of Business	Number of Enterprises
Site Preparation, Demolition, Earth Moving, Test Drilling and Boring	11
Building of Complete Constructions, or parts thereof; Civil Engineering, Construction of Highways, Roads, Water Projects	195
Building Installation, Installation of Electrical Wiring and Fittings, Installation, Plumbing and Other Installation	67
Building Completion, Plastering, Joinery Installation, Floor and Wall Covering, Painting and Glazing and Other Building Completion	18
Renting of Construction or Demolition Equipment with Operator	6

Source: Census of Building and Construction, 1993, *Irish Statistical Bulletin*, December 1995.

These are taken from the annual *Census of Building and Construction*. As with former CIP data, the data include only firms with more than 20 persons engaged. In this instance, the exclusion of smaller firms is probably an even greater deficiency than in the case of manufacturing. The figures show relatively large numbers of firms engaged in the construction of buildings, civil engineering and plumbing and electrical installation. There is only a relatively small number of firms in activities such as plastering, joinery, floor and wall coverings, although arguably such activities are the ones where small firms, which are excluded from the data, might be expected to predominate. International experience suggests that collusion in the form of bid-rigging is common in the construction industry.

Services

Distribution

Statistical information on the services sector is both relatively limited and, at least until fairly recently, was published very infrequently. According to the *Annual Services Inquiry*, there were 29,334 retail enterprises in the State in 1991, with a combined turnover of £9.4 billion (see Table 3.6). The average gross margin for all retail enterprises was 22.9 per cent, although there was a considerable variation between sectors ranging from 13.1 per cent in the case of garages and filling stations to almost 37 per cent in the case of pubs.

At first glance, the data suggest that the country is well served in terms of grocery shops and pubs, but electrical stores and shoe shops appear a little thin on the ground. From a competition viewpoint, however, what is relevant is the level of competition in specific markets. For example, consumers purchase electrical goods such as a freezer, washing machine or stereo system on a one-off basis. Such items tend to cost a significant amount of money and so it will make sense for customers to shop around and indeed to travel some distance if there are significant price savings to be made. As the Competition Authority noted in its first decision,[4] many consumers were prepared to travel to Northern Ireland to

---

[4]   Nallen/O'Toole, Competition Authority Decision No. 1 of 2.4.92.

purchase televisions and video recorders in the early 1980s because they believed that they could make significant savings by
doing so. This does not mean that every electrical store can be
considered to be part of a single market. Nevertheless it suggests
that even though there may be only one or two such stores in a
particular town, they still face competition from other stores. In
contrast, in the case of pubs, the market is predominantly a local
one. A pub in Castlebar, for example, is not really in competition
with one in Westport. Indeed, a pub in Rathfarnham is probably not
in competition with one in Blackrock. In this case, therefore, the
fact that the absolute number of pubs appears quite high does not
imply that competition in the sector is strong. The issue of competition in the drink trade is considered further in Chapter 12.

TABLE 3.6: RETAIL ENTERPRISES IN 1991

Description of Business	Number of Enterprises	Turnover (£m)	Gross Margin as % of Turnover
Grocery	5,429	2,858.7	19.5
Grocery with Pub	916	147.0	20.9
Pub and Off-licence	6450	915.6	36.7
Tobacco, Sweets and Newspapers	1,609	285.9	20.7
Fresh Meat	1,568	277.2	26.4
Other Food, Drink and Tobacco	1,479	293.8	21.3
Garages and Filling Stations	3,385	2054.4	13.1
Chemists	984	304.0	29.7
Hardware	756	252.0	26.2
Electrical Goods	532	196.6	26.4
Drapery and Apparel	2,246	796.9	32.7
Footwear	411	107.1	31.5
Other Non-Food	3,569	867.2	29.4
Total	29,334	9,356.4	22.9

Source: CSO, Annual Services Inquiry, 1991.

One area of distribution which has given rise to considerable concerns from a competition perspective over a long period of time in
Ireland is the grocery trade. The main reason for concern is the

fact that it is somewhat more concentrated than most other retail distribution sectors as can be seen from Table 3.7.

TABLE 3.7: IMPORTANCE OF MULTIPLE OUTLETS IN VARIOUS RETAIL SECTORS IN 1988.

Description of Business	*No. of Enterprises with More Than 10 Outlets*	*% Share of Turnover Held by Enterprises with More Than 10 Outlets*
Grocery	5	53.7
Public House	0	0
Other Food	4	3.0
Tobacco, Sweets and Newspapers	1	N/A
Clothing and Footwear	8	21.5
Motor Vehicles and Filling Stations	1	N/A
Chemist	1	N/A
Household Durables	2	N/A
Other Non-Food	5	10.8
Total	27	21.6

N/A.:   Not available. This data is not published by the CSO for reasons of confidentiality.
Source: CSO, *Census of Services 1988.*

In 1988, five enterprises in the grocery sector had 10 stores or more. This group, however, accounted for over half of total turnover of grocery enterprises. Arguably, such a level of concentration would not be regarded as excessive. The only other retail sector where enterprises with multiple stores had a significant market share is clothing and footwear. In this case, however, there were eight enterprises with more than 10 outlets but they accounted for just over 20 per cent of turnover in the sector. Unfortunately, comparable data were not included in the 1991 *Annual Services Inquiry* which shows that there were 17 enterprises in the grocery sector in 1991 with a turnover in excess of £5 million. These 17 enterprises had a total of 231 trading outlets and their turnover accounted for 58 per cent of total grocery turnover.

In addition to showing a trend toward concentration at the distribution level, the grocery sector in Ireland is also characterised by a high degree of concentration at the product level. Whelan (1995) found that in product areas such as breakfast cereals and cheese, just three suppliers accounted for 100 per cent of the market. In the case of detergents and medicinal products, two suppliers accounted for 100 per cent of the market. Products such as tea and coffee, soups and sauces, soft drinks, chocolate, butter and baby products all had three firm concentration ratios in excess of 75 per cent.

The *Annual Services Inquiry* indicated that there were 3,016 enterprises engaged in wholesale distribution in 1991. A breakdown of these into broad business categories is set out in Table 3.8 and indicates that in most categories there are large numbers of enterprises engaged at the wholesale level. The data in a number of cases, however, relate to very broad categories. For example, clothing and footwear are included in the same category as photographic and optical equipment. Thus, the large number of enterprises in some categories tells us very little about the level of competition at the wholesale level in respect of specific products. A final feature of the wholesale trade in the case of grocery products is the existence of vertical agreements between specific wholesalers and retailers, whereby the retailers operate under a common name or symbol and purchase all of their supplies through a particular wholesaler. The best-known example of this

TABLE 3.8: DETAILS OF WHOLESALE DISTRIBUTION ENTERPRISES IN 1991

Description of Business	Number of Enterprises	Turnover excl. VAT (£m)
Grocery	134	1,438.6
Other Food, Drink and Tobacco	613	1,659.7
Clothing, Footwear, Photographic and Optical	331	731.7
Builders' Materials	245	629.5
Hardware and Electrical	240	458.8
Motor Vehicles and Non-Agricultural Machinery	455	1,653.4
Agricultural Machinery	174	154.3
All Other Non-Food	824	3,393.0
Total	3,016	10,119.0

Source: CSO, Annual Services Inquiry 1991.

is the SuperValu and Centra stores which are linked to the Musgrave wholesale group. These outlets are estimated to have around 15 per cent of the retail grocery market.

Financial Services

The major financial institutions are ranked in Table 3.9 on the basis of their total assets. Again the data suffer from certain deficiencies. For example, total assets of institutions will include their overseas subsidiaries and thus provide a somewhat misleading picture of their position in the domestic market. Nevertheless, even allowing for this shortcoming, it is clear that the two largest banking groups are much bigger in size than all of their competitors. The combined assets of the two largest banks at the end of 1994 amounted to £38 billion, which represented 57 per cent of the total assets of the 25 financial institutions listed in Table 3.9. The assets of the third largest bank are equivalent to just over a quarter of those of the largest bank. Historically, the main financial groupings could be divided into separate categories, each of which was legally confined to particular lines of business. Thus, for example, the associated banks provided a broad range of retail and wholesale banking services and were traditionally responsible for the money transmission system, the building societies provided mortgage finance, the Trustee Savings Banks (TSBs) and Post Office Savings Bank were obliged to lend the bulk of their resources to the Exchequer, while the ACC and the ICC were originally established to provide credit in order to encourage the development of particular sectors, namely agriculture and small business. Most of these restrictions have now been removed.

A series of mergers during the 1960s reduced the number of associated banks from eight to four. The associated banks established an interest rate cartel in 1913 and from the mid-1950s onwards proposed changes to their agreed interest rates were approved by the Central Bank (McGowan, 1986a), thus providing the cartel with a form of official approval. The cartel was formally wound up in the mid-1980s. The TSBs have gradually expanded their branch network, while their number has declined as a result of a series of amalgamations. In 1992, the two remaining TSB groups combined to form a single entity.

Building societies traditionally specialised in raising funds from members and depositors for lending to members largely for house purchase by way of a mortgage. Prior to the passage of the Building Societies Act (1989) the societies were legally prevented from engaging in unsecured lending and were thus not in competition with banks in most areas of the lending market. For many years the societies were insulated from competition in the mortgage market.[5]

TABLE 3.9: IRISH FINANCIAL INSTITUTIONS AT 31 DECEMBER 1994

Name of Institution	Total Assets (£m)
AIB	21,036
Bank of Ireland	17,126
Ulster Bank	5,662
Banque Nationale de Paris	3,239
Irish Permanent	2,711
First National Building Society	1,752
Woodchester Investments	1,502
Irish Intercontinental Bank	1,440
Anglo Irish Bankcorp	1,407
Scotia Bank of Ireland	1,384
Educational Building Society	1,369
National Irish Bank	1,221
TSB Bank	1,129
ICC Bank	1,091
Post Office Savings Bank	1,004
ACC Bank	931
Barclays Bank	830
Irish Nationwide Building Society	690
Citibank	466
Westdeutsche Landesbank (Irl)	184
Ansbacher and Co.	183
Smurfit Paribas Bank	175
Bank of America	170
Guinness and Mahon(a)	100
Norwich Irish Building Society	95

(a) Guinness and Mahon was acquired by the Irish Permanent Building Society during the course of 1995.

Source: *Business and Finance,* Top 1,000 Companies.

---

[5]   Until the mid-1980s the favourable tax treatment of building society deposit interest meant that the societies could attract funds from depositors at rates of interest which allowed them to advance mortgage loans at interest rates which could not be matched by other institutions.

Prior to 1980 it was possible for new societies to enter the market and three new societies were formed during the 1970s (McGowan, 1988). Only one new society has been established since the passing of the Building Societies Act, 1976, and its establishment was challenged in the High Court by one of the existing societies in 1979,[6] with the result that while this society was permitted to carry on business, the prospect of further new entrants was effectively eliminated. The mutuality criteria with which a financial institution attempting to set up a society would have to comply would be such that it could not ensure that it would retain control of such a society (DKM, 1984).

Like the associated banks, the five largest building societies traditionally operated an interest-rate cartel (Thom, 1984). In 1981, this group accounted for more than 93 per cent of total building society assets, with the largest society on its own accounting for over 40 per cent of the total (see Table 3.10). The number of societies fell from 16 in 1981 to 6 in 1995 as a result of a series of amalgamations. Table 3.10 indicates that the societies that no longer operate between them accounted for only a small proportion of total society assets in 1981, so that the consolidation in the number of societies may not have increased concentration all that much. The only society not constituted as a mutual organisation was acquired by one of the larger associated banks in the mid-1980s. Since 1981 the share of the largest society has fallen significantly, while the ICS more than trebled its share during the period up to 1993. More importantly, while the number of societies has fallen, financial deregulation has resulted in other lending agencies entering the mortgage market and competing aggressively with the building societies.

The evidence on the level of competition in Irish financial markets is mixed. Guiomard (1995), for example, has pointed to the large market share held by the two largest banking groups and the fact that they are extremely profitable compared to banks in other countries. There is overseas evidence that banks in concentrated markets were slower to raise interest rates on deposits

---

[6] *Irish Permanent Building Society* v. *Registrar of Building Societies* (1981) ILRM 242.

in response to increases in market rates but were faster to reduce them when market rates fell, so that, in effect, such banks skimmed off a surplus on interest-rate movements in both directions (Neumark and Sharpe, 1992). At the same time, Nathan and Neave (1989) point out that concentration ratios are of little benefit as an indicator of firms' market power unless they refer to individual markets, since attempts to exercise market power must be implemented in given markets. Since 1984 there has been a significant deregulation of the financial sector, which had the effect of eliminating restrictions on the types of business in which different institutions could engage, a point that is considered at greater length in Chapter 12.

TABLE 3.10: DISTRIBUTION OF BUILDING SOCIETY ASSETS (% OF TOTAL)

Name of Society	1981	1993
Irish Permanent	40.4	34.8
First National	20.5	22.5
EBS	22.1	17.6
Irish Nationwide	6.0	8.8
ICS	4.3	15.2
Irish Life	2.0	*
Norwich Irish	1.3	1.2
Midland and Western	0.7	*
Irish Mutual	0.5	*
Ireland Benefit	0.6	*
O'Connell Benefit	0.5	*
Postal Service Permanent	0.4	*
Irish Savings	0.3	*
Garda	0.2	*
Guinness Permanent	0.1	*
Metropolitan	0.1	*
Total	100.0	100.0
Four Largest Societies	89.0	90.1

* Denotes societies which no longer operate.

Source: Annual Report of the Registrar of Building Societies 1981, *Business and Finance* (1994) and IPA (1993).

Financial institutions are multi-product firms. They compete to attract funds from depositors and to lend to various categories of borrower, for example. The deposit market can be further divided into markets for retail and wholesale deposits. On the lending side, there are distinct markets for lending to large and small firms and to personal customers. In addition, it is also possible to divide the lending market into markets for specific types of lending such as mortgage lending. In the case of the financial sector, there are data on individual product markets available which can shed some light on the level of competition.

Both the non-associated banks and the building societies have made significant inroads into the associated banks' share of the deposit market since the 1960s. This may be seen more clearly by considering trends over time in the public's holdings of money and other liquid assets (see Figure 3.1). The non-associated banks and buildings societies each had close to 20 per cent of the market in 1992, compared with shares of 5 and 4 per cent respectively in 1966. The combined share of the four associated banks had fallen to around 33 per cent. The State institutions, particularly the Post Office, also lost market share. Whether one is concerned with the market for retail or wholesale deposits, it is clear that there are large numbers of institutions competing with one another in those markets.

FIGURE 3.1: MONEY AND OTHER LIQUID ASSETS (% DISTRIBUTION)

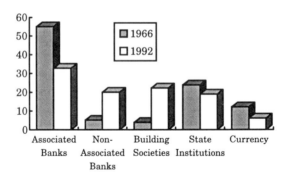

Source: Central Bank Bulletins.

Figure 3.2 shows how the associated banks also lost market share in the lending business. In 1992 they accounted for just over 40 per cent of total non-Government lending, compared with 76 per cent in 1966. Both the non-associated banks and building societies accounted for more than 20 per cent of lending to the private sector in 1992. In the latter case, of course, much of the increase resulted from increased home ownership as the societies were virtually confined to mortgage lending until 1989. The substantial erosion of the associated banks' share of both the deposit and lending markets suggests a significant increase in competition in financial markets.

FIGURE 3.2: NON-GOVERNMENT CREDIT (% DISTRIBUTION)

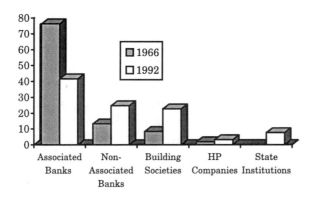

Source: Central Bank Bulletins.

Such conclusions must be subject to two caveats. Firstly, the figures may overstate the extent of the decline in importance of the associated banks because, as McGowan (1988) has pointed out, a significant part of the loss in market share was to their own non-associated bank subsidiaries. Secondly, the lending market can almost certainly be broken down into a series of separate distinct markets and it may well be that the level of competition varies considerably between these different markets. It seems reasonable to argue that the markets for large corporate loans and for small business loans are separate from one another. In the former case, Irish banks have always been exposed to external competition from foreign banks that did not have a presence in Ireland and, according to McGowan (1988: 47), such direct lending accounted for close to one-tenth of total private-sector borrowing from banks within Ireland during the 1980s. Irish-based institutions are probably not exposed to foreign competition in the case of small business loans. Traditionally, building societies and TSBs were effectively excluded from commercial lending. While they can now compete in the market for small business lending, their lack of experience in such business means that they may well be cautious about entering that market so that competition in that area may be less intense.

Similarly, the markets for unsecured personal lending and for mortgages would appear to constitute two further product markets. Figure 3.3 shows that banks and other non-traditional lenders have greatly increased their share of mortgage lending at the expense of building societies and state institutions since 1980. The number of mortgage loans has increased steadily since the early 1980s, indicating that increased competition means that mortgages are more readily available. There has also been a considerable expansion in the range of mortgage products offered, with the introduction of endowment mortgages, fixed-rate mortgages, low-start mortgages and a number of other variants, providing consumers with greater choice and with the option of choosing a mortgage more suited to their particular needs.

FIGURE 3.3: % DISTRIBUTION OF NEW MORTGAGE LOANS

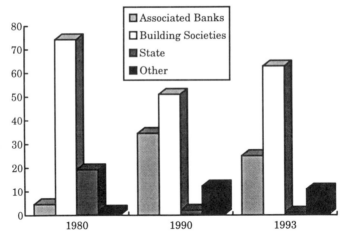

Source: Department of the Environment.

Building societies have begun to engage in unsecured lending while restrictions on personal and corporate lending by the TSB have also been eased. Building societies have also begun to compete more actively in the wholesale deposit market and to offer credit card services, while the largest society has recently announced plans to establish a leasing subsidiary. Over the past 20 years, there has also been a significant growth in credit unions, which compete in the retail deposit and personal-lending markets. The tendency for financial institutions to compete across a broader range of products has significantly increased consumer choice.

Conclusions

The present chapter sought to shed some light on the structure of the Irish economy. The picture that emerges is rather mixed. Clearly, Ireland has very few firms which are large by international standards. Nevertheless, there is a small number of firms which are quite large by Irish standards and it is possible that there are some markets where a small number of large firms would enjoy some degree of market power. In industries characterised by economies of scale it would appear, *a priori*, that the small size of the Irish economy would be reflected in high levels of concentration. There are serious data deficiencies which make it difficult to do more than offer some general broad-ranging comments on various sectors of the economy. It is difficult to see why some measures of concentration, such as the Herfindahl Hirschman Index, are not published by the CSO for both the manufacturing and distribution sectors. Such data would provide some useful additional insights into the structure of Irish business.

APPENDIX 3.1: DETAILS OF MANUFACTURING
ENTERPRISES BY SECTOR

Industry Sector	Number of Enterprises
Production & preserving of meat	65
Production & preserving of poultry	10
Meat & poultry products	59
Processing of fish & fish products	73
Fruit & vegetable processing	19
Dairy products	72
Grain mill products & starches	11
Farm animal feeds	51
Pet foods	4
Bread, fresh pastry & cakes	188
Biscuits & preserved pastry & cakes	13
Sugar, cocoa, chocolate etc.	24
Macaroni, noodles, couscous etc.	8
Processing of tea & coffee	5
Other foods	21
Distilled potable alcoholic drinks	7
Ethyl alcohol, cider, mineral waters & soft drinks	22
Beer & malt	11
Tobacco products	6
Textile preparation & spinning	8
Cotton & worsted weaving	6
Wool weaving	9
Other textile weaving	4
Textile finishing and made-up articles	61
Carpets & rugs	13
Cordage, rope, twine & netting	6
Other textiles	30
Knitted fabrics & hosiery	12
Knitted pullovers, cardigans etc.	40
Leather clothes & other apparel	33
Workwear	14
Other outerwear	144
Underwear	34
Fur & fur articles	8
Tanning & dressing of leather	6
Luggage, handbags, saddlery etc.	18
Footwear	18
Sawmilling & wood products	46
Builders carpentry & joinery	113
Wooden containers	21
Other wood products	33
Paper & Paperboard	9
Corrugated paper etc.	49
Paper stationery	13
Other paper articles	25

Industry Sector	Number of Enterprises
Printing & publishing of newspapers	333
Reproduction of recorded media	19
Industrial gases, dyes & pigments	6
Other inorganic basic chemicals	9
Other organic basic chemicals	19
Fertilisers & nitrogen compounds	16
Plastics in primary forms	7
Pesticides & other agro-chemicals	6
Paints, varnishes & inks	22
Basic pharmaceutical products	11
Pharmaceutical preparations	38
Soap, detergents, polishes etc.	17
Perfumes & toilet preparations	16
Other chemical products	37
Man-made fibres	5
Rubber products	37
Plastic plates, sheets, tubes etc.	26
Plastic packing goods	48
Builders plastic ware	53
Other plastic products	63
Shaping & processing of flat glass	15
Hollow glass	19
Glass fibres & other glass	9
Ceramic products	18
Bricks, tiles etc. in baked clay	5
Cement, lime & plaster	8
Concrete products	53
Furnaces & furnace burners	20
Lifting & handling equipment	43
Non-domestic cooling & ventilation equipment	31
Agricultural & forestry machinery	28
Machine tools	20
Mining, quarrying & construction machinery	11
Machinery for food, drink & tobacco processing	29
Special purpose machinery	49
Domestic appliances	15
Office machinery & computers	64
Electric motors, generators etc.	28
Electricity distribution apparatus	43
Insulated wire & cable	21
Accumulators, batteries etc.	7
Lighting equipment	18
Electrical equipment for engines, vehicles etc.	11
Other electrical equipment	18
Electronic valves, tubes & other electronic components	21
Television, radio transmitters & telephone equipment	18
Ready-mixed concrete	23

Industry Sector	Number of Enterprises
Cutting, shaping & finishing of stone	39
Other non-metallic mineral products	10
Basic metals	37
Metal structures & parts of structures	115
Builders carpentry & joinery of metal	96
Tanks, reservoirs & metal containers	31
Central heating boilers, radiators & steam generators	16
Forging, pressing etc. of metals	10
General mechanical engineering	21
Cutlery locks & hinges	10
Tools	50
Steel drums & containers	6
Light metal packaging	6
Wire products	22
Fasteners, screw machine products, chains & springs	20
Other fabricated metal products	95
Machinery for production/use of electrical power	52
Televisions & radios, recording equipment etc.	11
Medical & surgical equipment	39
Instruments for measuring, navigating etc.	60
Industrial process control equipment	6
Optical instruments, photo equipment, watches etc.	21
Motor vehicles	14
Motor vehicle bodies & trailers	43
Motor vehicle parts & accessories	37
Building & repairing of ships	19
Building & repairing of pleasure & sporting boats	9
Railway vehicles & aircraft	12
Other transport equipment	4
Chairs & seats	24
Other office & shop furniture	32
Other kitchen furniture	67
Other furniture	100
Mattresses	13
Jewellery & related articles	28
Musical instruments	8
Sports goods	14
Games & toys	14
Brooms & brushes	7
Other manufacturing	28
Total manufacturing	4126

Notes: A number of the industry groupings have been abbreviated.

Source: CSO, 1991 Census of Industrial Production: Provisional Overall Results for Industrial Enterprises.

4

COMPETITION RULES OVERSEAS

Antitrust in the United States

The United States is generally regarded as the home of modern competition law, or antitrust, and it has successfully exported the concept to many other countries throughout the world. As Scherer and Ross (1990) have observed, competition law in its modern form is a North American invention. This is evidenced by the fact that "strains of American antitrust can be discerned, in varying measure, in competition policies of nearly every nation" (Ahdar, 1991: 217).

The US legislation prompted the introduction of competition laws in New Zealand as early as 1908 (Ahdar, 1991). As Hogan (1989) points out, the EU competition rules, on which the Irish Competition Act is modelled, were themselves based on the US antitrust laws.

Antitrust laws were introduced in response to growing opposition to the problem of market dominance which began to emerge in the United States in the latter half of the nineteenth century, although Shenefield and Stelzer (1993) argue that their origins can in fact be traced back to the common-law proscriptions on restraints of trade which America's English settlers brought with them to the New World. The establishment of large-scale business organisations such as Standard Oil and others took the form of a trust under which shareholder voting powers were concentrated in the hands of a single managing trustee. As a result, legislative attempts to control such organisations came to be known as "antitrust" laws.

The basic elements of US antitrust law are to be found in the Sherman Act, 1890.[1] The legislation was introduced following calls by President Harrison for "penal legislation" to control

---

[1]   15 USCA, § 1–7.

"dangerous conspiracies against the public good" (*ibid.*: 8). Section 1 of the Sherman Act provides that:

> Every contract, combination in the form of trust or otherwise, or conspiracy, in restraint of trade or commerce among the several States, or with foreign nations, is hereby declared to be illegal.

Violations of this provision constitute a criminal offence and carry a maximum penalty, in the case of individuals, of a fine of $350,000 or up to three years imprisonment, or both, or, in the case of a company, a maximum fine of $10 million. Section 2 of the Act states that:

> Every person who shall monopolize, or attempt to monopolize, or combine or conspire with any other person or persons, to monopolize any part of the trade or commerce among the several States, or with any foreign nations, shall be deemed guilty of a felony. . . .

The basic form of Sections 1 and 2 of the Sherman Act will be recognisable to readers familiar with the competition rules set out in Articles 85 and 86 of the Treaty of Rome, and indeed in Sections 4 and 5 of the Competition Act, 1991. As with such provisions, the Sherman Act contains a broad sweeping prohibition of anti-competitive behaviour with no detailed list of the types of behaviour prohibited. Decisions on this were left completely up to the courts.

The US competition laws do not exist in a vacuum. There is, alongside the competition laws, a plethora of State intervention into markets by way of regulation in many sectors. The existence of regulation does not exempt a sector from the antitrust laws, but "actions undertaken at the behest or under the supervision of state or federal government authority" are exempt (White, 1993). There also has not always been one coherent philosophy behind US antitrust law, but a mixture of sometimes conflicting policies. Although it is not as important in shaping policy as the basic efficiency arguments for competition, an enduring element is "a distinct brand of American populism — favouring smallness and fearing bigness" (White, 1993).

Shenefield and Stelzer (1993) point out that those expecting the passage of the Act to be followed by a period of vigorous enforcement were disappointed. Siegfried and Mahony (1990) noted that following the passage of the Sherman Act, no instructions were issued to the various federal and state attorneys general regarding its implementation, nor were specific resources provided for enforcement. Undeterred by this, and despite encountering considerable difficulty in securing official authorisation and funding, John Ruhm, US district attorney for the middle district of Tennessee, initiated the first federal prosecution under the Act against a coal cartel in Nashville, Tennessee.

An interesting feature of *Jellico Mountain Coal*[2] was the question of whether the cartel constituted a restraint of trade or commerce among the several states. Although it is suggested that a major difference between US and EU competition rules is that the latter are concerned with preventing restrictions on trade between member states, Sherman Sections 1 and 2 also refer to trade between the several states of the US. In *Jellico Mountain Coal* the coal was in fact "imported" from mines in the state of Kentucky. Consequently, it was held that the arrangements constituted a restraint of trade among the several states. The cartel was found to be in violation of the Sherman Act and, as Siegfried and Mahony observe, "the rest is history".

Despite the successful prosecution of some of the major trusts, including Standard Oil, in the early part of the century, pressure mounted for the antitrust laws to be further strengthened. All three political parties supported tougher legislation in the 1912 presidential election campaign.[3] This was followed in 1914 by the passage of the Clayton Act[4] and the Federal Trade Commission Act.[5] The Clayton Act includes specific prohibitions on price discrimination, tying, and restrictions on mergers.[6] The Federal

---

[2]   *Jellico Mountain Coal*, 46F. 432 (C.C.M.D. Tenn. 1891).

[3]   In addition to the Democrats and Republicans, there was the Bull Moose party led by Theodore Roosevelt.

[4]   15 USCA § 12–27.

[5]   15 USCA §41–51.

[6]   The Clayton Act is the principal merger control statute in the United States. It is not proposed to consider the treatment of mergers under US law in the present text.

Trade Commission Act contains a prohibition on unfair competitive behaviour.[7] This Act also established the Federal Trade Commission (USFTC), which is one of two federal agencies responsible for enforcement of the antitrust laws.[8] The Robinson-Patman Act was introduced in 1936 to deal with price discrimination,[9] while the Celler-Kefauver Act, 1950 was designed to remedy perceived shortcomings in the merger provisions of the Clayton Act.

Per se v. **Rule of Reason**
In spite of the wide-ranging provisions, particularly of Section 1 of the Sherman Act, the courts decided at a relatively early stage against a literal interpretation of the Act. In *Addyston Pipe,*[10] Judge Taft referred to the common law as it applied in America and England at that time, noting that it permitted restraints of trade which were merely ancillary to some legitimate cause, but that it voided those whose main object was to restrict competition. He then distinguished between naked and ancillary restraints, concluding that the former so lacked any redeeming features that there was no need "to set sail on a sea of doubt" to establish whether or not the restraint was reasonable and that they were *per se* offensive. This distinction between offences which were *per se* or by their nature offensive and those which should be assessed on their merits on "a rule of reason" basis was confirmed by the Supreme Court in *Standard Oil*[11] in 1911. The *per se* rule was further enshrined in *Trenton Potteries*[12] where the Supreme Court rejected the view that price-fixing was not illegal if the prices fixed were reasonable. Justice Stone, delivering the verdict of the Court, stated:

---

[7]   15 USCA § 41–51.

[8]   The antitrust division of the Department of Justice is also responsible for enforcement. It has exclusive jurisdiction in the case of criminal offences, while the USFTC may only act in civil cases.

[9]   This legislation has not been actively enforced in recent years.

[10]   *United States* v. *Addyston Pipe and Steel Company et al.*, 85 Fed. 271 (6th Cir. 1898).

[11]   *Standard Oil Company of New Jersey et al.* v. *United States*, 221 US 1 (1911).

[12]   *United States* v. *Trenton Potteries Co. et al.* 273 US 392 (1927).

The aim and result of every price-fixing agreement, if effective, is the elimination of one form of competition. The power to fix prices, whether reasonably exercised or not, involves the power to control the market and to fix arbitrary and unreasonable prices. The reasonable price fixed today may through economic and business changes become the unreasonable price of tomorrow. Once established, it may be maintained unchanged because of the absence of competition secured by the agreement for a price reasonable when fixed.[13]

The Supreme Court appeared to row back from the *per se* prohibition on price-fixing just six years later in *Appalachian Coal.*[14] In that case the Court found that a cartel among coal mine operators formed during the depression was not illegal. In 1940, however, the Court in *Socony-Vacuum Oil* reasserted that price-fixing should be subject to a *per se* rule, essentially rejecting the earlier *Appalachian Coal* judgment. The judgment, delivered by Justice Douglas, stated that:

[For]over forty years this Court has consistently and without deviation adhered to the principle that price-fixing agreements are unlawful *per se* under the Sherman Act and that no showing of so-called competitive abuses or evils which those agreements were designed to eliminate or alleviate may be interposed as a defence.

He went on to point out that:

Ruinous competition, financial disaster, evils of price-cutting appear throughout our history as ostensible justifications for price-fixing. If the so-called competitive abuses were to be appraised here, the reasonableness of prices would necessarily become an issue in every price-fixing case. In that event the Sherman Act would soon be emasculated; its philosophy would be supplanted by one which is wholly alien to a system of free competition; it would not be the charter of freedom which its framers intended.[15]

---

[13] *United States* v. *Trenton Potteries Company et al.* 273 US 392 (1927).

[14] *Appalachian Coals Inc. et al.* v. *United States*, 288 US 344 (1933).

[15] *United States* v. *Socony-Vacuum Oil, Inc. et al.*, 310 US 150 (1940).

Agreements on maximum prices, market sharing and bid rigging
have all been found to be subject to the *per se* rule on price fixing.
There are some exceptions to the *per se* rule on price fixing. In
looking at collective musical copyright licensing, the Supreme
Court has indicated that a rule of reason test was the appropriate
one because such licensing systems were simply the most efficient
means for licensing use of copyright works.[16] Similarly, where it
was shown that the product could not be made available at all
without some form of restraint, the Supreme Court decided that
the appropriate rule to apply was a rule of reason test. The key
issue is whether there is a "naked" price restraint or whether the
restraint is justified on efficiency grounds.

While horizontal cartel arrangements have been subject to a
fairly consistent treatment, the position with respect to vertical
arrangements has shifted back and forth over time. The Supreme Court decided that these should be subject to a rule of
reason test in the early 1960s, only to come down subsequently
in favour of a *per se* prohibition, before deciding in *Sylvania*[17]
that non-price vertical restraints should be subject to a rule of
reason test. During the 1980s the authorities adopted a very
relaxed view of non-price vertical restraints with relatively few
enforcement actions against such arrangements. The Department of Justice 1985 Vertical Restraints Guidelines stated, for
example, that antitrust enforcement should focus on interbrand
restraint, because:

> . . . vertical restraints that only affect intrabrand competition
> generally represent little anticompetitive threat and involve
> some form of economic integration between different levels of
> production or distribution that tend to create efficiencies
> (Department of Justice, 1985, para. 2.1).

The Guidelines were rescinded in 1993 and the Department of

---

[16] *Broadcast Music Inc. et al.* v. *Columbia Broadcasting Systems et al.*, 441
US 1 (1979) and *Columbia Broadcasting System Inc.* v. *ASCAP et al.*, 450
US 970 (1981). Both decisions applied in the context of consent decrees
under which the copyright owners retained the right to grant individual
licences to users.

[17] *Continental TV Inc. et al.* v. *GTE Sylvania Inc.*, 433 US 36 (1977).

Justice has since opened a number of investigations into vertical restraints.

RPM was first subject to a *per se* prohibition in *Dr Miles Medical*.[18] In 1937, however, the position was altered dramatically by the passage by Congress of a rider to the D.C. Appropriations Act[19] which amended the Sherman Act and legalised RPM in states which had so-called "fair trading" laws.[20] Subsequent investigations revealed that at least one retail trade association which had lobbied for the passage of the Miller-Tydings amendment, as it was known, had bribed administration officials to help secure the passage of the legislation (Kramer, 1991). The Miller-Tydings provisions were eventually repealed in 1976, and in *Sylvania* the Court distinguished between price and non-price vertical restraints, and held that RPM was subject to the *per se* rule.

The 1985 Vertical Restraints Guidelines, while ostensibly only applying to non-price restraints, attempted to limit the situations in which a restraint would be considered a price as opposed to a non-price restraint, thus implying a less strict approach to RPM. The Justice Department had previously sought to persuade the Supreme Court to reverse its treatment of RPM by filing an *amicus curiae* brief in *Monsanto*.[21] This, however, prompted Congress to respond by prohibiting the Department from using any appropriated funds "for any activity to alter the *per se* prohibition on resale price maintenance in effect under Federal antitrust laws" (Dick, 1994: 4). As noted, the Vertical Restraints Guidelines have been rescinded and the Department has filed cases alleging RPM.

Market Dominance
Under Section 2 of the Sherman Act as with Article 86 of the Treaty of Rome, it is not mere size which is deemed offensive. This view was set out by Justice Learned Hand in *Alcoa* where he stated that:

---

[18] *Dr Miles Medical Co.* v. *John D. Park and Sons*, 220 US 373 (1911).

[19] This allowed the provision to escape the Presidential veto.

[20] It is interesting to note that RPM was justified on the grounds that it promoted fair trade.

[21] *Monsanto Co.,* v. *Spray-Rite Service Corp.*, 465 US 752 (1984).

A single producer may be the survivor out of a group of active competitors, merely by virtue of his superior skill, foresight and industry. In such cases a strong argument can be made that, although, the result may expose the public to the evils of monopoly, the Act does not mean to condemn the resultant of those very forces which it is its prime object to foster: finis opus coronat. The successful competitor, having been urged to compete, must not be turned upon when he wins.[22]

In *Standard Oil* the Supreme Court held that the creation by a series of mergers of a dominant firm with a 90 per cent share of the market constituted monopolisation within the meaning of Section 2. It endorsed the view of the lower court which held that the arrangements operated to destroy "the potentiality of competition".[23] The *Standard Oil* decision is seen as a landmark decision and led to the break-up of the undertaking. In 1982, proceedings taken by the Department of Justice against the AT&T telephone monopoly were settled by means of a consent decree which provided for the break-up of AT&T into a long-distance operator and a series of local regional monopolies, the "Baby Bells", along with the introduction of competing firms in the long-distance market.[24] In effect, the *AT&T* case resulted in the break-up of a dominant firm which had existed for decades. The case centred on the claim that entry into markets where competition was possible at the time (equipment and long-distance services) was prevented by the abuse by AT&T of its natural monopoly in the market for local services. The break-up into competitive and natural monopoly components was therefore deemed to be the remedy necessary to deal with the alleged form of abuse. The provisions of Article 86

---

[22] *United States* v. *Aluminium Company of America et al.*, 148 F.2d 416 (2nd Cir. 1945).

[23] *Standard Oil of New Jersey et al.* v. *United States,* 221 US 1 (1911). In fact the arrangements were held to infringe both Sections 1 and 2 of the Sherman Act. There are strong similarities between the judgment and the European Court of Justice judgment in *Continental Can.*

[24] *United States* v. *American Tel. and Tel. Co.,* 552 F. Supp. 131 (1982). The consent decree also prevented the Baby Bells from providing long-distance services in competition with other operators because of their natural monopoly in local services.

would appear not to go as far as requiring break-up of a dominant firm, although, theoretically at least, such a break-up might constitute the most appropriate remedy.[25] *Standard Oil* and *AT&T* are by far the most spectacular cases involving break-ups of dominant firms. The Section 2 actions for divestment which were instigated in the 1970s but dropped in the early 1980s, against IBM and other firms, indicate that the weapon of divestment, while very powerful, is also one that cannot be deployed as freely as the other sanctions in the antitrust battery. Posner (1970) found that structural adjustments were imposed in only 33 Section 2 cases since 1890 and that all but eight of these were decided prior to 1950. This issue is considered in Chapter 8. Private actions may also be brought under Section 2, typically in respect of specific alleged abuses such as predatory pricing or foreclosure.

Enforcement

A different feature of the US system is the multiplicity of modes of enforcement of the competition laws. The Justice Department has sole responsibility for enforcement of the Sherman Act, violations of which can be pursued by the Department as either criminal offences or civil matters. They thus have a range of sanctions from imprisonment, through fines, civil action for injunction or damages, to orders for divestment. The Federal Trade Commission and the Department of Justice both have enforcement responsibility for the Clayton Act and the Hart-Scott-Rodino mergers legislation, with responsibility for pursuing any given violation being allocated by agreement between the two agencies. Infringements of these Acts are civil matters, with the civil sanctions described above available to the enforcement bodies. The FTC Act, 1914 also gives the FTC a roving brief in respect of "unfair methods of competition". In the individual states, virtually all of which have a state antitrust law, the state Attorney General has responsibility for enforcement.

Private actions may be brought under the Sherman, Clayton

---

[25] It has been argued in the US that greater use could have been made of Section 2 to break up a number of other dominant firms and *AT&T* is admittedly something of an exception. As noted in Chapter 6, the Competition Act allows for the possibility of the break-up of a dominant firm by means of a Ministerial Order pursuant to Section 14.

and HSR legislation for damages or injunctions, or both, by any party suffering antitrust damage. Where an action by either of the enforcement bodies has already established the civil wrong, the private plaintiff need only prove their damage to succeed. The civil damages in all antitrust actions are tripled and this is seen to act as a strong deterrent to antitrust violations. The number of private actions tends to exceed greatly the number of actions brought by government agencies. Class actions are possible, which is of some significance in competition law generally. Actions may be taken under the state antitrust laws, by private litigants or by the state attorneys general as prosecutors, while the state attorneys may file treble damage actions on behalf of groups of citizens.

A final point worth noting is that the federal antitrust laws, like EU competition rules, operate alongside a system of state legislation. Folsom (1990) pointed out that 13 states had enacted antitrust laws in advance of the passage of the Sherman Act in 1890, and currently only Vermont and Pennsylvania do not have primary antitrust statutes. Traditionally, state antitrust actions have tended to be relatively limited. However, during the 1980s when federal antitrust enforcement waned, state action increased considerably. Following the introduction by the Department of Justice of its 1985 Vertical Restraint Guidelines, the state attorneys general agreed their own guidelines which represented a statement of common prosecutorial policy that openly ran counter to the Federal guidelines (Folsom, 1990). It seems unlikely that the rise in state action will be reversed in the years ahead. Co-operation between state and federal antitrust agencies has increased considerably in recent years and the state authorities also co-operate with each other in their investigations and cases. State enforcement is perceived to pay for itself. According to Folsom (1990), state antitrust laws rarely conflict with federal law and the application of state laws is pre-empted only in very rare circumstances, except in the case of sports cases. State laws extend to all activities, however national, provided that they affect commerce within the state. Similarly, the federal laws apply to all business activities, no matter how local they may be in nature, provided that they can be shown to have an effect on interstate commerce. The Supreme Court has held that even the activities of local real estate agents come within the scope of the Sherman Act.[26] In the case of 32 states, the state law formally requires adherence to federal antitrust precedents (Folsom, 1990).

Background to the EU Rules

In contrast to the US, cartels were widely encouraged in many European countries until after the Second World War. Examples of Government-sponsored or assisted cartels in the inter-war era existed in many European countries. Hardach (1975), for example, notes that "German industry . . . had organised competition since the late nineteenth century through a multitude of cartels under the benevolent eye of the State." Stockmann and Strauch (1984) noted that the number of known cartels in Germany increased from four in 1865 to 250 by 1896. Wiedenfeld (1927) reported that there were at least 100 international cartel agreements involving German firms, mainly in chemicals, in the early part of this century. Stockmann and Strauch (1984) observed that, prior to the outbreak of the First World War, legislation began to require compulsory cartelisation of industry. Hardach (op. cit.: 195) reports that the years following the 1920s hyper-inflation in Germany "were a period of strong and comprehensive cartelisation and concentration, since competition was felt to be troublesome and wasteful". Foreman-Peck (1983) reported that in Germany, by the early 1930s, about half of industrial raw materials and semi-manufactured goods was controlled by cartels or producers' associations. Stockmann and Strauch (1984) noted how, on assuming power, the Nazis introduced the Act on Compulsory Cartels in 1933.

The position in other countries was not remarkably different. According to Arndt (1944: 6):

> Government assistance to British industry during the 1930s largely served to speed the process of monopolisation and cartelisation which by the end of the decade covered all the most important industries of the country.

The combination of several large companies into the giant ICI chemicals group is one of the best-known examples of this approach. The UK Government supported a steel cartel in the

---

[26] Real Estate Board of New Orleans Inc., 444 US 232 (1980).

1930s, while the UK banks operated a cartel up to 1971. According to Caves (1968), "the deluge of restrictive agreements shaken from the branches of British industry confirmed the view that cartel-like trade associations had been essentially pervasive". Jorberg (1975) noted that cartels and price agreements in Sweden during the 1890s enabled a number of inefficient firms to operate.

Following the defeat of Germany in the Second World War, the Western Allied powers decided that the major German industrial cartels should be broken up. In a letter to Army Secretary Hull in 1944, President Roosevelt wrote that the defeat of Germany would need to be followed "by the eradication of these [cartel] weapons of economic warfare" (United States Army, 1949). The Potsdam Agreement between the victorious allies resolved that:

> At the earliest practicable date, the German economy should be decentralized for the purpose of eliminating excessive concentration of economic power, exemplified in particular by cartels, syndicates, trusts and other monopolistic arrangements (OG/CC, 1946).

This led to the enactment of separate competition laws in the British, US and subsequently French zones, based on the provisions of "The Havana Charter" (see below). These continued to apply following the establishment of the Federal Republic in 1949. Responsibility for their administration was transferred to the Federal Ministry of Economics in 1955. Under the Rome Convention the Allied laws remained in place as German law until the Federal Republic enacted its own competition laws. Although proposals for competition legislation were first proposed in 1940, the German legislation was not passed until 1957.

The important role played in the development of competition law in the Federal Republic of Germany by the competition legislation which was effectively imposed by the victorious Western Allies was summarised by Stockmann and Strauch (op. cit.: 1–20):

> Although the Allied decartelization and deconcentration laws have been criticised as failures, the regulation of deconcentration being regarded as the greater failure, it is fair to say that the present German cartel law, which is among the most comprehensive in the world, is unimaginable without this postwar experience. It is true that the Allied laws had little lasting direct

effect; they were unable to stop the general trend towards re-concentration, and they did not really prevent many kinds of restrictive arrangements. However, they provided the basis for the better understanding of the benefits to be derived from a free-market economy, an understanding which was borne out by the so-called "economic miracle" of the ensuing years. To summarise, when judged under long-term criteria, the Allied decartelization and deconcentration laws may be considered a political success.

In turn, German influence played an important role in shaping EU competition policy in its early years.

Principal Aspects of EU Competition Law

The European competition regime and substantive law are comprehensively covered by various text books and this summary is intended to give no more than a comparative broad overview of their nature and outline.[27] The greatest distinction between the European regime and all other competition regimes is that it is a supranational regime, which by virtue of Article 90 and Articles 92 to 94 has jurisdiction over not only the behaviour of undertakings, but also, to some extent, the laws of Member States and their industrial policy.

For the substantive law covering the actions of firms rather than the State, comparison with the other major competition regime, that of the US, may serve to illustrate the particular nature of the European system. There are two significant differences between Europe and the US. One is that the competition rules in the Rome Treaty create a blanket prohibition with the possibility of exemption where the US law creates only a blanket prohibition. Thus, where in the US the evolution of *per se* rules and the rule of reason approach has been the creation of the courts, in the EU the exemptions have been the creation of the Commission and a different type of distinction has evolved between what is offensive, and what is not. Although some Court and Commission decisions may look like rule of reason decisions, it is possible to identify a number of areas where European jurisprudence chooses to find

---

[27] A non-exhaustive list would include Whish (1993), Bellamy and Child (1993), Van Bael and Bellis (1993).

offensive, and exemptable, behaviour which under the US rule of reason would not be offensive in the first place, the obvious examples, discussed elsewhere in this book, being the treatment of vertical restraints. This is seen to be more true of the Commission than of the European Court of Justice.

Articles 85 and 86 are the core of the competition rules as affecting undertakings. Article 85(1) prohibits and Article 85(2) makes void agreements, decisions and concerted practices between undertakings which "may affect trade between Member States" and which have as their object or effect the prevention, restriction or distortion of competition. Article 86 prohibits the abuse of a dominant position within the common market or a substantial part of it "in so far as it may affect trade between Member States". Articles 85 and 86 do not cover every sector of industry in the Union. The European Coal and Steel Treaty contains its own competition rules, similar, but not identical to, Articles 85 and 86, which exclude the operation of the Rome Treaty rules, and indeed the national law of Member States.[28] Agricultural products which are covered by the Common Agricultural Policy are largely exempt from the provisions of Article 85.

The European enforcement regime is identifiably the product of civil law rather than the common law adversarial system. Responsibility for enforcing the Treaty rules lies with the Commission, which combines the functions of granting negative clearances or exemptions to agreements notified to it; the investigation of complaints; own-initiative investigation of possibly offensive agreements or behaviour; imposition of penalties, in the form of fines and orders; and the formulation of exemptions of general application (block exemptions). It is often described as being judge, jury and executioner, although it is also the case that the requirements of procedural fairness imposed upon the Commission by the accumulated jurisprudence of the Court of First Instance and the European Court of Justice are often onerous by comparison with Irish judicial review criteria.

Council Regulation 17/62 provides generally for the powers

---

[28] See Bord na Móna/Fuel Distributors, Competition Authority Decision No, 458 of 26.2.96.

and procedure of the Commission. The effect of Article 85(1) is to prohibit anti-competitive agreements; Article 85(3) states that 85(1) may be declared inapplicable. The Commission is the body that is given power by the Regulation to grant such exemptions. It may grant negative clearances, on the basis of a notification from the undertaking or undertakings concerned, certifying that on the basis of the facts in its possession there are no grounds for it taking action against the notified agreement. It may make orders for the cessation of an infringement, on application from Member States or persons with *locus standi*, or on its own initiative. On application by the parties concerned, it may apply Article 85(3), and it is the sole body with that competence; the European Courts cannot grant exemptions. It may also, without notification of particular agreements, grant block exemptions. The Commission has adopted block exemptions in a number of areas: exclusive purchasing (with special provision for beer and motor fuel supply agreements);[29] exclusive distribution;[30] franchises;[31] know-how licensing;[32] patent licensing;[33] research and development joint ventures;[34] specialisation agreements;[35] and selective distribution of motor vehicles.[36] Decisions of the Commission may be appealed to the Court of First Instance and thence to the European Court of Justice; and the EU law referred to *passim* throughout this book is composed of the accumulated jurisprudence of these three bodies. It is, of course, also the case that any person affected by a breach of Article 85 or 86 may bring an action in the Irish courts.

The relationship between EU and national competition laws is governed by Article 5 of the Rome Treaty:

---

[29] Commission Regulation (EEC) No. 1984/83.

[30] Commission Regulation (EEC) No. 1983/83.

[31] Commission Regulation (EEC) No. 4087/88.

[32] Commission Regulation (EEC) No. 556/89, replaced by No. 240/96.

[33] Commission Regulation (EEC) No. 2349/84/, replaced by No. 240/96.

[34] Commission Regulation (EEC) No. 418/85.

[35] Commission Regulation (EEC) No. 417/85.

[36] Commission Regulation (EEC) No. 1475/95.

> Member States shall take all appropriate measures . . . to en-
> sure fulfilment of the obligations arising out of this Treaty . . .
> (and) . . . shall abstain from any measure which could jeopard-
> ise the attainment of the objectives of the Treaty.

Thus, it can be argued, national legislation should not be interpreted or applied so as to impede the attainment of the goals of
the Treaty. There is continuing academic discussion of the extent
to which national competition legislation, and its mode of application or interpretation, can diverge from, and produce results
different from, those produced by the EU Commission without
impeding the application of the Treaty rules. Some of the less difficult questions have been answered. The Walt Wilhelm case[37] is
universally cited as authority for the, by now, unsurprising
proposition that a national competition authority may proceed
with an investigation while the same behaviour is under investigation in parallel by the Commission, and that the national
body may proceed to a decision, although if in due course that
decision is seen to be incompatible with the Commission decision, the national authority "is required to take proper account
of the effects of the latter decision". *Guerlain*,[38] more recently, is
authority that a Member State may take action under domestic
competition law against an agreement in respect of which the
Commission has issued a comfort letter. The Notice on Co-
operation between National Courts and the Commission in Applying Articles 85 and 86 of the EU Treaty[39] refers to this issue
but does not advance the discussion. Bellamy and Child (1993)
identify as one unresolved issue the interesting question of
whether a national authority can apply national law so as to
strike down an agreement which is exempted under Article
85(3). Temple Lang (1991) suggests an answer, which is that it
depends on whether the exemption in question is an indication
that the behaviour in question is merely considered not to be

---

[37] *Walt Wilhelm* v. *Bundeskartellamt* Case 14/68 [1969] ECR 1, [1969]
     CMLR 100.

[38] *Procureur de la République* v. *Giry and Guerlain* [1980] ECR 2327, [1981]
     2 CMLR 99.

[39] C39/6.

harmful, or whether it indicates that the behaviour is positively good and to be encouraged.

Article 90(1) is directed to the behaviour of Member States. It applies to "public undertakings, and undertakings to which Member States grant special or exclusive rights".[40] Undertakings to which the State has granted exclusive rights need not be "public" in the sense of ownership in order to be covered by Article 90(1). Article 90(2) provides a limited exclusion from the competition rules for a category of undertakings, not necessarily co-extensive with those dealt with in Article 90(1), which are those "entrusted with . . . services of general economic interest or . . . a revenue producing monopoly". These are stated to be subject to Articles 85 and 86 and, indeed, the other rules of the Treaty relating to competition, insofar as they do not obstruct the performance of the tasks assigned to them. The Commission and the Court have had occasion in the past to address, on an ad hoc basis, the question of whether the tasks of an enterprise relying on Article 90(2) are of general economic interest and have found public services such as post and electricity to come within the definition. Under Article 90(3), the Commission may act directly against a Member State for breach of Article 90(1) by way of decision or by directive.

States are subject not only to Article 90 and Articles 85 and 86, but also to the competition considerations involved in Articles 30 and 37. Article 37 applies the free movement of goods provisions to State monopolies of a commercial character. The obligation on Member States is to adjust progressively such monopolies, to the goal that there be "no discrimination regarding the conditions under which goods are procured and marketed . . . between nationals of Member States". Article 37 does not itself make the existence of a State monopoly offensive. Articles 37(1) and 37(2) are of direct effect and can be invoked before the Irish courts.

---

[40] A public undertaking has been defined in Directive 80/723, as one "over which the public authorities may exercise directly or indirectly a dominant influence by virtue of their ownership of it, their financial participation therein or the rules which govern it." This definition is specific to the directive in relation to financial services in which it is contained.

State Aids

Governments frequently provide aid to firms whether publicly or privately owned. State aid to industry can take various forms, including grants, tax breaks, subsidised loans and employment subsidies, to name but a few. Such aids may distort competition in a number of ways as they confer a competitive advantage on the recipients which allows them to undercut their rivals. Aid may enable the inefficient firm to survive at the expense of what was otherwise a more efficient rival, a clearly sub-optimal outcome. More importantly, a major incentive for firms to maximise efficiency is provided by the fact that failure to do so will ultimately lead to the demise of the firm. If the State is seen to bail out loss-making firms, this will reduce the incentive for management to operate efficiently. While allowing inefficient firms to escape the consequences of their failure to perform, it also means that efficient well-run firms will not benefit fully from operating efficiently. The provision of state aid by member states to domestic firms who have suffered because of competition from firms in other member states is simply inconsistent with the establishment of a single market. From an Irish perspective, effective EU controls on state aids are essential. As one of the smaller economies in the EU, it is highly unlikely that we could match the levels of aid that larger member states could provide to their domestic firms in the absence of controls. In such circumstances, Irish firms would almost certainly lose out while multinationals might be tempted by more attractive incentive packages to relocate elsewhere in the EU.

EU competition rules recognise that government actions may distort competition within the EU and the provisions of Articles 90–92 of the Treaty are designed to deal with this. Indeed, the payment of aids by national governments to shelter domestic firms from competition from firms in other Member States may be a form of "beggar thy neighbour" policy. Article 92(1) of the Treaty of Rome provides that:

> . . . any aid granted by a member state or through state resources in any form whatsoever which distorts or threatens to distort competition by favouring certain undertakings or the production of certain goods shall, in so far as it affects trade between member states, be incompatible with the common market. . . .

According to Korah (1990a), the concept of state aid under EU law is quite broad and covers grants, loans at low rates of interest and deferment of tax liabilities or any form of gratuitous advantage conferred by the State.

All new state aids are illegal unless notified by the government concerned to the Commission and approved by it. Governments do not always comply with such requirements. The Commission has on occasion compelled Member State governments to recover at least part of any illegally paid aid, even after it has been spent by the recipient. The Commission has been subject to criticism for a failure to take stronger action against state aid. The Commission has discretion to authorise state aid in individual cases. The provisions for authorising state aid differ from those for exempting an anti-competitive agreement under Article 85(3). Specifically, the Commission may approve aid if it finds that the interest of undistorted competition is outweighed by other community interests or objectives. This has given rise to concerns that decisions are based on non-economic considerations.

In the early 1990s, the Commission announced that national airlines would no longer qualify for state aid and proposed that aid could be given to assist with restructuring on a "one time, last time" basis. Under such arrangements, Iberia Airlines received almost $1 billion from the Spanish Government in 1992. By the end of 1994, however, the Spanish Government was arguing that it should be allowed to give Iberia another $1 billion on the grounds that it would otherwise face certain bankruptcy. In November 1994, the Commission changed its rules, effectively abandoning the "one-time, last-time" principle announced by Mr Van Miert, the then Transport Commissioner, when approving payment of aid to the Belgian airline, Sabena (*The Economist*, 19 November 1994). The change was announced by Mr Oreja, Transport Commissioner, on 16 November 1994 when he stated that:

> The one-time, last-time principle is the rule, the exceptions are those unexpected external conditions which are outside the control of (airlines) (*The Irish Times*, 17 November 1994).

Such arguments ignore the fact that every business is prone to be affected by unexpected developments which are outside its control. Mr Oreja reportedly indicated that he could not give a complete

list of events which would allow payments of new state aid, but
indicated that while a recession might not be regarded as sufficient, he felt that it might "be borne in mind" by the Commission.[41] The Commission frequently imposes stringent conditions
on companies receiving state aid in order to try to minimise any
adverse effect on competition. The approval of aid to Aer Lingus,
for example, was subject to restrictions on the airline increasing
its capacity on certain routes. Although such conditions are imposed in an attempt to prevent competitive distortions, they
themselves actually create new ones. They make it more difficult
for the firm to improve its performance, while they also introduce
a form of direct regulation of industries without any clear legal
basis for doing so.

International Co-operation and Convergence

The UN Conference on Trade and Employment, which was held in
Havana, Cuba from November 1947 to March 1948, included in its
Final Act and Related Documents ("The Havana Charter") proposals for international competition rules. Articles 46–52 included
a general policy statement on the control of restrictive business
practices and dealt with consultation procedure, investigation procedure, studies relating to restrictive business practices, obligations
of members of the International Trade Organisation, co-operative
remedial arrangements, domestic measures, special procedures
with respect to services, and interpretation and definition. The
Havana Charter and the proposed ITO failed to get off the
ground. The only part of the Charter that was implemented was
the General Agreement on Tariffs and Trade (GATT), which com-
menced operation in 1948. The Havana Charter provisions formed
the basis of the Allied laws imposed on West Germany after the
Second World War. They also influenced the wording of Articles 65
and 66 of the European Coal and Steel Community and Articles
85–90 of the Treaty of Rome.

The successful outcome to the GATT Uruguay Round has
brought back into focus the question of international co-operation
with respect to competition laws. This has occurred for two reasons.

---

[41] *The Irish Times,* 17 November 1994.

Firstly, the growing liberalisation of world trade has led to industry increasingly operating on a global scale. This in turn has created scope for cartel arrangements which extend beyond individual countries, prompting a need for co-operation between national competition agencies to counter such problems. Secondly, the reduction in Government-organised trade barriers arising from the Uruguay Round means that impediments to trade arising from private anti-competitive arrangements could emerge as a serious problem. In the past, the US has criticised Japan for an alleged failure to apply its competition laws. It seems inevitable that some mechanism will need to be devised to cope with such potential disputes. This is not, of course, to say that such measures are likely to be implemented in the very near future. Even if the political will currently existed, trying to secure agreement on a uniform code of international competition laws would represent a mammoth task. Equally, one must recognise that the tide is now flowing, however slowly, in that direction.

.

5

THE DEVELOPMENT OF COMPETITION LAW IN IRELAND

The Common Law Restraint of Trade Doctrine

Although restraints of trade were invalid under the common law, the common law doctrine of restraint of trade, as Hogan (1989) noted, did not outlaw most types of anti-competitive behaviour. The courts tended to regard restraints of trade as justified if they were "reasonable" in the sense of being in the interests of both parties to the agreement; and "reasonable" in the interest of society generally. A restraint of trade was presumed to be in the public interest, unless it could be clearly shown to be otherwise. In *Mogul Steamshipping Co.* v. *McGregor Gow & Co.,*[1] the House of Lords held that it was not unlawful for shipping lines to form a cartel which fixed freight rates, divided cargoes and engaged in predatory conduct against non-cartel lines. The effect of this judgment and a subsequent decision by the Supreme Court in *Macken* v. *O'Reilly,*[2] was "that the common law doctrine of restraints of trade is rather toothless and ineffective to prevent abuses by oligopolists and others determined to engage in anti-competitive and predatory conduct" (Hogan, 1989: 35).

The most recent occasion on which the Supreme Court was asked to consider the restraint of trade doctrine in detail was in *Kerry Co-op* v. *Bord Bainne.*[3] McCarthy, J., described the doctrine of restraint of trade as:

> a classic instance of the application of public policy; it has been part of the common law since the 16th century. It is desirable

---

[1] *Mogul Steamshipping Co.* v. *McGregor Gow & Co.* [1892] AC 25.

[2] *Macken* v. *Reilly* [1979] ILRM 79.

[3] *Kerry Co-operative Creameries* v. *An Bord Bainne; Avonmore Creameries* v. *An Bord Bainne* [1990] ILRM 664 and [1991] ILRM 851.

from the standpoint of the public good, to protect the right to
work of weaker parties from abuse *and to gain the economic
benefits of preventing such abuse* [emphasis added].

He set out the formulation of the test used in *Maxim Nordenfelt
Guns and Ammunition Co. v. Nordenfelt*[4], that the restriction was
required to be reasonable as between the parties, and reasonable
in the public interest, and noted that the doctrine was "peculiarly
related to the vagaries of economic philosophy". His view of the
public-good element in the specific case was:

> As to the second consideration of the public good, it is clear as a
> legitimate opinion to be held by the majority of the members
> that the national interests are best served by the promotion
> and expansion of Bord Bainne.

O'Flaherty, J. in the same case, while adopting the same two-
pronged test, indicated perhaps a different attitude to the "public
good" of gaining the economic benefits of competition by citing
Lord Diplock in *Schroeder Music Publishing Co. Ltd. v. Macaulay*:[5]

> the public policy which the court is implementing is not some
> 19th century economic theory about the benefit to the general
> public of freedom of trade, but the protection of those whose
> bargaining power is weak against being forced by those whose
> bargaining power is stronger to enter into bargains which are
> unconscionable.... If one looks at the reasoning of the 19th cen-
> tury judges in cases about contracts in restraint of trade, one
> finds lip service paid to current economic theories but ... one
> finds that they struck down a bargain if they thought it was
> unconscionable as between the parties to it, and upheld it if
> they thought that it was not.

The Competition Acts are not a natural extension of the policy set
out in the above passage, being concerned with effects on the
economy generally, rather than with fairness between parties.
However, the authors suggest that while the two regimes are different in nature, case law relating to the doctrine can still be of
interest, partly because the area covered by the Competition Acts

---

[4]   [1894] AC 535.

[5]   [1974] 3 All ER 616.

is not perfectly co-extensive with that affected by the common law doctrine, and partly because, in the areas of overlap, consideration of what is of benefit to society may in fact touch upon issues which are relevant under the new legislative regime.

The Restrictive Practices Legislation

The Restrictive Trade Practices Act, 1953 was based on what is known as the "control of abuse" principle. It was therefore quite different from the prohibition-based systems operated in the US and which were incorporated into the Treaty of Rome upon the establishment of the then Common Market. Under a control of abuse regime there is no automatic presumption regarding the illegality of any particular type of behaviour. Rather, every particular practice is examined in detail before deciding whether or not it should be specifically prohibited. Prohibition-based systems, in contrast, involve an automatic prohibition of any form of behaviour that is deemed to be anti-competitive, although some such systems, like the Competition Act, allow for the possibility of exemptions from this general prohibition.

The legislation was introduced at a time when restrictive practices were common in many sectors of the Irish economy. Hogan (1989) argues that the legislation reflected a cautious approach because such legislation was novel in Ireland. There were several amendments to the legislation and the original Restrictive Trade Practices Act was subsequently replaced by the Restrictive Practices Act, 1972. For most of this period, competition legislation operated alongside a detailed system of price controls. The scope of competition legislation was also broadened considerably with the introduction of the Mergers, Takeovers and Monopolies (Control) Act in 1978. The essential features of the system of competition legislation originally introduced in 1953 remained broadly unchanged for almost 40 years. It had certain advantages and achieved a degree of success, particularly in its early years, in eliminating entry barriers and liberalising entry to many trades. Nevertheless, it suffered from a number of shortcomings, not least the fact that it was slow and cumbersome. Calls for its replacement by a prohibition-based system were first made as early as 1977. These ultimately led to the introduction of the Competition Act in October 1991, which swept away most elements of the previous competition regime, although one major element remains, in the form of the Groceries Order, 1987.

Background to the 1953 Act

There are references to competition policy in certain articles of Bunreacht na hÉireann. Article 43, while guaranteeing private property rights, provides that the exercise of such rights should be regulated by the principles of social justice and that the State may delimit by law the exercise of such rights so as to reconcile such exercise "with the exigencies of the common good".[6] More explicit references to competition policy are contained in Article 45, which sets out Directive Principles of Social Policy. Article 45.2 states that the State shall direct its policy towards securing:

> That the ownership and control of the material resources of the community may be so distributed amongst private individuals and the various classes as best to subserve the common good.[7]

> That, especially, the operation of free competition shall not be allowed so to develop as to result in the concentration of the ownership or control of essential commodities in a few individuals to the common detriment.[8]

While Article 45.3 provides that:

> The State shall endeavour to secure that private enterprise shall be so conducted as to ensure reasonable efficiency in the production and distribution of goods and as to protect the public against unjust exploitation.[9]

The directive principles set out in Article 45 of the Constitution are, of course, not binding on the Oireachtas nor are they directly cognisable by the courts in interpreting legislation.[10] Nevertheless, these articles appear to indicate a view that is generally

---

[6]   Article 43.2.2.

[7]   Article 45.2.ii.

[8]   Article 45.2.iii.

[9]   Article 45.3.2.

[10]   A more detailed discussion on this point is outside the scope of this text.

supportive of the desirability of competition, which was arguably somewhat advanced for its time.[11] In the previous chapter it was noted that the inter-war era was a period when most European governments were actively promoting cartels and industrial concentration. Even in the United States, the Supreme Court in *Appalachian Coal* had decided that a cartel was acceptable as a means of countering depression in the coal mining industry.[12]

Fianna Fáil when it took office in 1932 adopted a policy of protectionism to promote the development of an indigenous manufacturing sector. Rationing had to be introduced to deal with shortages of many imported commodities during the Second World War. The Government of the time worked in co-operation with many trade associations as, according to Walsh (1974), such co-operation simplified the task of operating a rationing system. This in turn, however, strengthened those associations and enabled them to develop a high degree of cohesiveness. After the War many associations began to use their muscle to prevent the development of competition by the adoption of various restrictive practices, including restrictions on entry, collective resale price maintenance and, less frequently, collusive price fixing (see also Kennedy and Bruton, 1975). Such practices were facilitated by the fact that the domestic market was heavily protected and because the number of firms in many manufacturing sectors was relatively limited. Concern over such developments led to the introduction of legislation to deal with anti-competitive behaviour.

The Industrial Efficiency and Prices Bill was introduced in the Dáil in 1947. The Bill was primarily aimed at improving methods of price control in the context of continued shortages of certain imported goods and at introducing measures to make protected industries more efficient. Nevertheless, the Bill also contained measures to prohibit price fixing and limitations on entry to different trades, although such measures could obtain approval from the Minister

---

[11] Arguably Article 45.3.2 might equally be seen to favour a more interventionist approach to regulating economic activity.

[12] *Appalachian Coals Inc. et al.* v. *United States*, 288 US 344 (1933). As noted in Chapter 4, the decision in this case has subsequently come to be widely recognised as something of an aberration and is accepted as having no value as a judicial precedent.

for Industry and Commerce. The Bill lapsed upon the dissolution of the Dáil in 1948 and was not revived. Complaints about restrictive practices mounted in the Department of Industry and Commerce. Speaking on the introduction of the Restrictive Trade Practices Bill in the Dáil on 31 October 1952, the Minister for Industry and Commerce, Seán Lemass, observed that:

> For the past few years there has been a growing uneasiness among the public because of the development and extension of restrictive practices in the supply and distribution of goods. . . . Over that period there has flowed into the Department of Industry and Commerce a still larger volume of complaint about the operation of restrictive practices in trade — a volume of complaint which has shown no sign of diminution in recent months.[13]

Practices complained of included refusal to supply — which was stated to have accounted for the largest number of complaints — exclusive dealing, particularly in the case of petrol, and resale price maintenance.

Lemass informed the Dáil that the Bill was based on two principles:

> The first is, as a general rule and subject to public policy, to restrict imports by tariffs or quota arrangements in the interests of national economic development *that the fullest and freest competition in any trade is in the public interest.* Secondly, where there are special conditions which may justify some form of regulation, *then neither trade associations nor combinations of traders can be allowed to arrogate to themselves the right to impose these regulations or to limit competition.* We are framing this Bill on the assumption that *agreements between traders who should be in competition with one another must be treated with suspicion and that such agreements are an actual or a potential source of injury to the public as consumers*[14] [Emphasis added].

The aim of the legislation, according to the Minster, was "to smash trade rings".[15]

---

[13]   Dáil Debates 31.10.1952, col. 813.

[14]   *Ibid.*, at col. 821.

[15]   *Ibid.*, at col. 818.

In his speech, the Minister informed the Dáil that all the possible alternatives for dealing with the problem of restrictive practices had been considered before finalising the Bill. The Minister indicated that the idea of a prohibition-based system had been considered.

> The lawfulness of any practice could only be determined by litigation and only when some aggrieved citizen decided to put himself to the hazard of litigation in order to assert his rights. It is certain that in every case the proceedings would be long and costly, and the knowledge that they would be long and costly might easily deter many traders from asserting their rights, even though they were clear under the terms of the law. The more powerful the interests involved in maintaining restrictive trade practices, and the more profitable these restrictions were, the more certain it would be that the person who initiated the litigation under such a law to secure his rights would be harassed by every legal device. A verdict in his favour would be appealed from court to court and, even if, when all legal processes had been exhausted, the individual secured a verdict, the law would be settled only in his particular case.[16]

What makes such comments particularly interesting is the fact that this is exactly the approach that was adopted with the introduction of the Competition Act, 1991.

The Restrictive Trade Practices Acts

The 1953 Act established a body known as the Fair Trade Commission (FTC). Under the terms of the Act, the FTC could make Fair Trading Rules in respect of any goods, either on its own initiative or at the request of an association representing individuals trading in the goods concerned. Such rules did not have legal force but under the Act, if the rules were not being observed, the Minister could, following receipt of a report to that effect from the FTC, make an order, which, if confirmed by the Oireachtas, would have the force of law. No order was ever made on that basis. According to Walsh (1974), many observers believed that under the Act an order could only be made if recommended by the FTC following a

---

[16] Dáil Debates, 31.10.52, at col. 823.

public enquiry. A clear shortcoming of the Act was the exclusion of all services with the exception of distribution.

The FTC could hold a public enquiry on its own initiative or be directed to do so by the Minister. Of the 16 enquiries held under the Act, only two were held at the request of the Minister (Walsh, 1974). Any interested person could request the FTC to hold such an enquiry and, if the FTC refused the request, it had to give reasons for doing so to the person making the request. A report of an enquiry had to describe the conditions of supply and distribution of the relevant goods or of any services affecting their supply or distribution and to state whether the conditions "prevent or restrict competition or restrain trade or involve resale price maintenance". The report also had to state whether such interference with competition was unfair and operated against the public interest. The FTC could recommend that an Order be made and the Minister could make such an Order subject to confirmation by an Act of the Oireachtas. Reports had to be published, although commercially sensitive information could be omitted if it was not essential to understanding the report.

In September 1991, Restrictive Practices Orders were in force in respect of 11 trades. The orders contained specific prohibitions and requirements with which businesses engaged in the trade concerned had to comply. Hogan (1989), however, argued that the only Orders that could be said to have much practical importance were those that applied to building materials, motor fuels and groceries.

During the debate on the 1953 Act, the Minister stated that the option of a prohibition system with a schedule listing the specific practices which were prohibited had also been rejected by the Government since it would be difficult to secure agreements as to what practices should be outlawed in all cases, and because firms were likely to find ways around specific legislative prohibitions. Nevertheless, at the insistence of the opposition, a second schedule was added to the Act, defining certain unfair trading practices. This was intended as guidance for the FTC and was not to be taken as limiting its deliberations. Any enquiry under the original Act had to cover all aspects of supply and distribution, making the procedure unnecessarily long and complex. The Act was amended in 1959 to allow an enquiry to be held into one or more aspects of the supply and distribution of one or more kinds of goods (Restrictive Trade Practices (Amendment) Act, 1959, Section 2).

Under the Act a total of 22 sets of Fair Trading Rules were made in respect of a wide range of mainly consumer goods. (Two sets replaced existing rules). A large volume of complaints concerning various practices had built up prior to the establishment of the FTC. Walsh (1974) observed that the Fair Trading Rules procedure enabled the FTC to establish certain standards that discouraged undesirable restrictions over a relatively large number of products and trades in a relatively short period of time, when it would not have been possible within any reasonable time to hold public enquiries into all of the areas that had been the subject of complaint. Nevertheless, the fact that the rules lacked statutory backing and were essentially voluntary in nature was a weakness.

Many of the fair trading rules and enquiries undertaken in the early years of the legislation were prompted by concerns about measures designed to limit or restrict entry to particular trades. As already noted, the Act stemmed largely from concerns that various trade and representative bodies were seeking to exclude would-be competitors from particular trades. The first set of rules was introduced in respect of radios following numerous complaints regarding steps taken by a trade association (the Wireless Dealers' Association) to restrict entry. The rules included prohibitions on entry restrictions and price discrimination, the latter being influenced by the US Robinson Patman Act. The FTC consistently recommended the prohibition of horizontal price fixing and collective resale price maintenance and, in the rules for radios, recommended a prohibition on individual resale price maintenance. As Walsh (1974) points out, this decision was taken in spite of the fact that, at the time, Sweden was the only Western European country to have abolished the practice, and when there was considerable controversy regarding the merits and disadvantages of this practice emerging in many countries. Subsequently, individual resale price maintenance was permitted under some of the Fair Trading Rules, although these tended to be the exception.

The Restrictive Practices Acts

The *Third Programme for Economic and Social Development,* published in 1968, stated that the Government had decided that the Restrictive Trade Practices Acts would be amended to allow the FTC to investigate restrictive practices in a wider range of activities in the sheltered market sector of the economy. The Restrictive Trade Practices Acts were repealed and replaced by the Restrictive Practices Act, 1972 which introduced some important changes. For example, it extended coverage of the legislation to a number of services including professional services. Section 1 of the new Act, however, expressly excluded the key economic sectors of banking, electricity and transport from the scope of the legislation.[17]

The extension of the application of competition legislation to services was largely the result of a recommendation by the National Industrial Economic Council (NIEC). In considering the prospects for an agreed national prices and incomes policy, which at the time was seen as a means of countering the sharp increases in inflation recorded in Ireland from the late 1960s onwards, the NIEC expressed concern about the immunity of the professions from investigation into restrictive practices. The key change in the new Act, however, was the creation of the office of the Examiner of Restrictive Practices. Effectively, this separated the functions of investigation and adjudication under the Act. Such a separation of functions had been strongly advocated by the Federation of Trade Associations following an enquiry into electrical goods in 1968.

The 1972 Act conferred upon the Examiner sole responsibility for investigations into allegations of restrictive business practices. The power to undertake enquiries solely on its own initiative was removed from the Commission, which was renamed the Restrictive Practices Commission (RPC). Responsibility for enforcement of restrictive practices orders was transferred from the Minister to the Examiner, which was a significant improvement as Ministerial enforcement had been relatively lax. The procedures for

---

[17] It also excluded from the legislation services provided under a contract of employment.

making Fair Trading Rules were retained and such a procedure could be initiated by the Examiner or by a trade association, but not by the RPC. Similarly, the RPC could not undertake enquiries on its own initiative but could be required to do so following a report by the Examiner or at the request of the Minister. Under the new Act the content of the report of any enquiry was expanded so that the RPC was required to state whether, in its opinion, the conditions in a trade or service involved "practices (including arrangements, agreements or understandings) or methods of competition (whether or not relating to price) which are unfair or operate against the public interest".[18]

Whereas the original 1953 Act allowed the FTC to examine the effects of any orders, the 1972 Act greatly extended this to allow the RPC to:

> ... study and analyse (and report to the Minister when requested by him) the effect on the common good of the methods of competition, types of restrictive practice, monopolies, the structure of any markets, amalgamation of, or acquisition or control of, bodies corporate, the operation of multinational companies and relevant legislation....

including developments outside the State.[19] This provision gave the RPC wide scope for activity. Its effectiveness, however, was greatly curtailed by the fact that, for certain purposes, the RPC did not have powers to require the provision of information. Walsh (1974) observed that the shortcomings of this provision had proved to be a problem.

The National Planning Board (1984) criticised the RPC stating that its use of its extended powers under the 1972 Act had been disappointing. The Fine Gael/Labour Coalition Government subsequently announced proposals to strengthen competition policy through a restructuring of the agencies involved, while indicating plans to amend the 1972 Act to remove the remaining exemptions.[20] The 1972 Act was subsequently amended in 1987. The Restrictive

---

[18] Restrictive Practices Act, 1972, Section 7(d).

[19] Restrictive Practices Act, 1972, Section 12.

[20] *Building on Reality,* paras. 3.20-3.22.

Practices (Amendment) Act transferred the responsibilities of the Examiner to the Director of Consumer Affairs, who was renamed the Director of Consumer Affairs and Fair Trade. The Commission reverted to its original title of the Fair Trade Commission. The right to initiate investigations was restored. In part, this was prompted by the fact that, under the 1972 Act, the Examiner had consistently failed to request the RPC to undertake any investigations over a number of years, in effect rendering the RPC largely redundant. The 1987 Act removed all the remaining exempted sectors apart from the local authorities. According to the FTC (1991a), the amending legislation incorporated virtually all of the requests for additions to the 1972 Act made by the RPC over the previous 15 years. The one notable exception was the failure to adopt a prohibition-based system, which had been recommended by the FTC in an unpublished report in 1977 (FTC, 1991a). During the debate on the 1987 Act, the opposition spokesman, John Bruton TD, proposed an amendment incorporating prohibitions along the lines of those contained in Articles 85 and 86 of the Treaty of Rome. While this amendment was not accepted, the then Minister undertook to request a further FTC study of competition law. That report subsequently recommended the adoption of a prohibition-based system (FTC, 1991a).

Regulation of Monopolies

Competition legislation was further enhanced by the introduction of the Mergers, Take-overs and Monopolies (Control) Act, 1978. Consideration of the treatment of mergers is deferred until Chapter 10. The provisions of the 1978 Act with respect to monopolies, however, represented a significant addition to the framework of competition legislation. The focus of the restrictive practices legislation was on restrictive practices involving arrangements or understandings between firms. Technically, it could have been used to address issues arising from the behaviour of individual firms with a degree of market power. In practice, however, the focus of attention under the legislation was on the trading practices of all the firms in a particular sector rather than the behaviour of individual firms.

The 1978 Act provided that the Minister could ask the FTC to undertake an enquiry where he or she was of the opinion that an apparent monopoly needed to be investigated. The Act defined a monopoly as existing when:

> ... an enterprise or two or more enterprises under common control, which supply or provide, or to which is supplied or provided, not less than one-half of goods or services of a particular kind supplied or provided in the State in a particular year.

The FTC was obliged in the report of any such enquiry to state (a) whether a monopoly existed, (b) if it did, whether it prevented or restricted competition or endangered the continuity of supplies or services or restrained trade or the provision of any service or was likely to do any of those things, and (c) whether any of these was unfair and was likely to operate against the common good. On receiving a report from the FTC, the Minister could, after required consultations, by order, either, (a) prohibit the continuance of the monopoly except on conditions specified in the order, or, (b) require the division, in a manner and within a period specified in the order, of the monopoly by a sale of assets or as otherwise specified. While the monopoly provision of the 1978 Act contained quite severe powers to curtail monopolies, in fact no request for such an enquiry was ever made to the FTC under those provisions of the Act.

The Grocery Trade
The introduction of the Restrictive Trade Practices Act in 1953 was prompted by concerns regarding anti-competitive behaviour in many sectors of the economy. Concern regarding resale price maintenance in the grocery sector, however, played a key role. Over the subsequent 40 years, the grocery trade continued to pose serious problems, and a total of eight separate investigations into this sector were carried out by the FTC over the following 38 years. The first enquiry into the sector under the Restrictive Trade Practices Act was held in 1954–55. Walsh (1974) argued that this enquiry possibly had more influence over a wider range of products than any other enquiry. Measures such as blacklists of price-cutters, attempted boycotts of suppliers of those on such lists and aggressive publicity were employed to secure adherence to resale price maintenance. The FTC (1956) in its report dismissed claims that price competition would eliminate small traders as exaggerated. The FTC expressed the view that extreme

price competition, where it occurred, was likely to be of relatively short duration. Nevertheless, the resulting order allowed suppliers to withhold supplies from a retailer selling below a defined wholesale price.

Concern over so-called below-cost selling was a constant feature of enquiries into the trade. In its 1971 enquiry, the FTC (1972) accepted that widespread advertising of loss-leaders by some large retailers might give a misleading impression of the general level of prices in their shops. Nevertheless, it recommended that below-cost selling should not be prohibited but that advertising of such prices should be confined to the retailer's premises. A further enquiry in 1980 again concluded that the advertising of loss-leaders should be restricted, but considered that a prohibition of below-cost selling would entail "so radical an interference with trade" that it would not be justified (RPC, 1980). In 1972, and again in 1980, the Commission expressed fears that the fixing of minimum price involved in a ban on below-cost selling would constitute a form of official resale price maintenance which would represent a reversal of previous government policy. The Commission also expressed the view that below-cost selling benefited consumers, and that the immediate and only effect of any ban as far as consumers were concerned would be a blunting of competition between the major retailers. At the same time, however, it expressed the view that selling below cost was an artifice and that it was an undesirable practice involving a distinct element of unfairness, and on occasion presented some of the features of predatory pricing.

In 1987 the RPC again considered the question of below-cost selling in the grocery trade (RPC, 1987c). On this occasion it reversed the stance taken in previous enquiries and recommended an outright prohibition of below-cost selling of grocery goods. As it noted in its report, some of the parties who had given evidence at the previous enquiry were unhappy with its conclusions and continued to press for a prohibition on below-cost selling. The Joint Oireachtas Committee on Small Businesses recommended that a ban be imposed on below-cost selling. This was because, in its view, multiple stores had an unfair advantage through their inordinate strength. In April 1986, the Committee Chairman, Mr

Ivan Yates TD, introduced a private members Bill designed to outlaw below-cost selling.

The reasons advanced by the RPC for recommending a prohibition of below-cost selling were:

1. Multiple retailers had continued to increase their market share since 1980.

2. Rapid growth in sales of own-brand and generic products occurred because below-cost selling was concentrated on such products and this had distorted demand patterns.

3. Below-cost selling was unfair and contrary to the common good.

4. Below-cost selling caused problems to suppliers because rival retailers would pressurise them to withhold supplies from a multiple selling below cost, while it would also distort trade patterns if retailers sought to build up stocks in order to embark on a below-cost selling campaign

5. Below-cost selling led to unfair pressure on independent retailers by consumers who wrongly felt that such retailers were overcharging.

6. The ban on advertising below-cost sales was not effective because of inadequacies in enforcement mechanisms and because multiples' selling prices were widely known and so below-cost sales did not need to be advertised.

7. Below-cost selling confused consumers who were, as a result, unable to remember more than a few prices.

The FTC subsequently considered the issue of below-cost selling in the grocery trade again in 1991 (FTC, 1991b). On this occasion, a majority recommended that the ban on below-cost selling, along with most other provisions of the Groceries Order, should be abolished, since most instances of below-cost selling were not anti-competitive, while the newly introduced Competition Act would be capable of dealing with anti-competitive behaviour in the sector.[21] In fact, the majority concluded that the Groceries Order might

---

[21] One of the current authors was a member of the majority of the FTC who recommended in favour of an abolition of the Groceries Order.

actually reduce competition. Following publication of the Report, the Minister for Industry and Commerce announced that the Order would be retained for a time to allow for a detailed consideration of the FTC report. The Order is the only vestige of the old Restrictive Practices legislation that remains in place.

The Main Provisions of the Groceries Order

Perhaps the best-known element of the Groceries Order is the ban on below-cost selling. Although the order prohibits the sale below cost of grocery goods, it defines cost as the net invoice price of the goods. As the FTC discovered in its review of the Order, the net invoice price in many cases is higher than the actual cost of goods to retailers (FTC, 1991b). Significant discounts and rebates given by suppliers to retailers are not shown on the invoice. The practice of keeping discounts off invoice means that the legal minimum cost at which grocery goods may be sold may be significantly higher than the true cost to retailers. It is believed, for example, that multiple supermarkets obtain discounts of up to 35 per cent on milk, but such discounts are not reflected in the retail price. The range of goods to which the order applies is somewhat narrower than the normally accepted definition of grocery goods. Fresh meat, fish, fruit and vegetables are all excluded, and below-cost selling of such products is not prohibited by the Order.

The Groceries Order also includes prohibitions on RPM, price discrimination, refusal to supply and so-called "hello money".[22] It would appear that most such activities would also be prohibited under the terms of the Competition Act, 1991. Under Article 13(1)(a) of the Order, suppliers are obliged to supply goods. Where a manufacturer refuses to supply goods to a retailer as a result of pressure from other retailers, it can clearly be considered anticompetitive. As already noted, concerns about practices designed to prevent entry to various trades were a major consideration behind the introduction of the Restrictive Trade Practices Act in 1953. Suppliers, however, may unilaterally decide to refuse supplies on purely commercial grounds. For example, they may conclude

---

[22] Hello money refers to a practice whereby certain multiple supermarkets demand payments from manufacturers and suppliers to stock new products.

that supplying additional outlets may simply increase their distribution costs without resulting in any increase in overall sales. Article 13(1)(a) does not distinguish between these different types of situation which have very different implications from a competition point of view. In addition, the Order also sets maximum limits on the duration of credit afforded to retailers by suppliers. This provision reflects concerns that major multiple supermarket groups were demanding extended credit terms which created serious problems for suppliers. The FTC (1991b) concluded that the problem of excessive credit might not be covered by the Competition Act and that there may be some justification for specific legislation to deal with credit terms. The Director of Consumer Affairs retains responsibility for enforcement of the Order.

The Case Against Banning Below-Cost Selling

The ban on below-cost selling is designed to prevent grocery retailers from selling some items at a loss in order to attract consumers. The Competition Act would, on the basis of EU precedent, prohibit predatory pricing — that is, deliberate selling below cost by dominant firms in order to eliminate competitors. Many cases of below-cost selling in the grocery trade may not be predatory but may simply be a legitimate means of increasing market share, which is the objective of all competitive behaviour. Indeed this was the view taken by the majority in the last FTC review of the Order (FTC, 1991b). Such a view was supported by the OECD which observed in its 1993 Annual Survey of the Irish economy that:

> The order appears to have been designed to protect small grocers from predatory pricing, making no reference to the market power which is a precondition for such pricing. Given its structure, true predatory pricing — which requires the perpetrator to incur substantial losses or at least to forego present profits in the hope that those losses can be more than recouped in the future through the exercise of market power — would seem to be a remote possibility in the Irish retail grocery market, especially given that sunk costs are low compared with many other industries (OECD, 1993a: 86).

This is supported by economic research in the United States into below-cost selling which concluded that such activity was not predatory (Craswell and Fratrik, 1986). In the UK, the Director General of Fair Trading rejected calls for an investigation of below-cost selling by supermarkets in 1994. Explaining his decision in a letter to the *Financial Times*, he wrote:

> I do not believe that loss leading on selected products — as opposed to uneconomic pricing of the whole range of products — can be expected to drive rivals out of business and reduce competition to the detriment of consumers (*Financial Times*, 17 December 1994).

By preventing below-cost selling the ban actually restricts competition. Indeed the OECD concluded that "rescinding the Groceries Order would probably encourage greater price competition in a sector largely protected from international trade" (OECD, 1993a: 86). In particular, multiple supermarkets, which can purchase goods on better terms from suppliers because of their considerable buying power, cannot pass such benefits on to consumers when discounts are not shown on their invoices. Their ability to undercut other retailers' prices is thereby limited, which restricts competition. The losers are consumers who ultimately have to pay higher prices than they otherwise would. Whelan (1995) found that the ban on below-cost selling served to restrict competition in the grocery trade, while Brady (1994) came to a similar conclusion. The Director of Consumer Affairs (DCA), who is responsible for policing the order, wrote in his 1991 Annual Report that "the ban as it is presently constituted is too rigid and certainly does prevent consumers from obtaining the maximum advantage from the robust competition which occurs in the grocery trade" (DCA, 1991: 10). The Director rejected the view expressed in the minority FTC report that there should be specific legislation for the grocery sector, while indicating that the lack of state enforcement of the Competition Act would pose problems in the trade. The Director subsequently described the ban as "an interference in trade which should eventually be removed" (DCA, 1992: 5). In spite of the weight of independent evidence that the ban is detrimental to competition, it remains in place. As one observer so eloquently put it:

> That the Groceries Order is still in force is a tribute to the power and persuasiveness of those who lobbied for its retention (*Irish Times*, 6 October 1994).

The ban on below-cost selling enables grocery suppliers to establish the minimum price at which retailers can sell their
goods and effectively constitutes a form of RPM, a practice prohibited under the competition laws of virtually all developed
countries. It is ironic, therefore, that the ban on below-cost selling facilitates a practice that has long been regarded as seriously anti-competitive not just in Ireland but in most developed
countries. The problem is exacerbated by the fact that the Groceries Order defines cost as the net invoice price of the goods
which, as already stated, is, in many cases, considerably higher
than the actual cost of goods to retailers. A former Director of
Consumer Affairs, recalling his role in court actions to stop below-
cost selling, stated that:

> Most competition authorities throughout the world would not
> have been involved in that — they would have been encourag-
> ing shops to be more competitive rather than holding it back.

He went on in the course of the same interview to state that:

> I remember one time leaving an OECD meeting and being teased
> by colleagues from other countries because I was going back to
> Ireland to work on the fact that the price of bread had become too
> low. So there I was on a competition authority, flying back home
> to raise prices! (*Sunday Business Post*, 1 October 1995).

Representative bodies of suppliers and independent retailers
have argued that the ban on below-cost selling has had a number
of positive effects. In particular, it has been argued that the ban
on below-cost selling helped contain food price increases, preserved employment and enhanced the competitiveness of Irish
food processors. Quite how preventing retailers from selling goods
too cheaply keeps prices down is a mystery to the present authors.
Advocates of this position have not advanced any form of explanation of the causal links at work in this case but appear to rely
instead on the existence of an apparent correlation.[23] Such claims
would appear not to be compatible with most conventional explanations of causes of inflation. Official statistics indicated that retail grocery margins have increased since the introduction of the

---

[23] The existence of a correlation does not amount to evidence of causality.

ban on below-cost selling. The CSO's *Annual Services Inquiry* shows that average gross margins of grocery shops in 1991 were equivalent to 19.5 per cent of turnover. This compares with a figure of 15.8 per cent in 1988, a substantial increase in gross margins in just three years.

Supporters of the ban also argue that it is necessary to ensure the survival of small independent grocery retailers. In fact, as Walsh and Whelan (1996) noted, the numbers of such retailers have continued to decline. In addition, it was claimed that the Order protects jobs by protecting smaller retailers and suppliers and that the removal of the Order would have an adverse effect on food exports. In reality, many suppliers to the grocery trade have closed their domestic manufacturing operations since the Order came into force and are now distributors of imported goods. International experience shows that firms in the most successful exporting economies face very strong competition in their domestic markets.

One of the reasons advanced in favour of the Groceries Order in 1991 was the absence of an effective system of state enforcement under the Competition Act. It was argued that public enforcement, as provided for under the Order, was necessary to prevent anti-competitive behaviour in the grocery trade and that reliance on private actions would not prove effective. Following the introduction of the Competition (Amendment) Bill, 1994, which proposed to remedy this defect in the Competition Act, IBEC mounted a fresh campaign for the retention of the Order. While manufacturers and independent retailers favour its continuation, the majority of independent evidence would appear to be against it. Nevertheless, the Minister for Enterprise and Employment announced on 28 February 1995 that he had decided to retain the Order for a further two years in spite of expressing concern that "there is some evidence that the Groceries Order may be inhibiting desirable price competition to the disadvantage of the consumer" (Bruton, 1995). The Minister indicated that the Order needed to be retained until the Competition Act was amended to provide for effective enforcement, but stated that, when this was in place, he would consider revoking the Order.

Conclusions

The introduction of competition legislation in Ireland in the early 1950s had a significant positive impact, particularly in its early years (see Kennedy, 1960). It was successful in removing barriers to entry in many sectors and in reducing the incidence of RPM which was widespread prior to the enactment of the Restrictive Trade Practices Act. As Walsh (1974: 248) observed:

> While self-service and supermarkets would certainly have developed in the course of time, they would not have developed as rapidly, nor as extensively as they did had resale price maintenance continued in operation.

In the light of such sentiments it is highly ironic that the only element of the former legislation which remains in place facilitates the operation of resale price maintenance in the grocery trade. From 1953 until 1986 the legislation operated alongside a detailed system of price control enshrined in the Prices Acts.

The legislation was in essence a product of its time. It reflected notions of workable competition. The first FTC report on motor fuels, for example, concluded that there was an excessive number of filling stations. Curbs were introduced on the number of outlets in 1962. By 1971, attention had shifted to concern about vertical integration in the industry as indicated by the number of company-owned stations. This led to limits on the number of new company-owned stations in the 1972 Order. Contrary to Walsh's claims, the greater emphasis placed on equity in the 1972 Act weakened the pro-competition aspects of the legislation. This is most evident in the Groceries Order, 1987, with its ban on below-cost selling, designed to aid smaller retailers and to reduce pressure on suppliers to cut prices. As Mr Justice Stewart noted, in a dissenting judgment, in *Von's Grocery Store*:[24]

> Section 7 (of the Clayton Act) was never intended by Congress as a charter for the Court to roll back the supermarket revolution. . . . No action by this Court can resurrect the old single-line Los Angeles food stores that have been run over by the automobile or obliterated by the freeway.

---

[24] *United States* v. *Von's Grocery Company et al.*, 384 US 270 (1966).

The legislation also suffered from a number of limitations. Enquiries had to be carried out on a trade-by-trade basis by the FTC (in its various guises), into allegations of restrictive or anti-competitive practices. The FTC then reported to the Minister, recommending what measures, if any, might need to be incorporated into a Restrictive Practices Order for the trade concerned. If the Minister accepted the Commission's recommendation, she had to have the Order approved by the Dáil. It was therefore an extremely slow process. Thus, after 38 years, Restrictive Practices Orders were in operation for 11 trades covering, according to the FTC (1991a), about 35 per cent of total consumer expenditure.

In spite of the gradual extension of the provisions of the Acts to various services, no order was ever made in respect of such sectors. It was claimed that, on occasion, the threat of an enquiry was sufficient to put a halt to a particular practice (FTC, 1991a). Such claims are hard to reconcile with the fact that several trades were the subject of repeated enquiries, as the emergence of new or previously undetected practices required a fresh inquiry culminating in a new Order. The grocery trade was the subject of a total of eight investigations in one form or another under the terms of the various Restrictive Practices Acts. There were also several investigations into the distribution of motor fuels. For a long period of time enforcement was not as effective as it might have been, although this was largely overcome by amendments transferring responsibility for enforcement to the Director of Consumer Affairs and Fair Trade. Under the legislation different laws applied to different sectors of the economy. As the FTC (1991a) argued:

> It is difficult to understand why the competition laws should not be generally applicable as they are in the other countries examined in this study (para. 5.23(5)).

Hogan (1989) also argued that the legislation provided very little relief to victims of anti-competitive conduct. Over time the legislation proved to be cumbersome, applied different rules to different sectors of the economy and was ineffective in ensuring competitive markets.

6

THE COMPETITION ACTS

The Competition Act came into force on 1 October 1991. It represented an entirely different approach from that of the previous legislation described in the last chapter in that it created a blanket prohibition with automatic effect on all forms of anti-competitive behaviour. The EU and the United States, two long-established competition regimes, use forms of automatic prohibition. Ireland, by contrast, had for almost 40 years relied on the types of *ex post facto* control of abuse described in the previous chapter. The change in the Irish approach mirrors a general switch in a number of jurisdictions worldwide to prohibition-based systems. The introduction of the Act followed two FTC reports which had recommended the adoption of a prohibition system. A model for such a system existed in the Treaty of Rome, and in a number of the other EU Member States. The 1996 Act was designed primarily to provide for more effective enforcement.

The 1991 Act prohibits anti-competitive agreements, decisions and concerted practices between undertakings, making them automatically void and unenforceable. It also prohibits the abuse of a dominant position in a market for goods or services in any substantial part of the State. It creates a new tort-like right of action for any person aggrieved by such anti-competitive behaviour. The 1996 Act creates criminal offences of entering into or implementing anti-competitive agreements, decisions or concerted practices or of abusing a dominant position. The Competition Authority was set up by the 1991 Act and, under the 1996 Act, is given responsibility for enforcement, both civil and criminal. Its other functions are to deal with notifications, by which undertakings may seek certificates or licences for their agreements; to undertake studies and investigations under Sections 11 and 14 respectively, and to carry out investigations on referral by the Minister under the Mergers Act, 1978. The functions of the Authority are considered in detail below, except the role of the Authority under the Mergers Act which is considered in Chapter 10.

Choosing the EU Model

The wording of Sections 4 and 5 of the Competition Act is directly adopted from Articles 85 and 86 of the Treaty of Rome. The decision to take the EU wording is a choice that goes beyond convenience of drafting, as shown by the long title,[1] and it has had two specific effects. The first is that it has been treated by the Irish courts as bringing the European Commission and Court jurisprudence into the domestic arena. Judge Costello described it thus:

> Section 4 is in identical terms to Article 85 of the Treaty, around which has grown up in the past thirty years a very considerable volume of case law from decisions of the Commission and the Court of Justice. These decisions are not binding on our courts but in view of (a) the provisions of the Act's preamble which declares that its object is to prohibit by analogy with Article 85 the prevention, restriction and distortion of competition, and the fact that (b) Article 85 of the Treaty is part of Irish domestic law and the Irish courts are required to follow decisions of the Court of Justice in relation to it on inter-State trade, it seems to me that the decisions of both the Commission and the Court of Justice on the construction of Article 85 should have very strong persuasive force.[2]

However, in adopting any EU reasoning in the area of the competition rules, it is necessary to take into account that the Treaty rules have not one but two objectives. One is to prevent restrictions of competition and the other is the integration of the common market. The latter goal, argues Korah (1990a), has always been the more important of the two. There is, obviously, no equivalent purpose or element in the Irish Act. There is an

---

[1]   "An Act to prohibit, by analogy with Articles 85 and 86 of the Treaty establishing the European Economic Community, and in the interests of the common good, the prevention, restriction or distortion of competition and the abuse of dominant positions in trade in the State...".

[2]   *Donovan and others v. ESB* (1994) 2 IR 305.

interesting question, outside the scope of this book, as to the extent to which particular agreements or behaviour would have been found offensive by the Court or Commission, in the absence of a requirement for there to be an effect on trade between Member States. It is also worth noting that while the long title clearly intends to bring an EU reading into the Irish Act, the EU block exemptions were not incorporated into the domestic legislation. Models exist in other EU Member States for such incorporation, and the FTC (1991a) had recommended it as part of the Irish regime. It may also reflect a recognition that it was necessary for Irish agreements to be considered in the context of the Irish market before automatically applying to them rules formulated at EU level.

The Competition Authority has not declared a position on the extent to which it considers itself bound by the decisions of the European Commission and the European Courts. Its "Explanatory Note" for parties making a notification to it states:

> ... notifying parties might find it helpful to refer to appropriate decisions, block exemptions or notices of the EC Commission in respect of cases involving Article 85 of the Treaty . . . (upon which Sections 4(1) and (2) are closely based), and to any relevant judgments by the Court of Justice.[3]

An examination of the decisions of the Authority shows that it has, on a number of occasions, quoted and adopted EU reasoning. The Competition Authority has not had occasion to refuse a licence or certificate in respect of a notification of an agreement, decision or concerted practice granted an individual exemption by the Commission; it has, on the other hand, continued to examine notifications in respect of which individual exemptions existed,[4] rather than treat them as automatically licensable under Irish law. In fact, it has continued to examine *de novo* notifications in respect of which negative clearances, comfort letters or block exemption applied or were argued to apply.

---

[3] It may be relevant that the Explanatory Note predates the taking of any Authority decisions.

[4] Eurocheque Committee Decision No. 448 of 15.12.95.

Theory-neutral

The other effect of adopting the Rome Treaty wording is that it is a wording which is, to a fair extent, value-neutral as between schools of economic theory. It is possible, in considering whether specified behaviour does prevent, restrict or distort competition, to apply any one of the theories discussed in Chapter 2. Korah (1990a) argues that Articles 85 and 86 are based on a specific theory of workable competition, which was discussed in Chapter 2, but the authors would argue that this has not been treated, and Sections 4 and 5 should not be treated, as dictating a choice of theory. The forms of behaviour specified in Section 4(1)(a) to (e), and Section 5(2)(a) to (d) are not universally accepted to be offensive by all schools of economic theory. Thus, vertical price fixing is considered by a Chicago school analysis not to be restrictive of competition, whereas Section 4(1)(a) would appear to include both horizontal and vertical price fixing. Equally, "tying", which is described in Section 5(2)(d) is not considered by the Chicago school to be restrictive in any circumstances. Price discrimination is defined as offensive under both Sections 4 and 5 but, in fact, as noted in Chapter 2, economists generally recognise that price discrimination by a monopolist may on occasion increase efficiency. If the examples given in those sections were in fact thereby being defined as *per se* offensive, that would, at first sight, fix the Act with a strict Harvard approach, with some random divergences. However, it is also clear from the inclusion, in Section 4(1)(a), of agreements which "fix . . . any other trading conditions" that it cannot be intended to create a *per se* prohibition for a category so broadly defined. It is, of course, the case that individual decisions made by the Commission and the European Courts applying Articles 85 and 86 over the years have revealed choices and preferences of economic theory. Equally, the decisions of the Authority and the Irish courts applying Sections 4 and 5 show either choices of theory or the adoption of choices made in the EU context. However, as is discussed below, the decisions of the Irish courts, in the main, do not express the fact that such a choice of theory is being made, or make explicit the basis on which it is being made.

The Criminal Offences

The criminal provisions of the 1996 Act essentially make criminal offences of the Section 4 and Section 5 civil wrongs defined by the 1991 Act. Section 2(2) (b) of the 1996 Act creates the "Section 4" offence of entering into or implementing an agreement, making or implementing a decision or engaging in a concerted practice, "agreement", "decision" and "concerted practice" being defined as in Section 4 of 1991. Section 2(5) (b) of the 1996 Act creates the offence of not complying with the conditions of a licence granted by the Authority. Section 2(7) (a) creates the offence of acting in a manner prohibited by Section 5 of 1991, and the offence of not complying with an order made by the Minister under Section 14 of the 1991 Act.

The Act provides in some detail that it shall be a defence in respect of the Section 4 offence that a certificate or licence exists in respect of the agreement, decision or concerted practice[5]. Clearly, it is not the case that the Authority or the Minister would typically be proceeding to prosecute behaviour that it had certified or licensed. This is not to say that behaviour that has once been licensed or certified may not at a later date be found to be anti-competitive. The Authority has the function, and duty under the 1991 Act to revoke a certificate or licence where there has been a material change of circumstance, where it has been issued on the basis of misleading or incorrect information, or where the conditions attached to a licence are not being complied with, so that this defence is unlikely to arise in practice.

A defendant has a two-month period of grace defence in respect of prosecution where a certificate or licence is revoked by the Authority, or suspended by a Court,[6] or conditions are amended or inserted in a licence by the Authority,[7] under Section 8. This requires the defendant to show that it took steps to comply with the amended or inserted conditions within 14 days of their publication in Iris Oifigiúil, or, in the case of revocation or suspension, to cease the behaviour that is no longer licensed or

---

[5] Section 2(2) (c) (ii).

[6] Section 2(2) (c) (iii).

[7] Section 2(2) (c) (ii) II.

certified, and that it is proceeding with "due expedition" to complete its compliance. This defence is not available in respect of behaviour which caused the Authority to revoke a certificate or licence. It is difficult to see in exactly what practical circumstances the defence would arise.

Section 2(5), by making a criminal offence of non-compliance with licence conditions, is doing no more than logically completing the blanket Section 4 offence. However, in doing so, it changes the licensing function of the Authority in an important way. The function under the 1991 Act of granting a licence changed the standing of an agreement by making it enforceable and permitted where it would otherwise have been prohibited and void. The imposition by the Authority of conditions did no more than define the circumstances in which that permission would operate. The premise of the licence is that the agreement is otherwise void; but the view of the Authority does not itself make an agreement void. Any person in breach of licence conditions has been free still to argue in Section 6[8] proceedings, or in any proceedings involving the enforcement of the contract that the Authority's view is mistaken, that the agreement is not offensive in the first place, and the loss of the licence is therefore irrelevant. The 1996 Act by creating this offence gives the Authority the responsibility, in attaching conditions to a licence, of defining a criminal offence.

Two offences are created in respect of unilateral behaviour by dominant firms. One simply extends a criminal sanction to Section 5 of the 1991 Act. The other creates a criminal sanction for non-compliance with an order made by the Minister under Section 14 of the 1991 Act (or such an order amended after an appeal to the High Court). Section 14 gives power to the Minister to make any order, including divestment, in respect of a dominant position.[9] Section 2(7)(b) provides that in proceedings in respect of the Section 5 offence it will be a defence to show that the act was done in compliance with an order under Section 14. Again this can apply only to a relatively atypical situation where the Authority, or the Minister, seeks to prosecute an undertaking for

---

[8]   1991 Act.

[9]   See Chapter 8.

behaviour which has been imposed on the firm by Ministerial order. For both offences the two-month period of grace defence is provided for a situation where a second Section 14 order amends a first order. No Section 14 orders have been made since the coming into force of the 1991 Act.

Sections 2(2)(c) and 2(7)(b)(i) provide a defence, in respect of both the basic Section 4 offence and the basic Section 5 offence that "the defendant did not know, nor, in all the circumstances could the defendant be reasonably expected to have known" that "the effect of the agreement ... would be the prevention, restriction or distortion of trade alleged in the proceedings" or that "the act done by the defendant would constitute the abuse ... alleged in the proceedings". Clearly, this is an unusual provision. While the European Commission does take into account in considering a breach of the Treaty rules whether the behaviour has been clearly identified in the past as restrictive, it does so in the context of mitigation of fines and not as a defence.

Although the acts of the human persons who are its officers or employees are attributed to an undertaking for purposes of criminal liability, the four criminal offences discussed above can be committed only by an "undertaking".[10] It appears probable that the result of defining the criminal offence in this way will be that often the only potential defendant will be a company rather than the human persons who make its decisions. Apart from any wider public-policy considerations, this will mean that of the two criminal sanctions provided, imprisonment will not in practice be an available option for a court. Section 3(4) (a) creates an offence that can be committed by a human being who is not an undertaking, but it does not fill entirely the gap created. Section 3(4) provides that where an undertaking has committed any of the four offences described above, then any director, including shadow director, manager, secretary or other similar officer "... or any person purporting to act in such capacity" who authorised, consented to, or connived at, the acts that constitute the offence is also guilty of an offence. The same penalties are provided for this offence as for the four others. Clearly, this places the potential

---

[10]   See Chapter 7.

human defendant behind some kind of shield. It would seem that it must be shown, to some unspecified level of proof, that the undertaking has committed the offence before the human person can be convicted of the same offence. There is a presumption that the human person consented to or connived at the acts of the undertaking "until the contrary is proved".

The penalties provided for are, on summary conviction, a fine of £1,500, or, in the case of an individual, imprisonment for up to six months, or both. On indictment, the penalties are £3 million, or 10 per cent of turnover, or, in the case of an individual, imprisonment for up to two years, or both. Summary proceedings may be prosecuted by either the Minister or the Competition Authority.

The Statutory Right of Action

Section 6 provides that "any person aggrieved" by any action prohibited under Section 4 or 5 has a right of action for damages, injunctive relief or declaration against the undertaking or undertakings involved. The 1996 Act creates a wider personal liability for directors, shadow directors, managers and other officers of such undertakings. Actions for abuse of a dominant position may be brought in the Circuit or High Court. Actions against agreements, decisions and concerted practices may be brought only in the High Court.[11] It is difficult to guess at the reasoning behind the different jurisdictional provision for Sections 4 and 5. Given the concern expressed at the time of the introduction of the Act for small business and the consumer, there seems no good reason to limit recourse in respect of anti-competitive agreements to the High Court. It seems unlikely that it was considered that the High Court was the only appropriate forum for a new economic tort, given that the Circuit Court was considered appropriate in respect of an abuse of a dominant position.

A special *locus standi* was provided under the 1991 Act for the Minister for Enterprise and Employment to seek injunctive or declaratory relief, but not damages. This provision was intended as a form of State enforcement but was not used. Minister

---

[11]   Competition Act, 1991 Section 6(2). Section 6(2)(b) of the Act giving the Circuit Court jurisdiction in respect of Section 5 was not brought into force until 2.11.92 by SI 299/92.

O'Malley stated in the Dáil debates introducing the Competition Bill in 1991 that "the strength of the Bill is that it is self policing"[12] and, thus, the emphasis would not be on Ministerial action. In April 1995, Minister Bruton was advised by the Competition Authority (Competition Authority, 1995) that Independent Newspapers was in breach of Sections 4 and 5 and that a Section 6 enforcement action should be brought, but no action was brought. It is, of course, inherently problematic for any minister to bring this type of enforcement proceedings. This problem is recognised by the provision, by the Competition Act, 1996 of public enforcement by the Competition Authority using both criminal prosecution and civil actions under Section 6.

The Section 6 right of action has been successfully used for private litigation on a number of occasions. In fact, it is notable that the majority of actions have been run on the basis of Section 5 rather than Section 4, which contrasts with the experience in the EU and the US. Admittedly, the sample to date is small. In a number of that limited sample of cases the defendant was the State or a State body. The fact that the cases brought have been brought against the State may reflect a universal truth, not peculiar to competition litigation, that there is a greater willingness to sue the State than any other large defendant. It may also reflect the importance to the economy of semi-State firms or the fact that most of them are monopolies.

Functions of the Competition Authority
Section 10 of the 1991 Act established the Competition Authority, as an independent body, to consist of a chairman and no fewer than two and no more than four other members. Members of the Authority are appointed by the Minister for a maximum of five years and may be re-appointed. Under the 1991 Act, the primary function of the Authority was deciding on requests for the issuing of certificates and granting of licences for agreements notified to it under Section 7. The 1996 Act introduced criminal sanctions for breaches of Sections 4 and 5 and gave the Authority the power to bring both civil and criminal enforcement actions.

---

[12] Dáil debates 2.5.91 col. 1929.

The Authority also has a number of other functions. Under Section 11 as substituted by the 1996 Act, the Authority may carry out a study of "any practice or method of competition affecting the supply and distribution of goods or the provision of services". Prior to that, the Authority could only carry out studies when requested to do so by the Minister. It has carried out one study under Section 11 at the request of the Minister, concerning the newspaper industry (Competition Authority, 1995). Under Section 14 the Minister may ask the Authority to investigate an abuse of a dominant position. If the Authority finds that such abuse has taken place, the Minister may make various orders up to and including divestiture to break up the dominant position. At the time of the second reading of the Competition Bill, 1991, the then Minister Desmond O'Malley described Section 14 as being called in to play ". . . if there is a fundamental structural problem arising . . . I expect it to be used only in the gravest of cases, if at all".[13] To date, the Authority has not been requested to undertake an investigation of an abuse of a dominant position under Section 14. The Authority can be asked by the Minister to undertake an investigation of a merger under Section 7 of the Mergers, Take-overs and Monopolies (Control) Act, 1978. Four such referrals have been made since the coming into force of the Competition Act.[14]

Under Section 21, in order to obtain any information necessary for any of its functions under the 1991 or 1996 Act, the Authority may seek a warrant to enter premises or vehicles, require the production of documents and information, and take copies of documents. The criterion for the issue of a warrant is that a District Justice be satisfied that it is proper to do so for the obtaining of information which is necessary for the exercise by the Authority of any of its functions. The Authority, to carry out its functions under the 1991 Act, may also summon witnesses before it, examine them on oath and require the production of documents by them.[15] Failure to attend, or produce documents, or any

---

[13] Dáil Debates 30.4.91.

[14] See Chapter 10.

[15] Competition Act, 1991, Schedule, para. 7.

behaviour which would, if the Authority were a court, be contempt of court, carries the criminal sanction of a £1,000 fine or six months' imprisonment, or both. The Authority has indicated that it has issued a summons on at least one occasion.[16] The Section 21 powers have not been used to date. It has not used any of the above powers in relation to merger investigations or in the only Section 11 study carried out to date.

Where the powers of the Authority are used to obtain information, it is a criminal offence[17] for any person to disclose such information. In *Irish Press plc* v. *Minister for Enterprise and Employment,*[18] Keane J. refused to make an order requiring the Minister to disclose to Irish Press plc the unedited Report of the Competition Authority on the newspaper industry, referring to the need for the Authority to be able to ensure the confidentiality of commercially sensitive material supplied to it by business people or firms who expected that their confidence would be respected.

The quorum for the Authority is three. Prior to the 1996 Act, the Authority consisted of only three members. If necessary, it is possible for the Minister to permit the Authority to act with a lesser quorum for any of its functions other than decisions in respect of Section 4.[19] The Competition (Amendment) Act, 1996 provides for the Minister to assign the title of Director of Competition Enforcement to one permanent member of the Authority, who is given specified tasks of investigation in relation to enforcement but may also act as a member of the Authority for all other Authority functions under the Act. There is a parallel provision for investigation by the Authority of the criminal offences.

At the date of going to press, no criminal offences have been prosecuted by the Authority, and no civil actions have been brought under Section 6. While the Director of Competition Enforcement is given the role of investigation of both civil and

---

[16] Booksellers Currency Conversion Agreement, Decision No. 348 of 2.9.94.

[17] Schedule, para. 9 of 1991.

[18] *The Irish Times*, 31 May 1995.

[19] Schedule, para. 6(4) of 1991.

criminal offences, the decision to bring proceedings is a decision of the Authority. Minister Bruton introduced the extension of the right of civil action to the Authority as being the most important element of the 1996 Act, and the form of enforcement which he expected would be predominantly used. The relative merits of civil and criminal sanctions are discussed in Chapter 9.

The 1991 Act operates by making agreements automatically void and actionable if anti-competitive. It provides for the parties thereto, the option of notifying to the Authority agreements, decisions or concerted practices, seeking a certificate, or licence, or both. The Authority has stated a view that agreements which could in no sense be considered to prevent, restrict or distort competition are not notifiable.[20] It might be argued that the Authority's interpretation, while practical, is not immediately obvious on the face of the 1991 Act. For the purposes of notification, the 1991 Act distinguishes between agreements in existence at the date of its coming into force,[21] and agreements created subsequently ("old" and "new" agreements). Section 7(1) created a cut-off date for the notification of "old" agreements.[22] The vast majority of notifications made to the Authority were of "old" agreements, notified immediately before the deadline. No relief can be granted in a Section 6 action in respect of notified "old" agreements for the period prior to an Authority decision.[23]

Certificates

Section 4(4) of the 1991 Act provides for the issue of a certificate where, in the opinion of the Authority, the notified agreement does not offend against Section 4(1). The 1996 Act provides for the issue of a certificate in respect of a category of agreements.[24] The

---

[20] Thoroughbred Ltd./Grenfell Ltd.; Firestone/Aga Khan, Decision No. 11 of 5.11.92.

[21] 1.10.91.

[22] 30.9.92.

[23] s. 6(7) as amended by s. 6 of 1996.

[24] s. 5 of 1996. s. 5 also substitutes the word "contravene" in place of "offend against".

Authority may revoke a certificate where there has been a material change of circumstance or where the certificate has been issued on the basis of misleading or incorrect information.[25] A certificate is a protection against damages in Section 6 proceedings,[26] but it is not in any way conclusive or binding on a court, and is not a protection in such proceedings from the granting of an injunction or declaration. Equally, the Act does not give a certificate any legal effect in any other form of proceedings arising out of the certified contract, such as action for performance or payment. A general consideration, applicable here, is that a party to a contract, seeking to avoid it in reliance on the Competition Act, might arguably be considered to have benefited from an illegal contract and be subject to return to the other party monies or benefit received thereunder. Section 4(8) of the Act provides that a court may make such order for recovery or restitution as may seem just, in respect of an offensive agreement. While the topic of statutory illegality is beyond the scope of this book, the issue has arisen to some extent in two cases since the coming into force of the Act. In *RGDATA* v. *Tara Publishing Ltd.*,[27] RGDATA obtained a declaration under Section 6 that a 20-year exclusive licence granted by them 10 years previously was void. The issue of the original payment received by RGDATA for its grant of 20-year exclusivity was not canvassed in the judgment. In *Premier Dairies* v. *Doyle and Harries*,[28] however, an injunction was sought to enforce a post-termination non-compete clause in a distribution agreement, and resisted on the grounds that the clause was void by operation of the Competition Act. The judge granted the injunction, stating:

> In this case the Defendants are proposing to repudiate a contract which they signed with open eyes and which they worked for years and which they purchased for value. . . . What prevented

---

[25] s. 8(6) of 1991.

[26] s. 6(6) of 1991.

[27] *RGDATA* v. *Tara Publishing Co. Ltd.*, [1995] 1 IR 89.

[28] High Court, Kinlen J. 29.9.95.

the Defendants from suffering any competition from outsiders was the original agreement which they signed and used. The exclusivity was part of the benefit which they had purchased. . . . (H)aving regard to . . . the fact that they signed this negative covenant freely and exercised it, they cannot now repudiate it.

While noting that the judgment relates to the grant of an interlocutory injunction only, the authors respectfully suggest that repudiation does not arise. The Supreme Court on appeal[29] did not refer to this particular issue, taking the view that the covenant might be found void as a result of the 1991 Act, at a plenary hearing.

Licences

Section 4(2) of the 1991 Act provides for the Authority to license agreements, decisions or concerted practices which offend under Section 4. The Authority may:

> . . . grant a licence . . . in the case of . . . any agreement . . . which . . . contributes to improving the production or distribution of goods or provision of services or to promoting technical or economic progress, while allowing consumers a fair share of the resulting benefit and which does not —
>
> (i) impose on the undertakings concerned terms which are not indispensable to the attainment of those objectives;
>
> (ii) afford the undertakings the possibility of eliminating competition in respect of a substantial part of the products or services in question.

The grant of a licence permits an agreement which would otherwise be void, and thus in practice a licence from the Authority is a more comprehensive protection of a contract from possible challenge than a certificate. It is a complete defence to a Section 6 action, and to any other form of action relying on the Act. There is no provision for a court to apply the four licence criteria, with the result that, where proceedings are brought against an anti-competitive but licensable agreement which was not notified, it is not possible for a court itself to exempt the agreement.

---

[29]   [1996] 1 ILRM 453.

A licence may be made retrospective to the date of notification, but no earlier, in the case of a "new" agreement. "Old" agreements notified under Section 7(1) of the 1991 Act cannot obtain a licence for any date earlier than the date of the Authority's decision. Section 4(2) provides for the grant of a licence to an agreement "or category of agreements". This power mirrors the power of the Commission to make block exemptions for categories of agreements, but whereas the Commission acts under Council Regulations,[30] the Authority's scope to grant category licences is not further elaborated in any way in the Act or otherwise, save for a passing reference in Section 4(3)(b). The Authority has used the power in two distinct ways: to grant licences for categories of similar agreements, such as the exclusive distribution category licence; and as a basis for licensing multiples of standard form agreements. The latter have not always been described as category licences but appear to operate in practice in the same way. The question as to whether a licence granted for the text of a standard agreement can be taken to license any example of that text signed between the notifying party and a new party remains to be considered by the courts. Category licences of the first type have been granted for exclusive purchasing of motor fuel,[31] exclusive distribution agreements,[32] cylinder LPG dealer agreements[33] and franchise agreements.[34] The content of the licences is discussed in Chapter 7. Licences may be made subject to conditions, and the cylinder LPG category licence,[35] for example, is subject to the obligation to report annual sales of cylinder LPG. The Authority has power under Section 8 of the 1991 Act to revoke or amend any licence it has granted, or any conditions of a licence where, inter alia, there is a material change of circumstance or where the licence conditions are breached. As

---

[30] Regulation 19/65, OJ (1965–66), p. 35, for example.

[31] Decision No. 25 of 1.7.93.

[32] Decision No. 144 of 5.11.93.

[33] Decision No. 364 of 28.10.94.

[34] Decision No. 372 of 17.11.94.

[35] Decision No. 364.

it happens, the only licence that has been amended to date is the cylinder LPG category licence.[36]

The Authority has issued Notices in respect of employment agreements, mergers pre-dating the Act and shopping centre leases.[37] Notices were not provided for under the 1991 Act and have no legal standing but merely give an indication of the Authority's views. The provision in the 1996 Act for "category certificates" could potentially be useful in disposing of, or making unnecessary, notifications of agreements that turn out to be inoffensive, such as the large number of shopping centre leases certified by the Authority during 1994. The agreements currently before the Authority do not appear to contain any category so large and homogeneous as the shopping centre leases. However, given that the Authority must proceed to a decision in respect of every notification, a category certificate which might pre-empt unnecessary notifications would be a useful tool. The EU has no equivalent category negative clearance, but in the different EU enforcement regimes, reliance on a Commission Notice may be put forward as grounds for resisting a fine. It is also open to the Commission, as the enforcement body, not to proceed to a decision on an agreement notified by the parties, but to issue what is known as a comfort letter, confirming that an agreement does not appear to offend. Arguably, an Authority with enforcement powers can properly do the same.

The Notification System
Section 7(6) of the 1991 Act provides that the functions of the Authority "shall be carried out in accordance with such procedures, if any, as may be prescribed". The Minister may make regulations in respect of "any matter referred to in this Act as prescribed or to be prescribed".[38] The fees payable in respect of a notification are prescribed[39] and the method of giving notice of a

---

[36]   Decision No. 402 of 19.6.95.

[37]   15.9.92, 4.5.93 and 2.9.93 respectively.

[38]   s. 23(1) of 1991.

[39]   Competition (Notification Fee) Regulations 1991 SI No. 250 of 1991 sets the fee at £100.

decision.[40] Apart from that, no procedures have been prescribed for the Authority. Paragraph 6(3) of the Schedule to the 1991 Act provides that "subject to this Act, the Authority may regulate its own procedure" which it has done, evolving a notification form, Form CA, and a series of procedural steps, including the possibility of an oral hearing. It has been argued[41] that the Minister is obliged to prescribe procedures but:

> It is perfectly clear that the Oireachtas contemplated that the Authority could carry out its functions even if the Minister did not prescribe procedures.

For notification of an agreement, the Authority requires the notifying party to supply the contract, a completed Form CA, and an Annexe describing the nature of the agreement and giving other specified information, while the 1991 Act requires that the notification be accompanied by the statutory fee.[42] The Form CA corresponds closely to Form AB used by the Commission, and seeks similar information, requiring the notifying party to state the relevant product or service, and market, and their argument(s) for a certificate or licence. The practice of the Authority has been that notification of a contract may be initiated by either party thereto, without the involvement at that stage of the other contract party or parties. The alternative would be to require all parties to an agreement to join in a notification, effectively giving any one party a right of veto on recourse to the notification process. The 1996 Act provides that unilateral notifications shall be deemed, and be deemed always to have been, valid.[43] It also provides for the notification of proposed agreements.[44]

The subject matter of a notification must be an agreement,

---

[40] Competition Act 1991 (Notice of Licences and Certificates) Regulations 1993 SI No. 293 of 93.

[41] *Cronin and others* v. *Competition Authority and others.* Unreported, High Court, Costello J. 24.6.94.

[42] s.7(4) of 1991.

[43] s.12(1)(a).

[44] s.12(1)(b).

decision or concerted practice, between undertakings, and must be complete. The Authority has rejected the notification of the Charter of the Worshipful Company of Goldsmiths, as being neither an agreement, decision or concerted practice. Only agreements, decisions and concerted practices made between undertakings are notifiable. The Authority has by Notice of 18 September 1992 stated that it does not consider that employees are undertakings, and thus that employment agreements are not capable of notification. A number of agreements were notified to the Authority to which a Minister is a party. The Authority has rejected one such notification made between the Minister for Health and the Federation of the Irish Chemical Industry (FICI), on the grounds that the Minister was not, in the context of the notified FICI agreement, an undertaking. The Authority's notice of rejection also stated that Ministers would not typically be undertakings, a formulation which does not preclude the possibility that they might be such, in some circumstances.[45] The Authority has stated that consumers are not undertakings (Competition Authority Annual Report, 1992: 5).

Authority Procedure After Notification

After accepting a notification as being of a complete, notifiable agreement between undertakings, the Authority makes public the fact of notification in a standard advertisement in a daily national newspaper.[46] It is provided in paragraph 8 of the Schedule to the 1991 Act that interested parties may make submissions to the Authority, and one reason for making notifications public is to inform interested parties. One member of the Authority takes primary responsibility for each notification. At that point, the Authority's practice is to advise the notifying party, and any non-notifying parties to the agreement, that consideration of the agreement has begun, and the name of the member of the

---

[45] See also Chapter 7. The Authority subsequently rejected notification of an agreement between the Minister for Transport, Energy and Communications and licensed MMDS operators.

[46] To date, *The Irish Times*, and to date, on the second Friday of the month, with some exceptions.

Authority dealing with it. The Authority may seek more information from the notifying party. The next formal step is for an initial assessment to be agreed by the Authority, either to issue a certificate or grant a licence, or to refuse either. Where the Authority agrees a negative assessment, a Statement of Objections issues to the parties to the contract. The parties are offered a period of 28 days to reply to the Statement of Objections, and either party may request an oral hearing. The reply to a Statement of Objections or, where it is granted, an oral hearing, is the penultimate stage of a notification. The Authority view either is changed by the argument of the party, and the notification proceeds to a certificate or licence decision, or it is not, and it proceeds to a refusal decision. Where the Authority agrees that a notified agreement can be certified, or licensed, either it proceeds to do so directly or, where the decision involves a new issue of principle, it issues a Notice of Intention seeking submissions from third parties and making available a synopsis of the facts on which it has based its positive assessment. On the basis of the submissions received, it may still proceed to a positive decision, or it may change to taking a negative view. In the latter case, it will proceed to deal with the notification according to the negative procedure outlined above and issue a Statement of Objections. There is a third route which the Authority has taken on many occasions, where the notified agreement is amended by the parties, removing the elements that offend — for example, after the issue of a Statement of Objections. The Authority has then decided on the basis of the amended agreement whether to certify or license. The question as to whether the Authority should be considered in those circumstances to have certified or licensed the amended agreement rather than the original, which by implication, in the Authority's view, was offensive and did not qualify for a licence, has not been considered by a court, nor has the question of whether, for the purposes of Section 6(6) of the 1991 Act, the date from which the protection from damages arises is the date of notification or of amendment.

The Acts do not make provision for oral hearings and it is thus a matter for the Authority to exercise its discretion as to whether a hearing is required. There will be circumstances where natural justice will require that the parties be heard orally. However, the decision that the Authority is required to make does not, in the authors' view, necessarily of its nature require oral argumentation. The practice of the Authority to date has been to establish no formal procedure. It has treated the hearing as an opportunity for the interested party or parties to make a case orally, with or without legal representation and with or without witnesses. Making a case, in the context of something that is not an adversarial process, requires the interested party to discharge some onus of proof which is measured not by reference to the proofs of an adversary, but to some objective standard. The Authority in practice asks questions to elicit facts or argument, but takes the view that there is an onus on notifying parties to make their case for the certificate or licence which they have requested. The level of proof required may be deduced from the language of Section 4 which requires the Authority to "form an opinion"; in the case of a certificate "on the basis of the facts in its possession", and in the case of a licence "having regard to all relevant market conditions". It has not to date either required or agreed to an oral hearing attended both by a notifying party, and a party opposing the notification, although no formal statement of the policy of the Authority has been made as to whether this might ever be appropriate. Section 4(5) of the 1991 Act provides that the Authority may, "before granting a licence or issuing a certificate . . . invite any Minister of the Government concerned with the matter to offer such observations as he may wish to make". The Authority has sought the views of Ministers in a number of instances.

The Authority view is that as the notification system is voluntary, a notification can be withdrawn at any stage before it reaches a decision. In its 1993 Annual Report, the Authority has expressed its view on the potential waste of State resources that this may involve.

Decisions and Appeals

Section 4(6) of the 1991 Act requires that the Authority give notice of its decisions "in the prescribed manner". SI 293/1993 provides for giving of notice by registered post to "every party thereto seeking the licence or certificate", or, in the case of a category licence, by publication in Iris Oifigiúil. The Authority has two statutory obligations of publication. S.4(6) requires it:

> ... on granting a licence or issuing a certificate ... (to) ... give notice ... stating the terms and the date thereof and the reasons therefor ... to be published in Iris Oifigiúil and cause notice of the grant ... or issue ... to be published in one daily newspaper published in the State.

This creates an obligation to publish notice of a positive decision, but not of a negative one. Separately, Section 6(8) of the 1991 Act provides that "The Authority shall as soon as may be cause to be published in Iris Oifigiúil" all decisions, positive or negative, in respect of "old" agreements — those in existence on 1 October 1991. The combination of the two requirements results in the anomaly that there is no apparent obligation to publish notice of a negative decision in respect of a "new" notification. In practice, the Authority has published all decisions on notifications in a national newspaper and publishes a notice containing reasons for each decision in Iris Oifigiúil. The anomaly may be explained by the idea, discernible at certain points in the Act, that a positive decision changes the status of an agreement, whereas a negative decision does not. There is also a specific reason why it is necessary to give public notice of the conclusion of an "old" notification, which is that, at that point, its protection from Section 6 action expires. The Authority in practice publishes notice of the conclusion of all notifications, old and new, whether by decision, rejection or withdrawal.

Section 9 of 1991 provides for an appeal against a positive decision. This is an appeal on the merits of the Authority decision, and is open not just to the parties to the notified agreement but to "any undertaking or association of undertakings concerned, or any other person aggrieved". The appeal must be made within 28 days of the statutory publication of the Authority decision, a period which may be extended at the discretion of the court. There is no provision for an appeal on the merits against a negative decision.

There is, of course, the possibility of challenging an Authority decision by way of judicial review and to date this has been done twice. It is not intended to consider the many issues potentially relevant to judicial review of a body such as the Authority.[47] An *ex parte* injunction was obtained by Newspread Ltd. in June 1993 restraining the publication by the Authority of notice of a decision refusing a certificate or a licence to the agreement between Newspread and Easons on their agreed mode of conversion of the sterling prices of newspapers and magazines for distribution in Ireland. The issue was settled without proceeding to judgment.[48] In July 1993 the Authority issued a category licence for exclusive purchase agreements for motor fuels[49] which disposed of a number of notifications made by the major oil companies of their standard form agreements with retailers. The Authority had previously published a draft of the category licence and had invited submissions from interested parties. The decision was challenged by the Texaco Retailers Association on the grounds that the Authority refused to supply the Association with the text, or a summary of the text, of the agreements notified by Texaco, or a copy of, or a summary of, the notification made by Texaco — that is, the argument made in Texaco's submission. It was also argued that the Association should have been permitted to reply to the Texaco submissions.

> The draft is a very detailed appraisal by the Competition Authority of the operation of the Act, and of the existing contracts Texaco had with retailers, and of proposals for new agreements that might be entered into. The Authority then indicated its view of whether a licence should issue, the economic grounds, and the proposed form of the category licence. . . . Persons interested . . . including Mr Cronin, would see the view the Authority had taken of submissions made to it.

Thus:

> There was nothing unjust in the way the procedures were followed and they were eminently fair.[50]

---

[47]   The reader is referred generally to Hogan and Morgan (1991).

[48]   See Competition Authority (1993).

[49]   Decision No. 25 of 1.7.93.

[50]   *Cronin* v. *Competition Authority*, High Court unreported, Costello, J., 24.6.94.

It is worth noting also, that the issue arose in the same case, of the Applicant's *locus standi* insofar as the claim related to the text of agreements, notified by Texaco, to which they were not themselves party.

> On the issue of locus standi I am not expressing a concluding view but I do think the Applicant was very concerned indeed with the decision.

Studies

In keeping with the minimalist nature of the Acts, no provision is made for procedures to be followed in a Section 11 study. Unlike a decision under Section 4, or an opinion under Section 14, a study by the Authority under Section 11 does not in itself have legal consequences for any party. In the only Section 11 study undertaken to date, the Authority published the terms of reference set by the Minister, sought submissions, and held oral hearings, as described in the study itself.

7

SECTION 4: AGREEMENTS, DECISIONS AND CONCERTED PRACTICES

The long title of the Competition Act, 1991 describes it as "An Act to prohibit, by analogy with Articles 85 and 86 of the Treaty (of Rome) . . . and in the interests of the common good, the prevention, restriction or distortion of competition. . . ." The core substantive provisions of the Act are Section 4, which prohibits and makes void anti-competitive agreements, decisions and concerted practices, and Section 5 which prohibits the abuse of a dominant position. The latter topic is considered in the next chapter. The present chapter looks at the substantive law of Section 4 as it has been applied in what is now a large number of decisions by the Competition Authority and the Irish courts. Some EU decisions under Articles 85 and 86 are referred to but the purpose of the chapter is to show the implementation in Ireland of the prohibition.

Given that the Acts have only been in force for a limited period of time and that, prior to the 1996 Act, the Competition Authority did not have powers to consider any arrangement other than those notified by one of the parties involved, an examination of Authority decisions cannot provide comprehensive coverage of the types of behaviour prohibited by Section 4. Nevertheless, many forms of common commercial agreement have been addressed.

The Scope of the Act — "Undertakings"
The Act applies to "undertakings", defined as:

> a person being an individual, a body corporate or an unincorporated body of persons engaged for gain in the production supply or distribution of goods or the provision of a service.[1]

---

[1]   Section 3.

The word "undertaking" is the word used in Articles 85 and 86, but the Treaty contains no definition of it. A working definition has emerged through the implementation of Articles 85 and 86, but the Irish Act includes the phrase "for gain", adding a concept that is not derived from the EU jurisprudence. A body is not caught by the Act merely by virtue of being a body corporate:

> The function of the . . . companies was simply to hold land and to dispose of the land and they are not in any sense within the meaning of that section (section 3) bodies engaged in the production, supply or distribution of goods or the provision of a service.[2]

The scope of the definition was considered in detail at an early stage in the life of the Act in relation to the Voluntary Health Insurance Board, a statutory corporation established by the VHI Act, 1957. Section 4(4) of that Act provides that:

> The Board shall so fix the subscriptions . . . that . . . the revenue of the Board from the subscriptions, together with its other revenues (if any) shall be sufficient, but only sufficient . . . after the Board has made such allowances as it thinks proper for reserves, depreciations and other like purposes, to meet the charges (including repayment of loans to the Minister) properly chargeable to revenue.

Similar provisions exist in other statutes establishing some semi-State companies, such as the ESB. Costello, J. found[3] that the words "engaged for gain" which appear in the wording of the Irish Act, and not in Articles 85 or 86, were intended to catch only those bodies whose *object* was that of gain; and that the VHI "merely provides a service in the public interest". The Supreme Court, reversing the High Court decision, found:

> . . . the words "for gain" connote merely an activity carried on or a service supplied, as it is in this case, which is done in return for a charge or payment, and that, accordingly, the Defendant does come within the definition of an undertaking. . . . What

---

[2] *Sibra Building Company Ltd. and others* v. *Palmerstown Centre Development Ltd. and others.* High Court, Keane, J., unreported, 24.11.92.

[3] *Deane and others* v. *VHI*, unreported, High Court, Costello, J., 9.4.92.

would be saved from application of the Act ... is ... a charitable association providing the spending of money and the supply of goods or services free of any charge or payment.[4]

The equation of "for gain" with "for profit" was specifically rejected. The argument was made that the addition, in the Irish Act, of the words "for gain" was intended to mirror the provisions of Articles 90(2) and 92 to 94 (which make special provision for undertakings to which Member States grant special or exclusive rights, typically the State companies). That argument was rejected on the basis that that reading would exempt from the provisions of the Act not only the VHI or the ESB, but many statutory corporations, and:

> ... if the construction of this section contended for by the Respondents is correct, then it is probable that its consequence in Ireland would be that the Act of 1991, so far from being a prohibition of distortion and abuse of a dominant position by way of analogy to Articles 85 and 86 would be very extensively limited indeed in its application ....

Subsequently, the ESB has also been found to be an undertaking[5] and it is clear that other State companies, and not-for-profit companies, are also within the scope of the Act. This still leaves unanswered some of the questions raised at the time of the VHI case, regarding the status of bodies like local authorities and Ministers. A view appears from some of the decisions of the courts concerning Ministers as undertakings, that the answer to the question may be dependent on the activity in which the Minister is engaged. It is not clear whether that approach would be adopted in considering other persons or bodies. The Authority found Waterford Harbour Commissioners to be an undertaking,[6] noting that harbour authorities are empowered to charge for the services they supply, are not subject to any obligation not to make a profit, and according to the policy stated in the 1985 Green

---

[4] *Deane and others* v. *VHI* (1992) 2 IR 319.

[5] *Donovan and others* v. *ESB* (1994) 2 IR 305

[6] Decision No. 7 of 4.8.92.

Paper on Transport Policy are expected to make a realistic return on investment.

The question as to whether Ministers could be undertakings was not discussed in the course of the Dáil debates at the stage where concern was expressed as to whether local authorities or trade unions were within the scope of the Act. This might reflect an assumption that Ministers were clearly outside the definition, but if so, that assumption has been questioned a number of times in cases brought against Ministers under Section 6.

> The Minister is a statutory corporation and his objects are set out in the terms of s.1 of the Ministers and Secretaries Act 1924. There may be circumstances in which the Minister is engaged in activities which would constitute her as an "undertaking". That is not the case here. If she is a party to the agreement, she is not a party to commercial activity of any sort and is not engaged in trade.[7]

In *Carrigaline Community TV and others* v. *Minister for Transport, Energy and Communication*,[8] Keane J. found (obiter) that a Minister:

> ... whether as individual or as an undertaking, is an undertaking within the meaning of Sections 4 and 5 of the 1991 Act, if he is engaged for gain. That expression is interpreted by the Supreme Court in dealing with the VHI. It appears from that decision that if a body such as the Minister supplies a service in return for a charge or payment, he will be engaged for gain, and hence within the ambit of Sections 4 and 5.

On the facts of the case he found:

> It is also clear, however, that if the Minister in granting licences for transmissions is engaged in no more than a regulatory or administrative function then the fact that he imposes a charge for the granting of the licence does not in itself mean that he is engaged for gain.

---

[7] *Greally* v. *Minister for Education, ASTI and others*, High Court, Costello J., unreported 27.2.95 Counsel's note. The authors are grateful to Gerard Hogan BL for providing his note of the decision.

[8] High Court, unreported, Keane, J. 10.11.95.

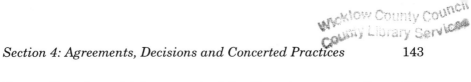

Proceedings brought in respect of the licensing system for artificial insemination[9] pleaded that the Minister was in breach of Sections 4 and 5 of the Act, but the judgment deals exclusively with the Article 85 and 86, and Article 90 arguments in the case. As noted in Chapter 6, the Competition Authority has rejected notifications of agreements involving the Ministers for Health and Communications.

It was stated by the then Minister in the Dáil debates on the 1991 Act that trade unions were intended to be taken out of the scope of the Act and that the phrase "for gain" was intended to achieve this objective. Peter Barry, TD, however, also warned in the same debates that exemptions from the Act should be made explicit, rather than relying on the future interpretation of an inexplicit phrase. Judge Costello has found in respect of trade unions that:

> This section (section 3) must be read in the light of the long title to the Act which refers to its object being "the prevention, restriction or distortion of competition and the abuse of dominant positions *in trade*". This means that an association of undertakings which is providing services for gain must be doing so in the course of trade to be within the statutory definition . . . . Here the trade union is not engaged in any commercial activity, rather it is providing a service for its members for a common purpose.[10] [emphasis in the original]

The concept of providing goods or services in the course of trade, as distinct from doing so for a common purpose with members has not been explored further in litigation. However, it can be seen that if extrapolated to other bodies corporate, it could result in a limit to the scope of the Act not unlike that which would have been produced by the reading, rejected by the Supreme Court in *Deane* v. *VHI*, of "for gain" in the sense of "for profit" rather than the sense of "for any monetary return". This is an interpretation of the phrase "for gain" which treats "gain" as a necessary motive, as distinct from considering whether "gain" was factually present

---

[9] *O'Neill* v. *Minister for Agriculture*, High Court, unreported, Budd, J., 5.7.95.

[10] *Greally* v. *Minister for Education* op. cit.

or not. The authors suggest that if such a test of motive were to be
applied, it could result in exactly the limiting of the scope of the
Act ruled out in *Deane* v. *VHI.*[11]

Restraint of trade clauses in employment agreements had been
litigated in the past under the common law rules so it was not
surprising that lawyers would identify it as a possible area of concern under the Act. A number of notifications of such agreements
were made. However, the Authority has issued a Notice in respect of
employment agreements,[12] stating that employees are not undertakings, for the reason that they carry on business not on their own
behalf but for their employer. The Notice quotes the European
Court of Justice view in *Suiker Unie.*[13] It also states that an employee who has left an employer and is in business on his or her
own account may thereby be constituted an undertaking, and their
contract with the erstwhile employer then comes within the scope
of the Act. This view has since been questioned (Callanan, 1991).
Subsequently, the Authority rejected a notification of an employment contract where the employee had left and immediately been
employed by another employer, on the basis that the employee had
not been and never became an undertaking[14] but accepted a notification where a former employee did set up in business on their own
account.[15] A person who makes an agreement when an employee
may nonetheless be treated as an undertaking where, by virtue of
the very agreement, they set up in business for themselves.[16] The
Authority has also treated some employment contracts as falling
within the Act by virtue of their being made a condition of an
agreement which is between undertakings. This may occur, for
example, in the course of the sale of a business where two firms
agree that one firm will employ a person on specified terms,[17] or

---

[11]   [1992] 2 IR 319.

[12]   Iris Oifigiúil, 18.9. 92. pp. 632–3.

[13]   *Suiker Unie* v. *Commission* [1975] ECR 1663.

[14]   Peter Mark/Majella Stapleton, Decision No. 13 of 18.2.93.

[15]   Apex/Murtagh, Decision No. 20 of 10.6.93.

[16]   Phil Fortune/Budget Travel, Decision No. 9 of 14.9.92.

[17]   Rohan/Rohcon, Decision No. 301 of 25.3.94.

where the seller remains as the employee of the buyer.[18]

In ACT/Kindle,[19] the Authority stated that the seven share-holders who controlled the company were undertakings because of that ownership and control although the seven were not each individually controllers of the company. The Authority has since then treated as agreements between undertakings agreements with groups of controlling shareholders. It might be questioned whether the individual shareholders in a group that has collective control can properly be said to be engaged for gain, and be undertakings, when they are not economically independent of one another in doing so, nor intended to be so. On the other hand, EU jurisprudence recognises that bodies can be integrated in the same economic endeavour and still be distinct undertakings, as in principal/agent and parent/subsidiary relationships. It is also relevant to consider the operation of the Act in the context of Irish company law if agreements framed as being made between groups of shareholders, and third parties, fell outside the scope of the Act. Given that it is very common in any case for agreements that could be made between companies to be made instead between the members, for various commercial reasons, then even without deliberate anti-trust engineering the Act could be rendered ineffective in respect of many agreements, in a way, it is suggested, not contemplated by the legislators.

Two undertakings may be separate legal persons, while forming only one economic unit. Thus two companies in a parent/subsidiary relationship, or two subsidiaries of the same parent, are legally separate persons, but are, as it were, one economic person. The EU approach to agency agreements is that the agent, although an undertaking, is by definition integrated into the principal's economic enterprise.

There is no *de minimis* provision in the Act, so that the size of an undertaking does not affect its being caught by the Act. The Authority stated in its first decision, Nallen/O'Toole, that excluding agreements between small undertakings could deny consumers in rural areas the protection the Act was designed to give. The FTC

---

[18]   Carroll Catering/Sutcliffe, Decision No. 29 of 9.9.93.

[19]   Decision No. 8 of 4.9.92.

(1991a) had recommended the inclusion of a *de minimis* provision for all forms of behaviour except price-fixing and collusive tendering, but that option was specifically rejected in the Dáil debate on the then Bill.

Agreements, Decisions and Concerted Practices

The Authority's decisions concern primarily agreements between undertakings, and these are discussed throughout. It has considered the question of an association of undertakings on a lesser number of occasions, most notably in its decision on the Code of Ethics of the Association of Optometrists.[20] The decision stated that as most of the optometrists who were members of the association were undertakings in their own right, it constituted an association of undertakings. It noted that, while EU decisions in this area generally involved trade associations, a professional association was not excluded. The rules, or in this case, the Code of Ethics, constituted a decision of the association. By their nature, concerted practices are unlikely to be notified to the Authority. The level of co-ordination necessary to amount to a concerted practice is a matter of discussion at EU level, but the issue arises typically in the context of enforcement rather than voluntary notification. The Guide to the Competition Act (Competition Authority, 1991) notes that there is no definition in the Act of the term "concerted practice" and refers to the definition contained in the Dyestuffs case.[21]

> A form of co-ordination between undertakings which without having reached the stage where an agreement properly s) called has been concluded, knowingly substitutes practical co-operation between them for the risks of competition.

The Irish Booksellers[22] arrangement in relation to their currency conversion chart was dealt with by the Authority as a concerted practice.

---

[20]   Decision No. 16 of 29.4.93.

[21]   *ICI and Others* v. *Commission* [1972] ECR 619.

[22]   Decision No. 348 of 2.9.94.

Section 4(1) — The Basic Prohibition

The basic prohibition on anti-competitive agreements set out in Section 4(1) is extremely brief:

> Subject to the provisions of this section, all agreements between undertakings, decisions by associations of undertakings and concerted practices which have as their object or effect the prevention, restriction or distortion of competition in trade in any goods or services in the State or in any part of the State are prohibited and void . . . .

The section contains a non-exhaustive list of anti-competitive behaviour:

> . . . including in particular, without prejudice to the generality of the subsection, those which —
>
> (a) directly or indirectly fix purchase or selling prices or any other trading conditions;
>
> (b) limit or control production, markets, technical development or investment;
>
> (c) share markets or sources of supply;
>
> (d) apply dissimilar conditions to equivalent transactions with other trading parties thereby placing them at a competitive disadvantage;
>
> (e) make the conclusion of contracts subject to acceptance by the other parties of supplementary obligations which by their nature or according to commercial usage have no connection with the subject of such contracts.

There are certain forms of agreements which are almost universally understood to be anti-competitive and therefore offensive, under both Article 85, and Section 4. As noted in Chapter 2, economic theory tends to regard horizontal[23] arrangements between competitors with more concern than vertical[24] agreements, in that the former are rarely innocuous, whereas, although some vertical agreements are considered to be seriously offensive, there are many

---

[23]   Agreements between firms at the same level of production or distribution.

[24]   Agreements between firms at different levels in the production or distribution process.

which are not. Agreements between competitors in respect of selling price — a cartel — have been considered offensive by the
Authority. This view is in accordance with EU jurisprudence and
with competition laws in most OECD countries. Under US law
price-fixing arrangements are unlawful *per se* and engaging in such
agreements can constitute a criminal offence. Other forms of horizontal behaviour which are virtually always considered offensive
are market sharing and limiting production, since for the most part
these are merely alternatives to price-fixing. It is possible for a
horizontal agreement to co-operate to be inoffensive, or to be offensive but licensable. The EU, for example, grants a block exemption
for R&D agreements[25] and the Authority granted a licence in respect of the agreement between creators of copyright music and
IMRO, although it involved joint selling by competitors.[26]

The Authority has found vertical restrictions on price to be offensive on all occasions to date.[27] The Commission at one stage
considered that resale price maintenance in distribution agreements did not affect trade between Member States, and it therefore did not proceed to consider whether it was also anti-
competitive. This appears to have been misunderstood to be a
Commission finding that resale price maintenance was on the
merits not anti-competitive, but the present position is that the
EU block exemptions for exclusive distribution, exclusive purchasing, franchising and motor vehicle distribution do not permit RPM
clauses. The position for non-price vertical restrictions is less
clear-cut and the Authority's treatment of them has varied in
different circumstances.

Notwithstanding the long title of the Act, examination of the
decisions of the Authority shows that in the main they are
evolved from first principles, although on many occasions reference is made to the reasoning of the EU or other competition
jurisdictions. For a number of the notifications this is necessarily
so, since they have raised questions for which there is no EU
precedent. However, it has also been the case that where EU

---

[25] Commission Regulation (EEC) No. 418/85.

[26] IMRO/creators, Decision No 445 of 15.12.95.

[27] The first decision on this was Esso Solus agreement, Decision No. 4 of 25.6.92.

precedent exists the Authority has chosen on some occasions not to adopt it. Thus, while the exclusive distribution category licence[28] expressly refers to, and adopts the reasoning of, Regulation 1983/83, and the motor fuels category licence[29] refers to and adopts the reasoning of Regulation 1984/83, the franchise category licence[30] differs from the EU franchise block exemption, Regulation 4087/88, in that it does not make a blanket finding that franchise agreements necessarily offend under Section 4(1); it finds, rather, that they may or may not offend. The Authority has not stated a preference for particular schools of economic theory but it can be deduced without difficulty from its condemnation of vertical price restraints that it is not applying a rigid Chicago school doctrine in that area. It has also cited US precedent and in some instances that of other countries. It has had occasion to decide on notifications of agreements which previously would have been subject to the common-law restraint of trade doctrine, and it appears from those decisions that, while there is no great divergence of result, it does not feel tied to the principles evolved under that doctrine.

The Nature of the Prohibition

In its first decision, Nallen/O'Toole,[31] the Authority stated a number of general principles, and made clear that it considered that Section 4(1) had to be interpreted on a "rule of reason" basis.

> If Section 4(1) were to be interpreted literally then virtually every form of business agreement could be argued to prevent, restrict or distort competition because any agreement effectively prohibits others from concluding the very same contract with the original parties.

The standard illustration of the situation where a rule of reason approach produces a different result from the literal approach arises where the agreement under consideration might restrict competition in one form, but enhances competition in other ways.

---

[28] Decision No. 144 of 5.11.93.

[29] Decision No. 25 of 1.7.93.

[30] Decision No. 372 of 17.11.94.

[31] Decision No. 1 of 2.4.92.

The argument that exclusive patent licences should be considered inoffensive if they would not be granted, without exclusivity, and information therefore would not be disseminated, is an argument that the improvement in dynamic competition more than offsets the restriction on static competition. Equally, the argument that distributors of a product need territorial exclusivity in order to encourage them to focus their efforts on promoting that product, is an argument that the lessening of intra-brand competition is offset by increased inter-brand competition.

An example of the same reasoning is visible in Waterford Harbour Authority/Bell Lines.[32] At the time of the building of a new container port in Waterford harbour for which the necessary capital was put up by the Harbour Authority, the authority agreed with Bell Lines to grant it priority use of the new facilities. In return, Bell Lines would pay to the Harbour Authority, over the period of the agreement, sufficient monies to cover the capital outlay and associated interest costs incurred in the building. The Competition Authority assessed this as an agreement which restricted behaviour in relation to one port but which did not restrict competition, since competition in this field was more widely dispersed than one port:

> The Authority nevertheless believes that there are a number of competing ports through which goods may be shipped to and from Britain and mainland Europe by Lo/Lo and Ro/Ro modes both within the State and in Northern Ireland. In its opinion these ports should all be regarded as part of the market. Competition takes place largely between the various ports which can handle Lo/Lo and Ro/Ro traffic. . . . As the Authority believes that the market is that for shipping goods either by Lo/Lo or Ro/Ro through ports in the entire island of Ireland, and that the notified agreement does not prevent, restrict or distort competition in that market, the agreement does not offend against Section 4(1) of the Competition Act. Indeed, as the agreement only involves giving Bell Lines priority access rather than exclusive use of the facilities, the development of the new terminal may allow other shipping lines access to Waterford harbour for container traffic and could increase competition.[33]

---

[32] Decision No. 7 of 4.8.92.

[33] Waterford Harbour Commissioners/Bell Lines Ltd., Decision No. 7 of 4.8.92.

This was elaborated further in later Authority decisions:

> Such an approach is well established in competition law following the US Supreme Court decision in the Standard Oil[34] case in 1911. In that case (which involved a merger), White CJ, in delivering the opinion of the Court, rejected the view that the blanket prohibition in Section 1 of the Sherman Act applied to every contract in restraint of trade and imposed the plain duty of applying its prohibitions to every case within its literal language. [35]

The US Supreme Court in that decision effectively endorsed the decision of Taft, J. in *Addyston Pipe*[36] where he distinguished between "naked" and "ancillary" restraints. Keane, J., applying Article 85 in *Masterfoods* v. *H.B.*[37] refers to the approach of the United States Courts and notes that the Court of Justice and the Court of First Instance have also, notwithstanding the more elaborate construction of the EU competition rules, applied a rule of reason approach in respect of vertical restraints in a number of circumstances; and he also chose to apply that test to Articles 85 and 86. It is also implicit in *RGDATA* v. *Tara Publishing Co. Ltd.*[38]

> The fact that . . . RGDATA . . . would be precluded from publishing a magazine under a particular title or with a particular accolade may in theory restrict competition but only in the sense that the vendor cannot reclaim and exploit the asset of which he has disposed. Any additional restriction which would impose wider restrictions of a lengthy nature would offend the Treaty of Rome, the 1991 Act and at common law.

The same reasoning can be found in the multiple shopping centre lease decisions of the Authority, where the restraint on change of user was found not to be a restriction of competition, but a restraint ancillary to the inoffensive purpose of creating a mix of retailers. It also arises in the context of the grant of exclusive right. The FAI agreed with Adidas for the exclusive supply of

---

[34] *Standard Oil Company of New Jersey* v. *United States*, 221 US 1(1911).

[35] Scully Tyrrell and Company/Edberg Limited, Decision No. 12 of 29.1.93.

[36] *United States* v. *Addyston Pipe and Steel Company* 85 Fed. 271 (6th Cir.1898).

[37] (1993) ILRM 145.

[38] (1995) 1 IR 89.

football kit for its international teams, and granted Adidas the exclusive right to market replicas:

> The net issue is whether, by denying other suppliers the right to promote their products by supplying them to the FAI, such an agreement prevented, restricted or distorted competition. In the Authority's opinion it did not do so. Of course Adidas benefited from the fact that what it was selling was a reproduction of the kit worn by the international team ... (but) there are many other teams and individuals that other sportswear manufacturers can enter into similar agreements with. . . . As the notified arrangements were limited in time, competition between suppliers to secure rights to supply the FAI occurs at regular intervals. . . . It is relevant that following the expiry of this agreement the FAI have switched to another sportswear supplier. . . . Adidas undoubtedly secured some competitive advantage over its rivals as a result of the arrangement. It is, however, an essential feature of competition that firms will attempt to gain some edge over their competitors. . . . It is only where they could be shown to prevent other suppliers from entering the sportswear market that such arrangements could be deemed anti-competitive.[39]

The analysis here illustrates the important point that competition can take many forms, and any evaluation of whether or not an agreement is anti-competitive must take this into account. In this instance the suppliers compete for the contract to supply when it comes up for renewal and as long as the duration of the agreement is not unduly long, competition may not be impaired.

The literal interpretation of section 4(1) seems to equate a restraint on the commercial freedom of an individual party with a restriction of competition. One reason for this may be the length of establishment of the restraint of trade rules, concerned primarily with the restraint on an individual, and reasonableness between the parties. The concern with the effect on public good, although it is notionally a component in the restraint of trade rules is often expressed in terms of supplies of products reaching consumers, rather than in terms of prices, or effect on other competitors.

---

[39] Adidas/FAI Decision No. 421 of 12.9.95; see also Adidas/Sports Stars Decision No. 422 of 12.9.95.

> An agreement is unlikely to be invalidated by a common law court because it is alleged to infringe some wider public interest, e.g. because it might lead to an improper allocation of economic resources or prove inflationary. Such allegations often lack precision and courts of law are not well equipped to evaluate them (Treitel, 1988).

Competition is a complex process which involves business firms constantly seeking to gain some advantage over their rivals by developing better ways to present their products and attract customers. There is no simple straightforward definition of what constitutes competition, thus establishing whether particular forms of behaviour are restrictive is not a straightforward exercise, save in the case of blatantly anti-competitive practices such as price-fixing and collective boycotts. In very many instances it will only be possible to come to a conclusion as to the intended object or actual effect on the basis of a detailed economic analysis. The so-called rule of reason is little more than a recognition that each case must be considered on its merits.

In Nallen/O'Toole, the Authority also stated the general principle that "competition" includes potential competition; i.e. that Section 4 prohibits not only behaviour that prevents, restricts or distorts the competition actually taking place in the market, but also behaviour that stifles competition that would otherwise emerge. This is a proposition that is limited by the caveat that the potential competition has to amount to a "real likelihood" that competition would emerge, but for the behaviour condemned. In Cooley[40] the Authority considered that in order to find an "effect" of restricting potential competition there would have to be such a "real likelihood" but that an object of restricting potential competition could exist where there was a less certain expectation of the translation of that potential into actual competition.

Section 4(2) — Licences

The existence of a licensing provision means necessarily that it is envisaged that agreements the net effect of which is to restrict competition may be licensed. The scope to permit anti-

---

[40]   Decision 285 of 25.2.94.

competitive agreements, by means of a licence, is a recognition that the conclusion that such agreements are harmful is of necessity a general rule to which there are real-world exceptions. The Authority decisions in which licences have been granted to date contain some broad similarities insofar as many of them deal with various forms of vertical restraints which the Authority has found enhance efficiency. Thus, for example, a number of licences have been granted in respect of exclusive purchasing agreements in the LPG and oil markets. The Authority has found the agreements offensive on the basis, inter alia, that networks of such agreements exist in those markets, making them difficult to enter, but proceeded to grant licences on the grounds that there are efficiency gains in the distribution of those products in being able to plan deliveries and future levels of sales.

Horizontal Price-fixing and Other Offensive Agreements

The Authority decisions on horizontal price-fixing have in each case found it offensive and not licensable. While cartels were not typically notified, for obvious reasons, the Authority has dealt with agreements which it found to produce the same effect and to be offensive. The Irish Booksellers Association[41] notified the agreement by which they prepared and circulated for their members a currency conversion chart, for the conversion of printed sterling prices on books. The purpose of the ready reckoner was stated by the notifying party to be "so as to ensure minimum disparities in the retail price of books in Ireland" and was treated by the Authority as horizontal price-fixing. It was found to be offensive and, since no argument had been advanced for a licence, a licence was not granted. The rules of the Irish Stock Exchange on trading in Government gilts included an agreement between brokers on fixed minimum commissions, which was found to be a horizontal agreement on price, offensive and not licensable.[42] The decision notes that in the absence of fixed commissions, competition might drive commission rates to a uniform level, but stated that there was

---

[41] Decision No. 348 of 2.9.94.

[42] Decision No. 335 of 10.6.94.

a fundamental difference between prices which were set competitively and those which were based on an agreement between competitors or rules of an association. In Supertoys:[43]

> The arrangements described involved an agreement between retailers, who were competitors, on the prices which they proposed to apply to a range of products and an understanding that none of the retailers would depart from such agreed prices except in response to local competition. In the Authority's opinion, such an arrangement amounts to an agreement to fix the retail selling prices of such goods.

The mere exchange of price information was found by the Authority to be offensive,[44] a position consistent with the EU and the US.

Section 4 specifies agreements between competitors to take specific forms of action such as share markets, limit production or fix other trading conditions. These are no more than illustrations of a potentially infinite variety of ways for competitors to restrict competition between them in respect of any element of competition. In PRS/creators,[45] the PRS itself constituted an agreement between competitors, i.e. the creators and owners of music copyrights, to sell their product, i.e. use of the copyright material, through the Society. The Authority found the existence of such a collecting society to be offensive, but potentially capable of being licensed as contributing to an improvement in distribution of the copyright material. The same reasoning was applied in IMRO/Cable TV[46] where the UK TV companies agreed with a number of TV rediffusion companies for the licensing of their copyright material, and appointed IMRO as their agent for the collection and distribution of royalties and making any further agreements with new rediffusion companies. The agreement had the effect that the TV companies did not compete with each other in setting rates or conditions for the use of their material, and as such it restricted competition. As with PRS/creators, it was licensed on the grounds that it created

---

[43] Decision No. 304 of 21.4.94.

[44] Esso Solus Agreement, Decision No. 4 of 25.6.92.

[45] Decision No. 326 of 18.5.94.

[46] Decision Nos. 383 and 384 of 16.12.94.

an improvement in distribution. An agreement between competitors that one will allow the other to exploit its plant or assets is, on the face of it, offensive. In David Allen/Adsites,[47] parties in direct competition in the market for 48-sheet poster advertising sites in the State agreed that one would license to the other its sites to be marketed with the former's own. The agreement was found offensive and not licensable. In the same vein, it is implicit in Cerestar/BetCo.[48] that an agency relationship made between two existing competitors will, or at least can, be offensive.

The members of trade or professional associations will by their nature be competitors, so that decisions of such associations of undertakings which restrict competition are considered in the same way as horizontal agreements between competitors. In the case of the Association of Optometrists,[49] the Authority cited the view of the European Court of Justice that:

> A recommendation of an association of undertakings, even if it has no binding effect, cannot escape (Article 85(1)) where compliance with the recommendations by the undertakings to which it is addressed has an appreciable influence on competition in the market in question.[50]

The restrictions of the Association on price advertising were found to restrict competition:

> (T)he requirement to observe the Board's rules by which members of the Association were precluded from . . . (b) quoting prices in media advertisements . . . also constituted a restriction of competition which offended against Section 4(1) . . . The Authority notes that overseas evidence indicates that restrictions on price advertising by health care service providers, and by optometrists in particular, have been found to result in higher prices to consumers than would otherwise be the case.[51]

---

[47] Decision No. 378 of 21.11.94.

[48] Decision No. 374 of 21.11.94.

[49] Decision No. 16 of 29.4.93.

[50] *IAZ International Belgium NV and others* v. *Commission* (1983) ECR 3369.

[51] These rules were in fact amended by the date of the Authority's decision.

But the rules for calculation of fees also indirectly affected price:

> The Association's Code of Ethics required that practitioners
> should charge on a professional fee system e.g. fee for exami-
> nation, fee for dispensing, plus the cost of appliances and ma-
> terial supplied . . . . (The Authority) is concerned that requiring
> members to set charges in a particular way could facilitate
> agreements between some or all of the members of the Asso-
> ciation on prices.

The decision also highlights the concerns that arise regarding the
criteria for membership of a professional body since these could
involve a restriction on competition:

> While membership of the Optometrists' Association is not com-
> pulsory in order to compete in the relevant market, it may be
> that individuals unable to join would be placed at a serious
> competitive disadvantage relative to members. In particular, if
> the public felt that non-members were in some sense less
> qualified than members, then restrictions on entry to the Asso-
> ciation could distort competition.

This is an idea which was echoed in *Donovan* v. *ESB*[52] in con-
demning restrictions on entry to a trade association. In the same
case it was found also to be an abuse of a dominant position of
the ESB that radio and television advertising described unregistered contractors as "cowboys".[53] The Authority had expressed a similar view in Optometrists:

> Provided the Association does not seek to create the impres-
> sion that Fellows of the Association are more highly skilled
> than overseas trained optometrists, thereby placing the latter
> group at a competitive disadvantage, the Authority believes
> that the restriction of the title of Fellow to those who have
> passed the Association's examination does not offend against
> Section 4(1).

The Authority also condemned restrictions which required that
services be carried out only in the patient's home or in offices
designed to a specified level of privacy:

---

[52]   [1994] 2 IR 305.

[53]   This is discussed in Chapter 8.

Patients are quite capable of deciding for themselves to what extent they require privacy when obtaining such services. Such rules may in fact prevent, restrict or distort competition in so far as they could prevent new entrants or existing practitioners from offering services in a new or innovative way, or in a manner or setting which would be more convenient to the customer.

Horizontal Agreements which Do Not Offend

There are horizontal agreements between undertakings, and indeed competing undertakings, which do not restrict competition. Co-operation between competitors can be inoffensive where it does not affect their competing with one another. There is a brief reference in *Carna Foods and Mallon* v. *Eagle Star*[54] to an alleged concerted practice of insurance companies. The plaintiff's complaint was that his insurance company had cancelled his policy and refused to give reasons, and that he was advised that he would not then be able to obtain insurance from other insurers in those circumstances. However, the judgment refers only to a concerted practice of refusing reasons:

> On the evidence I am satisfied that there was no concerted practice between the insurance companies nor was there any practice organised by the Insurance Federation of Ireland. Furthermore, even if it was established that the refusal to give reasons was in some way agreed between the companies or done on the advice of the Insurance Federation, I cannot see how such a refusal distorts or restricts trade.

In Gill and Macmillan/publishers,[55] an agreement by one competitor to extend its own delivery service to its competitors was found inoffensive since it did not affect competition between the parties in relation to the sale of their goods. The Clearing Rules of the Dublin Bankers Clearing Committee[56] were certified by the Authority as inoffensive. The member banks agree common rules for clearing, exchange and settlement of paper and electronic

---

[54]   *Carna Foods and Mallon* v. *Eagle Star Insurance Co.* [1995] 1 IR 526.

[55]   Decision No. 366 of 28.10.94.

[56]   Decision No. 441 of 23.11.95.

transactions. Membership is open to all credit institutions which comply with criteria of size and supervision, and they all contribute to the administrative costs of the system. The decision states that the agreement does not prevent members from making bilateral agreements if they prefer. Similarly, the Rules of the Direct Debit Committee,[57] and those of the Cheque Card Committee,[58] were found inoffensive. The Rules, which provide for co-ordinating conditions for direct debits, and paper and electronic formats, and the issuing of cheque guarantee cards, respectively, did not affect member banks in competing in offering those services to their customers. Again, the criteria for membership were objectively justified, although this was not explored in detail in the decision. The Authority has found an agreement between competitors to co-operate to be inoffensive, and, in fact, pro-competitive where it was satisfied that the co-operation was limited to a specific project which would have been too large for the co-operating competitors to have undertaken alone.[59]

Non-Price Vertical Restraints

The main guidance as to the view taken in the Irish courts of vertical restraints comes from the one Article 85 case, *Masterfoods v. HB*,[60] in which a non-price vertical restraint, of freezer exclusivity, was considered in some detail. HB, the largest incumbent ice-cream supplier in Ireland, had agreements with many of its retail stockists (typically tobacco, sweet and newsagent shops) to provide them with freezers. It was a condition of supply that the freezer could be used only to stock HB ice-cream. Retailers were free to take another freezer from another supplier, and stock its rival products, but were unlikely to do so in their typical constraints on space. They were also free to buy a freezer outright, obtain HB ice-cream and sell it from their freezer on a non-exclusive basis, but for reasons of cost did not in practice typically

---

[57] Decision No. 442 of 23.11.95.

[58] Decision No. 427 of 2.10.95.

[59] Group 91 Architects, Decision No. 433 of 20.10.95.

[60] [1993] ILRM 145.

do so. Retailers were free to end the agreement by giving two months' notice. Mars, entering the Irish market, took proceedings on the basis, inter alia, that HB's freezer agreements were in breach of Article 85(1) (b), and 85(1) (e).[61] Having taken the view, as discussed earlier, that the rule of reason approach was appropriate, Judge Keane considered the object, and the effect, of the freezer exclusivity provision. He found that it was "similar in nature" to an exclusive purchasing obligation, but that that did not determine the issue since the EC jurisprudence was to the effect that exclusive purchasing was not necessarily restrictive of competition. He cited *Delimitis*[62] and *Brasserie de Haecht*.[63] In the light of the facts given above, and the fact that the retailers did not have to take all, or any specified share, of their ice-cream orders from HB, he considered that the agreement was "different in character" and not "in any way equivalent" to the categories of exclusive distribution, selective distribution or franchising, or tied house agreements for beer or petrol, which had been considered by the Commission for individual or block exemption. He took the view that rather than considering the history of the agreements and the probable intention of HB in entering into them:

> . . . it is clear that, in determining whether a particular agreement has an anti-competitive object within the meaning of Article 85(1), the agreement should be considered objectively and without regard to what the intention of the undertaking concerned may have been.

By that test, the object of the agreement was to prevent HB's competitors having the use of space in HB's freezer cabinets; to ensure that storage and display would be available for HB products; and to facilitate quality control. These were not in themselves objects of restricting competition. In considering the effect, it was relevant to take into account HB's dominance, the existence of the network of retailers in the exclusivity contracts, the relatively weak bargaining position of the retailers *vis-à-vis* suppliers

---

[61] The Article 86 issues in the case are considered in Chapter 8.

[62] *Delimitis* v. *Henninger Brau* [1991] 1 ECR 935.

[63] *Brasserie de Haecht* v. *Wilkin* [1967] ECR 407.

and the substantial volume of products affected by the agreement. It was also relevant that one effect of the agreements was to confer on HB "significant commercial advantages", which were not anti-competitive "except, of course, to the extent that every practice by a business which increases its sales and maximises its profits is likely to be to the disadvantage of its competitors." These are the efficient and economical distribution of products, the opportunity to display advertising, and the guarantee of space for display and storage of HB products. There were also the advantages for retailers of not having to buy freezers for themselves, and of being more assured of supplies than if they owned their own freezer. He found that the agreements, not being of a type considered *per se* offensive in the EC jurisprudence "on the basis of the analysis already conducted are not captured" under Article 85(1) (b). It appears from this formulation that he considered that in order to come to a view on Article 85(1) (b) it was both necessary and sufficient to consider the wider question of the object and effect of the agreements on competition, rather than any narrower question. He also found that the agreements did not offend under Article 85(1) (e) specifically because they were not "contrary to normal commercial usage"; and because they were not "supplementary obligations which by their nature . . . have no connection with the subject of such contracts". It was the case that such agreements had been the norm in the industry, not only for HB but for all its competitors and had been so for some years prior to HB becoming the leading firm. It was also the case that "the exclusivity term is of the essence of the contract". The agreements therefore did not offend under Article 85(1) (e).

Exclusive Distribution

The Authority has issued a licence for exclusive distribution agreements[64] which follows closely the EU block exemption for exclusive distribution.[65] It finds that exclusive distribution:

> . . . prevents the supplier supplying the goods . . . for resale to any other distributor in the territory . . . and it prevents any other

---

[64] Decision No. 144 of 5.11.93.

[65] Regulation 1983/83 OJ. [1983] L173/1, as amended.

> distributor in the territory from obtaining the goods. . . . It intro-
> duces a degree of rigidity into the market, since distribution ar-
> rangements are established for . . . relatively long periods of time
> and since many goods are already tied under such agreements.
> The fact that the products are available from only one source in
> the territory also tends to restrict intra-brand competition

and is therefore offensive. However, it is licensable:

> Exclusive distribution agreements generally lead to an im-
> provement in distribution because the supplier is able to con-
> centrate his sales activities and he does not need to maintain
> numerous business relations with a large number of dealers. . . .
> (I)t is often preferable for the supplier to concentrate on pro-
> duction and to delegate the distribution function to a specialist
> distributor who already possesses the necessary organisation
> and dealer contacts.

The obligation that resellers refrain from active sales outside
their territory is also offensive, since it affords territorial protection to other distributors within the network, but it is licensable,
as obliging distributors to concentrate their active efforts on their
allotted territory, and thereby effect the improvement in distribution for which the licence is granted. It appears from this that any
exclusive distribution agreement by definition will be offensive
under the reasoning of the category licence; while not every offensive agreement will be licensable, where it does not in fact
create the improvement in distribution described.

The category licence also deals with other restrictions typical
in distribution agreements, listing those that do and do not disentitle an agreement to the benefit of the licence. A ban on passive sales out of the territory is found offensive, since its existence in a network of distribution agreements ensures that each
distribution area has absolute territorial protection, and competition in respect of the products in question is completely
eliminated. Unlike the ban on active sales, the category licence
does not license a ban on passive sales, since it does not improve
the distributor's concentration on his or her own area. The common thread of the other restrictions which lose an agreement
the benefit of the licence are attempts by the supplier to control
the commercial freedom of the distributor in selling on the

goods. The setting of resale prices by the supplier, or a post-termination non-compete restriction, take an agreement outside the scope of the licence, as does a restriction on the distributor's freedom to choose customers, appoint agents and sub-distributors. The distributor may, however, be restricted from supplying dealers who are unsuitable, as defined on objectively justifiable grounds; and a supplier may reserve to themselves the right to deal with specified customers.

Franchise Category Licence

The Authority issued a category licence for franchise agreements[66] which, like the EU block exemption for franchise agreements,[67] deals with a specific type of franchise, defined for the purposes of the licence. The word "franchise" is not itself a term in Irish law, except insofar as it is imported into it by the EU block exemption. The licence therefore differs slightly from the exclusive distribution category licence which applies to an existing form of relationship, familiar in Ireland. The franchise category licence is intended to cover not every type of agreement described as a franchise, in commercial use in Ireland, but only that narrow band of agreements which are defined by it. That definition is:

> . . . an agreement whereby one undertaking, the franchisor, grants the other, the franchisee, in exchange for direct or indirect financial consideration, the right to exploit a franchise for the purpose of marketing specified types of goods and/or services. . . .

with a franchise being defined as:

> . . . a package of industrial or intellectual property rights relating to trade marks, trade names, shop signs, utility models, designs, copyrights, know-how or patents. . . .

The Authority has found agreements, described by the parties as franchises, not to be within the scope of the licence[68] where no

---

[66] Decision No. 372 of 17.11.94.

[67] Regulation 4087/88.

[68] Griffin/O'Connor, Decision No. 416 of 4.9.95. Brooks Thomas/franchisees, Decision No. 410 of 30.6.95.

intellectual property was being granted. It should also be noted that the category licence does not find franchise agreements, as defined, *per se* offensive, merely that they may be so.

Like the exclusive distribution category licence, the franchise category licence lists types of restrictions which are licensed, and those which take an agreement out of the scope of the licence. Thus, the licence permits agreements by which the franchisor recommends a retail price, but not one where the franchisee is not free to set their own price. A post-termination non-compete clause which is limited to the area in which the franchisee operated, and which is limited to a reasonable period not exceeding one year, is licensed, but a post-termination clause which exceeds those limits of geography and duration deprives the agreement of the benefit of the licence.

Exclusive Purchasing

Unlike the European Commission, the Authority has not issued a category licence for exclusive purchasing generally. It has issued two, for the motor fuels sector and LPG, and it has taken a number of individual decisions. In different circumstances, the Authority has found exclusive purchasing variously to be inoffensive,[69] offensive but licensable,[70] and unlicensable.[71] Exclusive purchasing was found to be inoffensive where only a single retailer or distributor was involved, and other retailers were not prevented from obtaining supplies of the product. In the case of motor fuels,[72] the Authority found the agreement to purchase supplies exclusively from one supplier to be offensive since it closes off the buyer from other suppliers, and vice versa. This is not necessarily offensive where the buyer is open to competition from other resellers who can seek supplies from the same supplier[73]

---

[69] Johnston Brothers/Campbell, Decision 368 of 28.10.94; Griffin/O'Connor, Decision 416 of 4.9.95; Carlton Cards/Balladeer, Decision 434 of 20.10.95.

[70] Conoco distributor agreement, Decision No. 413 of 25.8.95,.

[71] The cylinder LPG category licence provides that a tie exceeding two years would not be licensable. Decision No. 364 of 28.10.94.

[72] Esso Solus, Decision No. 4, 25.6.92.

[73] Johnson Brothers/Campbells, Decision No. 368 of 28.10.94.

and where there is not a danger that the supplier will tie a network of resellers in exclusive purchase obligations, making entry by other suppliers more difficult. In the motor fuels sector, virtually all suppliers tie virtually all retailers with exclusive purchase obligations for up to 10 years, creating a closed network for any new entrant.[74] In *Delimitis* v. *Henninger Brau AG,*[75] the ECJ had held that an exclusive purchasing obligation did not automatically restrict competition but that it should be considered in context, specifically in the light of whether the restriction formed part of a network of restrictions, inhibiting entry to the market by other suppliers. The Authority subsequently issued the motor fuels category licence,[76] licensing solus agreements. It found that solus agreements whereby retailers agree to purchase exclusively from a supplier for 10 years in return for the financing by the supplier of the cost of upgrading the filling station contributed to the improvement in distribution which made the agreement licensable.

In subsequent individual decisions where the supplier was not investing money or equipment in the buyer, the Authority has still found exclusive purchasing to be in principle capable of being licensed:

> The exclusive purchase arrangements . . . contribute to reducing cost and improving the distribution of grocery goods. The combined purchasing power of the retailers through Musgraves enables the best possible price to be obtained from suppliers. . . . Consumers benefit to the extent that some part of the savings accruing to the retailers is passed on in the form of lower prices. . . . The Authority accepts that consumers have gained from the competition which Musgraves has provided for the multiples particularly in rural areas. . . . If the retailers order stock other than through Musgraves, the whole group is weakened and its viability would be threatened. Accordingly, the

---

[74] There are other forms of retail distribution used in the motor fuels sector, including agency agreements and supplier-owned stores staffed by employees. However, all retail distributors, properly so-called, for the major oil companies are in solus agreements.

[75] [1991] 1 ECR 935.

[76] Decision No. 25 of 1.7.93.

Authority believes that the purchasing obligation is indispensable to the attainment of the objectives of the agreement.[77]

As with motor fuels, the Authority considered that there was a danger that agreements of indefinite duration could foreclose entry by other suppliers who would be prevented from finding outlets. In Supertoys,[78] the Authority has also found inoffensive a looser form of exclusive purchasing, by which the member toyshops were bound to buy specified toys only from specified suppliers with which Musgraves had concluded an agreement. The agreement was closer to being a group purchase scheme than exclusive purchase and was thus found not to offend.[79]

Apart from agreements formally framed as exclusive purchasing, the Authority has found that agreements for the exclusive use of equipment may have the same effect and has treated them as such. In Burmah Castrol/hire purchase and equipment loan and Burmah Castrol/new cash loan,[80] the agreements, for the financing of equipment for the display, storage and dispensing of lubricating oil, contained an explicit exclusive purchasing requirement but also provided that the distributor could use the equipment supplied or financed only for the supplier's product. The Authority found that this obligation by itself could operate to effect an exclusive purchase obligation.

> If exclusive use of the equipment, however, meant . . . that the goods of only one supplier could be handled by the reseller, this would amount to exclusive purchasing . . . .

Thus, as with an explicit exclusive purchasing obligation, if it is offensive, it may be licensable, where the equipment supplied does produce a legitimate improvement in distribution and where:

---

[77] Decision No. 354, Musgraves Ltd. Licensee and Franchise Agreements, 19.9.94.

[78] Decision No. 304 of 21.4.94.

[79] But note earlier discussion of the horizontal price-fixing element of the agreement.

[80] Decision No. 361 of 13.10.94 and Decision No. 380 of 15.12.94.

> . . . [the supplier] would have been unlikely to provide such loans or equipment if they could have been used freely for competitive products.

Again foreclosure is an issue relevant in the granting of a licence:

> . . . the problem of foreclosure is considerably reduced since . . . the equipment can be used for any lubricants of the workshop's choosing [after expiry of a fixed term] . . . [at] a maximum duration of five years, this does not afford the possibility of eliminating competition to a substantial degree.[81]

In the LPG industry exclusive purchasing operates at a number of levels. The Authority has granted licences for some manifestations of exclusive purchasing and refused them for others in the LPG sector. The agreements whereby retailers are bound to buy cylinder LPG from one supplier only are dealt with by category licence.[82] The licence applies only where the agreement does not exceed two years. Suppliers may not foreclose access to their existing dealers beyond a two-year term by signing them up in advance for consecutive terms, but may do so once agreement has expired. The licence constituted a refusal for the three LPG companies which had notified agreements of five years duration. It is worth noting that one of the three, Blugas, had argued that exclusive purchasing was not indispensable for the improvements in gas distribution attributed to it. The category licence lasts until 31 October 1999, but the Authority has said that it is continuing to review the LPG market, and the category licence has attached to it annual reporting conditions. The Authority subsequently granted licences for the exclusive purchase agreements used for customers of bulk LPG,[83] finding a term of five years licensable for all three companies. This was closer to exclusive supply than exclusive purchase, since it was supply for use and not resale.

---

[81] Burmah Castrol, Decision No. 407 of 30.6.95.

[82] Cylinder LPG category licence, Decision No. 364 of 28.10.94 as amended by Decision No. 402 of 19.6.95.

[83] Flogas/bulk customers, Decision No. 388 of 10.4.95; Blugas/bulk customers, Decision No. 389 of 10.4.95.; Calor/industrial customers, Decision No. 408 of 22.6.95.

Selective Distribution

The Authority has taken no decisions to date on selective distribution agreements, and there have been no reported court cases. A number of selective distribution agreements, specifically in the motor car sector as well as several relating to cosmetics, have been notified to the Authority.

Exclusive Supply

An agreement to supply exclusively one person may be offensive, but is not necessarily so. It may close off supplies to parties who would otherwise be competing with the buyer; on the other hand, there may be copious stocks of the same goods from other sources. There can also be a legitimate object for an exclusive supply agreement, other than the intention to distort competition, which is to ensure sufficient and/or regular supplies. In Hickson/Angus,[84] a sale of business notification, AFCL agreed to purchase 90 per cent of its requirements of a particular raw material (nitromethane) from Angus, its former parent, for a period of three years, with automatic renewal thereafter on an annual basis. The obligation was found to be offensive on the basis that it limited the freedom of AFCL to approach other suppliers. It was, however, licensable for a period, on the basis that AFCL might not otherwise have the security of supply necessary to guarantee production to its customers, having previously relied on its former parent for supplies; and on the basis that without guaranteed supplies of raw material from Angus to AFCL, AFCL might have been less valuable to Hickson, its purchaser. In ESB IH/ICL,[85] which was not as such an exclusive supply agreement but rather a long-term fixed-quantity contract, ICL contracted for 10 years to buy minimum quantities of fuel ash, amounting to 50 per cent of total output, from the ESB. The Authority found that although this would result in ICL being the only producer of processed fuel ash in the State, this was not offensive. It did not prevent any other

---

[84] Decision No. 353 of 7.9.94, Hickson International plc/Angus Fine Chemicals Ltd.

[85] Decision No. 390 of 12.4.95, ESB Industrial Holdings Ltd/Irish Cement Ltd — Pulverised Fuel Ash.

person from buying the remaining 50 per cent of the raw material and processing it.

Agency

The Authority dealt with an agency relationship first in the Conoco consignee agreements[86] where it set out the general principle that the relationship of agency was not itself offensive. It also stated that the use or absence of the word agency in the agreement was not decisive; and, in fact, the Conoco agreement stated that it was not an agency relationship. The Authority found that the consignee was in fact an auxiliary organ, forming an integral part of the principal's business and carrying no risk in the business, never taking property in the goods, and acting on behalf of Conoco, and therefore the relationship, despite the disclaimer, was that of agency. This might be treated as an extreme instance of the application by the Authority of the principle that the name applied is not decisive. It is not decisive, but it is significant in indicating the intention of the parties.[87]

The Authority has separately said that it is possible for the relationship of agency to be offensive, for example, where an agent dealt in a wide range of competing goods or where two direct competitors appointed the same agent.[88] It has also suggested[89] that it could be offensive where the agent operated as an independent trader in goods which competed with the agency goods. Where the relationship was not offensive, individual clauses could still be so. However, to date the Authority has found that in agency agreements clauses giving absolute territorial protection, and price-fixing by the principal are inoffensive. The Authority has not explicitly stated that it is relying on EU precedent in this area, and indeed the EU view is unclear. The Authority must therefore be taken to be acting on a first-principles basis. The treatment of post-termination non-compete clauses in agency agreements is considered below.

---

[86] Decision No. 286 of 25.2.94.

[87] North Western Cattle Breeders, Decision No. 446 of 15.12.95.

[88] Cerestar/BetCo., Decision No. 374 of 21.11.94.

[89] Irish Ropes/Newtec, Decision No. 397 of 26.4.95.

Delivery

In Murphy Brewery/Clada[90] the Authority found that Clada's agreement with Murphy to take and fill orders from Murphy customers was no more than a delivery service. Clada was not involved in the purchase and resale of the goods, and not acting as the agent of Murphy. It was therefore not offensive to define an exclusive territory, nor was the nature of the agreement itself offensive.[91]

Resale Price Maintenance

The imposition of a price by a seller on a reseller is discussed in Chapter 2. The Authority has stated consistently in its decisions that resale price maintenance is offensive, and it has not licensed it. The Net Book Agreement decision[92] sets out at length the Authority's views. The Authority outlined the conflicting economic views on RPM, along with EU decisions and the legal position in several other countries before concluding that:

> The Authority considers that the weight of evidence indicates that RPM is generally restrictive of competition. Consequently, in its view, agreements involving RPM will generally offend against section 4(1).

No licence was granted. In Gill and Macmillan/Booksellers,[93] an obligation on booksellers not to sell books for less than "the unit price indicated on the invoice", imposed by all publishers using a delivery service provided by another publisher was found by the Authority to be offensive as direct RPM.[94] The NBA was also considered to have a horizontal aspect:

> Once a book is designated as a net book by a publisher, the publishers of rival titles can set their prices in the knowledge that the designated book will not be sold below the designated

---

[90]   Decision No. 362 of 13.10.94.

[91]   See also Gill and Macmillan/Publishers, Decision No. 366 of 28.10.94.

[92]   Publishers' Association, Decision No. 336 of 10.6.94.

[93]   Gill and Macmillan/Booksellers, Decision No. 365 of 28.10.94.

[94]   Op. cit.

net price. Consequently the agreement reduces the element of uncertainty regarding a competitor's response to a firm's marketing strategy which is an essential feature of competitive markets.

In support of its view the Authority referred to a study of the NBA, by Allen and Curwen (1991), which found that:

> In general, given the existence of the NBA, we would expect publishers to price similar products as though they were operating a cartel. The fact that they can fix the price of a specific title at any level they wish is very far from what is meant by "conditions of free competition". In conditions of free competition there would be constant downward pressure upon prices in order to clear the market, so that over time prices, on average, would rise more slowly than elsewhere in the economy where free competition did not exist.

The Authority concluded:

> While the Authority does not consider that the NBA necessarily amounts to a fully fledged horizontal price-fixing arrangement, it nevertheless believes that it does go some considerable way towards reducing uncertainty regarding competitors' pricing decisions. . . .

It was also relevant that while not obliged to net any particular book, the UK publishers chose to net of the order of 75 per cent of books published.

The line between recommendation of prices and price-fixing can be fine. An agreement by retailers to issue a catalogue for toys, listing a price suggested by the wholesaler, was found by the Authority to be offensive:

> The fact that the agreed prices were suggested to the Council of Supertoys and the members by Musgraves indicates that the agreement also includes some element of vertical price-fixing or resale price maintenance.[95]

The agreement also required the retailers to advertise prices of a selection of toys, and then abide by the advertised price, a requirement which, as already noted, the Authority considered to

---

[95] Musgraves/Supertoys, Decision No. 304 of 21.4.94.

amount to horizontal price-fixing and not merely a recommendation. The Authority has found recommended retail prices to be
inoffensive, if genuinely no more than a recommended price. The
motor fuels category licence[96] citing the Esso solus decision[97]
stated that informing independent resellers of a RRP did not
amount to RPM and was not necessarily offensive, so long as the
resellers were informed that they were free to set their own
prices. The benefit of the exclusive distribution category licence
does not apply to an agreement where:

> . . . the supplier recommends to the exclusive distributor a
> specified resale price or a specified maximum or minimum re-
> sale price, unless the reseller is informed that he is free to de-
> termine his own resale prices . . . .[98]

The franchise category licence provides that it will not apply to
franchise agreements where:

> . . . the franchisee is restricted by the franchisor, directly or indi-
> rectly, in the determination of sale prices . . . without prejudice to
> the possibility for the franchisor of recommending sale prices.[99]

The Authority has found that an obligation on a master franchisee to agree with the franchisor, and publish to the sub franchisees a list of recommended prices brings the agreement outside
the category licence, and is not individually licensable.[100]

Miscellaneous Agreements

Tied Sales

Tied sales are listed under Section 4 as an example of an anti-
competitive restriction, but it has not typically come before the
Authority as an issue. Falcon Holidays notified an agreement with

---

[96]   Decision No. 25 of 1.7.93.

[97]   Decision No. 4 of 25.6.92.

[98]   Decision No. 144 of 5.11.93, Article 3(g).

[99]   Decision No. 372 of 17.11.94, Article 5(e).

[100] Computa Tune, Decision No. 447 of 15.12.95.

an insurance broker, Ben McArdle, under which Falcon agreed to make it mandatory for all buyers of foreign holidays to buy holiday insurance, and to do so from McArdle's. The Authority considered that the obligation to buy insurance alone might limit consumer choice but it did not restrict competition. There were evident reasons of prudence why a holiday operator would insist that travellers be insured. The requirement that all insurance bought had to be bought from McArdle's did, however, clearly prevent competition from other insurance brokers and insurers, and from travel agents who had previously sold insurance, in respect of a significant share of the package-holiday market. The agreement was considered to be offensive and unlicensable, until amended to permit holiday buyers to arrange for their own insurance.

Shopping Centres, Leases and Sales of Land

While sales and leases of land can contain covenants which are, in the common-law sense, in restraint of trade, a restraint on the use of any parcel of land is unlikely, by definition, to restrict competition. The fullest exploration of the view of the Authority on this point is its Notice in relation to Shopping Centres.[101] The Notice states that the existence and development of shopping centres improved competition in retail outlets. This appears to be an argument for finding an ancillary restriction inoffensive. However, the Notice goes on to state that the restriction on change of user for individual units in shopping centres does not restrict competition in the relevant geographical market, which would be a wider area than the centre alone. Obviously, this is a statement of fact, relating to the size of shopping centres typical in Ireland, and their situation usually close to a town or city main street retail area. The Authority has dealt with a large number of shopping centre leases on the basis of the Notice and has also taken individual decisions on leases and sales of land, on the same principle that where use of any piece of land for any trade or business is restricted, this does not prevent that trade or business from being carried on from any other location in the State.

---

[101] Notice in respect of Shopping Centre Leases, Iris Oifigiúil, 10.9.93, pp. 665–667, and numerous subsequent decisions on shopping centre leases.

Investment Share Purchases

There are large numbers of Authority decisions on investment share purchases — that is, the purchase of minority shareholdings. Where the investor is not a competitor of the investee, the transaction is virtually by definition not restrictive of competition. It may in fact be pro-competitive in permitting the investee company to compete in a market where it otherwise would not be able to. The restrictions which are inoffensive as ancillary to such an investment are explored below in the context of non-compete and non-solicit post-termination clauses. The situation, obviously, is different where the investor and investee are competitors. In the Newspaper Study (Competition Authority, 1995), the Authority expressed the view that the purchase by one competitor of a 24.9 per cent stake in another, apart from being an abuse of dominance, was also an agreement that was offensive under Section 4. The question of a licence did not arise, since the context was a study under Section 11 and not a notification under Section 7. By implication, since the Authority recommended strongly that the Minister take action, it might be assumed that it did not consider the agreement licensable.

Non-compete Clauses

The Competition Act prohibits agreements which restrict competition, so it might be expected that it prohibits agreements not to compete. However, it is possible for explicit agreements not to compete to be inoffensive in particular circumstances.

Sale of Business. The Authority in its first decision[102] certified a post-term non-compete clause on the sale of a business. It found that the transfer of goodwill on the sale of a business was an inherently inoffensive transaction; and that a restriction which did not exceed the duration, and geographical scope necessary to effect that transfer was also therefore inoffensive. A similar view was expressed in *RGDATA* v. *Tara Publishing Co. Ltd.*:[103]

---

[102] Nallen/O'Toole, Decision No. 1 of 2.4.92.

[103] (1995) 1 IR 89.

> Insofar as a vendor is selling the goodwill attaching to a named publication it would be justifiable to require the vendor to covenant against competing in the same business for such reasonable period as might be necessary to ensure that the purchaser achieved the goodwill in the enterprise which he had purchased.

This view of ancillary restraints is an application of the rule of reason discussed earlier in the chapter. One relevant factor in considering the time necessary to transfer goodwill was how often the goods or services sold by the business are bought by consumers — for example, daily or very infrequently. The non-compete clause certified in Nallen/O'Toole was three years. In a number of subsequent decisions the Authority has said that two years is the maximum necessary to effect a transfer of goodwill in most businesses, although the possibility exists that a longer or shorter period will be appropriate in the context of a particular business. The Authority has said that the duration of the non-compete clause will be considered from the date of actual completion, and rejected the idea that a non-compete clause should run from the date of the last instalment, where the consideration was paid in instalments.[104]

In the specific case of the transfer of technical know-how on the sale of a business, where the transferor is restrained from using the transferred know-how by a non-compete clause, a longer period of up to five years has been found inoffensive. The Authority first stated this view in ACT/Kindle,[105] and in a number of decisions since. In Hickson International/Angus Fine Chemicals[106] the Authority:

> ... agrees with the EC Commission view in *Reuter/BASF* that an obligation to keep know-how secret from third parties, imposed on the transfer of an undertaking, may not be used to prevent the transferor, after the expiry of the reasonable term of a non-competition clause, from competing with the transferee by means of new and further developments of such know-how.

---

[104] FBH/Harty Security, Decision No. 444 of 30.11.95.

[105] Decision No. 8 of 4.9.92.

[106] Decision No. 353 of 7.9.94.

The Hickson/Angus decision cites the definition of technical know how given in EU Commission Regulation 556/89. The Authority has rejected some claims that expertise specific to a particular business amounted to technical know how — for example, in travel agency,[107] credit insurance[108] and for "information used in the production of goods or the provision of services" in the catering business.[109] It has accepted that there is technical know-how involved in "the creation, development and application of computer software",[110] protection devices for use in electronic circuits,[111] the production of high-grade organic chemicals (custom fine chemicals),[112] the production and preparation of chemicals for use in seed treatment,[113] "the operation and processes involved in the manufacture of packaging for food" and chemicals for food.[114]

Clauses providing that a vendor of a business shall not use technical know-how to compete are sometimes accompanied by confidentiality clauses of unlimited duration in respect of the same technical know-how. The Authority has dealt with these[115] by stating that they cannot be used to prevent re-entry by a vendor after the permitted period for transfer of goodwill has expired.

Where after a sale of business the vendors remain as shareholders, the Authority has said that a non-compete clause for the duration of the shareholding is not offensive, provided that the arrangements are not an artificial construction to evade the Act. It has found it offensive to tie vendors in such an arrangement so that they could not dispose of their shares, and therefore

---

[107] Phil Fortune/Budget Travel, Decision No. 9 of 14.9.92.

[108] Sedgewick Dineen/Legal and Commercial Insurances, Decision No. 332 of 19.5.94.

[109] Carroll Catering/Sutcliffe, Decision No. 29 of 9.9.93.

[110] ACT/Kindle, op. cit. and Mentec/Online, Decision No. 141 of 27.10.93.

[111] GI Corporation/General Semiconductor, Decision No. 10 of 23.10.92.

[112] Hickson/Angus, op. cit.

[113] Rhône Poulenc/Shell, Decision No. 273 of 3.2.94.

[114] Azinger/Fispak, Decision No. 414 of 25.8.95.

[115] Hickson/Angus, op. cit.; Rhône Poulenc/Shell, op. cit.

could not compete with the company, for a fixed period of three years and six months.[116]

Investment Share Purchases. A typical restraint in such agreements is that imposed by the investor to keep the key personnel of the investee company in place, by employment contracts, fixed-term directorships or shareholdings, or a combination of the three. In Cambridge-ACT/Imari,[117] the investor restricted the key member of the investee company from leaving, and competing with the company, for five years from completion or two years from ceasing to be employed by it. The parties amended the clause to apply for 915 days after the director in question sold his shares; or immediately on his ceasing to be employed by the company, whichever was the later, and this was found to be inoffensive. The Authority has subsequently taken a number of decisions in the context of investment share purchases, mainly under the Business Expansion Scheme, on post-termination non-compete clauses. It has found that non-compete clauses binding the key personnel of the investee company from competing with it after they leave are not offensive if they do not exceed the fixed term of the loan or other investment. The rationale is that the restriction is ancillary to the investment, which would not be made without it.

> Taking into account the particular nature of the BES investment involved, the Authority considers that where the duration of the non-compete or non-solicit clause equates with or is less than the estimated duration of the Fund's subscription to the company, this does not offend against Section 4(1).[118]

Employment Agreements. In Apex/Murtagh[119] the Authority stated that an employer had a legitimate proprietary interest in

---

[116] Scully Tyrrell/Edberg, Decision No. 12 of 29.1.93.

[117] Decision No. 24 of 21.6.93.

[118] Cambridge Business Expansion Fund/Standard Subscription Agreement with Investee Companies, Decision No. 404 of 22.6.95.

[119] Decision No. 20 of 10.6.93.

the goodwill of his customers, and in placing some restriction on an employee. An employer had to be free to disclose to an employee details of customers and other business information which the employee would not otherwise acquire, and then must be free to protect that information. Thus, the employee could be restrained from taking the information and using it in competition with the employer. However, this did not justify a general post-termination restriction on the employee competing with the employer. It would, rather, justify a more narrow restriction on the employee soliciting customers with whom he or she had dealt. In the instant case, the clause was a post-termination non-solicit clause for two years, covering all customers of the employer. This would have covered customers with whom the employee had not dealt, and customers who had become such after the employee had left, and customers who ceased to be such of their own initiative; and the Authority indicated to the parties that this was offensive. The employer proposed to amend the agreement to customers with whom the employee had dealt, and for a period of 18 months after termination. The Authority found the duration of the clause as amended still offensive. Where the restriction is embodied in some way other than the contract of employment, as it was in the Rules of the Association of Optometrists, the reasoning is still the same:

> The Code states that a practitioner employed in a practice shall not, on leaving such employment, strive to entice patients away from his former employer. Proximity of premises to his former employers for the purpose of enticing patients is unethical . . . the Authority accepts that a restriction on former employee ; directly soliciting their former employers' customers is not of itself anti-competitive.

However:

> If this requirement were to be used to restrict former employees from competing with the business of their former employers the Authority would regard it as offending against section 4(1).

In the case where an employee has become privy to confidential information or technical know-how of the employer, the Authority has found that a restriction on use of the information, unlimited as to time, is not offensive.[120]

Agency Agreements. The reasoning applied to employees has also been applied to the relationship of agency.[121] Where the principal must give the agent information about his business and his clients, he is entitled to protect that information by a non-solicit clause limited to those clients and, where there is one, the agent's geographical area of operation.

Category Licences. The benefit of the exclusive distribution category licence does not, however, apply to agreements that contain a post-termination non-compete clause.

> Article 1 shall not apply where . . .
>
> (i) the supplier imposes any restriction on the reseller after the date of termination of the agreement, except in the case of prohibiting the use or disclosure of confidential information, provided that such prohibition does not prevent the exclusive distributor from competing after such termination.[122]

The franchise category licence permits a restriction on the franchisee competing with the franchisor or other franchisees during the term of the franchise, and permits a one-year post-termination non-compete clause, limited to the franchisee's own former franchise area. Thus, a commonly occurring form of post-termination non-compete clause, preventing the franchisee from competing with the franchisor or other franchisees, exceeds what is permitted by the licence.

In respect of such clauses in exclusive purchase agreements, the motor fuels category licence[123] provides:

> Article 1 shall not apply where:
>
> (f) the supplier imposes any restriction on the reseller after the date of expiry of the exclusive purchasing agreement, and

---

[120] Apex/Murtagh, Decision No. 20 of 10.6.93.

[121] Cross Vetpharm, Decision No. 412 of 25.8.95.

[122] Article 3(i).

[123] Decision No. 25 of 1.7.93.

in particular imposes an obligation: . . . not to engage in the purchase and resale of competing goods.

First Refusal on Sale of Business or Premises

In Griffin/O'Connor[124] the Authority stated its view that:

> The obligation . . . to give first refusal (which) refers both to the business and the premises . . . can have the effect of preventing other people coming into this market by way of buying Mr O'Connor's business. In Musgraves Ltd./Licensee and Franchisee Agreements[125] the Authority considered that the object and possibly the effect of a clause requiring licensees to give first refusal of premises to Musgraves to be to prevent competitors acquiring the premises, with, implicitly the goodwill and benefit of location. In this case the location of an electrical goods store is not as crucial as that of a convenience supermarket; and here only one premises is affected, unlike the network of premises of Musgraves licensees and franchisees.

The clause was, however, found to be offensive since there was no discernible object or effect other than to restrict competition, and, as in Musgraves, none of the criteria for a licence were fulfilled. The two examples above relate to retail premises, where location within a retail area might be considered important. The Authority took a similar view in respect of petrol stations in the Motor Fuels Category Licence. Such clauses have been found inoffensive in other circumstances where the nature of the premises was such that a new entrant could easily replicate it as, for example, sites for oil depots.

Conclusion

The applications of Section 4 in Ireland to date, by the Courts and the Authority, reveal some tendencies as to the legal and economic approaches that will be used. The Courts have not in any reported case to date identified a school of economic theory as being applied. The Authority has not overtly adopted a preferred school of

---

[124] Griffin/O'Connor, Decision 416 of 4.9.95.

[125] Decision No. 354 of 19.9.94.

theory, beyond references to "mainstream" economic thought, but in the limited number of situations where it identified a choice of theory as arising it has chosen not to apply a Chicago approach. The Courts have stated that EU precedents, if not binding, are strongly persuasive. The Authority has applied EU reasoning in a number of decisions, but it has also, albeit in a smaller number of decisions, chosen not to apply it. No pattern can be said to have been established in relation either to the legal or the economic theory which will be applied.

8

SECTION 5: ABUSE OF DOMINANCE

Introduction

In addition to the prohibition on anti-competitive agreements between undertakings described in the previous chapter, the 1991 Act also prohibits unilateral behaviour which constitutes an abuse of market power. Section 5 provides:

> (1) Any abuse by one or more undertakings of a dominant position in trade for any goods or services in the State or in a substantial part of the State is prohibited.

Section 5, like Section 4, gives a non-exhaustive list of forms of abuse.

> (2) Without prejudice to the generality of *subsection (1)*, such abuse may, in particular, consist in —
>
> (a) directly or indirectly imposing unfair purchase or selling prices or other unfair trading conditions;
>
> (b) limiting production, markets or technical development to the prejudice of customers;
>
> (c) applying dissimilar conditions to equivalent transactions with other trading parties, thereby placing them at a competitive disadvantage;
>
> (d) making the conclusion of contracts subject to the acceptance by other parties of supplementary obligations which by their nature or according to commercial usage have no connection with the subject of such contracts.

These are examples of types of behaviour which may be, although they are not inevitably, abuses of a dominant position. Abuse of a dominant position may be manifested in dealings with existing suppliers or customers, by the imposition of unfair trading terms; or *vis-à-vis* other competitors in the market, by predatory pricing;

or in seeking to change the structure of the market. There is also, clearly, a broad overlap with breaches of Section 4 as Judge Costello stated:

> I agree . . . if it could be shown that the ESB entered into agreements, decisions or concerted practices which were prohibited by section 4, this would amount to the imposition of unfair trading conditions within the meaning of section 5(2) (a) and therefore an abuse of its dominant position.[1]

There has been a small number of private actions brought under Section 6 alleging Section 5 abuses. The Authority has not had occasion to consider Section 5 issues other than in the context of the Newspaper Study (Competition Authority, 1995). Thus, in contrast to Section 4, there is only a limited volume of Irish material available on abuse of a dominant position. There is a danger with any form of anti-competitive behaviour that it may not be discovered or may not be realised to be anti-competitive. This is particularly true of unilateral behaviour. However, with abuse of a dominant position the opposite danger also exists that genuine though aggressive competitive behaviour may be treated as behaviour that is intended or is likely to exclude legitimate and equally efficient competitors. Experience in other countries shows that there are far more complaints about abuse of a dominant position than there are findings of abuse.

Defining the Market
The starting point for establishing abuse of dominance logically is to identify whether or not a firm is in a dominant position, or, to put it another way, whether it can exercise market power. In order to do so, it is necessary to define the market or markets within which the firm is allegedly dominant. The question of market definition is therefore the point of departure for a discussion of abuse of dominance. However, defining the market is also an important factor in establishing whether or not arrangements can be regarded as anti-competitive and therefore in breach of Section 4(1). Identifying and defining a market poses several problems. At the outset one must establish what products should properly be

---

[1] *Donovan* v. *ESB* (1994) 2 IR 305.

included in the relevant market and what is the geographical extent of the market. For example, should butter be regarded as a unique product market? The answer would depend on whether a large number of customers would use margarine instead of butter at a small but significant price differential. This example serves to illustrate an important concept in defining relevant markets, namely the existence of goods which are substitutes for one another. It is widely accepted that the relevant product market should be defined in such a way that only goods which are very close substitutes for one another are included. The point was well summarised by the US Supreme Court in *Times-Picayune* where it stated:

> For every product substitutes exist, but a relevant market cannot meaningfully encompass that infinite range, the circle must be drawn narrowly to exclude any other products to which, within reasonable variations in price, only a limited number of buyers will turn.[2]

It has been argued that economists have failed to develop adequate mechanisms for defining a market.

> Because economists, from Adam Smith forward, have with confidence and enthusiasm, although not necessarily with shared views, written about markets, it is plausible to expect that they would have had quite a bit to contribute to the resolution of the market-definition issue. Plausible, but erroneous (Horowitz, 1981).

Consequently, it is argued that courts have had little help from economists in defining markets, with the result that "while paying obeisance to the relevant economics concepts, the courts have had to adopt solely legal criteria in defining the relevant market in any particular (antitrust) case" (Schrank and Roy, 1991). Economists have certainly sought to devise means of ascertaining whether or not certain products should be considered substitutes for one another. One approach is to measure the cross-price elasticity of demand. Put simply, this measures the responsiveness of the change in demand for a product to changes in the price of

---

[2] *United States* v. *Times-Picayune Publishing Company*, 345 US 594 (1953).

another product.[3] If the price of one good increases and this leads to a fall in demand for the good and a proportionate increase in demand for another, then the two goods are substitutes and are part of the same market. As in many areas of economics, however, things are not quite that simple in practice. Data may not be available to enable accurate estimation of cross price elasticities. Other factors such as increased incomes or changes in consumer tastes because of advertising campaigns may impact on sales. There is also the question of how high the cross price elasticity of demand needs to be before goods are deemed to be part of the same market.

The long history of anti-trust legislation in the US has prompted economists to come up with various alternative methods of defining markets. These fall into two broad categories: those that focus on price and those that focus on trade flows. Those in the former category have their origins in neo-classical economics theory. A key feature of markets, according to economists such as Alfred Marshall, is that the price of a particular good will be the same throughout the market.[4] Essentially, such approaches argue that if prices are uniform throughout a market, then prices of substitute products cannot move too much out of line with one another. There have been several variants on this approach involving tests for correlation between prices of goods and between changes in prices and tests for relative price stability. All of these approaches suffer from some shortcomings.

The point to emphasise is that for goods to be regarded as close substitutes and part of the same market, consumers must respond to small changes in relative price. This is a point that is often overlooked. The fact that at some level of price consumers might switch from product A to product B does not mean that they are in the same market. If in fact the producer of product A can set prices at a level that yields monopoly profits it does not matter if there is some absolute level beyond which the price

---

[3]   The cross price elasticity of demand is defined as the percentage change in quantity sold of good A divided by the percentage change in price of good B.

[4]   Neo-classical writers such as Marshall were primarily concerned with the geographical extent of a market.

cannot be raised without causing consumers to shift to product B. There is after all ultimately a limit to the price that a pure monopolist can charge. Up to that point producer A is able to exercise a degree of market power because product B is not a sufficiently close substitute to act as a constraint on the exercise of such power. If, for example, there were a bread monopoly, undoubtedly at some price consumers would simply decide to eat cake.

Price-based methods of defining markets have been formally incorporated in the US Department of Justice Merger Guidelines. In establishing whether or not the products of a merged firm constitute a unique market, the crucial question is whether the firm could sustain a significant non-transitory price increase. This is usually interpreted to mean an increase in price of at least 5 per cent for more than one year. If such an increase could not be sustained because consumers would switch to other products in sufficient numbers, or new suppliers would enter, forcing the firm to lower prices, then the authorities add the closest substitute product to their definition of the relevant market and apply the test again. Successive iterations are performed until they arrive at the situation where a 5 per cent price increase could be sustained for more than one year. The Competition Authority has cited this approach for defining a market in a number of decisions as described below.

In the United States the courts have shown a greater tendency than the EU to rely on objective tests in order to arrive at a definition of a market. The use of cross-price elasticities of demand received the imprimatur of the Supreme Court in *Times-Picayune* and again in the *du Pont* cellophane case,[5] where Mr Justice Reed stated that, in order to define a market and ascertain whether or not Du Pont had a monopoly, "what is called for is an appraisal of the 'cross-elasticity' of demand in the trade". In a dissenting judgment, however, Mr Chief Justice Warren stated that:

> In defining the market in which du Pont's economic power is to be measured, the majority virtually emasculated Section 2 of the Sherman Act.

---

[5]   *United States* v. *E.I. du Pont de Nemours and Company* 351 US 377 (1956).

In defining a market in *United Brands*,[6] the key EU case relating to an abuse of a dominant position, the European Court of Justice declined to apply a cross-elasticity of demand test, opting instead for a more subjective test which emphasised what the Court regarded as the special characteristics of the banana.

> The banana has certain characteristics, appearance, taste, softness, seedlessness, easy handling and a constant level of production which enables it to satisfy the constant needs of an important section of the population consisting of the very young, the old and the sick.

Korah has expressed strong criticism of this judgment, arguing that there was considerable economic evidence to indicate that United Brands did not enjoy any significant degree of market power and also that:

> the interests of the toothless are sufficiently protected by the inability of the dominant firm to discriminate against them. It would lose so much market share from the rest of the population that it would not be worth raising prices to exploit the weak (Korah, 1990a: 59).

Price-based theories have also been adopted in Australia where the Trade Practices Tribunal set out a detailed definition of a market in *Queensland Co-operative Milling*.

> Within the bounds of a market there is substitution — substitution between one product and another, and between one source of supply and another, in response to changing prices. So a market is the field of actual or potential transactions between buyers and sellers amongst whom there can be strong substitution, at least in the long run, if given a sufficient price incentive. Let us suppose that the price of a supplier goes up. Then on the demand side buyers may switch their patronage from this firm's product to another, or from this geographic source of supply to another. As well, on the supply side, sellers can adjust their production plans, substituting one product for another in their output mix, or substituting one geographic source of supply for another. Whether such substitution is feasible or likely

---

6   *United Brands Co* v. *Commission* Case 27/72/[1978], ECR 207.

depends ultimately on consumer attitudes, technology, distance and cost and price incentives.[7]

An interesting feature of the Australian legislation is that Section 4(E) of the Trade Practices Act includes a definition of a market. The term is defined as:

> ... a market in Australia and, when used in relation to any goods and services, includes a market for those goods or services or other goods and services that are substitutes for, or otherwise competitive with, the first mentioned goods or services.[8]

Product flows approaches to defining markets focus on the extent of product movement between different areas in order to establish whether, in fact, the two areas should be considered a single market. Such tests are more concerned with the geographical definition of the market. Large movements between areas are taken as an indication that they are part of the same market. Such theories have also been accepted by US courts. In *Pabst*[9] it was successfully argued that the appropriate market was that for beer in the State of Wisconsin. This view was justified on the basis that Wisconsin had the highest per capita beer consumption in the US and relatively little beer was imported into Wisconsin. The decision was criticised for ignoring the fact that 75 per cent of the beer brewed in Wisconsin was shipped out of the state (Schrank and Roy, 1991).

Up to now we have focused on the concept of goods being substitutes for one another from a demand or customer perspective. Goods may also, however, be substitutes from the supply side, as noted in *Queensland Co-operative Milling* cited above. For example, a firm making men's shoes may well be able to switch from producing men's to women's shoes. Does this mean that men's and women's shoes constitute a single market? If a small increase in the price of women's shoes would cause a significant switch by producers from making men's to women's shoes, then most

---

[7] *Queensland Co-operative Milling Association Ltd.* (1976) 25 FLR 169; 8 ALR 481.

[8] Australian Trade Practices Act 1974 s. 4(E).

[9] *United States* v. *Pabst Brewing Co.*, 384 US 546 (1966).

economists would answer in the affirmative.

The Irish courts had been asked on a small number of occasions prior to 1991 to consider the question of market definition in cases involving Article 86 of the Rome Treaty. In *Kerry Co-op* v. *An Bord Bainne*[10] the complaint made by Kerry Co-op, and Avonmore, in relation to Article 86, was that Bord Bainne was abusing a dominant position in obliging Kerry and Avonmore to export through it, at, it was argued, a loss in relation to the price they would obtain exporting directly. Costello found that the relevant geographical market was Ireland, rather than the Community. He found that the product market was that for dairy products, other than milk because "the Board is in the market of buying and selling dairy produce and not in the market of supplying specialist services for exporters". However, this did not mean that the market was the market for dairy products, other than milk, in Ireland, since Bord Bainne does not sell dairy products in Ireland; it only exports. The market Costello was finding was the market for Irish companies exporting dairy products, other than milk, from Ireland. He did not refer to any principle involved in finding this to be the market, and if Bord Bainne made an argument that the geographical market was the wider European market, this does not appear from the judgment.

The plaintiffs in *Deane* v. *VHI*[11] argued that the relevant market was that for insurance for health care, in which the VHI had 92 per cent of the business. The defendants argued that there was no relevant market; that the VHI was caught by Section 5 only in relation to the trade or business which constituted it an undertaking and that no abuse was alleged in the insurance market. Judge Keane did not explicitly reject this argument but may be taken to have done so implicitly since the judgment proceeds to consider the questions as to whether the VHI is dominant and the forms of behaviour that constitute an abuse of dominance. He made a finding that the VHI was dominant in the market for insurance

---

[10] *Kerry Co-operative Creameries* v. *An Bord Bainne*; *Avonmore Creameries* v. *An Bord Bainne* [1990] ILRM 664.

[11] *Deane and others* v. *Voluntary Health Insurance Board*, unreported High Court, Keane, J. 22.4.93.

for health care, and went on to consider whether it had committed an abuse of that position by indirectly damaging the interests of the plaintiffs as providers of health care. The entire part of the judgment dealing with the Section 5 arguments, however, must be taken to be to some extent obiter since Keane considered that the behaviour complained of as the Section 5 abuse was in any case behaviour that the VHI was permitted and required by the VHI Act to carry out.

In *Donovan and others* v. *ESB*,[12] the harm alleged to the plaintiffs was in their ability to compete as electrical contractors. Costello, J., found:

> The evidence . . . establishes that the market for the supply of electrical contracting services is a very segmented one . . . [T]he market for low voltage installations . . . is the market in which the Plaintiffs mainly engaged and . . . is the relevant market for the purposes of this case.

In this market, he found the ESB to have no more than a 1 to 2 per cent share.

The striking feature of the cases that have come before the Irish courts is that they have required judges to consider the question of market definition and dominance in circumstances where it appeared very obvious that the defendant had overwhelming control of at least one market, and also had power over firms operating in a related market; so obvious that it did not seem necessary to spell out principles of market definition. In *O'Neill* v. *Minister for Agriculture*,[13] the State conceded the existence of a dominant position held by the regional monopolies created by the Livestock (Artificial Insemination) Act, 1947, without any explicit statement at any point in the judgment as to the market that had been found to be the relevant market. It appears by implication to have been that for the State service of AI.

It was only in *Masterfoods* v. *HB*[14] that the issue of market definition gave rise to more detailed consideration. Mars' case was

---

[12] [1994] 2 IR 305.

[13] High Court, unreported, Budd, J., 5.7.95.

[14] Masterfoods Ltd v. HB Ltd. [1993] ILRM 145.

that the relevant market was that for ice-cream impulse products, while HB's was that it was the market for impulse products generally; including soft drinks, sweets, crisps, chewing gum and ice cream. Mars argued that the test of the product market was substitutability. It put forward three ways of measuring this:

(i)   Common sense as to the characteristics of the product in the eyes of consumers, i.e. coldness, sweetness etc.

(ii) Ice cream is seasonal, but confectionery is not; there is no correlation between increases in sales of ice cream in summer, and confectionery sales which stay constant

(iii) Cross price elasticity of demand, as found using a multiple regression analysis.

The common sense or consumer's view was also illustrated by a direct survey of consumer preferences (replies to the question asking what they would have bought if there hadn't been a Mars ice cream available). Supply-side substitutability was stated to be very low since producers of dairy or chocolate products could not easily switch to producing ice cream.

HB challenged each of the components of Mars argument. It argued that "common sense" as to market definition, in the sense of consumer perception of characteristics of goods was unreliable. Consumers might consider the energy sources gas, oil or coal to have different characteristics but suppliers consider them all to be in the same market. Seasonality was also a flawed test since petrol and ice cream showed the same seasonal pattern but were not in the same market. The cross price elasticity test was challenged on two grounds. One ground was that the particular log linear model used did not remove the peculiarities of individual shops, their product mix and customer income distribution. A more general criticism of the cross price elasticity test was made, that the difficulty of using it at all was deciding what the correct correlation was between prices and sales to indicate that products were substitutes. The test used was flawed in that it did not show that the correlation worked both ways.

Judge Keane noted that the European Commission had found

the relevant product market to be impulse ice-cream products. He came to the same conclusion:

> . . . largely on what has been described as the "common sense" or "innate characteristics" test. I do not think that someone going into a confectioner's or newsagent to buy an ice cream who finds the cabinet temporarily empty would treat their appetite as slaked by a can of coke or a bag of crisps . . . . This conclusion is undoubtedly borne out by some of the marketing surveys . . . . It is also confirmed, but to a limited extent only by the seasonal factor. As to the cross elasticity of demand criterion . . . it may be that Doctor Bishop's econometric study could be said at least in a negative sense to confirm the "common sense" test. Ultimately, however, I think the acknowledged incapacity of that procedure to embrace all the significant variables which would have to be taken into account significantly reduces its value.

If this is a finding that cross price elasticity tests can be discounted as of no or little value, the authors suggest that this is a luxury available only in those cases where common sense unaided is genuinely capable of finding the relevant market.

In the Newspaper Study (Competition Authority, 1995), the Authority stated that there is no simple clear-cut definition of a market, but that the question of product substitutability is crucial. The question of product substitutability is one that is intuitively easy to understand but the actual measuring of a sufficient degree of substitutability cannot be done merely on an intuitive basis. The Study describes the methods of measurement used theoretically, and in application in other competition jurisdictions. The Authority looked at the US Department of Justice Merger Guidelines test for market definition, described above. The Authority also referred to those Guidelines in Cooley/Irish Distillers.[15]

The Authority in the Newspaper Study also noted that the US Department of Justice chooses the smallest product market as the relevant market. The European Commission and Courts are considered to define product markets more narrowly again than the US, although they are then more prepared not to find dominance in the narrowly defined market until a higher level of market share is reached. Apart from price movements, the Commission

---

[15] Decision No. 285 of 25.2.94.

takes into account product characteristics, and intended use, and implicitly the subjective view of consumers. The Commission has also taken into account the view of the firm itself (as shown by its behaviour rather than in the sense of asking the firm) as to the market in which it is competing.

In Cooley,[16] the Authority stated that it took into account the Commission position that the market is "all those products which are regarded as interchangeable or substitutable by the consumer, by reason of the products' characteristics, their prices and their intended use" and cited the view of the US Supreme Court in *Times-Picayune*. The Authority noted that the Irish Whiskey Act, 1980 defines the product which can be described as Irish whiskey. It also noted that the main drinks suppliers were increasingly involved in producing and distributing different kinds of drinks, indicating that such products were not substitutes for one another. The fact that "customers specify . . . particular brands when buying whiskey" indicated that whiskey was not treated as generic, or as a commodity. The Authority referred to the European Commission decision in *Bells*,[17] where it was found that a prohibition on exports "affected the structure of competition on the Scotch whisky or non-Scotch whisky market", indicating that Scotch whisky constituted a separate market from other whiskeys. The Authority stated that:

> (It) believes that in the event of a small increase in whisk(e)y prices relative to that of other spirits, there would be a very limited shift in consumption away from whisk(e)y to such products. Consequently the Authority does not believe that there is a single spirits market.

And as between Irish and Scotch:

> . . . in Ireland, although perhaps not elsewhere, Irish whiskey and Scotch whisky may constitute separate markets . . . [because] . . . a small increase in the price of Irish whiskey would not lead to any significant shift in consumption from Irish to Scotch whisk(e)y. The Authority believes that the entry of a new Irish whiskey producer onto the market would have a

---

[16]   Decision No. 285 of 25.2.94.

[17]   [1978] 3 CMLR 298.

far greater impact on the price and level of sales of IDG's products than would the entry of a new brand of imported whisky.

IDG had argued that one adverse effect of Cooley, as a failing firm being sold in a "fire sale", was the damage that the sale of its stocks would do to the world image of Irish whiskey. By implication, it would not have harmed the world image of Scotch.

In *Woodchester*,[18] the Authority had occasion to consider the fact that banks, as noted in Chapter 3, are multi-product firms competing in several distinct markets. This illustrates the point that a market is not necessarily co-extensive with a sector. It is possible for a multi-product firm to be dominant in some markets and not in others.

In Waterford Harbour/Bell Lines,[19] the notification was concerned with the provision of shipping services to and from Britain and mainland Europe. The Authority distinguished between airports and seaports as catering for different types of goods, on the basis that air freight was not economically viable for heavy or bulky exports. The Authority also distinguished between exports leaving the State for Britain and for other destinations. The Authority went on to distinguish between types of loads coming into seaports, bulk and container traffic, and to distinguish between container Ro/Ro and Lo/Lo.[20] The Authority regarded Lo/Lo and Ro/Ro as easily interchangeable for trucks loaded with containers. Waterford Harbour was in competition with all Lo/Lo and Ro/Ro ports in the island of Ireland from which goods were shipped to Britain and mainland Europe, on the basis that traffic from all parts of Ireland went through ports throughout the island. In effect, the Authority's decision indicates that the relevant geographical market was the island of Ireland, rather than Waterford.[21]

---

[18] Decision No. 6 of 4.8.92.

[19] Decision No. 7 of 4.8.92.

[20] The former refers to containers driven onto ferries by trucks; the latter to the removal and loading of the container from the trucks onto the boat.

[21] In Nallen/O'Toole, the Authority indicated that the relevant geographical market extended beyond the town where the business concerned was located.

The approaches to market definition described above are all of them ways of analysing the behaviour of actual buyers. As such, they require replicating the considerations that affect a real buyer, such as technical substitutability, switching costs[22] and price. In order to compare prices as a buyer actually does, the person attempting to define the market needs to know whether a more expensive version of a product, with some more convenient or attractive feature, is considered by a buyer to be equivalent in value to the cheaper version without the added feature. Generally, this kind of decision making requires the competition agency to obtain the same information that a buyer within the market would have and take a subjective view. It is of course also possible to identify the actual behaviour of real buyers objectively, whether by observation of the interaction of price and demand, or by means of a survey. The latter may appear an easier solution, but is difficult to do correctly, since the question has to be put in such a way that the buyers are genuinely answering the question the answer to which the competition agency, or court, needs to determine. Having said that, the difficulty of obtaining price information as an aid to market definition should not be exaggerated. Even where it is not possible to run a full cross price elasticity test, there will in many situations be some data for price changes and sales figures over a period of time, which will be a useful indicator in arriving at a market definition. On occasion, it is necessary to fall back upon commonsense methods such as trying to establish whether there is a clear qualitative gap between products (Robinson, 1934).

Dominance

Broadly speaking, a firm that can act without regard to its competitors, its suppliers or its customers is considered to be dominant. Large market share is an indicator, although not conclusive proof, of dominance. The extent to which large market share indicates dominance may be determined by the nature of the market. Contestability theory would say that, where it is easy for other

---

[22] The cost of switching from one product to another — for example, in switching from fuel A to fuel B for central heating, the switching cost might involve that of changing the hardware of the heating system.

firms to enter a market, an incumbent firm with high market share will nonetheless be inhibited from setting high or monopoly prices, or acting inefficiently. The rationale is that if it did so, it would be susceptible to "hit and run" entry from new entrants, and it is therefore obliged, by the threat of entry to act as though it were in a competitive market. It has an incentive not to deploy its market power, and thus is unlikely to exert dominance. However, as noted in Chapter 2, not all real-world markets are contestable. The useful application of contestability theory depends on being able to determine whether barriers to entry in fact exist.

As noted above, there is little authority from the Irish courts on market definition; there is correspondingly little on dominance. The lowest market share examined in the context of dominance was 49 per cent, in *Kerry Co-op* v. *Bord Bainne*[23] where Costello, J. found:

> With some considerable hesitation and notwithstanding the liberalisation of the trading rules brought about in 1988 and the drop in Bord Bainne's share of exports of dairy produce I have come to the conclusion that it can be said factually that Bord Bainne is presently in a dominant position in the market to which I have referred.

The figures given elsewhere in the judgment were that "in 1979 (Bord Bainne) handled 75 per cent (in value terms) of all dairy exports but by 1988 . . . this figure had declined to 60 per cent and in 1989 to about 49 per cent. There is now a considerable number of companies and, in addition, a number of Bord Bainne's own members who are engaged in the export of Irish dairy products in competition with Bord Bainne on foreign markets."

In *Masterfoods* v. *HB*[24] Keane, J. found HB to be dominant in the market for impulse ice creams in Ireland. The grounds for the finding were that it had had a market share rarely less than 70 per cent for nearly a quarter century; the small number of competitors and their relatively low market shares; the fact that HB's share was several times larger than its nearest competitors

---

[23]   [1990] ILRM 664.

[24]   [1993] ILRM 145.

(Valley or Mars); and the efficient vertically integrated distribution system it operated through retail TSN shops. He noted that HB did not, however, own its distributors. It was also relevant that HB operated independently of its competitors, customers and ultimate consumers and that it had "at all times effectively dictated the level of prices for all ice-cream products and . . . never felt the need to reduce prices in order to compete more effectively with others in the market." In *Deane* v. *VHI*,[25] Keane, J. found the VHI to be dominant with 92 per cent of the market.

The question was raised in the VHI case as to whether the use of power in one market in such a way as to affect firms in another market, in which the alleged abuser was not dominant could constitute an abuse. The question is implicitly answered in *Donovan* v. *ESB*[26] and in *Deane* v. *VHI*[27] in the affirmative, although given that the question is not explored in either case, it cannot be taken to be anything as definite as a ruling that abuse can be found in any market where the alleged abuser is not dominant.

There is a fleeting reference in *Carna Foods and Mallon* v. *Eagle Star*[28] to the possibility of finding collective dominance:

> To claim that two or more undertakings are abusing a dominant position, it would be necessary to show collusion . . .

but the idea is not further explored. In *A & N Pharmacy Ltd.* v. *United Drug Ltd.,*[29] Carroll, J., took the view, in the context of an interlocutory, but mandatory, injunction that there was a serious issue to be tried as to whether the defendant, as one of three oligopolists who collectively controlled over 90 per cent of the business in wholesale pharmaceutical drugs in Limerick, was abusing a dominant position.

---

[25] High Court, unreported, Keane, J., 22.4.93.

[26] [1994] 2 IR 305.

[27] High Court, unreported, Keane, J., 22.4.93.

[28] *Carna Foods and Mallon* v. *Eagle Star Insurance Co.* [1995] 1 IR 526.

[29] *A&N Pharmacy Ltd.* v. *United Drug Wholesale Ltd.* [1996] 2 ILRM 42.

In *Donovan and others* v. *ESB*,[30] Costello, J. found that the ESB "is not a serious competitor in this (contracting services) market" having a market share of between 1 and 2¼ per cent but "the ESB is in a dominant position in the market for the supply of electrical contracting services". The reasoning of the decision, it must be inferred, is that the ESB had a controlling influence on behaviour in the market for services by reason of its statutory monopoly position in the market for supply.

The formulation of dominance in European law, repeated in *Hoffman La Roche*[31] and a number of EU cases and adopted by Keane J. in *Mars*,[32] is:

> A position of economic strength enjoyed by an undertaking which enables it to prevent effective competition being maintained on the relevant market by affording it the power to behave to an appreciable extent independently of its competitors, its customers and ultimately of the consumers.

Market shares of 40 to 45 per cent have been found by the European Court of Justice to constitute dominance[33] and the Commission (1980) has stated that it does not consider 40 per cent to be the lowest level at which dominance can be found, but rather that 20 per cent could in some circumstances constitute dominance.

The Commission has also taken into account contestability arguments, in *Tetra-Pak I*,[34] in looking at the market for aseptic packaging machines and finding that technology was a barrier to entry. In *British Midland* v. *Aer Lingus*,[35] the Commission identified as a barrier to entry the opportunity costs involved in entering the market. For any airline operating out of Heathrow, the decision to operate on the London–Dublin route necessarily involved using slots which the airline could otherwise use for other,

---

[30] *Donovan and others* v. *ESB* [1995] 2 IR 305.

[31] *Hoffman LaRoche* v. *Commission* [1979] ECR 461.

[32] *Masterfoods* v. *HB Ice Cream Ltd.* [1993] 1 ILRM 145.

[33] *United Brands Co.* v. *Commission* [1978] ECR 207.

[34] [1990] 4 CMLR 47.

[35] [1993] 4 CMLR 596.

more profitable routes; the loss of that opportunity would inhibit new entry into the market. Contestability arguments have, as noted in Chapter 2, been accepted quite readily in the US Courts. The Competition Authority in its Newspaper Study (1995) pointed out:

> . . . if an incumbent perceives that new entry is unlikely and acts with disregard for potential competitors, then the fact that new entry is feasible may well not be all that relevant.

The abuse of a dominant position may itself constitute proof of the dominant position. This apparently circular approach is based on the idea that the firm is only able to act abusively because it has a dominant position, and it has been accepted by the European Commission and the Court, and cited by the Fair Trade Commission (1991c). It has been criticised (Whish, 1993; and others) as being circular but the authors suggest that it is to some extent implicit in the first definition of dominance cited above of a firm able to act in disregard of its competitors.

Abuse of Dominance

As noted in Chapter 2, dominant firms may engage in various forms of strategic behaviour that may adversely affect competition. The treatment of such behaviour by competition law is now considered. Although there is not a great volume of case law to date under the 1991 Act, more Section 5 than Section 4 actions have been brought by private litigants. As above, the approach of the Irish Courts to Article 86 of the Rome Treaty is relevant.[36] In *Kerry Co-op* v. *Bord Bainne*,[37] Costello found that it was not an abuse (under Article 86) for Bord Bainne to require its members to trade with it because the obligation to trade was nominal and because the sanction for failure to trade was merely the loss of membership, which he had found not to constitute a loss of their property rights. "There is an objective justification for the Bord, in selling its members' products giving most control to those using it

---

[36] *O'Neill* v. *Minister for Agriculture*, High Court, unreported, Budd, J., 5.7.95 is not discussed in this context. While Article 86 was pleaded, the case deals essentially with Article 90 issues.

[37] [1990] ILRM 664

as their central marketing organisation." He also found that the pricing policy of Bord Bainne was to obtain the best prices for exports; there was no evidence that it resulted in members getting lower prices than if they sold alone. He also found that there was no detriment to the Irish consumer. This seems to indicate that a finding of such detriment would have contributed towards the behaviour being abusive. He did also, however, indicate that his views on dominance and abuse of dominance were being given in the context that his order in the case would anyway be to refer to the European Court a question as to whether the competition rules of the Treaty applied in the first place to these products.

In *Deane* v. *VHI*,[38] Keane cited *Hoffman la Roche* to say that changing the structure of the market to the effect that competition was weakened was abusive. While he indicated that he did not need to decide the issue, he stated that abuse consisted of behaviour "(a) to weaken competition in the relevant market or (b) directly damage the interests of those dependent on the supply or acquisition of the goods or services in question." The Plaintiff's allegation had been that the VHI abused a dominant position because they caused damage in an indirect manner to the Plaintiffs in their capacity as providers of health care. "If that contention were correct in law, it would follow that the action of the VHI . . . was also an abuse."

In *Masterfoods* v. *HB*,[39] Keane, J. stated: "I approach the question [of abuse] on the basis that, if the practices complained of create what has been described as a strategic barrier to entry, designed to make the market significantly less contestable, they would constitute an abuse of HB's dominant position." He considered the history of HB's behaviour relevant: both HB, before it was dominant, and all its competitors always had freezer exclusivity. HB would have been abandoning unilaterally a practice universal in the industry, to the benefit of their competitors. He noted that retailers wanted to stock HB, and that that in itself was an obstacle for its rivals. "HB's dominant position in the market will continue to present a crucial difficulty for new entrants, at least

---

[38] High Court, unreported, Keane, J., 22.4.93.

[39] [1993] ILRM 145.

in the short term. But it does not follow from that that they are required to act in a way . . . which makes no economic sense and is against their legitimate interest."

Judge Carroll, granting an interlocutory mandatory injunction to supply, found that there was a serious issue to be tried as to whether a refusal to supply pharmaceutical drugs, where the plaintiff is unable to obtain supplies elsewhere, is an abuse of a dominant position:

> In my opinion, since the advent of competition law, commercial enterprises are being forced to do business with other persons against their will. Since the defendant is a commercial enterprise supplying drugs there would be no inconvenience to it if cash is forthcoming for orders from the plaintiff.[40]

In *Donovan* v. *ESB*,[41] the most detailed consideration to date of Section 5, it was found that the ESB, as a dominant firm, had abused its dominant position in entering into an agreement with the Register of Electrical Contractors of Ireland (RECI), under which only RECI members would be able to certify premises for connection to the ESB grid; and by the unilateral action of refusing interconnection other than in accordance with that agreement. Unregistered contractors were obliged to obtain a certificate by inspection by a RECI contractor, at a significant cost, before connection would be granted. Clearly, this gave RECI members a competitive advantage over non-members. In those circumstances, the exclusion of any competitors from the trade association was a serious competitive disadvantage, and the criteria for membership would therefore be offensive unless "based on objective criteria with a proper appeal procedure."[42] In the unusual circumstance that an agreement, rather than unilateral action, was under consideration under Section 5, the analysis applied was directed towards whether the agreement between ESB and RECI offended under Section 4. If so, it would then consequentially offend

---

[40] *A&N Pharmacy Ltd* v. *United Drug Wholesale Ltd.* [1996] 2 ILRM 42.

[41] (1994) 2 IR 305.

[42] *Donovan* v. *ESB* (1994) 2 IR 305.

under Section 5, as stated in the quotation earlier in the chapter. It was found that the intention of the agreement was to promote safety, and not to prevent, restrict or distort competition. However, it did have the effect of restricting competition:

> The decision by RECI to charge an inspection fee of £85 to non-registered contractors . . . did have the effect of restricting the ability of a significant number of small contractors to compete . . . because of the extra costs involved which would have to be passed on to the customer . . .

RECI had also organised an advertising campaign promoting its members by comparison with non-members, described in the advertising as "cowboys", which was also found to restrict the ability of non-members to compete. However, Costello, J. found that the restrictions on the ability of non-members to compete "would be obviated if there were no restrictions on enrolment on the RECI register". The restrictions were:

> . . . the imprecision of the criteria for registration, the arbitrary power to refuse enrolment, the absence of any appeals procedure, the existence of a requirement for enrolment not required for the objects for which the Register was formed . . .

and, in aggregate, "these resulted in a restriction on competition".

It was found not to be offensive that the four founding members of RECI (including two existing trade associations) controlled the company and the register, nor that members of those trade associations were charged lower entry and annual subscription rates. The latter was justified by reference to administrative savings, and the former was found not to be offensive in itself without proof of abuse. Control, it was suggested is not the same as abuse of control, just as dominance is not offensive, but abuse of dominance is.

The Authority was required in the Newspaper Study (Competition Authority, 1995) to consider two possible abuses of dominant position. One concerned the allegation by National Newspapers of Ireland that News International was engaged in predatory pricing. The view of the Authority was that predation was not occurring. Predatory pricing:

> . . . has a very specific meaning in both economic and legal contexts. It entails deliberately selling below cost in order to

eliminate one or more competitors or to weaken them to such a degree that they can no longer offer strong competition to the predator so that prices can then be increased in order to provide supra-normal profits (Competition Authority, 1995, para. 8.44).

The Authority concluded that News International could not literally eliminate any of the Irish newspapers. Moreover, if it did, there was no reason to think that it would benefit from the custom of former readers of the eliminated paper, in preference to the other competitors in the market.

> It is irrational to engage in predatory behaviour unless the predator is going to recoup the losses sustained in such an exercise through higher prices in the future (*ibid.*).

In looking at the purchase by Independent Newspapers of a minority shareholding of 24.9 per cent in Irish Press Newspapers Ltd. and Irish Press Publishing Ltd. the Authority referred to the view of the European Commission and the Court of Justice that strategic behaviour by which a dominant firm modifies market structure in its favour can be an abuse. It found that this share purchase had the effect of strengthening the dominant position of Independent Newspapers. It also found that the object of the share purchase was to prevent any rival of Independent Newspapers acquiring control of the Press newspapers.

> The Independent purchase . . . has already enabled Irish Press plc to reject a rival bid. . . . It has therefore already had the effect of preventing the acquisition of the Press newspapers by a rival group. Arguably the Independent's minority shareholding cannot prevent a rival acquiring the remaining shares. . . . It nevertheless represents a strong deterrent to other investors interested in acquiring outright or substantial control of those newspapers in order to compete head on with Independent Newspapers (*ibid.*, para 8.54).

It came to the conclusion that the acquisition of the shareholding was an abuse of a dominant position.

Overview
The concept of abuse of dominance is widely recognised as notoriously difficult to prove. George and Jacquemin (1992) argue that

alleged abuses would require a full-blown investigation to identify both the intent behind any particular type of conduct and to establish its effect and, as a result, there were likely to be relatively few cases. They note that the application of Article 86 was slow to get off the mark and that there were only 50 such cases in the period up to 1989. The US experience of the operation of Section 2 of the Sherman Act is broadly similar in this respect, although arguably the relative paucity of such cases in recent years reflects policy choices as much as any other consideration. Shepherd (1990) notes that Section 2 cases tend to be extremely lengthy. Ferrands and Totterdill (1993) have gone so far as to argue that Article 86 is "almost useless".

A second problem arises in respect of remedies for dealing with abuse of dominance. George and Jacquemin (1992), for example, argue that fines for abusive behaviour are subject to the criticism that they merely constitute tinkering with the problem and, in some cases at least, are unlikely to provide an adequate remedy as long as the underlying market structure remains unchanged. In effect, there will be some occasions when the most appropriate remedy involves structural adjustment of the dominant position. Such a remedy is not provided under Article 86 but is one that exists and, as noted in Chapter 4, has been implemented under US law, albeit in a limited number of cases. The possibility of structural adjustment of a dominant position exists under Section 14 of the Competition Act, which provides that the Minister may order the break-up of a dominant position, by a sale of assets or otherwise, following a finding by the Competition Authority that there has been an abuse of the dominant position.

Structural Adjustment

Section 14 has not been invoked to date. It is in keeping with the experience of enforcement in other jurisdictions that structural problems are tackled less often than problems of behaviour, and that there is a reluctance to change existing structures by ordering divestment. Shepherd (1990) has been critical of the failure by the US authorities to seek divestment under Section 2 more frequently, while conceding that the overall number of cases where such remedies are appropriate is rather small. As noted in Chapter 6, Minister O'Malley indicated during the course of the debate on the Act that it was envisaged that this provision would be used only rarely.

Although in Ireland divestment is a remedy to be ordered by a Minister, rather than granted by a court, it is subject to a perception, not confined to Ireland and influenced by the approach of courts to enforcement, that any remedy, civil or criminal, should be directly addressed to the identified harmful activity. Divestment of a block of property is not, however, ordered on the basis that the ownership of that block is itself the wrongful act, but rather that divestment will permit competition to flow where previously it was blocked. It thus may appear to be a more serious interference with property rights than prohibiting identifiably harmful behaviour. The mistake inherent in this is that competition law is not primarily concerned with individual wrongs and harms so much as with effect on the economy; so that it is correct to have a remedy that is directed to fixing the harm to the economy rather than to being a punishment fitted to a crime.

Another reason why divestment is not a frequently used weapon may be that it is perceived as involving a more serious interference in a business than, for example, requiring alteration of contract terms. In *United Shoe*,[43] for example, Judge Wyzanski observed:

> In the antitrust field the courts have been accorded . . . an authority they have in no other branch of enacted law . . . . They would not have been given, or allowed to keep, such authority in the antitrust field, and they would not so freely have altered from time to time the interpretation of its substantive provisions, if courts were in the habit of proceeding with the surgical ruthlessness that might commend itself to those seeking absolute assurances that there will be workable competition.

Nevertheless, it remains the case that in a small number of cases divestment may well be the most appropriate remedy and its application should not be ruled out entirely.

---

[43] *United States* v. *United Shoe Machinery Corporation* 110 F. Supp. 295, 348 (1953).

9

LEGAL CERTAINTY AND
EFFECTIVE ENFORCEMENT

The previous three chapters have described in some detail the main features of the Competition Acts. In analysing the operation of the legislation to date, three main issues are examined. Firstly, as it applies specifically to business activity, there is a need for a degree of legal certainty. Secondly, it is obviously important that aggressive competition not be confused with anti-competitive behaviour and that, while the latter should be penalised, the former should not. The third issue relates to the effectiveness of the legislation in deterring anti-competitive activity in the economy.

Legal Certainty

There are several sources of uncertainty in competition law; some peculiar to the area and some exacerbated manifestations of problems that arise in other areas of law.[1] The dividing line between aggressive competition and anti-competitive behaviour can be a thin one on occasion. As a result, there are two types of error that may arise in applying competition law. Firstly, behaviour may, on occasion, be mistakenly identified as anti-competitive, with the result that such behaviour may be prohibited even though it may actually be beneficial. Secondly, genuinely anti-competitive actions may not be recognised and go unpenalised. It is important that both types of mistake should be avoided. Necessarily, where legislation cannot define behaviour except by its effects, uncertainty is created. It is fundamental, in a social contract sense, that citizens should be able to obey the law, and not unwittingly breach it because of its lack of clarity. There is also a connection between the clarity of a law and its observance by citizens. The behaviour

---

[1] "The natural and reasonable desire that statutes should be easily understood is doomed to disappointment" (Bennion, 1992).

in question here is commercial behaviour of businesses, where certainty also has a financial value. Specifically, under the Irish Acts, contracts that restrict competition are not enforceable by the courts. For all these reasons, it is important that firms be able to determine, or have determined for them, the effect of competition regulation on their behaviour. Apart from any other reason, economists would say that uncertainty can defeat the purpose of competition legislation, because uncertainty has what is called a chilling effect on business behaviour. It is an obvious pitfall of unclear provisions that firms will act anti-competitively. What is not so obvious is that it will also cause firms, from excess of caution, to refrain from behaviour which would not be anti-competitive, and which might in fact be pro-competitive.

The second difficulty is one that is true of all law, but especially so of competition law. "All laws are pigeon holes" (Korah, 1990b) and any law prohibiting anti-competitive behaviour of necessity is an attempt to build the right-size pigeon hole for behaviour about which experts disagree. This is a problem that goes a step beyond the problem, with all laws, of the preliminary investigation of facts which is necessary to know if a law applies to the fact situation. Competition law prohibits certain behaviour, which it defines by reference to *effects*. The Competition Act, 1991 prohibits any behaviour that has the object or effect of preventing, restricting or distorting competition; an *ex post facto* test. So also do the European Treaty Rules on which the Irish Act is based, and the US antitrust statutes. The comparison required to be made, in each case, is whether the behaviour under scrutiny prevents, restricts or distorts competition by reference to a hypothetical situation where this behaviour was stopped, or had never happened. Sometimes there will be a real-life comparator, as where it is possible to consider the same market prior to the behaviour taking place. Where there is not, the court, or enforcement agency as the case may be, is being asked to consider the likely state of competition in the market in the absence of the behaviour complained of, and can do so only by making assumptions as to how markets work, based either on how markets usually appear to work, or evidence of economic theory predicting the likely effects of the behaviour under scrutiny.

In part, such difficulties arise because anti-competitive behaviour can take many forms and any attempt to enshrine in legislation a comprehensive list of anti-competitive behaviour would be quite a complex task. Given the ingenuity of the human mind in devising avoidance behaviour, it would also be a virtually useless one. In addition, however, whether particular arrangements are anti-competitive or not will frequently depend on the circumstances in which they operate. Thus, in the case of certain types of behaviour, it is not possible to say *a priori* whether or not the practice is anti-competitive. Vertical restraints are one example which we consider below. Also, economic theory evolves over time. Research into firm behaviour is ongoing. The result of such study is that new types of anti-competitive behaviour will be identified and behaviour previously considered offensive may come to be seen in a more benign light. Competition law must therefore be flexible enough to recognise and cope with such considerations.

Economists, like any expert witnesses, offer a view that may not be based on empirical evidence. In the case of economists considering the effect of behaviour on competition, it is just as likely to be one that is entirely theory based. There are some questions in the application of competition law where the ultimate issue is one that is reached entirely by the application of economic theory. Bok (1960) argues, in the context of mergers, that economist witnesses, unless clearly directed otherwise, will often want to have taken into account a multiplicity of relevant factors so that there is a gap between the normal endeavour of economists to make predictions at varying levels of certainty, and the endeavour of lawyers to prove matters to a specific level of certainty, such as, for example, a balance of probabilities. The risk, he suggests, of searching for some absolute truth by way of taking into account all possible factors, is that sufficient information on all factors will not be available, and their introduction will do no more than add to uncertainty. He argues that in the specific context of mergers, the need for certainty for business is great enough that it is correct to choose two or three key factors, and deliberately leave all others out of the scope of judicial inquiry.

> Lawyers have perhaps not always been explicit enough in articulating the peculiar qualifications which their institutions

place upon the unbridled pursuit of truth and this failure may in some measure explain the irritation with which their handiwork is so often greeted by even thoughtful economists (Bok, 1960).

There are different approaches to providing certainty. One is to attempt to formalise economic theory into white-line rules. Korah (1990b) argues that the European Commission has done this, mistakenly, in respect of vertical restraints in its block exemptions; this is discussed as a substantive issue below. The explanation, she says, for so distorting the economic rules in turning them into legal rules is:

> Many officials would not find it easy to apply such broad (economic) tests, and think that lawyers advising business would find similar difficulty. In practice, however, in-house lawyers are usually very quick to see the commercial and economic consequences of their firm's agreement and specialist competition lawyers soon pick up the skill and are educated by their clients.

To this the authors would add that it is a self-fulfilling prophecy for rule-makers to say that lawyers would not understand or apply economic tests, and to invent a bowdlerised version for their convenience. Lawyers, of course, will simply learn to apply whatever rules have the force of law.

> In 1982, when the Herfindahl index was introduced to the anti-trust world through its inclusion in that year's Merger Guidelines, the anti-trust bar . . . quickly adjusted. After a very short period antitrust lawyers and their clients discussed Herfindahls as if they had been using them all of their lives (Lande, 1994).

If the above is true, and if Korah's criticism is correct, the Commission is in fact only choosing to oblige lawyers to learn the wrong test, rather than the right one.

Under the US approach as described in Chapter 4, some forms of behaviour, very limited in number, are established as being *per se* offensive. This approach brings certainty into some areas, although by definition it is not intended to do so for all areas. The lure of any *per se* rule is that it seems to offer certainty. However, it is subject to the risk, common to any white-line test, of being drawn in the wrong place. Clearly, there may be circumstances in which behaviour that is subject to the *per se* rule is not anti-competitive so that the application of the rule may on occasion result in errors of the first type. Nevertheless, given the degree of acceptance that price fixing and market sharing will almost always prove anti-competitive, the US *per se* rule which is limited to such behaviour is unlikely to result in many innocent agreements being deemed illegal.[2]

> *Per se* rules always contain a degree of arbitrariness. They are justified on the assumption that the gains from imposition of the rule far outweigh the losses and that significant administrative advantages will result. In other words, the potential competitive harm plus the administrative costs of determining in what particular situations the practice may be harmful must far outweigh the benefits that may result. If the potential benefits in the aggregate are outweighed to this degree, then they are simply not worth identifying in individual cases.[3]

The Competition Act, 1991 contains no *per se* rules. Being based on the existing European model, it instead provides to some extent for the resolution of uncertainty in individual cases by allowing parties to notify agreements to the Competition Authority for the purpose of obtaining a certificate or a licence, as detailed in Chapter 6. A certificate is a statement of the view of the Competition Authority, on the basis of the facts in its possession, that the notified agreement does not prevent, restrict or distort competition. In a Section 6 action or an action for enforcement of an agreement, which has been notified to, and certified by, the Authority, it is a matter to be considered *de novo* by the court whether the agreement is or is not anti-competitive, and whether it is enforceable. The qualified nature of the certificate as protection is emphasised by the fact that where it is found, in Section 6 proceedings, that an agreement was in fact anti-competitive, "any

---

[2] As noted in Chapter 2, some economists would not regard RPM as anti-competitive, and would presumably feel that the application of the *per se* rule to RPM is a mistake. In the Supreme Court decisions in cases regarding musical copyright the *per se* rule was not applied to horizontal agreements on price.

[3] *United States* v. *Container Corporation of America et al.* 393 US 333, 341 (1969) Marshall, J. (dissenting on other issues).

certificate in force . . . in relation to that agreement . . . shall thereupon cease to have force and effect". In that respect, a licence provides a more certain result for a notifying party in that it does "permit the doing of acts which would otherwise be prohibited and void". Thus, it is a barrier to an action under Section 6, and a complete reply to a party seeking to rely on Section 4 as a defence to the enforcement of the agreement. Refusal decisions by the Authority do not provide any ultimate certainty in that they do not have any legal effect in court proceedings in respect of the same agreement. Finally, while the view of the Authority as to which elements of an agreement are offensive will be clear from refusal decisions, the issue of severance is one for determination by the courts.[4]

Legal certainty is more easily attained in a mature system of competition law so that some uncertainty is a necessary feature of a new regime. There has been legislation in force only since 1991, and at the date hereof very few cases have been decided by the courts.

Striking the Right Balance

Licences, as noted in Chapter 6, may be granted to categories of agreements as well as to individual agreements. This provision appears to be modelled on the EU block exemption approach for dealing with commonly occurring agreements. Several of these block exemptions apply to different forms of vertical restraints, such as exclusive distribution, exclusive purchasing and franchising. The two broad messages which emerged from our review of the economics literature on non-price vertical restraints in Chapter 2 were that:

• Whether non-price vertical restraints will prove beneficial depends to a large extent on the characteristics of the goods in question and various other market conditions; and

• At the very least, vertical restraints involve some trade-off between inter and intra-brand competition. The outcome of such a trade-off again will vary depending on the circumstances in each individual case.

---

[4] s.4 (7).

The European Commission in its block exemptions appears to conclude that non-price vertical restraints infringe Article 85(1) of the Treaty of Rome — that is, they are anti-competitive and restrict trade between member states. This appears to amount to a *per se* rather than a "rule of reason" approach.[5] Korah (1990b) argues that by so doing, the Commission, in trying to provide clear legal rules and avoid individual consideration of every fact situation, has erred first in the direction of finding offensive behaviour that may not be so, and then in granting blanket exemptions to behaviour that may in some circumstances be restrictive. It is worth noting that at the First European Competition Forum organised by DG-IV in April 1995 for the national competition authorities and courts of Member States, the panel discussion by national authorities on vertical restraints criticised the Commission's approach, the views expressed being that vertical restraints were not automatically offensive, that there was excessive reliance on block exemptions and that the preferable approach was a case-by-case analysis (Commission, 1995).

A block exemption would appear to be an inappropriate means of dealing with arrangements which should properly be dealt with on a case-by-case or "rule of reason" basis. The block exemption implies that such restraints are *per se* desirable, a view that is generally confined to adherents of the Chicago school. A block exemption may not only permit such agreements but its existence may provide firms with an incentive to engage in anti-competitive

---

[5] In fact the preamble to a number of the Regulations qualifies this somewhat. The preamble to 1983/83 states that:

- whereas exclusive distribution agreements of the category defined in Article 1 of this regulation *may fall within the prohibition contained in Article 85(1)* of the Treaty;

- whereas *this will apply only in exceptional cases* to exclusive agreements of this kind to which *only undertakings from one member State are party* . . .

- Whereas *it is not necessary expressly to exclude from the defined category those agreements which do not fulfil the conditions of Article 85(1)* of the Treaty [emphasis added].

In effect, the wording appears to recognise that not all exclusive distribution agreements infringe against Article 85(1) but this appears to be contradicted in the operative part of the regulation.

agreements when they might not otherwise do so. There seems to be a strong probability that the block exemptions result in the second type of error identified earlier — that is, in some cases at least they permit arrangements that are anti-competitive and have no offsetting beneficial features. The Commission decisions withdrawing the benefit of the exemption in Mars/Langnese and Mars/Schöller represent a welcome recognition of such problems but there are almost certainly many more such cases.

> The conclusion that interbrand restraints are generally more pernicious than intrabrand restraints does not, however, compel the conclusion that the latter pose a trivial threat to competition. Similarly the conclusion that some, or even many, intrabrand vertical restraints are either pro competitive or competitively neutral does not compel the conclusion that they are benign in almost every case. Our recent experience . . . indicates that some vertical intrabrand restraints have substantial anti competitive potential and that the existence of concomitant efficiencies should not be assumed (Dick, 1994: 3).

In one sense, Korah's criticism may be unduly harsh. At the time of the original block exemption for exclusive distribution in 1967, mainstream economic thinking would have been quite hostile to most non-price vertical restraints. The US Supreme Court, for example, ruled in 1967 that non-price vertical restraints were *per se* illegal. The continued adherence to the view that non-price vertical restraints are anti-competitive reflects a failure by the Commission to modify its views as economic theory has evolved over the past 25 years or so. This is in contrast to the US where both the courts and the authorities have altered their views over time. Thus in 1963 the US Supreme Court, by a five to three majority, refused to condemn territorial and customer restrictions included in motor vehicle distribution agreements, on the grounds that it did not "know enough of the economic and business stuff out of which these arrangements emerge"[6] to be certain whether they restricted competition or represented "the only practicable means a small company has for breaking into or staying in business." It referred the matter back to the District Court for a

---

6   *White Motor Co.* v. *United States*, 372 US 253 (1963).

thorough exploration of the facts, — that is, the application of a rule of reason rather than a *per se* test. Four years later, however, the Court did an about turn, ruling that manufacturers which imposed territorial and other restrictions upon resale committed *per se* violations of the Sherman Act.[7] This proved to be an extremely controversial decision and was subject to widespread criticism. Ten years later, the Court again reversed its view, in the *Sylvania*[8] case. The case involved a TV manufacturer (Sylvania) whose dealer contracts restricted selected retailers to store locations specified by the manufacturer. The Court held that vertical restraints could promote inter-brand competition by enabling the manufacturer to achieve efficiencies in distribution. It stated that "when interbrand competition exists . . . it provides a significant check on the exploitation of intra-brand market power because of the ability of consumers to substitute a different brand of the same product." The Court concluded that in the particular case there was no evidence that the restrictions had or were likely to have "a pernicious effect on competition" or that they lack "any redeeming value". It concluded that while particular vertical restraints may well be anti-competitive, such restraints should be judged on the basis of a rule of reason approach. The Sylvania decision was seen by some commentators as marking the coming of age of economic analysis in its application in US antitrust law.

Korah (1990a) has argued that the Court of Justice has tended to take a less restrictive approach to exclusive distribution than the Commission, notably in *Technique Minière*.[9] There the Court expressed the view that:

> In particular it may be doubted whether there is an interference with competition if the said agreement seems really necessary for the penetration of a new area by an undertaking.

The Court indicated that a detailed analysis of market conditions would be necessary to establish whether an agreement had the

---

[7]   *United States* v. *Arnold, Schwinn et al.*, 388 US 365 (1967).

[8]   *Continental TV* v. *GTE Sylvania*, 433 US 36 (1977).

[9]   *Société Technique Minière* v. *Maschinenbau Ulm GmbH*, S6/65 [1966] ECR 234.

effect of preventing, restricting or distorting competition, which seems to imply a "rule of reason" approach to vertical restraints. Shortly afterwards, the Court appeared to take a somewhat different view in *Consten/Grundig*.[10] Significantly, however, the arrangements in that instance included an absolute ban on parallel imports. It is widely recognised that the Commission and the Court have, over the years, tended to give greater priority to preventing market segmentation than to competition *per se*. In the latter case, the Court indicated that if an exclusive distribution agreement was essential for a supplier to gain access to the market, then it did not infringe Article 85(1). Regulation 1983/83 advances this argument to justify exemption under Article 85(3). If the rationale for permitting such agreements is that they are essential for a new firm to enter the market, can such justification continue to apply after they have become well-established?

In part, the EU approach may have been driven as much by administrative considerations as anything else. The large volume of exclusive distribution agreements notified to the Commission resulted in it being given the power to grant block exemptions to categories of agreements. Thus, in 1967 it introduced a block exemption for exclusive distribution agreements. Administrative convenience is hardly a sound criterion on which to base legal principles. The block exemption was subsequently renewed with some amendments in 1983 and remains in force today. The Commission simultaneously issued a block exemption for exclusive purchasing agreements.

The Competition Authority exclusive distribution category licence follows the EU Commission approach in finding that exclusive distribution agreements are anti-competitive and offend against Section 4(1) "as the supplier's commercial freedom is limited by virtue of the agreement, since he is unable to appoint other distributors, while other distributors are prevented from obtaining the goods for resale from the supplier."[11] The licence also speaks of such arrangements introducing a degree of rigidity into the market. It therefore is closer to a *per se* rather than a rule

---

[10] *Consten and Grundig* v. *Commission* [1966] ECR 299.

[11] Decision No. 144 of 5.11.93.

of reason approach, in contrast with the Authority's general approach. It then, however, goes on to find that such arrangements are generally acceptable. The category licence is arguably subject to the same criticism as the EU block exemption for exclusive distribution — it fails to analyse such agreements on the basis of a rule of reason and errs in licensing agreements that are anti-competitive and not efficiency enhancing. As noted in Chapter 7, the Authority has adopted a less strict approach in the franchise category licence, while its treatment of exclusive purchasing, where it has taken decisions on individual agreements or networks of agreements in particular market sectors, has been clearly based on a case-by-case analysis.

It may be argued that the block exemptions are nevertheless useful to business and advisers in providing a set of clear rules. This may well be achieved at the expense of errors of the second type because they may well permit non-price vertical restraints in circumstances where they are genuinely anti-competitive and have no beneficial effects. Legal certainty, while desirable, is not an end in itself, and competition policy should not permit anti-competitive behaviour in order to achieve legal certainty. The authors would also argue, however, that the wording used in some of the EU block exemptions is vague, raising questions as to how much legal certainty they provide in reality.

A large number of exclusive distribution agreements were notified to the Competition Authority and it granted a category licence for such agreements which was based largely on the EU block exemption. The Authority, however, found that approximately 30 per cent of exclusive distribution agreements notified to it did not satisfy the category licence because they contained one or more of the following restrictions on competition:

1. Absolute territorial protection for the distributor

2. Limitations on the freedom of the distributor to set resale prices

3. Limitations on the freedom of the distributor to choose customers, and

4. Post-termination prohibition on competition by the distributor.

All of these provisions are excluded by the relevant EU regulation. Such a high "failure" rate is an indication either of serious non-adherence to the EU Regulation or that the Regulation is itself rather unclear, in which case, by definition, it cannot be claimed to afford legal certainty.

The dilemma faced by competition authorities in dealing with vertical restraints is well summarised by Tirole (1988: 186):

> Theoretically, the only defensible position on vertical restraints seems to be the rule of reason. Most vertical restraints can increase or decrease welfare, depending on the environment. Legality or illegality *per se* thus seems unwarranted. At the same time, this conclusion puts far too heavy a burden on the antitrust authorities. It seems important for economic theorists to develop a careful classification and operative criteria to determine in which environments certain vertical restraints are likely to lower social welfare.

Nature of Agreements Notified to the Authority

The large number of commercial agreements notified to, and considered by, the Authority since its establishment provides some useful insights on the impact of the legislation. Some further insights are provided by the relatively small number of actions brought under Section 6, as mentioned below. The Authority's decisions relate only to agreements notified to it. One would not *a priori* expect seriously anti-competitive arrangements to be notified to the Authority unless the parties thought that action by a third party in the courts was likely or one of the parties wished to have the agreement declared void.

Between 1 October 1991 and 31 December 1995, 1,312 agreements were notified to the Authority requesting either a certificate or licence. During this period the Authority dealt with 984 of these agreements. The Authority issued certificates to 463 agreements — that is, it decided that they were not anti-competitive. In contrast, only 37 agreements were refused a certificate or licence. However, the picture is more complex than these figures at first suggest.

Just under half of the agreements certified by the Authority were in respect of shop lease agreements, the vast majority in respect of retail outlets in shopping centres. Of the remaining 240 agreements certified by the Authority, 78 required amendment before certification. A reading of the Authority's decisions in such cases indicates that such agreements, as originally notified, were considered not only to be anti-competitive, but not to satisfy the requirements for a licence. Nevertheless, this implies that in total 385 (almost 40 per cent) of the agreements decided upon by the Authority were not anti-competitive to begin with, raising questions as to why they were notified. If the large number of shopping centre notifications are extracted from the total decisions, however, that percentage changes to 21 per cent of agreements decided on.

Up to 31 December 1995, the Authority had dealt with 241 exclusive distribution agreements. Almost 70 per cent of these satisfied the provisions of the Authority's category licence. It has been argued that the Authority should have issued a category licence for such agreements at the very outset. Certainly this might have greatly reduced the number of such agreements notified. As against that, in the absence of any information on the type of agreements that were in existence, it would have been very difficult to frame a category licence. More importantly, almost 12 per cent of exclusive distribution agreements dealt with were only cleared after the agreements had been amended because they originally contained restrictions not permitted by the licence. Another 18 per cent of the exclusive distribution agreements notified to the Authority were withdrawn following the grant of the licence, mainly because they did not satisfy its provisions. Thus, almost 30 per cent of exclusive distribution agreements, as originally notified, did not satisfy the requirements of the category licence and were either amended or withdrawn following the grant of the licence.

In total, around 200 agreements (almost 25 per cent of those decided upon by the Authority) were refused, amended or withdrawn following objections by the Authority. Such a figure goes some way towards contradicting the hypothesis that the low failure rate reflects a lenient approach by the Authority. Equally, the high pass rate reflects the fact that a large proportion of the agreements notified to, and dealt with, by the Authority were genuinely not anti-competitive. The Act, therefore, involved a considerable amount of unnecessary notifications, which represented a burden on business. However, the alternatives, such as, for example, the option of making a prohibition without exemptions, might have resulted in more prolonged uncertainty. The court system might not have dealt with all the issues covered by the Authority in the same timeframe; and the subsequent lack of legal certainty would have resulted in the danger of some firms being inhibited from making agreements which, in fact, were not anti-competitive. Guidelines issued by an enforcement agency could mitigate this effect to some extent.

If a competition law is based on a prohibition system with the possibility of exemption, then some official body is required to perform the task of deciding upon exemptions and there must be a system for notifying agreements to that body. The large number of harmless agreements notified may therefore be an inevitable start-up cost attaching to such a system, although it is probably also attributable to the lack of effective enforcement which reduced the incentive to notify more harmful agreements. The fact that the Authority expended considerable time and effort in dealing with agreements that were not anti-competitive, while it was largely powerless to deal with those that were, obviously raised questions about the effectiveness of the Act and the use of State resources. The Authority observed in its annual report for 1993:

> From the perspective of the Government and the economy generally, the Authority's resources, limited as they are, would probably be better employed in tackling even a small number of seriously anti-competitive agreements rather than issuing formal decisions approving innocuous agreements (Competition Authority, 1993: 13).

To the extent that the refusal decisions of the Authority have caused firms to amend or terminate anti-competitive agreements, then its activities, and the 1991 Competition Act itself, had some beneficial impact on the economy. However, the Authority's lack of enforcement powers meant that it could not ensure that particular practices had been terminated after a refusal decision. Where a refusal decision issued, there was no sanction to require the parties to abandon their offensive agreement, beyond the sanction of the risk of Section 6 action, or unenforceability, which would have applied to the agreement whether notified or not. Perhaps the publication requirements on the Authority might have been considered a risk, if not a sanction, insofar as they made publicly visible the fact of notification and alerted potential litigants to agreements the existence of which they might not otherwise have been aware of. However, it could certainly not be argued that the full benefits of the 1991 Act were realised by way of the notification system.

As an enforcement mechanism, private litigation equally could not be considered to have been particularly successful in the first years of the 1991 Act as relatively few cases were brought. While the number of actions brought under the 1991 Act has obviously increased, it will also be the case that actions brought by private litigants will not necessarily coincide with the practices of greatest harm to the economy. Another relevant consideration is that "persons aggrieved" might well have no realistic possibility of bringing proceedings and might not do so; and that serious abuses could go unchallenged by the private right of action. It is also clear that a more effective enforcement regime was required.

The Competition (Amendment) Act, 1996

The core provisions of the Act give the Competition Authority civil and criminal enforcement powers and create five new criminal offences. There are some general points to be made about the creation of overlapping criminal and civil sanctions for economic wrongs. One is that it is a growing feature of Irish legislation to create criminal offences in new, white-collar areas and give responsibility for their prosecution to bodies other than the Gardaí.[12] Arguably, this operates as a delay on prosecutions since each new prosecutor will have a "running in" or learning period before it will be possible for them to mount successful prosecutions. McDowell (1995) outlines the problems inherent in creating a criminal offence out of a general prohibition. Another specific problem, identified in the context of the Companies Act, 1990 by Murray (1993), is that where there are powers to compel attendance of witnesses, production of documents, and answers to

---

[12] The Companies Act, 1990 being one example.

questions in respect of civil matters, as there are under the Competition Act, 1991, the right to silence may arise, or be invoked, because of the existence of an overlapping criminal sanction, even where the criminal penalty is not being pursued.

Economic theory would suggest that the penalties for breaches of competition rules should be sufficient to deter such behaviour. Firms have clear incentives to infringe the Acts since there are considerable benefits accruing to firms from engaging in anti-competitive behaviour. At the same time, unduly severe penalties could deter firms from engaging in behaviour where there is even the slightest possibility of it being deemed anti-competitive. In the latter case, the legislation will deter many types of behaviour which are not anti-competitive. The optimal penalty is one that achieves an adequate balance between these two extremes.

It is clear that the use of the private, tort-like civil action as a sanction, where damages are calculated so as to put an injured party back in the position they would be in had the injury not been inflicted, would be no threat to deter an economic tort. The offending firm would risk nothing more by behaving to repress competition than it would by letting competition develop. This incentive structure is taken into account in the US provision for the successful plaintiff to be awarded triple damages. However, it has been suggested that even this may underestimate the profitability of some forms of anti-competitive behaviour, and that the measure of damages to be a true deterrent should be a multiple, not of the plaintiff's loss but of the defendant's gain (White, 1993).

It could be argued, in the case of civil enforcement that an injunction would constitute a still less serious sanction than tort damages. The threat of an injunction is not a real disincentive to engage in anti-competitive behaviour. An undertaking that has chosen to carry on a profitable course of conduct which impedes competition has no reason to stop, rather than wait to see whether a High Court action is brought. Arguably, the worst loss of any firm, in the event that the Authority pursues it successfully to an injunction, will be its own legal costs and possibly, but not necessarily, those of the Authority. It will make sense to continue until an injunction is obtained and indeed it will make sense to appeal. Having said that, the absence of a deterrent effect does not prevent the injunction from being a useful instrument for an enforcement agency. Given that for abuse of a dominant position there will sometimes be a fine dividing line between aggressive competitive behaviour and abusive behaviour, where not only the enforcement agency and the dominant firm but also independent economists might legitimately disagree as to whether behaviour is offensive, it is appropriate to have the option of a remedy that is not punitive in nature. An injunction can be an effective remedy for a private litigant in the specific circumstances where they take action to prevent a dominant competitor from blocking their entry or forcing their exit from a market. There is a certain inherent advantage on the side of the non-dominant firm being forced from the market in that, by definition, in most instances the status quo is better preserved by ensuring that it is not removed from the market, and if necessary ultimately paying damages to the dominant firm, than by allowing it to exit from the market, or never enter it, suffering unquantifiable damage.[13]

It is commonplace in the US for successful prosecutions by the state authorities for breaches of the antitrust laws to lead to the filing of cases for damages by affected parties. While it is possible that this would happen in Ireland in some circumstances, it is also easy to anticipate a number of circumstances where there will be no individual, undertaking or group able to act collectively. In the United States, the attorneys general of the individual states have *locus standi* to bring actions for damages on behalf of the citizens of the State, but this is in the nature of an enforcement measure rather than a true action for damages. It does not extend to identifying individual aggrieved consumers and allotting damages between them. It is not, however, easy to construct an Irish equivalent that would not be open to the challenge that it constituted a penal sanction. The same would possibly be true of the US provision for triple damages in private actions. As a separate consideration, an injunction can only be obtained to restrain the specific course of anti-competitive behaviour shown in the

---

[13] See, for example, *Private Research Ltd.* v. *Brosnan and Network Financial Services Ltd.* [1996] 1 ILRM 27; *Donovan* v. *ESB,* High Court, Lardner, J., 2.11.92; and *A&N Pharmacy Ltd.* v. *United Drug Wholesale Ltd.* [1996] 2 ILRM 42.

proceedings. Not unlike the old Restrictive Practices Orders, they can deal with the present offensive conduct, but may not be able to provide for evasive action taken in the future.

On the face of it, therefore, fines would appear to constitute a more effective deterrent to firms engaging in anti-competitive behaviour. However, fines also suffer from certain shortcomings. Presumably it is the firm that would bear the cost of any fines, but as Blair (1985) points out, it is the natural persons who control the firm who take decisions to engage in anti-competitive activity. Managers may have incentives to engage in anti-competitive behaviour if the higher profits accruing from such behaviour have a positive impact on their remuneration. Thus it may be that penalising firms for anti-competitive behaviour may prove a less effective deterrent than sanctions against the individuals responsible for firms' behaviour. Werden and Simon (1987) argue that imprisonment is an appropriate sanction for certain anti-competitive practices such as price fixing. Indeed, individuals may be imprisoned for such activities in the US.

It is necessary that fines be set at a level such that, notwithstanding the difficulty of prosecution, they would still constitute a deterrent. More than any other behaviour defined as criminal, anti-competitive conduct is decided upon purely to maximise profit of a business. In the US, in spite of quite substantial penalties for breaches of the antitrust legislation, some firms have been found to have been repeatedly involved in violations of the antitrust laws. Carlton and Perloff (1990), for example, reported that there were 13 US Department of Justice and three Federal Trade Commission antitrust cases against General Electric and Westinghouse over the 1911–52 period, all of which the authorities essentially won. Yet this would not appear to have discouraged these firms from continuing such behaviour. In part, this may suggest that penalties need to be quite high to deter anti-competitive behaviour. In addition to the level of penalties, deterrence also depends on the likelihood of being apprehended. Posner (1970) has shown that, in the US, price-fixing conspiracies have been more prevalent during periods of lax antitrust enforcement.

Finally, in considering the relative merits of private civil action, state civil action, and state criminal prosecutions, it should perhaps be mentioned that, in the US, actions brought by private parties outnumber state actions, by a multiple of between 5 and 10 (White, 1993); and that it has often been private actions which have given rise to precedents of wider importance. The private civil action may not be a substitute for state enforcement but it can be an adjunct to it with a usefulness which goes beyond the remedy for the individual plaintiff.

As noted, the 1996 Act also provides for the Authority to undertake studies under Section 11 of the 1991 Act on its own initiative, a power that could potentially be a very useful tool in the context of an active enforcement regime. The Office of Fair Trading in the UK has the highly useful power to conduct own-initiative studies in respect of oligopolistic markets, a power that it finds more useful than investigations into specific offences by individual firms.

10

MERGERS

An effective merger control regime is an essential element of competition law and policy. Mergers and acquisitions constitute an integral part of the competitive process, since they provide one mechanism by which the control of assets can be transferred to more efficient management. Merger controls are designed to prevent firms from eliminating competitors by taking them over and achieving a dominant position, which they can later abuse. As noted in Chapter 8, it can frequently prove difficult to control the exercise of market power once it has been acquired. Many of the early US antitrust cases such as *Northern Securities*[1] and *Standard Oil*[2] were concerned with mergers. As Wiedenfeld (1927) noted:

> The substitutability between mergers and cartels as alternative means of securing market power explains the strength of the American merger boom of 1899–1900 in comparison to the British. In the United States the anti-trust legislation of 1890 made cartel agreements more difficult and therefore encouraged mergers.

The Rationale for Mergers
Mergers and takeovers take place for a large number of reasons. Cable (1986), for example, noted that empirical research had failed to develop a single dominant motive for mergers. One motive for mergers is a desire to lessen competition and indeed to establish a dominant if not an outright monopoly position. Scherer and Ross (1990) note that the desire to achieve or strengthen monopoly power played a prominent role in the US horizontal merger wave that took place around the turn of the

---

[1]   *United States* v. *Northern Securities Co. et al.*, 193 US 197 (1904).

[2]   *Standard Oil Company of New Jersey et al.* v. *United States*, 221 US 1 (1911).

century. The *New York Times,* for example, quoted Thomas Edison as stating that the creation of the General Electric Company in 1892 was based on such considerations:

> Recently there has been sharp rivalry between (Thomson-Houston and Edison General Electric), and prices have been cut so that there has been little profit in the manufacture of electrical machinery for anybody. The consolidation of the companies. . . will do away with a competition which has become so sharp that the product of the factories has been worth little more than ordinary hardware (*New York Times*, 21 February 1892).[3]

Merger controls are a precautionary measure. They exist to prevent firms from reducing the degree of competition in the market by eliminating competitors (horizontal mergers), while takeovers of suppliers/customers (vertical mergers) may present an opportunity to deny competitors access to raw materials or distribution outlets. Conglomerate mergers, involving firms in different sectors, may not have a direct effect on competition, but the parent may use profits in one industry to cross-subsidise attempts to dominate another industry.

Mergers also occur for quite legitimate reasons. They may be prompted by a desire to achieve economies of scale or other efficiencies. Economies of scale arise where unit costs are reduced because of an increase in firm size. Production economies may be limited since the merging firms' plants already exist and economies could be more easily achieved by expanding a single plant than by trying to co-ordinate activities in two separate plants post acquisition. However, the merged firm will be able to re-organise its activities, closing the least efficient plants and retaining or even expanding the more efficient units. Mergers can also achieve efficiencies in respect of administration, marketing and other ancillary activities, since the size of such operations in the merged firm may well be less than the combined size of such operations in the two firms prior to the merger. As against this, however, larger firms may well suffer from increased levels of internal bureaucracy, with consequent negative effects on performance.

The analysis of mergers and their effects in many instances

---

[3]　Cited in Scherer and Ross (1990).

tends to focus on the trade-offs between any increase in market power and economies of scale, following the Williamson (1968) "trade-off" model. The model represented a useful and influential means of analysing mergers but suffered from some serious limitations. In particular, it was a static, partial equilibrium model which failed to take account of dynamic effects of mergers on technical progress, investment, growth and other factors. It is worth noting that mergers are not the only factor which affect market concentration and in spite of the merger waves of the 1970s and 1980s, Singh (1993) notes that there was little evidence of increased concentration in either the UK or US. Nevertheless, it is argued that mergers will tend to increase the market power of the merged firm. One school of thought argues that, as there is a body of evidence that mergers have little positive impact (see below), they should be tightly regulated (Fairburn and Kay, 1989).

The alternative approach favours a more *laissez-faire* attitude to mergers and this has influenced policy in the UK and US over the past 15 years. This approach, which is advanced by corporate finance specialists, focuses on the market for corporate control. Mergers and takeovers allow control of assets to be transferred to owners who believe that they will be able to make more productive use of them — that is, they can operate them more profitably than the existing owners and managers. The possibility of a transfer of control is seen as providing an important spur to efficiency in modern business firms which are seen to suffer from a serious principal-agent problem because of the separation of ownership and control. The threat of takeovers provides an important discipline on managements to maximise efficiency since their position is likely to be in doubt in the event of any takeover. Therefore, it is argued that mergers and takeovers can play a useful and important role in increasing efficiency, thereby adding to overall economic welfare. Merger and acquisition activity is likely to be greater in a more dynamic economy where firms are constantly on the look-out for acquisition opportunities. Critics, however, argue that the market for corporate control may not work very efficiently in the real world. It is far easier for a larger firm to take over a smaller one than the other way around, regardless of the relative efficiency of the two firms. Research shows that large inefficient firms are far more likely to survive than smaller more profitable ones, a result which is at variance with the view that mergers encourage efficiency (Singh, 1993). Models of the market for corporate control also assume that share prices are efficient, in that they provide an accurate indicator of the fundamental value of businesses. This is unlikely to be true. The market is characterised by information asymmetries since internal management knows more about the business than anyone on the outside. It is also argued that the threat of takeover can prompt short-term behaviour by management as a means of guarding against takeover, so that the threat of a take-over will not act as a spur to efficiency.

The present chapter focuses primarily on the question of horizontal mergers, since these are more frequently seen to pose problems from a competition perspective than other types of mergers. Nevertheless, it is important to recognise that other types of mergers may also pose problems from a competition perspective. Vertical mergers involve firms integrating into upstream (input) or downstream (final product) markets. Such mergers may be prompted by a desire to block rivals' access to essential raw materials or to block access to retail outlets, forcing competitors to establish their own distribution network, thereby raising their costs. Vertical integration may also reflect the fact that a vertically integrated firm can secure significant economies of scope and can reduce transactions costs. Mergers between firms in different industries would appear less likely to pose a threat to competition, although there may be the risk that the merged firm will use profits in one sector to finance predatory pricing in another. Some commentators argue that reciprocal buying arrangements between various divisions in a conglomerate might also pose a threat to competition. Conglomerate mergers may enable the realisation of firm-level scale economies — for example, large conglomerate firms may face lower capital costs. Such arrangements also offer firms an opportunity of moving into different markets. By so doing, a firm can reduce its dependence on a single market and spread risk. For example, a firm engaged in a product market that is particularly prone to cyclical fluctuations might wish to reduce its exposure to such fluctuations by moving into other product markets.

It is frequently argued in support of mergers in Ireland that only firms that are so large as to be dominant in the domestic market will be capable of competing with larger foreign firms in international markets. On that basis, it is argued that the establishment of dominant firms should be permitted and indeed perhaps encouraged and that domestic competition considerations should be subordinated to the need to promote "national champions". In practice, such arguments are not confined to Ireland. They are frequently advanced in much larger economies. They have been advanced at EU level, on the grounds that Europe needs very large firms to compete with the US and Japan, and in the US and Japan for similar reasons. Baldrige (1985) notes that such arguments were an important factor in causing the decline in antitrust activity against mergers under the Reagan administration. Assuming for the moment that such arguments have some validity, one must wonder, given the small size of the Irish market, whether even a firm that is dominant in Ireland would be large enough to compete at international level.

A merger or take-over may provide a means of preventing company collapse. Scherer and Ross (1990) observe that there are unlikely to be large numbers of such cases, as acquiring firms normally seek healthy acquisition targets. Nevertheless, take-overs of so-called failing firms do occur and frequently such mergers may be permitted even though they might lead to a significant diminution of competition. The failing firm issue has arisen in respect of a number of mergers considered by the Competition Authority. The Authority refused a certificate in IDG/Cooley[4] but accepted the failing-firm argument in Barlo/Veha.[5] In its report on Tribune Newspapers, the majority of the Authority recommended against allowing Independent Newspapers to increase its shareholding in *The Sunday Tribune*, while recognising that there was a distinct risk that this could lead to the closure of that newspaper (Competition Authority, 1992).

---

[4] Competition Authority Decision No. 285 of 25.2.94.

[5] Competition Authority Decision No. 302 of 25.3.94.

Evidence on Merger Outcomes

There has been considerable empirical research into the effects of mergers, indicating that mergers tend to produce mixed results. Magenheim and Mueller (1988), for example, found that, while target-firm shareholders enjoyed short-term gains, shareholders in (normally larger) acquiring firms appeared to lose out over the longer term as the share-price tended to decline following the merger. A study of post-merger company performance by Ravenscraft and Scherer (1987), which covered almost 6,000 US mergers concluded between 1950 and 1976, found that:

> The picture that emerges is a pessimistic one: widespread failure, considerable mediocrity, and occasional successes (Scherer and Ross, 1990: 173).

The study found, for example, that around 47 per cent of acquired business units were subsequently sold off. While these units had enjoyed profits above their industry norms prior to the merger, they recorded negative profits in the year prior to sell-off, indicating a serious decline in performance. In the case of UK mergers, Meeks (1977: 66) concluded that:

> . . . efficiency gains, which in public policy statements have been assumed to be the saving grace of growth by takeover, cannot . . . be relied upon: strong evidence was reported that the efficiency of the typical amalgamation, did not improve after merger . . . it actually appears to have declined.

Arguments that large firms will be better equipped to compete on world markets are undermined by evidence that dominant or monopoly firms frequently prove to be inefficient and thus less capable of competing internationally. Several US studies have contrasted the performance of entities such as US Steel, General Motors and IBM with the likes of Standard Oil and AT&T, which were broken up as a result of antitrust actions. Shepherd (1994: 204) observed that:

> The divestiture that AT&T was forced to accept is widely credited — by AT&T's own top officials as well as most antitrust scholars — with improving its performance.

Ten years after the break-up of AT&T and the decision not to pursue an antitrust action against IBM, the *Wall Street Journal* reported that:

> In October 1982, AT&T and IBM were running neck-and-neck for the honor of being the biggest US stock. The government had just ordered the break-up of AT&T, while leaving giant IBM intact. . . . Ten years later, AT&T's stock has been a winner. Counting the seven Baby Bells, whose shares were distributed to AT&T holders in 1984, AT&T's stockmarket value soared 272 per cent from October 1982 to October 1992. And IBM? Its market value fell 20 per cent (*Wall Street Journal,* 19 November 1992).

Shepherd (1994) concluded that, in the case of both General Motors and IBM, their dominant position simply fostered inefficient behaviour. General Motors was far less efficient than its smaller Japanese rivals and suffered a serious loss of market share once Japanese producers began to compete in the US market. Adams and Brock (1994: 243) found that:

> The presumption that massive corporate size and high market concentration are conducive to good economic performance is no more than that — an a priori assumption unsubstantiated by the facts. To the contrary, the weight of the evidence shows that noncompetitive industry structure breeds noncompetitive industry behaviour, and culminates in noncompetitive performance.

In support of this they also cite the experience of US Steel, GM and IBM. They note how US Steel was created almost overnight by the consolidation of 180 formerly independent plants. The result, they argue, was the creation of an inefficient, technologically-backward firm with a bloated bureaucracy which has suffered large declines in market share and required sustained government protection to survive. In contrast, smaller, independently-owned minimills flourished and are highly profitable. In the case of Europe, Geroski and Jacquemin (1985: 175) concluded that policies of promoting national champions pursued by various EU member states "may have left Europe with a population of sleepy industrial giants who were ill-equipped to meet the challenge of the 1970s and 1980s".

There are domestic examples of dominant firms which are insulated from competition in their home market and not very

successful at competing internationally. Irish Distillers, for example, emerged following a series of mergers during the 1960s. It
was, until relatively recently, the only producer of Irish whiskey.
The bulk of Irish Distillers revenue and profits is generated in the
domestic market.[6] It is also the case that it accounts for only a
small proportion of world whisky consumption. A monopoly of the
domestic market did not help it to make any impact on international markets and it was ultimately acquired by a French drinks
company following an attempted hostile takeover by a combination
of UK firms. Goodman International expanded through a series of
acquisitions in the 1980s. The Dáil had to be recalled to pass special
legislation to prevent its collapse in 1990.

Merger Control in Ireland

Most OECD countries, with greater or lesser degrees of strictness,
control or monitor mergers in some way. There are elements that
recur in most merger jurisdictions, such as thresholds of turnover
or market share below which the control is not applied, political
involvement in keeping the decision-making process with or close
to a Minister, and the involvement of considerations other than
pure competition efficiency criteria, such as broad "public interest" or explicit employment considerations in permitting or
disallowing mergers. In deference to the time sensitivity and
commercial sensitivity of mergers, there is also typically a time
limit on the decision-making body and a guarantee of confidentiality for business secrets. Thus, for example, under the Irish
Act the fact of notification for clearance is not required to be
published by the Minister, although the parties can and do
sometimes choose to do so.

The merger control regime in Ireland comprises two parallel
jurisdictions, the second of which might be described as acciden-
tal, being the capture of mergers by the Competition Act, 1991.
Under the Mergers, Takeovers and Monopolies (Control) Act,
1978, as amended by the Competition Act, 1991, responsibility for
deciding whether or not to permit mergers involving firms above a

---

[6] According to its 1992 Annual Report, 80 per cent of the firm's turnover
was attributable to the Republic of Ireland market.

certain size lies with the Minister for Enterprise and Employment. Over the years, the Department has published relatively little information regarding its assessment of mergers. The 1978 Act operates by making automatically void any transaction within its scope which is not notified. Ireland is unusual, but not unique, among OECD countries in having a merger jurisdiction where notification is a precondition to validity of the transaction.[7] Failure to notify creates an "eternal shadow on title" to the transferred shares. Notification is to the Minister for Enterprise and Employment. The scope of the Act covers all "enterprises", defined as "a person or partnership engaged for profit in the supply or distribution of goods or the provision of services . . .". It is specified that this includes building societies, friendly societies, and credit unions, and it also specifically includes holding companies. This last inclusion is presumably considered necessary on the basis that otherwise a holding company might not appear to be directly "engaged . . . in the supply . . . of goods or . . . services". The definition of service excludes banking services, including trustee savings banks, employment services, and services provided by Local Authorities. There are additional requirements for mergers of banks, building societies, stockbrokers, and insurance companies.

A merger is defined as occurring when "two or more enterprises, at least one of which carries on business in the State, come under common control".[8] Enterprises are deemed to come under common control where one enterprise obtains the right to appoint or remove a majority of the board of the other; or acquires a substantial part of the assets of the other so as to result in the buyer being placed in a position to replace, or substantially to replace the vendor in the business in which the vendor was engaged immediately before the acquisition. They are also deemed to come under common control by acquiring control over voting shares, except where the voting rights are not after the acquisition more than 25 per cent of the total voting rights. There is a popular understanding

---

[7] According to Whish and Wood (1994), who surveyed merger control regimes in 24 OECD countries, notification was a precondition to validity in only Ireland, Germany and Portugal.

[8] s. 1(3) (a).

that this is a white-line point at which a purchase of shares is deemed to be a merger and is caught by the Act, and that, correspondingly, involvement below that point is clearly not caught by the Act. The authors' view is that the deemed control at 25 per cent does not preclude the possibility of a finding of actual control below that level. It is clearly possible for a shareholder holding less than 25 per cent of voting shares to have true control of a company, where, for example, control of the management is given to that shareholder by means of contractual rights. The overall test under s. 1(3) (b) is "if decisions as to how or by whom each (enterprise) shall be managed can be made either by the same person, or by the same group of persons acting in concert" and s. 1(3) (c), deeming control to exist at 25 per cent, is stated to be without prejudice to that paragraph. An interesting comparison is that the EU Merger Regulation[9] applies to mergers defined as the acquiring of "decisive control", and the Merger Control Task Force has found "decisive control" in a number of instances where the shareholding acquired was not itself decisive of control but was supplemented by contractual rights over, for instance, particular commercial decisions[10] or the identity of manager of the company.[11] The Merger Regulation covers, but distinguishes between, takeovers and concentrative joint ventures, and for joint ventures it applies the question of whether there is joint control of the new entity. It has found joint control between a 90 per cent shareholder and 10 per cent shareholder where under the shareholding agreement the latter had the right (which would have constituted this a merger under the Irish Act in any case) to appoint five of 10 board members, and a chairperson with casting vote, but it also took into account a contractual right for the 10 per cent shareholder to veto annual and five-year business plans, material changes in the business of the new entity, and hiring and firing of senior employees. It was also considered relevant that the 10 per cent shareholder had provided the funds, by way of loan, for the

---

[9]   Council Regulation 4064/89 (1990) OJ L257/14.

[10] Volkswagen AG/VAG(UK) Ltd. Case IV/M304 [1993] 4 CMLR 237.

[11] Ericsson/Hewlett-Packard Case IV/M292 [1993] 4 CMLR 300.

90 per cent shareholder to acquire its shares.[12] In CCIE/GTE,[13] the Commission found a 19 per cent shareholder to be exercising sole control where the 81 per cent shareholder had ceded veto rights over all board and shareholder decisions.

The only publishing obligation apart from the obligation to publish Authority reports themselves, is in Section 15 of the Act which states that the Minister must furnish an annual report of the number and nature of investigations undertaken by the Competition Authority. The details of notifications are not made public by the Minister, so it is not possible to know the view of any Minister as to whether, or the extent to which, the 25 per cent operates as a necessary as well as a sufficient condition for common control to exist. Still less is it possible to estimate the extent to which it is relied on as a threshold by advisers, for the purpose of advising against notification. Decisions of the Minister are published only as an annual list of mergers notified and action, if any, taken.

The Act applies to all mergers, as defined, where the value of the gross assets of two of the enterprises involved exceeds £10 million, or the turnover of two enterprises exceeds £20 million. The threshold does not apply to newspapers.[14] This is a recurring theme of many merger regimes, that there is political concern with concentration of firms in the media sector, which goes beyond competition rationale to the view that a diversity of firms in any medium is a good thing in its own right. Since 1991, of the four mergers that have been referred by the Minister for investigation by the Competition Authority under the 1978 Act, as amended, one involved the proposed increase by the Independent Group of its share in the *Sunday Tribune* from 29.9 per cent to over 50 per cent, while another involved the proposed takeover of a cable television company.[15]

The thresholds set in the Act can be changed by order of the

---

[12]   Thomas Cook/LTV/West LB [1992] 5 CMLR 202.

[13]   CCIE/GTE [1992] 5 CMLR 299.

[14]   Mergers Takeovers and Monopolies (Control) Act (Newspapers) Order 1979.

[15]   The proposed takeover did not proceed in this case and the notification was withdrawn.

Minister under Section 2(4), the most recent being the Mergers, Takeovers and Monopolies (Control) Act, 1978 (Section 2) Order 1993. Orders changing the thresholds must be laid before the Dáil. The formula for calculating the threshold is by reference to the gross assets of any two of the companies involved, or the gross turnover of any two companies involved. It should be noted that the method of calculation of turnover on the face of it catches all mergers involving two large companies, even if the two large companies are on the same side of the merger, and the merger is the acquisition of a third, smaller company. However, according to the then Minister, Ruairí Quinn, introducing the Competition Amendment Bill, 1994,[16] the approach "which in practice, has been applied by my Department" was to apply this as a requirement that both sides of a merger, the vendor and the purchaser, were above the threshold level. Both Fine Gael and the Progressive Democrats suggested calculating thresholds by reference to percentage of market share instead of having absolute financial limits. The idea is deployed in a number of countries in combination with financial thresholds, but it is not, except in the case of Austria, used as the sole criterion. The two measures are combined either as alternative or combined requirements for notification. Neither the EU nor the US merger jurisdictions use market share as a test for compulsory notification. One reason for that is that market share is a measure that cannot be taken until a market definition is chosen, and the choice of market definition is an area that is often contentious as between the regulator and regulated. Indeed, the Belgian merger notification threshold, measured by reference to joint turnover and joint market share,[17] is currently criticised on this specific ground (Ysewyn, 1994). It would not provide a white-line test, and where there is an automatic penalty for failure to notify, the authors suggest that it is not appropriate to make the decision to notify dependent on a judgment by the firm or its advisers, which carries a high chance of being different from that of the regulator.

The initial notification to the Minister must be made within

---

[16] Dáil Debates 28.6.94 col. 977.

[17] The Law of 5.8.91 on Protection of Economic Competition.

one month of there having been an offer, capable of acceptance, which would bring the enterprises under common control. The Competition (Amendment) Act, 1996 provides for the first time that the Minister may prescribe fees for notification. The notification obligation is on all enterprises involved, and the criminal sanction for failure to notify applies to all parties to the transaction. The offence is committed by "the person in control of an enterprise failing to notify" or to supply information required, being any officer, or partner or other individual in control of an enterprise. The possible penalties are £1,000 on summary conviction and a £100 daily fine; or, on indictment, £200,000 and a £20,000 daily fine. There is no penalty of imprisonment. No prosecutions have ever been brought.

The procedure under the Act involves fixed time limits for the Minister to make decisions. This is similar to most other jurisdictions, and reflects the recognition that mergers are time-sensitive and may be affected by any delay involved in compliance. The sequence and time limits of a merger notification are as follows. Section 7 provides that the Minister shall "as soon as practicable" inform the enterprises if he or she has decided not to make an order prohibiting the transaction or within 30 days of the commencement of the relevant period — that is, after all relevant information has been supplied — refer the notification to the Authority for investigation. This is not a binding time limit obviously, but it is also made devoid of any significance by the provision of other, specific time limits within which the Minister must take specified steps, in default of which the merger obtains a default permission. The basic limitation period after which a default permission arises is three months. However, the Minister may within the first month require further information and impose a time limit on the parties for its supply, in which case the three months does not start to run until the Minister has received the information requested (s. 6(1)).

These periods compare with a norm of 30 to 60 days among European OECD countries, with the lowest limit of seven days in Canada.[18] There is no public record in Ireland of the time taken

---

[18] There is a choice of modes of notification in Canada, and this limit only applies where a short-form notification may be made.

between notification and decision, although it is possible in some instances to deduce from announcements by firms of their clearances that a decision has been reached in a shorter, and sometimes very much shorter period. In contrast to the detailed criteria which the Authority must take into account if asked to investigate a merger, no criteria are specified for application by the Minister. The Minister may either inform the notifying enterprises that he or she has decided not to make an order or refer the merger to the Authority for investigation after which the Minister may make an order or conditional order under Section 9. None of these has attached to them an explicit obligation to state reasons. The requirement that the Minister publish the reports of the Authority of its investigation into a merger which has been referred to it, results in some increase in transparency.

In a reference to the Authority for investigation the Authority is subject to a time limit set by the Minister but which may not be less than 30 days and is ultimately bounded by the overall time limit of three months. Section 8 requires the Authority to state its opinion as to whether or not the proposed merger or takeover concerned "would be likely to prevent, restrict or distort competition or restrain trade in any goods or services and would be likely to operate against the common good". The Authority is required to give its views on the likely effect of the merger on "the common good in respect of" a large number of areas, some of which are relevant to competition *per se* and some of which are not, but are relevant to other Government policies. Thus the investigation must cover continuity of supplies or services, rationalisation of operations in the interest of greater efficiency, research and development, increased production, access to markets and consumers, all of which would be relevant to an investigation of the effects of the merger on competition.[19] It must also, however, cover "level of employment", regional development, and shareholders, partners, and employees.[20] Merger legislation in many jurisdictions includes a "common good" or "public interest" test. The Minister is obliged to publish the report of the Authority within two months

---

[19] s. 8(2) (a) as substituted by the Competition Act, 1991.

[20] *Ibid.*

of receiving it, "with due regard to commercial confidentiality". The Minister may, after receiving the report, while still within the time limit of three months (and any extension resulting from seeking information), make an order under Section 9. An order may "prohibit a proposed merger . . . either absolutely or except on conditions specified in the order". A conditional order, which is in effect a conditional permission, must be used within 12 months, and it is provided that that will be a condition of any conditional order (s.9(1)(b)). During 1990, a proposed change in control of the Master Meat Group and the proposed acquisition of the entire issued share capital of DJS Meats Limited by Anglo Irish Beef Processors were prohibited subject to conditions (Mergers Report, 1991). After the investigation by the Authority of the proposed increase by the Independent Group of its share holding in the *Sunday Tribune* (see above), the Minister made an Order blocking the proposal. Independent issued proceedings to have the Order quashed which have been served but not further pursued. Ministerial orders must be laid before both Houses of the Oireachtas, where they pass by default, unless resolutions annulling them are made by either House within 21 days. There is a limited appeal to the High Court on a point of law, which can be invoked only within one month of the coming into force of an order by any enterprise referred to in the order.

Under Section 13, Orders may be enforced by the Minister or the Director of Consumer Affairs seeking an injunction in the High Court, or by prosecution. The criminal sanction for breach of an order is £500 on summary conviction with a £100 for each day of continuing default; and £5,000 on indictment, with a fine for continuing default of £500. Unlike the offence of failing to notify, there is also a sanction of imprisonment of six months on summary conviction and two years on indictment. The Director of Consumer Affairs is the authority designated to prosecute summary offences under Section 13. The Director's role under Section 13 now appears anomalous given that the primary responsibility for the Act and other types of prosecutions under it lies with the Minister, but is a remnant from the time when the Director had a wider involvement in the application of competition law.

Analysis of the Operation of the Mergers Act

Figure 10.1 analyses notifications made to the Minister in accordance with the provisions of Section 5 of the 1978 Act as amended. A number of points may be made on the data. Firstly, it is clear that a large number of merger agreements notified do not come within the scope of the Act. Indeed, in recent years the number of non-notifiable agreements has consistently outnumbered the amount of notifiable agreements. The data for the period since the 1978 Act came into force show that around 50 per cent of all notifications made to the Minister were deemed not to be notifiable.[21] The fact that most of the mergers notified to the Minister under the Act are not notifiable raises the obvious question as to why the parties involved attempted to notify them. Notification involves various costs for business. Such costs include legal and other advisors as well as the internal costs, in the form of management and staff time, involved in compiling and preparing information required as part of the notification. Even if the initial notification was not comprehensive, it would still involve costs.

Figure 10.1: Analysis of Mergers Notified under the Mergers Acts

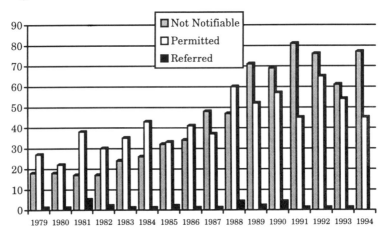

Source: Department of Enterprise and Employment, various years.

---

[21] This includes a small number of notifications that were withdrawn or did not proceed.

The thresholds for notification relate to turnover or value of the assets of the firms involved. This should provide a clear indication to firms of whether or not there was a need to notify a merger. The relatively high level of what are, in effect, unnecessary notifications is therefore puzzling. It may indicate that the penalties for failure to notify, where there is a legitimate requirement to do so, are so severe as to prompt firms to adopt an extremely cautious attitude. The existence of any potential doubt about the transfer of title may well prompt business to adopt a cautious approach on the grounds that it is better to notify in order to be sure. The second feature of the data is the fact that the vast majority of notified mergers are cleared at the first stage of the process — without referral to the Competition Authority. In fact, since 1978, only a handful of all mergers have been referred for a more detailed analysis in accordance with Section 7 of the Act.

As noted above, the Mergers Act does not require the Minister to disclose details of mergers notified or to publish reasons for not referring a merger to the Authority. It could be argued that the fact that such a small number of mergers have been referred indicates a relatively lax approach to merger control with little evidence that many anti-competitive mergers are challenged. Such a conclusion may be mistaken. It is possible, for example, that if the authorities are known to adopt a strict approach to merger control, seriously anti-competitive mergers may simply not be notified, as business recognises that such mergers are unlikely to be approved. Thus, a low referral rate should not automatically be interpreted as indicating a lax approach to merger control. Howe (1995) reported that only a small proportion of mergers which could have been referred to the Monopolies and Mergers Commission (MMC) for detailed scrutiny under the UK legislation were, in fact, referred. Similarly, most notifications under the EU Regulation are cleared following a preliminary examination. Nevertheless, the lack of information and transparency in the operation of the Mergers Act makes it difficult to assess the strictness with which the Act is applied. There has been some increase in transparency in recent years. Section 17(5) of the Competition Act, 1991 provides that, where a merger is referred to the Competition

Authority, the Authority's report must be published by the Minister within two months of receiving it. This at least has the benefit of indicating whether or not the Minister has accepted the advice of the Authority. So far, however, this provision has had only limited effect because, as already noted, very few mergers have been referred to the Authority for investigation by the Minister since the introduction of the 1991 Act.

Mergers and the Competition Act

The position of mergers under the Competition Act is unclear. The Competition Authority stated in Woodchester[22] that it believes that mergers may offend against Section 4(1), and indeed it has found that some mergers actually did offend. In Woodchester, the parties argued that, as this was an agreement which had been notified to, and approved by, the Minister for Industry and Commerce under the Mergers Act, it did not come within the scope of the Competition Act. The Authority stated, in a lengthy decision, that, in its view, a merger was not automatically outside the scope of the Competition Act by virtue of its having been approved under the Mergers Act. It went on to conclude, on the basis of a detailed economic analysis of the relevant markets, that the notified arrangements would not have any appreciable effect on competition, and indeed in some markets could be pro-competitive, and therefore it issued a certificate indicating that the notified agreement did not offend against Section 4(1) of the Competition Act. The Authority's decision was perhaps not that surprising. The FTC (1991a) in its study of Competition Law stated that "mergers and takeovers may be agreements which would be caught by Article 85 if they restrict or distort competition . . .".

The Authority also cited the European Court of Justice decision in *Philip Morris*[23] that the acquisition of shares in a competitor could infringe Article 85(1). The Court decision raised the possibility of Article 85 being applied to mergers but this was never pursued to its logical conclusion under EU law, as the

---

[22] Competition Authority Decision No. 6 of 4.8.92.

[23] *BAT and Reynolds* v. *Commission* Case 142 and 156/84 [1987] ECR 4487.

judgment itself provided the spur for the introduction of the EU Merger Regulation.[24]

The Authority clearly indicated in Woodchester that it did not believe that Section 4(1) was designed to provide a *per se* prohibition of mergers. It indicated that where a merger resulted in a lessening of competition it would, in its view, offend against Section 4(1). The mere reduction in the number of competitors or enlarged market share of the merged entity was not sufficient to establish a lessening of competition. The Authority indicated in Woodchester and subsequently in Scully-Tyrrell[25] that unless the market following the merger was likely to be fairly concentrated it would not regard the merger as offending against Section 4(1) of the Competition Act. Specifically, in the latter decision it indicated that, in the event of a horizontal merger, if the four-firm concentration ratio following a merger was less than 40 per cent it would see no need for any further analysis.[26] Even where the market was found to be concentrated following the merger the Authority indicated that it would not consider the merger to be offensive in the absence of barriers to entry by new firms, or if there was a significant level of competition from imports.

The first merger found to be offensive by the Competition Authority under Section 4 of the Competition Act concerned an agreement whereby Irish Distillers Group agreed to make an offer for the whole of the existing share capital of Cooley Distillery, subject to obtaining valid acceptances for shares representing more than 50 per cent of such issued share capital and to certain other conditions.[27] IDG had been the only producer of Irish whiskey for many years. Cooley was established in 1987 and acquired an alcohol plant owned by a state company, Ceimicí Teo, which was in liquidation. The parties argued that Cooley was in financial difficulties and that it had been for sale at various stages

---

[24]   Regulation No. 4064/89, OJ [1990] L257/14.

[25]   Competition Authority Decision No. 12 of 29.1.93.

[26]   The Authority also indicated that where the data was available it would use the Herfindahl-Hirschman Index to assess the level of market concentration.

[27]   Decision No. 285 of 25.2.94.

since 1991. It was also submitted that Cooley could not survive unless it was purchased by a major international drinks company. IDG expressed concern that the financial difficulties besetting Cooley could lead to the disposal of whiskey stocks which could be sub-standard and that this would damage the image of Irish whiskey overseas, thereby having an adverse effect on IDG itself. The group stated that, in its view, the stock was not suitable for any purpose other than sale as a bulk ingredient product. IDG's stated intention was that the Cooley plant should remain closed. IDG's Chief Executive agreed that IDG did not need and could not use the plant, but wanted to stop anyone else using it. The Authority concluded that the arrangements had the object and the effect of preventing or restricting competition.

The Authority recognised that the situation was complicated by Cooley's financial difficulties. It cited the US Department of Justice Merger Guidelines on the failing firm defence. The Authority concluded that if the arrangements proceeded, any possibility of Cooley becoming a competitor would have been eliminated, while it was unlikely that any other new entrant would emerge. It noted that the acquisition would not result in the retention of the assets within the industry since IDG's stated intention was to close Cooley's production and storage facilities. In the Authority's view, if Cooley were to survive, this would certainly enhance competition in the whiskey market, and it believed that there was a very real possibility that, in the absence of its acquisition by IDG, Cooley would be able to secure distribution deals for a number of major international markets and that such deals would provide additional funding for the company. In the Authority's opinion, there was a reasonable prospect that an overseas drinks producer would be interested in having an Irish whiskey operation within its portfolio of activities and, if IDG were not a potential buyer, Cooley could be acquired by another firm, albeit at a lower price. Indeed the fact that IDG was prepared to pay an inflated price to acquire Cooley and its assets and the fact that among the reasons given by its Chief Executive for doing so was to ensure that no one else could acquire the plant, suggested that IDG at least considered that there was a possibility of Cooley being purchased by someone else.

The only other merger found by the Authority to offend against Section 4(1) *per se* involved an acquisition by David Allen,[28] a firm with a 56 per cent share of the large outdoor-poster market, of a smaller rival.[29] The parties had a combined market share of 64 per cent. The Authority considered that large outdoor advertising posters constituted a distinct product market and the market following the merger would have been highly concentrated, while there was clearly no possibility of competition from imports. The Authority also concluded that it would not be easy for new firms to enter the market. In addition, it noted that since the larger firm had begun to market the poster sites of the smaller firm in conjunction with its own, there was evidence of a significant increase in poster rental prices.

The Authority's approach has been criticised on the grounds that it has created a double jeopardy for mergers, in that even mergers approved by the Minister under the Mergers Act, could be in breach of Section 4(1) and, by implication, Section 5 of the Competition Act. Such an interpretation, if correct means that third parties, notably competitors, could initiate court proceedings to block or possibly unscramble a merger. This clearly results in some degree of uncertainty. Just as it is undesirable for firms to make unnecessary notifications under the Mergers Act, it would appear to be equally undesirable to have a two-stage notification process allied to a risk of private actions. As against this, it is clear that the Authority's views indicate that only very few mergers are likely to be caught by Section 4(1). In addition, in *Cooley*, the proposed merger was below the Mergers Act thresholds and could not have been tackled under the provisions of that Act. The Authority in its published decisions has also shed some light on merger agreements and sets out its reasons for finding them anti-competitive or not as the case may be. Thus, unlike the Mergers Act, there is greater transparency under the Competition Act because of the requirement for the Authority to publish reasons for

---

[28] David Allen/Adsites, Decision No. 381 of 15.12.94.

[29] The Authority has refused certificates to a small number of other mergers on the grounds that the non-compete provisions contained in agreements went beyond what was necessary to secure the transfer of goodwill to the purchaser.

its decisions. The disadvantage is that the requirement to publish decisions with reasons, combined with the Authority's limited resources, means that it cannot always deal with mergers as quickly as business might wish.

The EU Merger Regulation 4064/89

No specific legislative control of mergers existed in the EEC from 1958 until 1989. In Continental Can[30] the Court had held that mergers came within Article 86, where a dominant firm by acquiring another firm would substantially reduce competition. This formulation is more limited than that of the domestic laws of many OECD states, which would typically control the creation as well as the enhancement of a dominant position. The limit on jurisdiction resulted in relatively few mergers being scrutinised by the Commission between 1972 and the date of the Philip Morris[31] case. The decision found that the acquisition by a competitor of a minority shareholding could be considered under Article 85 and would infringe it if the acquisition of control resulted in a restriction of competition. Voluminous academic writing, expressing in equal measure the two opposing views,[32] already exists on the question as to whether this, by logical extension, meant that the Commission could look at full mergers under Article 85. The question was resolved with a political rather than a legal answer when EU Merger Regulation 4064/89[33] was introduced. The Merger Regulation explicitly states that Articles 85 and 86 are not appropriate in their form to deal with mergers. The Regulation is made by reference to Article 235.

The Merger Regulation came into force in 1990. It provides that "whereas . . . concentrations . . . must be welcomed . . ." nonetheless a ". . . concentration which creates or strengthens a position as a result of which effective competition in the common market or a substantial part of it is significantly impeded" will

---

[30] Case 6/72 [1973] ECR 215.

[31] *BAT and Reynolds* v. *Commission* Case 142 and 156/84 [1987] ECR 4487.

[32] See Bos, Stuyck and Wyndck (1992) pp. 69 et seq. for a summary of the discussion.

[33] OJ [1990] L257/14.

infringe the Treaty Rules. It makes a jurisdictional distinction between "durable change in the structure of the undertakings" and the "co-ordination of competitive behaviour of independent undertakings". The latter are co-operative joint ventures and fall to be dealt with under Articles 85 or 86. The former are either traditional mergers, or "concentrative joint ventures". A concentrative joint venture is one that performs "on a lasting basis all the functions of an autonomous economic entity which does not result in the co-ordination of the competitive behaviour of the parties themselves or with the joint venture". The distinction between concentrative and co-operative has been criticised (Hawke and Huser, 1993) as illogical in itself but also as requiring the Merger Task Force to deal with the substantive issues in a merger/joint venture before being able to allocate jurisdiction. The criticism is that a view has to be taken as to whether there will be ongoing co-operation between the parties to the transaction before it is known whether it is to be treated as a concentration or a co-operative joint venture.

The Regulation applies only to mergers where the aggregate worldwide turnover of all the parties involved exceeds ECU 5000 million; and the aggregate Community-wide turnover of each of at least two of the undertakings involved exceeds ECU 250 million. Member States may request the Commission to deal under the Regulation with a merger which falls below the thresholds insofar as the merger creates or strengthens a dominant position in the Member State. The Regulation excludes the jurisdiction of national law for any merger coming within its scope. The consequential amendment to the Irish Mergers Act, 1978 provides that notification to the Commission of a merger coming within the Merger Regulation will satisfy and render unnecessary notification under the Irish Act. Both the European thresholds, and therefore the European jurisdiction, are white-line tests, which, as discussed above, are of greater importance in merger control than in competition control generally.

The Regulation led to the creation of a Merger Task Force within DG IV of the Commission with exclusive responsibility for mergers. As with most national merger control, decisions are to be taken within fixed time limits. The initial investigation must be concluded within one month from notification, or six weeks where a Member State has requested the Commission to take action. It appears that negotiation with the parties can take place during that time if there are changes which could remove the concerns of the Commission, although the legal status, and specifically the enforceability of any undertakings given, as distinct from actual action taken or amendments made, is "unclear" (Bellamy and Child, 1993). After the initial investigation the Commission either proceeds or does not proceed to a more detailed examination. If it does so, it must take a decision within four months of the date of original notification. As with the Mergers Act, if no decision is taken within the time limit, a default permission arises.

George and Jacquemin (1992) note that the Merger Regulation includes no explicit efficiencies defence. It was in an earlier draft but was, they report, dropped on the grounds that it might give the Commission too much power in determining industrial strategy. It is difficult to see what useful role efficiency arguments could play since, under the letter of the Regulation, competition considerations must prevail in the event of a conflict.

Toward a More Rational Treatment of Mergers
Merger regulation is unique in competition regulation in that it is preventative. By contrast with the difficulties of divestment of dominant undertakings, it is comparatively simple to provide a regime for the prior scrutiny of structural changes in markets which detects changes that may restrict competition, while not imposing large compliance costs on business. Bok (1960) argued that merger jurisdiction is one area of competition regulation where legislators can give free rein to the wish for legal certainty (discussed in Chapter 9) by imposing white-line rules. Bok claimed that this is not unfairly arbitrary because there is no particular harm in having a rule that errs on the side of leniency, since the control is a preventative control. In the event of missing a harmful merger, there are other competition laws in place which can control the behaviour of the merged entity. It is equally not particularly harmful to err on the side of strictness in a bright-line test since there are no personal freedoms affected, no divestment of property is involved and there will be alternative business options available for a firm that is able to merge either horizontally

or vertically. It will, that is, most probably also be in a position to expand internally in a horizontal or vertical direction.

From a public policy perspective the rationale for merger control is to identify and, where appropriate, to stop those mergers that would allow a firm to acquire undue market power and thus allow it to affect adversely the interests of consumers, and possibly other firms, and to put the minimum of difficulties in the way of all other mergers. There appears to be a significant number of unnecessary notifications under the Mergers Act. The lack of transparency in the operation of the Act makes it difficult to assess how effectively the legislation is applied. Coupled with this, there is an overlap between the Mergers Act and the Competition Act, 1991, which again may involve some degree of unnecessary notification and which also raises the threat of blocking actions by rivals in the Courts. The authors do not think that there is any evidence of a significant degree of failure to notify mergers under the Mergers Act. The severe penalties involved, which include both an eternal shadow over the transfer of title along with provision for jail terms for company officers, provide a strong incentive to notify.[34] For the first time, the 1994 Report of the Minister for Enterprise and Employment listed the mergers notified to the Minister, which would allow outside parties to establish if a merger had not been notified.

It is difficult to see what could be done to reduce the number of unnecessary notifications under the Mergers Act. The notification thresholds appear relatively straightforward and the Department issues guidelines to firms. If in fact the reason for such notifications is the high penalties for failure to notify, then obviously a relaxation of such penalties might ease this problem, but at a risk of reducing compliance. It is arguable from a public policy perspective that competition should not be the only, or indeed the decisive, factor in deciding whether or not to approve a merger. Nevertheless, the lack of transparency raises some concerns that, on occasion, too little emphasis may be placed on competition considerations. This is particularly true given the lack of strong

---

[34] Murphy (1994) has also suggested that the threat to title may give rise to many unnecessary notifications.

commitment to competition which has traditionally been evident in Ireland. Logic would also suggest that the problem of double notification under both the Mergers and Competition Acts should be resolved.

The present authors' preference is for a system that would require that mergers be notified under the Mergers Act to an independent agency such as the Competition Authority.[35] The Authority would have to decide within 30 days of receipt of all relevant information whether the merger required a detailed examination — the same time period as at present afforded to the Minister for deciding whether or not to make a referral. If it decided that a more detailed examination was required, this would have to be completed within a further 30 days. The Authority could refuse approval to a merger that it considered would lead to a significant lessening of competition. The Authority would be required to announce its decision at both the first and second stage. Given that it is argued that other considerations besides competition should be taken into account when assessing a merger, the final decision would rest with the Minister who could reject the Authority's findings by putting an Order before the Dáil, either permitting or prohibiting a merger contrary to the Authority's recommendations. Any such order would have to be put before the Dáil within 30 days of the announcement of the Authority decision. The aim of this proposal, as already stated, is to increase transparency and ensure that competition considerations are at least fully considered in all merger cases. As it involves the same time limits as under the present arrangements, there is no obvious reason why such a scheme would not deal with legitimate business concerns, while allowing greater transparency.

In addition, mergers should be removed from the scope of Section 4(1). If the Authority were responsible for the initial consideration of mergers under the Mergers Act, the possibility that the parties might try and include anti-competitive arrangements in a merger agreement would be lessened. The proposal by Minister Quinn to amend the Competition Act to exclude mergers from the

---

[35] The authors point out that of course such a task could be discharged by a separate independent agency with sole responsibility for considering mergers.

scope of Section 4(1) would only have excluded the actual merger element, while leaving other aspects of the arrangements within the scope of Section 4(1). It is not clear that such a scheme would have resolved the double notification problem. Under the proposal advanced here, mergers could be excluded totally. Section 5 of the Act should continue to apply as this would guard against the type of situation that emerged in Cooley/Irish Distillers. However, since the Authority has responsibility for enforcement of the Competition Act, the right to take private actions should not be permitted in the case of mergers under Section 5. A similar provision applies under the New Zealand Commerce Act. Such a provision would ensure that, while the Authority could take action where there was a genuine competition concern, business rivals could not initiate court proceedings, perhaps some time after the merger had been completed, in an attempt to inflict harm on the merged firm. Certainly there is evidence that, in the US, private actions were used to hinder proposed mergers. As against that, it may be argued that the penalties for taking unfounded cases in Irish law would act as a considerable deterrent to actions prompted by a desire to harm a competitor, and that private rights of action should be retained in order to guard against cases where there is genuine competitive harm to a third party.

As noted in Chapter 6, in dealing with requests for certificates or licences in the context of notified agreements, the Authority does not proceed to take refusal decisions without first affording the parties an opportunity to amend their agreements in order to satisfy the requirements of Section 4(1) or 4(2). In the context of the scheme proposed above for mergers, it would appear desirable for the Authority to be able to explore with the parties ways of overcoming any concerns that it might have regarding potential adverse implications for competition. Indeed, it would appear desirable if this could be done at either stage of the process. Howe (1995) outlined the benefits of such a "fix-it-first" approach. Generally, this would involve the parties giving binding undertakings. These would usually involve making structural adjustments — for example, agreeing to divest themselves of certain assets within a set period of time in return for approval of the merger. Theoretically, undertakings could apply to future behaviour, but these raise problems of ongoing policing and involve a form of more direct regulation. Obviously, a mechanism would need to be provided to ensure that any undertakings were complied with.

Acquisitions of a shareholding in a competitor below the Mergers Act thresholds should continue to come within the aegis of the Competition Act. This would act to deter firms trying to construct arrangements artificially to avoid antitrust scrutiny. If such arrangements remain subject to the Competition Act, while merger control remains vested with the Minister, there is a related danger of firms tailoring their agreements to come under what they perceive to be the more lenient of the two regimes — that is, forum-shopping. The proposals outlined above would avoid such behaviour.

Conclusions

It is clear that current aspects of the Irish merger control regime are not entirely satisfactory, from the point of view of both competition agencies and business. In the present chapter, we have outlined proposals for an alternative regime which would give more visible recognition to competition issues while retaining to Ministers the right to take the ultimate decision in respect of mergers above a certain size. It might be argued that there is no need for such a far-reaching reform, that the proposals outlined here place too much emphasis on competition considerations. In the authors' opinion, such arguments miss the point. The primary, and indeed in most instances the only, rationale for merger control is a competition one: to protect against the acquisition of excessive market power. In deciding whether or not to allow a merger, other factors arguably should be balanced against the competition considerations. While that is undoubtedly true, there is a need to place greater emphasis on competition in assessing mergers, since a merger regime which does not place considerable weight on competition matters is largely a pointless exercise. Although the Competition Act contains a prohibition on abuse of dominance, such a provision may, as noted in Chapter 8, not be wholly effective. Merger controls are based on the recognition that, on occasion, it is better to prevent a dominant position from being established at all, than to attempt to police it subsequently.

11

INTELLECTUAL PROPERTY

Intellectual property, in all its manifestations, raises complex issues for competition regulation.[1] Intellectual property law protects ownership of intellectual property by affording its owners certain monopoly-type rights. Affording such monopoly rights to owners can have both good and bad effects. As noted below, the protection afforded to intellectual property provides a strong incentive towards innovation and technological progress, which is generally desirable. As against that, intellectual-property owners may abuse their monopoly rights, thereby harming consumers and rivals. The interaction between competition law and intellectual property law thus involves a difficult balancing act.

Patents, copyright and trademarks confer exclusive property rights on their owners but differ in the nature of the protection they provide. Copyright protects original literary, dramatic, musical or artistic work, published or unpublished, by making any unauthorised use a criminal offence. Protection runs for 70 years from the date of death of the creator, or from the date of publication if that is after the creator's death. Patent protection gives novel, non-obvious inventions 20 years' protection from the date of registration, and requires the invention to be published in the Patents Office. There is a form of compulsory licensing in respect of "sleeping" patents which are not implemented by their holder. Trademark registration protects indefinitely the use of a registered mark on specified goods or a specified class of goods. There is no compulsory licensing but trademarks can be removed from the register if there appears to be no bona fide intention to use them.

---

[1] The discussion in this Chapter is intended to be relevant to all forms of intellectual property protected under Irish or EU law.

The Rationale for Statutory Protection

The nature of intellectual property is that using it, unlike with most other goods, does not destroy it; it is a form of public good. No matter how many people "use" a patented invention, or a novel, they do not use it up. Thus, in order to exploit intellectual property commercially, the creator must be able to make it available to users who will pay for it, while simultaneously having some way to exclude some users, and ensuring that paying users cannot simply give it away to others. Laws protecting intellectual property are intended to enable creators and owners to do exactly that. Thus, to some extent, statutory protection is based on a form of economic efficiency argument, balancing the public interest in having access to newly-created intellectual property, with the incentive to creators to create, which is given by allowing them some form of monopoly protection. Protection may also be justified on the grounds that creators have a moral right in respect of their creation, as can be seen in the Continental approach to literary copyright.

It is generally accepted that all creators of intellectual property incur costs in its creation which cannot be recouped without monopoly rights. Firms spend money on research and development in order to develop new products and new ways of doing things. Such expenditure constitutes a sunk cost, as, once it has been incurred, it cannot be recovered. If firms could not recoup the costs of such expenditure, they would have little incentive to engage in R&D activities. The costs of such expenditure can only be recouped if the subsequent price is greater than the post-invention production and marketing costs — there must be some monopoly profits. The same considerations apply to any sole inventor who uses their own unpaid time to invent. In the absence of protection, the rate of invention would be less than the level desired by society. In economic terms, there is a market failure, since the market left to itself would produce a sub-optimal outcome. As noted in Chapter 2, the Austrian viewpoint is that without the possibility of a temporary monopoly, many (perhaps most) products might never exist as it would be in no one's interest to invent them. Thus, the view that the statutory protection of intellectual property rights restricts competition is only valid when considered *ex post* — that is, after time and effort have been expended developing new inventions or creating original work,[2] whereas the correct approach is to consider the position *ex ante*.

> The condemnation of monopolies ought not to extend to patents, by which the originator of an improved process is allowed to enjoy, for a limited period, the exclusive privilege of using his own improvement. This is not making the commodity dear for his benefit, but merely postponing a part of the increased cheapness which the public owe to the inventor, in order to compensate and reward him for the service. That he ought to be both rewarded and compensated for it, will not be denied, and also that if all were at once allowed to avail themselves of his ingenuity, without having shared the labours or the expenses which he had to incur in bringing his idea into a practical shape, either such expenses and labours would be undergone by nobody except the very opulent and very public-spirited persons, or the state must put a value on the service rendered by an inventor, and make him a pecuniary grant (Mill, 1848: 295).

The protections afforded to intellectual property cannot be viewed in purely static terms. Competition is also a dynamic process involving the introduction of new products or services, or new methods of production. It is this innovation which the protection of intellectual property is designed to encourage and foster. Thus, in considering the impact of such protections, it is important to look at both static and dynamic effects. Statutory protection creates both an incentive to innovate, and, in some cases, an obligation to diffuse the innovation. Under different national patent systems, either the first party to invent or the first to file details of an innovation obtains the benefit of any patent. This provides a strong spur to innovation since there is a clear benefit to being first. The publication requirement of patent registration prevents rivals from copying the patented process, but provides them with information regarding product and process developments which may in turn lead to further innovation.

There can of course be innovation without the incentive of statutory protection. Know-how, the knowledge accumulated

---

[2] Of course it could be argued that even in the absence of patent protection, copying a competitor's invention is not costless.

within a business of methods of work or other techniques, is not given any statutory protection in Ireland, but clearly it is of value to producers. The obligations of disclosure associated with patent protection may in some cases have the effect that the protection is not attractive to a creator and a creator may choose not to patent material that would be entitled to registration, treating it instead as know-how.

The Limits of Statutory Protection
The definition of the individual intellectual property rights is, of course, already established by statute in most countries. However, the statutory protections of exclusivity for the creator of intellectual property are not designed to take into account competition considerations. Protection is a fixed 20-year time limit for patents and 70-year time limit, from the death of the creator, for copyright.[3] The statutory periods of protection are not chosen or designed as exactly correlating to the necessary incentive to the inventor. More recently evolved forms of intellectual property, such as plant breeders' rights,[4] attempt a more sophisticated balancing of the public good with the private property rights, by granting different terms of years for the protection of different plants. For most other forms of intellectual property, however, at this initial level of control it is not within the bounds of practical possibility to put in place a mechanism to control the amount of protection granted. Arguably, some patents do not deserve 20 years' protection; arguably, some deserve longer. Not only is it not practically possible to have the grant of rights subject in the first instance to assessment by a tribunal competent to give the necessary level of protection and no more, but if it were possible, it would be self-defeating. The lack of legal certainty prior to a grant would itself be an inhibition to creation or invention. A balance is struck: but it is not a balance which does, or can, refer to the value of, and public interest in, the specific intellectual property protected.

For all forms of intellectual property there is an initial threshold of value in the definition of what can be protected, but that

---

[3]   Patents Act, 1992, Council Directive 93/98/EEC.

[4]   Plant Varieties (Proprietary Rights) Act, 1980.

definition does not necessarily correspond exactly with what one would choose to protect if designing the optimum regime for the encouragement of dynamic competition. Patent protection does provide for the diffusion of ideas by the requirement at the time of patenting to supply a description of the invention, for public registration, sufficiently clear and complete that it can, on the expiry of protection, be carried out by any person skilled in the relevant art. However, the protection is available only for inventions capable of industrial application, which are new and which involve an inventive step.[5] Kingston (1987) argues that the protection of the idea, rather than its implementation, has the result that the mere existence of the idea, or any of its components, in unimplemented form, anywhere in the world, prevents a person who wishes to invest and implement it from obtaining any statutory protection. The requirement that it be beyond the state of the art — that is, that it not be a step obvious to persons skilled in the area — has the result that there is no protection for investment in an idea which is state of the art but which no-one else is exploiting. Obviously, this argument rests on an assumption that there is no incentive to invest without statutory protection, which may not always be the case. Beath et al. (1994) argue that patent protection does not prevent "inventing around" and thus does not in practice give the protection of a monopoly-type right. Because rivals do in fact invent around patents, firms lodge blocking patents and then do not exploit them, resulting in so-called "sleeping patents". The patent laws of some countries, including Ireland[6] require the owners of "sleeping patents" to license them on reasonable terms to other users, recognising both that protection is merited only where society has the benefit of implementation of the protected idea, and that protection may be used anti-competitively. However, the filing of sleeping patents may be innocent of anti-competitive intent. One claim that a dominant firm had filed large numbers of patents to block entry was rejected by the US courts.[7] The defendant, Xerox, had filed over 1,000 patents in a particular

---

[5]   Patents Act, 1992 s. 9(1).

[6]   Patents Act, 1992 s. 70.

[7]   *SCM Corp.* v. *Xerox Corp.*, 645 F.2d 1195, 2nd Cir., (1981).

area by the mid-1970s, but 60–65 per cent of these were not used. Scherer (1981) reported, however, that the plaintiff had a history of failing to have patents registered, indicating that its problems may have reflected poor innovation rather than abusive behaviour by its dominant rival. Patent protection can also have a further effect beyond the 20 years of protection from rivals; at the expiry of the 20-year period, despite the public availability of the patent, the original patentor may have the benefit of a 20-year learning curve, and it may have the benefit of the effect of first-mover advantage.[8]

Copyright, in Ireland and the UK protects an original form of expression of literary or dramatic, musical or other artistic works.[9] In Ireland, this includes mechanical compilations of mundane facts, the property for which protection was asserted in the *Magill* case. There is an argument, considered later, that such compilations do not merit or require the same level of protection as creative works. The possibility of such gradations of protection is recognised in the existing Irish Act in that a lesser level of protection is given to sound recordings, which are subject to a form of compulsory licensing. Burke et al. (1988) argue that car-door designs ought not to have had had copyright protection (as opposed to industrial design protection) in the UK, and that the rationale for copyright protection does not properly apply to that kind of design. The House of Lords found to that effect in *British Leyland* v. *Armstrong Patents*,[10] in holding that the holder of such a copyright would not be permitted to rely on it in such a way as to interfere with consumers obtaining spare parts. The European Commission has in the past appeared to take the view that trademarks do not themselves add any value to goods, which is of benefit to the consumer. It has moved to accepting that trademarks may not add value but are useful to protect and to identify to customers other kinds of added value and quality that customers

---

[8]   Discussed in Chapter 2. There is, however, also some indication that first-mover advantage may not always benefit the first to market innovation; see Tellis and Golder (1996).

[9]   Copyright Act, 1963.

[10]   [1986] AC 577; [1986] 1 All ER 850.

wish to choose. However, it has also expressed the view that trademarks, like other forms of intellectual property and like advertising, can create barriers to entry. The Competition Authority, referring to the Commission decision in Moosehead/Whitbread,[11] considered in the context of non-exclusive trademark licences, that trademarks could have the effect of barriers to entry, although on the facts they did not do so in the markets in which the notified agreements operated.[12]

Part of the premise for statutory protection is that the creation of intellectual property is generally beneficial to the public good. The assumption that intellectual property is always beneficial is subject to the qualification that there will be intellectual property created which has no identifiable useful purpose, and indeed it can be created and used deliberately for anti-competitive purposes. In the particular case of R&D, it is recognised that more is not necessarily better and that there is a tendency to duplication in R&D by competing firms. Galbraith (1970) states, in respect of product diversification generally: "It requires an exercise of imagination to suppose that the taste so expressed originates with the consumer." Dealing more specifically with trademarks, Carlton and Perloff (1990) refer to empirical studies which show consumer preference for branded drugs not to be replicated in blind tests; and to the US Bayer aspirin case, where Bayer was found not to be either qualitatively superior, nor superior as a placebo, to generic aspirin. They report that Bayer, although "relatively expensive", is nonetheless the best-selling form of aspirin, out of 400 forms. They conclude that "...[c]onsumers cannot always tell similar products apart and would not buy one product instead of another in the absence of brandnames." On the other hand, the Federal Trade Commission was unsuccessful in an action brought against the three largest breakfast cereal manufacturing firms in the US, alleging that the firms proliferated varieties

---

[11]   OJ [1990] L100/32 [1991] 391 4 CMLR.

[12]   Old Bushmills/Celtic Glass; Irish Distillers/Celtic Glass/LLEDO/Lough Derg/Tobler Decision No 284 of 7.2.94; Irish Distillers/Mileeven/ Thompson/O'Lionard Decision No. 287 of 25.2.94

of cereals in order to "pack the product space"[13] and thereby make new entry more difficult.[14]

There is a danger in considering the effect on competition of arrangements involving intellectual property that the existence of the statutory right will be taken as a given which must be left out of calculation, and the competition rules applied mechanically around it, to every exercise that goes beyond its scope. Thus, for example, the former EU block exemption for patent licensing[15] did not apply where royalty payments, or any restrictions, were imposed for a period longer than the period of the relevant patent. This is now removed from the block exemption for technology transfer[16] so as to permit payments to be staggered past the date of expiry of statutory protection. The previous approach indicated a view that the statutory protection period must not be extended in any way, including contractual. Arguably, the patent protection period may be a shorter period than the licensor needs, in order to recover the true value from the licensee. The nature of the patent may be that the licensee cannot derive value from it within the arbitrary period of time, and all that is achieved by requiring royalty payments to be made only within the statutory patent protection period is to oblige the licensee to advance capital on the basis of a guess as to future profitability or returns which neither the licensee nor the licensor may want to, or be able to, make accurately. The activities of firms attempting to extend contractual protection so as to fill the gaps in statutory protection give rise to behaviour which can look suspiciously like attempts to restrict competition, although that is not necessarily the intention.

---

[13] The concept of "packing product space" refers not to the abuse of physically filling the space that supermarkets are able to allocate to the product, but rather describes excessive product differentiation so that any new variety is pre-empted. For a discussion on the concept of product space, see Tirole (1988).

[14] In the Matter of Kellogg's et al., 99 FTC 8 (1982). See also Schmalensee (1978) for a more detailed discussion of this case.

[15] Regulation 2349/84, as amended by Regulation 151/93, OJ [1993] L 21/8; and Regulation 556/89, OJ [1989] L61/1 respectively.

[16] Regulation 240/96, OJ 1996 L31/2.

Horizontal Agreements

As discussed in Chapter 2 and passim, economists consider horizontal agreements to be subject to a higher presumption of anti-competitive effect than vertical agreements. Given that intellectual property can be a barrier to entry to a market, a horizontal agreement to share or acquire intellectual property can be highly anti-competitive.[17] Most horizontal agreements which come under scrutiny involve either co-operation in creating new intellectual property, or the acquisition or pooling of existing intellectual property for the purposes of exploiting it at the level of production. There are, however, many valid reasons for licensing.

Patent licensing is a convenient mechanism by which new discoveries can be implemented throughout the world. Transport costs may make it unfeasible for a firm in one country to produce domestically to supply foreign markets. In such circumstances it makes sense for it to license production in other countries. Firms other than the patent holder may be more efficient at exploiting its innovation, in which case it will again make sense for it to license its use to others. According to economic theory, a profit-maximising inventor will be indifferent between being the only seller of a new product and licensing others to sell it, so long as the product market was competitive prior to the invention.[18] Technological developments are cumulative. Thus, company B may develop and patent an improvement on company A's invention. In such circumstances, it would make sense to combine the two. Each firm may, however, choose to block the other. Often, however, holders of complementary patents will agree to cross-license each other. This enables both to achieve state-of-the-art technology. Clearly, it is in the interest of society to allow patent licensing, and such licensing may prove beneficial. At the same time, from a competition viewpoint, vigilance is required to ensure that such arrangements do not result in anti-competitive behaviour. Such cross-licensing agreements have sometimes been used as a mechanism for cartel-type behaviour, either through price fixing or preventing entry. Such practices may result in greater

---

[17] *Tetra-Pak Rausing* v. *Commission* T-51/89 [1991] 4 CMLR 334.

[18] For a discussion of this point, see Carlton and Perloff (1990: 676).

restrictions on competition than would have arisen if each firm
had exploited its own patented technology separately. Patent licensing, apart from being abused, may also simply be used as a
protective colouring for market sharing, as it was in *National
Lead*,[19] to divide markets on the basis of "patents not yet issued
and . . . inventions not yet imagined".

Scherer and Ross (1990) point out that cartelisation through
reciprocal licensing of patents has tended to be treated harshly
under US law. Ordover and Baumol's view (1988) that licensing
should be viewed positively leads them to argue that, in intellectual property licensing, price-fixing may be a rational way for a
licensor, who is an actual or potential competitor of the licensee, to
deal with the situation. This could arise where the licensor is also
in production using the patent, and grants a non-exclusive licence, or where the licensor and licensee are producing in territo-
ries between which there may be scope for arbitrage. This is particularly pertinent within the EU where parallel imports will be
effectively impossible to prevent. The Ordover-Baumol argument
is that if the licensee is free to use the technology in a way damaging to the licensor's interests, the licence may not be granted. If
the licensor can fix the price, they will grant the licence, and fix
the price, rather than the potentially more restrictive option of
fixing the patent licence fee at a level calculated such that the licensee cannot undercut them. Price fixing is marginally less restrictive since the licensee has an incentive to cheat on it. The
authors note that an assumption that a contract will not be enforced, or will be cheated on, is one which may be made in economic theory but which cannot properly be made in applying
competition law. This argument is made within the overall argument of Ordover and Baumol that dynamic competition, from innovation, is very much more important than static competition
(price competition), and that automatic application of rules to protect the latter may inhibit the former.

One unique form of collusion between holders of intellectual
property, which has been found permissible, in limited circumstances, in a number of competition jurisdictions, is the phenome-

---

[19] *United States* v. *National Lead Co.*, 63 F. Supp. 513 (S.D.N.Y. 1945).

non of the copyright collecting society, which is essentially a co-
operation agreement between holders of created intellectual property for the purposes of collective marketing. Because of the nature of copyright music, a comprehensive repertoire of music is a
valuable item to a vast range of customers. Copyright collection
societies have on a number of occasions been the subject of antitrust attention in the US, both at the instigation of the enforcement agencies and by way of private actions by customers of their
product. They have been treated by the US Supreme Court[20] as
rare exceptions to the US *per se* rule on horizontal price fixing, in
the very specific context of an amended consent decree accepted
by ASCAP in 1950 and a consent judgment accepted by BMI in
1966, requiring the Societies not to exclude the possibility of creators negotiating for direct sale to individual users.

In Ireland, the Competition Authority considered the terms on
which creators and publishers assign copyright to the Performing
Rights Society (PRS) for collection of royalties,[21] and refused a
certificate or licence. The collective enforcement of copyright was
found to be offensive, as being co-operation between competitors
(i.e. the creators, *inter se*, and publishers, *inter se*) but licensable
in principle. It would not be possible, or certainly not easy, for users to buy a comprehensive repertoire of music in the absence of a
collecting society. The agreement between creators was therefore
indispensable to the improvement in distribution of that product.
Certain of the restrictions contained in the PRS Rules and Articles of Association were found to be offensive, and not licensable,.
The PRS practice was to refuse to grant back to the member creators the assigned right, so as to permit them to negotiate to license their work to individual users. The Rules also limited to
three-year intervals the opportunity for members to resign from
membership or to divide rights into subdivisions of the full performing right for the world. The Authority stated that these restrictions were not indispensable for the organisation of the collecting

---

[20] *Columbia Broadcasting System Inc.* v. *ASCAP et al.* 620 F 2d 930 (1980)
and 450 US 970 (1981); *Broadcast Music Inc. et al.* v. *Columbia Broadcasting Systems et al.* 441 US (1979).

[21] PRS/creators, Decision No. 326 of 18.5.94.

society, and completely eliminated the possibility of competition between the individual members. Subsequently, the Authority issued a licence for a similar agreement between the Irish Music Rights Organisation (IMRO) and creators and publishers.[22] The agreement was similar to the agreement found unlicensable in PRS/creators,[23] but with the variation that having assigned copyright to the society, the owner could, by agreement with all other owners involved in the same work (for example, the lyricist in agreement with the composer, together with a publisher), require IMRO to license the work back so that the owner(s) could independently negotiate its non-exclusive licence to any user. The Authority found this licensable once it had been amended to reduce the period of notice required by IMRO to two months and amended so that the owner was not required to identify all works and all performers involved, only the time and place of performance. The agreement also differed from the PRS/creators agreement in reducing from three years to one year the intervals at which a creator or owner could leave membership of IMRO and require reassignment of their works. An earlier version of the agreement obliged the owner(s) also to prove that all works to be performed on the occasion would be licensed under the same rule — that is, by their owners and not through IMRO. This provision was not included in the agreement licensed. The Authority had previously found offensive, but licensable,[24] the agreement whereby a number of television companies, such as ITV and the BBC, grant a non-exclusive licence and, using IMRO as an agent, collect royalties from cable TV retransmission companies for the use of their broadcasts. The Authority stated that collective licensing agreements between actual or potential competitors, as here the television companies, were on the face of it restrictive of competition; but because of the number and diversity of copyright interests involved, the collective system was the most efficient method of distribution and as such, licensable.

---

[22] Decision No. 445 of 15.12.95. PRS and IMRO had in the interim separated into two national collecting societies.

[23] Decision No. 326 of 18.5.94.

[24] Decision No. 384 of 16.12.94.

Apart from the unusual case of music copyright, the US and the EU competition regimes both recognise the R&D joint venture as a potentially useful type of horizontal agreement in relation to intellectual property, which can be encouraged, or at least permitted. In many industries, R&D is a very costly activity. As a result, firms will seek to form joint ventures to engage in R&D. Ordover and Baumol (1988) argue that competition policy should generally take a benevolent view of joint ventures, while recognising that there are risks. Baumol (1992) points out that horizontal co-operation may lessen competition in R&D markets themselves, or lead to co-ordinated behaviour in the downstream product market, strengthened by the threat of exclusion from shared information. As Ordover and Baumol (1988: 21) also observe:

> Plainly dominant firms have incentives to induce exit and discourage entry of technologically capable rivals. R&D competition affords plenty of possibilities in this regard.

The European Commission, where it considers the research would not be carried out at all without a particular joint venture, takes the view that the joint venture is inoffensive. Otherwise, R&D joint ventures are permitted, both individually and under a block exemption[25] not only to co-operate on specified research but to impose restrictions on their other research, and to co-operate in production, marketing and distribution. What they may not do, predictably, is fix prices or impose limits on production, share customers or share markets. The essential rationale for exemption, individually or under the block exemption, is the recognition, stated above, that, in practice, firms in competition with one another engage in R&D which is often duplicative, and that a joint venture may have the beneficial effect of eliminating wasteful parallel research.

The US approach to mergers or joint ventures involving intellectual property is a useful illustration of the difficult analysis required by intellectual property. The US DOJ/FTC Merger Guidelines distinguish between markets for innovation and markets for created technology or goods. The US Intellectual Property Guidelines (1993, 3.2.3) consider as a separate market the market

---

[25] Regulation 418/85 and Regulation 151/93.

for innovation where "the capacity for research and development activity that likely will produce innovation in technology is scarce and can be associated with identifiable specialised assets or characteristics of specific firms". This identification of innovation markets is intuitively appealing in that it recognises the difference in nature of intellectual property which has been safely created and can be valued, and the more speculative business of setting out to prospect for something new. As against that, it has been suggested (Addanki, 1995) that it is of limited usefulness, in that no enforcement agency can possibly have enough information to second guess firms as to the R&D that "likely will produce innovation," still less be able to know the effect of permitting or forbidding such a merger or joint venture. Fogt and Gotts (1995) are also critical of the US approach to technology market definition, in the DOJ/FTC Merger Guidelines. The Guidelines, they argue, define markets primarily in terms of substitutability measured in terms of shifts in price; whereas for intellectual property products, which by definition will often be new products, it is unlikely that price data will exist or be easily obtainable.

Vertical Agreements: Licensing

Where the licensor is not an actual or potential competitor of the licensee, the licensing relationship is vertical. As noted earlier, one approach to the consideration of licensing of intellectual property begins from the basis that licensing is better than not licensing from the point of view of the diffusion of the intellectual property for the common good (Ordover and Baumol, 1988). Therefore, they argue, a more benevolent approach should be taken to vertical restrictions in licensing agreements than should be taken to such restraints in the context of the distribution of goods or services. The US Intellectual Property Guidelines state that intellectual property will be treated no differently from other forms of property, but it is clear that this is an indication that it will be treated, as a minimum, no less favourably than goods or services.

The EU exemption for technology transfer[26] is very directly analogous to the block exemptions dealing with vertical restraints

---

[26]   Regulation No. 240/96 OJ (1996) L31/2.

on the purchasing[27] and distribution[28] of goods or services. In the block exemptions, clauses which fix prices or create absolute territorial protection disentitle an agreement to the benefit of the exemption. Korah (1990a) argues that the German authorities, in particular, have tended to be suspicious of intellectual property rights and of restrictive aspects of intellectual property licensing arrangements, and that such thinking has strongly influenced the Commission and possibly the European Court of Justice. However, a progression in the language of the block exemptions is discernible between 1985 and 1996. The previous patent licensing block exemption states that exclusive patent licences as defined in the Regulation are no more than "capable of falling within the scope of Article 85(1)" and that they do not do so:

> ... where they are concerned with the introduction and protection of a new technology in the licensed territory, by reason of the scale of the research which has been undertaken and of the risk that is involved in manufacturing and marketing a product which is unfamiliar to users in the licensed territory at the time the agreement is made.

As expressed, this could be intended as a recognition of dynamic as opposed to static competition, but it can equally be read as an expression of the Treaty aim of forwarding market integration. The previous block exemption for technical know-how[29] and the block exemption for technology transfer[30] both state that the licences defined do not fall under Article 85(1):

> ... where they are concerned with the introduction and protection of a new technology in the licensed territory, by reason of the scale of the research which has been undertaken, and of the increase in the level of competition, in particular interbrand competition, and in the competitiveness of the undertakings concerned resulting from the dissemination of innovation within the Community.

---

[27] Regulation 1984/83 OJ L 1735, 30.6.83, p. 5 amended by OJ L 281 13.10.83, p. 24.

[28] Regulation 1983/83 OJ [1983] L173/1.

[29] Regulation 2349/84, as amended by Regulation 151/93, OJ (1993) L 21/8; and Regulation 556/89, OJ (1989) L61/1 respectively.

[30] OJ (1996) L31/2.

Abuse of a Dominant Position

Apart from the risk of cartel-type behaviour, intellectual property affords scope for abusive behaviour by a dominant firm. Ordover and Baumol (1988) note inventive uses of intellectual property in this way, such as the choice by a dominant firm to alter component standards in order to harm, or with the effect of harming, competing suppliers of such components — for example, where a dominant firm in the markets for cameras and/or film chooses to change the physical design of its cameras so as to make existing substitute films obsolete. Pre-announcements of new-product launches may be a means of deterring consumers from purchasing existing products of smaller rivals. Among the allegations made by Novell, competitors of Microsoft, to the US FTC and Department of Justice investigations in 1994 were that Microsoft intentionally designed its Windows products so that they could not be used with Novell's DR-DOS system.

The distinction evolved in European law between the existence of an intellectual property right and its exercise can sometimes seem to be no more, in the context of vertical licensing agreements, than the distinction between having a statutory intellectual property right, and having additional contractual restrictions imposed on its use by a licensor. What has been startling in the European jurisprudence has been its application to merely having an intellectual property right, and refusing to license it. In Volvo/ Veng,[31] the ECJ held that the mere refusal to license intellectual property is not itself abuse of a dominant position. The idea that it could be combined with other behaviour to add up to an abuse of a dominant position was striking enough in itself, even though the Court on the facts did not impose licensing. The intellectual property in question was that necessary for the manufacturing of spare parts for Volvo cars. The Court suggested that the kind of behaviour, which, taken together with refusing to license, would amount to abuse would be increasing the price for Volvo manufactured spares, refusing to supply manufactured spare parts to independent repairers, or ceasing to manufacture spares for still-current car models.

---

[31] Case 238/87 (1988) ECR 6211, [1989] 4 CMLR 122.

In May 1985, *Magill*, a magazine publisher in Dublin, published a magazine of forward weekly listings of BBC, ITV and RTÉ television programmes. All three television companies moved, successfully, to stop the publication by injunction in the Irish courts as an infringement of their respective copyrights. The practice of the three companies was to publish their own listings separately, either directly or by licensing-related companies, in a one-week format, and they each permitted newspapers to publish a compendium of their listings but only for one day forward and two days at weekends. The products available to consumers, therefore, were non-comprehensive weekly forward listings, or comprehensive listings for one or two days.

Television programme listings are essentially the by-product of the programme production process. Arguably, they are not the sort of original creative work for which copyright protection is normally justified on the basis of the arguments outlined earlier. To the extent that programmers compete for viewers in their primary market, the production of television programmes, it is essential for them to advertise their programme schedules in order to attract viewers. It is not clear, therefore, that television programmers would face little incentive to produce programme listings if such material were not subject to copyright protection. Indeed, the fact that they license daily newspapers to reproduce their schedules free of charge confirms that they have an interest in publicising their programme listings. Thus, the threat of market failure, or lack of incentive for creators, which characterises other areas of copyright would not appear to arise in this case.

Lardner, J. held that the Irish Copyright Act, 1963 did protect mechanical compilations of banal facts and said:

> I am satisfied . . . that (the) arrangements which it is said constitute an abuse . . . are correctly to be attributed to RTE's determination . . . to enforce the copyright given to them in Irish law . . . and to exploit their labour in the preparation of these schedules. . . . If they are to be denied this system securing to themselves first publication . . . they will be deprived of an important element of the substance of their copyright and of the right of first exploitation of their own labour.[32]

---

[32] *RTE and others* v. *Magill and others* [1990] ILRM 534.

The Commission found that the factual and legal monopoly together constituted a dominant position.[33] It further found that
there was a demand from consumers for a comprehensive weekly
forward guide which was not being met, but which would be met if
the licence were granted. It found that the object of the television
companies in refusing to license was to protect their own guides
which did not compete with each other, and that this was a use of
copyright as an instrument of abuse. Thus, it found that the television companies were acting in abuse of their dominant position
in refusing to license.

On appeal, the Court of First Instance (CFI) affirmed the decision of the Commission as to (a) the product markets, (b) the existence of a dominant position in those markets, and (c) the fact of
abuse. The Court stated that it was a matter for the national law
of each Member State to determine the conditions and procedures
under which copyright is protected. It also stated, in apparent
contradiction, that exercise of rights given by national copyright
law can be an abuse of a dominant position when "the copyright is
no longer exercised in a manner which corresponds to its essential
function . . . which is to protect the moral right in the work and
ensure a reward for creative effort". However, mechanical compilations of banal facts are in fact protected under the Irish Copyright Act, 1963. It might be desirable for copyright protection to be
granted only to works which entailed a "creative effort", but that
is not the limiting factor in the Irish Act. It cannot therefore be
said that the "essential function" of the Copyright Act is, in respect of all material protected by it, as described by the CFI.

The Advocate General in his Opinion still recognised the theoretical possibility that a refusal by a copyright owner to license
could, in limited circumstances, be an abuse of a dominant position.

---

[33] The Australian Price Surveillance Authority notes in its survey of book
prices (PSA, 1989) that copyright protects originality of expression, rather
than originality of ideas so that it permits the emergence of a number of
similar products from different sources, i.e. copyright protection does not
necessarily create a monopoly of a product market. Without diverging
into literary appreciation, this will obviously not hold where the form of
expression differentiates the work to the extent that it has no substitute,
but the comment points up the different nature of the monopoly of the
television companies here.

The Court of Justice held that the legal and factual monopoly which RTÉ and ITV had over access to the facts which they compiled to make their copyright work gave them a dominant position.[34] The CFI conclusion, it held, was therefore correct. The CFI had taken into account the fact that there were no substitutes — that is, the refusal to license prevented any competing product from ever coming onto the market. It also took into account that the television companies, at that time, only published forward weekly listing of their own respective programmes; there was therefore no comprehensive forward weekly listing, although there was a reliably predictable consumer demand for such a product. Finally, and it appears now in the light of the tenor of the ECJ judgment most importantly, they took into account the fact that the television companies had monopoly control of the factual information to be compiled. The ECJ reiterated that a mere refusal to license could not constitute an abuse, but that maintaining the monopoly intellectual property right, while not providing the product that consumers wanted, was an abuse.

The significance of the distinction should be noted. If refusal to license could itself be an abuse of a dominant position, then compulsory licensing might be imposed. Unlike compulsory licensing for sleeping patents, compulsory licensing on the basis of Article 86 would not be a predictable component of national legislation. Potentially, the effect on the incentives for creators could be great. However, in *Magill* the necessary component of the dominance of the television companies was their monopoly access to the factual raw material. The facts compiled were not in the public domain but were completely within the control of the television companies. The "facts" being compiled were effectively the policy decisions of the executives of the television companies, as on a yearly and then a monthly and finally weekly basis they worked out their programming schedules. In this case, the "work" of compiling them, which copyright law protects and rewards, is indistinguishable from the necessary recording of the decision. In other words, the programmers would have to compile the material anyway. Just as importantly, they also needed to publicise it in order to attract

---

[34] Case C. 241/91 P of 6.4.95.

viewers. It is not necessary that the material be protected by copyright in order to provide the necessary incentive for the programmers to compile and publish it.

A similar value judgment, as to what merits absolute protection as distinct from protection subject to compulsory licensing, is made in the proposed European Commission directive on database copyright.[35] This proposes the creation of an EU protection for the compilation on a database of material that is not itself in copyright — for example, the compilation of a street directory. Where the compilation itself, by reason of its selection or arrangement, constitutes the author's own intellectual creation, the draft directive would give it the protection of database copyright. Where the compilation does not evince intellectual creation in its selection or arrangement, the draft directive would only protect such a compilation to the extent of prohibiting unauthorised extraction. Such a compilation may be made subject to a compulsory licence, entitling extraction and re-use of the material for commercial use, subject to a fee. It is suggested that there can be a situation where the author falls short of the draft directive threshold of "intellectual creation", but satisfies the requirement of the Copyright Act, 1963 for "originality", which is no more than a requirement that the author not have copied the compilation from any other person. Indeed, the facts of *Magill* might be considered to be exactly that. The two different levels of protection proposed in the draft directive are perhaps a more fine-tuned recognition of the relative incentives required by creativity, on the one hand, and "sweat of the brow" on the other, than was possible within the particular facts of the *Magill* case.

The judgment should perhaps also be considered in the light of the essential facilities doctrine.[36] Denying a competitor access to an essential facility, defined as a facility the use of which is essential for the competitor to operate in a market, can be an abuse of a dominant position. Under the essential facilities doctrine, the owner of an essential facility must make it available to competitors although the owner is entitled to be remunerated for granting

---

[35] OJ C 308 of 15.11.93.

[36] See Chapter 2.

such access. The question of the appropriate charge for such use is itself a complex and interesting one, and is considered further in Chapter 13 in the context of vertically integrated utilities. There is, however, a more fundamental question about the application of the essential facilities doctrine to intellectual property, which is that compulsory access changes the incentives to invest in creation in a way that regulators cannot easily predict.

National Laws and Parallel Imports

Apart from problems in the nature of intellectual property as subject to externalities, there is a problem peculiar at the moment to the EU, as the only operating supranational competition regime, that its competition rules must interact with intellectual property rights which are created on a national basis. By definition, national intellectual property rights include within them the right to block importation into that country of any products containing or using the same intellectual property. Normally such provisions would prevent parallel imports of such products — for example, books and musical recordings — thereby segmenting national markets. The way in which the Commission and the European Courts have dealt with this is discussed briefly below. Although it is only in the EU that there is a regime with legal competence to deal with intellectual property rights as barriers to importation, obviously the same effect operates between all non-EU countries and between Member States and third countries as a restraint on competition from imports.[37] Within the General Agreement on Tariffs and Trade (GATT), the TRIPS agreement (on trade-related aspects of intellectual property) involved discussions of the principle of exhaustion of rights but, occupied by its primary task of achieving international agreement to a minimum standard of protection of intellectual property in all countries, it was obliged to leave the secondary issue unresolved for the time being. International agreement in TRIPS to the principles of national treatment (States shall give the nationals of other

---

[37] The Australian Prices Surveillance Authority recommended in a series of reports that provisions of the Copyright Act, 1968 preventing parallel imports of books, sound recordings and computer software should be removed (PSA, 1989, 1990 and 1992).

countries the minimum protections set out in the Agreement) and the "most favoured nation" principle (States shall give non-nationals the same protection given to nationals, and to nationals of any other State) impinge upon the EU exhaustion of rights approach to the extent that the EU may apply it only on the same non-discriminatory basis.

The EU general approach to intellectual property licensing is very much shaped by the fact that intellectual property rights add an extra facet of difficulty to the integration of the single market. The Community law has evolved ways of overcoming this effect in the doctrines of exhaustion of rights and of common origin. It is not intended here to discuss these rules in their full complexity.[38] Both doctrines involve the development by the European Court of Justice of a distinction between the existence of an intellectual property right and its exercise. Thus, although the "essential subject matter" of the national intellectual property right could not give rise to a breach of Article 85, the exercise of the right could. The doctrine did not grow unaided out of Articles 85 and 86, but rather out of the free movement of goods provisions, Articles 30 and 37. The doctrine of exhaustion of rights, first born in *Deutsche Grammophon GmbH* v. *Metro-SB-Grossmarkte*,[39] is that where an intellectual property owner, or a person deriving title from the owner, puts goods on the market in any Member State, they may not rely on a national intellectual property right in another Member State to prevent the importation of the goods into the second country. The doctrine of common origin, created in the *Hag* cases, I and II,[40] and also more in the context of Articles 30 and 37 than 85 and 86, is that where intellectual property rights are owned in different Member States by different persons, but the rights derive from a common origin, one right may not be used to resist the importation of goods containing the other right. The significance of the two doctrines is that having been born, as it were, out of the Rome Treaty goal of market integration, they

---

[38] They are dealt with in detail in, for example, Rothnie (1993).

[39] Case 78/70 [1971] ECR 487; [1971] CMLR 631.

[40] *Van Zuylen* v. *Hag* (192/73) [1974] ECR 731 [1974] CMLR 127; *CNL-SUCAL* v. *Hag* GF AG (C-10/89) [1990] I ECR 3711, [1990] 3 CMLR 571.

have cross-pollinated into the inter-related competition goal of Articles 85 and 86, so as now to affect consideration of competition issues even where the effect on inter-State trade is no more than notional. The authors suggest that while the distinction between existence and exercise of an intellectual property right could, of course, evolve spontaneously out of national competition law, the existence of the European jurisprudence might be expected to be relevant to its evolution in the context of the Competition Act.

12

REGULATION VERSUS COMPETITION

Competition policy does not work in a vacuum. In all developed
economies, governments intervene in the economy in all sorts of
ways. Ireland is no exception in this regard. Business activity is
subject to a whole raft of statutorily imposed regulations, covering
such diverse matters as pub opening hours, restrictions on advertising and employment conditions. Regulations may be deliberately designed to restrict competition or may be the result of a
belief that competition is undesirable in particular sectors. Such
views were more common in the past than today. Anti-competitive
regulations may be imposed in response to lobbying by vested interests, or restrictions on competition may be an unintended side
effect of regulation. Nevertheless, the fact that regulations restrict
competition confers considerable benefits on incumbent firms in
regulated sectors. This may frequently result in such firms favouring the retention of the existing regulatory *status quo*, long
after the original rationale for regulation has ceased to apply. As
noted in Chapter 2, one of the most effective ways to establish or
maintain a monopoly is to pressure government to enact legislation. Galbraith (1987) notes how the English Parliament passed
the Statute of Monopolies in 1623–4 to curb the fairly common
royal practice of granting monopoly rights to producers of goods of
all sorts. The adverse effects of many regulatory regimes on competition was highlighted in the Culliton Report. The Government
responded by stating that it:

> . . . accepts these recommendations and has mandated the De-
> partment of Enterprise and Employment to examine a number of
> areas, including sheltered or not-traded services, where controls.
> restrictions, licences or other limitations inhibit the creation of a
> competitive environment (*Employment through Enterprise*: 43).

The present chapter begins by looking at the economic arguments
for and against regulation. It then considers a number of specific

areas where regulation has an adverse effect on competition and asks whether such restrictions are justified, and whether legitimate regulatory objectives could be achieved in a less restrictive fashion. Where they have been introduced, regulatory reforms which have permitted greater competition have proven to be beneficial to consumers and to the overall economy.

The Case for Intervention — Market Failure
Governments intervene in the workings of the market in various ways for all sorts of reasons. Commenting on the reasons for such intervention, Scherer and Ross (1990: 9) note that "the list of justifications, plausible and not so, could be proliferated almost without end".

Peltzman (1989) notes that until the 1960s economists regarded market failure as the motivating primary rationale for government regulation. It is recognised that, on occasion, markets may fail but there is some disagreement about the extent to which market failure occurs. Market failure may arise because of information asymmetries or the existence of externalities. Information asymmetries arise when consumers do not have adequate information regarding products. Regulation may be justified in such circumstances to protect consumers from being exploited by producers who have far more information concerning the product in question. For example, it is not easy for consumers, or their doctors, to obtain adequate information regarding drugs and medicines. Suppliers have an incentive to be somewhat economical in the information they provide given their desire to maximise profits. Externalities arise where the private and social costs of production diverge. The example most commonly used in economics textbooks is environmental pollution. Pollution imposes a cost on society as a whole rather than the individual polluter.

Regulatory Failure
More recently, there has been a growing recognition in the economics literature of what may best be described as "government failure" (see, for example, Stiglitz, 1990). This recognises that governments can make mistakes and set inappropriate policy objectives or choose inappropriate means of achieving their objectives.

Regulation frequently imposes unintended costs, thereby altering incentives and producing results that may be quite different from what was originally intended. In addition, regulation has a tendency to favour particular types of activity and thus benefit certain sectors of the community at the expense of others. It needs to be borne in mind that restrictions on competition primarily benefit the suppliers of goods and services in the protected market sector, at the expense of the consumer and the economy as a whole.

> Regulation may also take place because, even though markets are working well, those who have political power are displeased with the results, or they may consider some good or service to be too important to be priced and allocated by unfettered market processes (Scherer and Ross, 1990: 9).

The essential message to emerge from developments in the economics literature on regulation over the past 20 years is that private market failure may not, of itself, constitute a sufficient justification for state intervention. Rather, it needs to be established that such intervention will actually lead to a better outcome than that produced by the market and, where it is justified on such grounds, the preferred option is that which imposes least cost. This is not a totally new idea. Pigou (1924) observed that:

> It is not sufficient to contrast the imperfect adjustments of unfettered private enterprise with the best adjustment that economists in their studies can imagine. For we cannot expect that any State authority will attain, or even whole-heartedly seek that ideal. Such authorities are liable alike to ignorance, to sectional pressures and to personal corruption by private interest. A loud-voiced part of their constituents, if organised for votes, may easily outweigh the whole.

Such theoretical developments have resulted in a re-appraisal of regulatory frameworks in many developed economies since the early 1980s. This re-appraisal has resulted in the easing of regulations in many areas of economic activity with market forces being given a freer rein. Although this process has generally been referred to as deregulation, this is not a wholly accurate description of the process. Rather than simply abolishing regulations entirely, the process in most countries has involved a reform of the regulatory framework, with a greater emphasis being placed on market forces.

Licensing

Licensing is a frequently chosen method of regulation. Classically, it consists of criminalising an existing field of activity, permitting access back into it with a licence and setting criteria for the grant of the licence. There will usually be qualitative criteria, relating to the perceived mischief or danger that the licensing is intended to control. A commonly used criterion is fitness to undertake the particular business. Quantitative criteria may be imposed as well. The reasons for wanting to control sectors in this particular way are as various as the reasons discussed above for wanting to regulate any industry, but licensing as a mechanism deserves consideration in its own right because it provides useful illustrations of the adverse effects of regulation. Licensing often favours the incumbents at the time the licensing scheme is introduced, is in itself inhibiting of new entry, and is a continuing distortion of the field of activity in question. Specific examples include public houses, passenger road transport and professional services, which are dealt with in this chapter.

Hogan and Morgan (1991) note that licensing as a form of control is not intended to operate anti-competitively, and that the presumption is that licensing is on a qualitative and not quantitative basis unless otherwise specified in the enabling legislation. However, the evidence is that any licensing system contains the danger of operating as an interruption and distortion of competition which extends beyond the effect of removing unlicensed competitors from the market. The introduction of a licensing system inevitably favours incumbents in the market. Sometimes it is designed to do so, as where there is provision for incumbents who have been in the relevant area of activity for a specified period of time to be licensed automatically, or on a more favourable basis than new entrants. This may correspond with an explicit aim of the licensing regime, as where it is intended to ensure a level of qualification in the interests of public safety and experience is accepted as a substitute, perhaps during a transition period, for an academic qualification. On the other hand, it may not correspond to an explicit aim, or be explicit in the licensing regime, but it may simply be the case that incumbents are already in a better position than new entrants to comply with licensing criteria. This may be an inevitable result of the introduction of licensing into a sphere where it did not previously exist, but it may also nonetheless inhibit new and competent entry, and that may be detrimental to the sector in question. New entry may also be stultified by a perception by the licensing body that only the incumbents are or can be competent to be licensed:

> (T)he officials in the Department considered that the establishment of the MMDS system was a logical extension of the existing cable system and that the existing cable operators would be in the best position to provide an early service.[1]

And, therefore, those existing operators should be invited to apply for authorisation.

There is another kind of entry barrier with licensing which is that where proof of fitness, necessarily amounting to proof of experience, in the licensed field is a component of the criteria for a licence (as it is, for example, for pub licences and professional services) entry is not only costly but is to some extent under the informal control of incumbents in their decisions to accept trainees. This is not a high barrier to entry in some situations. The authors are not seriously suggesting that publicans, in choosing their bar staff, are consciously and effectively screening potential new applicants for pub licences. It is, however, suggested that, where entry into a sector is dependent on the co-operation of the incumbents, a culture is created in which new entrants are less likely to want to disturb any status quo. Intuition also suggests that all entrants who have overcome barriers to entry have an incentive not to see subsequent new entrants incur less cost than themselves.

Moore (1961) criticises the traditional rationales for licensing regimes in those areas of commerce where the customer is considered to be unable to conduct a search for a qualified provider of the service, either because of lack of competence to evaluate the

---

[1]   *Carrigaline Community Television Ltd. and Gabriel Hurley* v. *Minister for Transport Energy and Communication and others*, unreported, High Court, Keane J., 10.11.95.

qualification of practitioners or because the service is used rarely and search costs would be disproportionate. This, for example, is the rationale for maintaining registers of practitioners of specific professions, as discussed below, such as medicine, dentistry or veterinary medicine where unqualified exponents would be a public danger. In a sense, the consumer search is undertaken by the State instead and search costs borne by the licensed sector, and ultimately spread back over its customers. Moore's criticism is that inevitably the licensing cost becomes a cost of entry to the sector, inhibiting new entry.

A licensing system may also give licensed incumbents an extra weapon with which to fend off potential new entrants. It appears often to be the case that there is perceived to be a property right in the licence, or rather, by a process of osmosis, a perception of a property right in the exclusivity of the licence, as has occurred, for example, in practice in relation to taxis. Where there is a criminal sanction created by the enabling legislation, the incumbents may seek to have it invoked. There may also be, in some form, a right for the licensed competitors to take civil action in their own right for injunctive relief against any unlicensed operators. The idea of a private right of action arising out of the mere creation of a licensing scheme was rejected, in the context of passenger road transport, where the plaintiff "being apprehensive of the impact the defendants' competition would have on her business" sought an injunction restraining their unlicensed operation on the grounds, inter alia:

> . . . that the Road Transport Acts were passed not merely for the benefit of the public at large but for the protection of those to whom passenger carriage licences were granted against uncontrolled competition from unauthorised operators who were not subject to any of the conditions imposed under the Acts on licensees for the safeguarding of the interests of the public.

It was held that the Acts did not themselves create a right of civil action for the class of persons who were licence holders.[2] However, the plaintiff was able to enforce the Acts against the unlicensed

---

[2] *Parsons* v. *Kavanagh* [1990] ILRM 561.

competitor in reliance on the principle that the Constitutional right to earn a livelihood extends to a right to be protected from unlawful competition with that livelihood. The decision did not involve any consideration of whether the unlicensed operator was in fact a source of the dangers the Act was intended to prevent. In May 1996, the members of the Consultative Committee of Accountancy Bodies, Ireland, which represents the main accountancy bodies authorised by the Department for Enterprise and Employment to undertake auditing work under the Companies Acts, began judicial review proceedings of a decision by the Minister to add the Institute of Incorporated Public Accountants to the authorised category. In *O'Connor and others* v. *Williams and others*,[3] a group of Limerick taxi drivers brought proceedings to enforce against rival hackney drivers the provisions of the Road Traffic (Public Service Vehicles) Regulations, 1963 and 1983, prohibiting the use of radios other than by taxis. Judge Barron found that since, in this instance, the criminal sanctions in the Regulations were effective and were capable of being invoked, the plaintiffs did not have the *locus standi* of the plaintiff in *Parsons* v. *Kavanagh*. The incentive for incumbents to use the licensing system as a barrier to entry is obvious. In *Carrigaline*,[4] it appears from the judgment that the Department of Transport Energy and Communication was heavily lobbied by the cable companies to bring prosecutions and seize equipment. The incumbents asserted economic loss from the activities of the unlicensed operators, which on examination the Court found to be unfounded.

In *Carrigaline*, the Department wished to encourage incumbents to provide national television coverage, so that a Government objective of coverage for four national television channels, when those came into existence, might be achieved. The fulfilment of a State objective, by private investment, may be a valid component in a licensing decision, but where it exists, it ought to be transparent. The then Minister wrote to one of the cable operators:

---

[3]   High Court, unreported, Barron J., 15.5.96.

[4]   *Carrigaline Community Television Ltd. and Gabriel Hurley* v. *Minister for Transport Energy and Communication and others*, op. cit.

> You were invited to apply for exclusive franchises and it is accepted that no further licences for (other forms of retransmission) within or throughout your franchise regions will be granted for the duration of your ... licences ... my Department will apply the full rigours of the law to illegal operations affecting that franchise region. . . . Once the . . . systems are established . . . licensees may apply for a renewal of the ten-year agreement period. . . . I should say that I do not see changes of franchise being made simply for the sake of change.[5]

It is noted, in relation to the last assurance given in the above quotation that, where there is a compelling reason for exclusive licensing, as, for example, for true natural monopolies, competition for licences at regular intervals is considered to be valuable in itself as a surrogate form of competition, in the absence of competition for the actual service.

In *O'Neill* v. *Minister for Agriculture*[6] the system for licensing of artificial insemination services under the 1947 Livestock (Artificial Insemination) Act and 1948 Regulations was challenged as, inter alia, in breach of Article 90 of the Rome Treaty in creating a collective dominant position for the licensed Societies. It was argued that it was not necessary for the stated aims of the licensing system to create a closed monopoly system. The argument was rejected at the High Court but the case is under appeal. Without suggesting that all, or any, of the numerous other licensing powers of Ministers are subject to challenge under Article 90 as being restrictive of competition, or that a geographical monopoly provision might not be justified for any one of a number of reasons, it may be that one appeal of monopoly for an administrator is that it simplifies the task of monitoring compliance with licence criteria. The restriction on competition produced by regulation may be inadvertent; it may be unnecessary; and it may never have been part of the consideration in the framing of the licence system.

Every decision to introduce licensing potentially contains one or more of the costs or distortions referred to here. One option

---

[5] *Ibid.*

[6] High Court, unreported, Budd, J., 5.7.95.

suggested by Moore (1961) is that where the rationale for licensing is lack of consumer information as to qualifications of the operators in the sector, certification is a less distorting mechanism. By certification, he means a system of public certification of the qualifications that would be thought necessary under a licensing system. There would then be no prohibition on uncertified practitioners also competing, an option also referred to as registration of title (as opposed to registration of function). This removes the inhibiting effect on entry of qualification, the use by incumbents of the licensing legislation as a barrier both civil and criminal; and avoids the danger of taking away from consumers a choice they might wish to make, of cheap and possibly risky goods or services, rather than expensive and safe ones. There are some areas at least where such proposals would appear to be appropriate.

Professional Services

In many countries, competition regulation has not until recently addressed itself to competition in professional services. Some competition laws have been made explicitly inapplicable to professional services, and some have not in practice been applied. The reasons, like the reasons for interference with markets for goods and non-professional services, range from being well-founded in reasons of maintenance of standards of quality and consumer protection, to being simply mistaken. It is common in many countries for professions to be self-regulating, and for that self-regulation to become elevated to the level of statutory control of the profession, thus removing it, to a greater or lesser extent, from the general competition law. As stated above, one reason for the failure of legislators to apply competition law to professions in the same way as to other services has been the recognition of the asymmetry of information between professions and their clients. This rationale is used to justify having the profession itself control entry, have a monopoly of training, control use of a professional title or hierarchy of titles, set maximum or minimum fees, restrict the form of legal personality under which a member of the profession may carry on business, prohibit carrying on business in partnership with non-members of the profession, prohibit or limit the delegation of work to para-professionals or control advertising.

Any of these might be justifiable in itself; what is relevant from the point of view of competition in a profession is that they may also be an effective means of reducing or eliminating competition between members, and reducing the entry by new competitors which would otherwise occur.

In countries where professions have been subject in the ordinary course to competition law, some of the above recurring features of professional self-regulation have been found to be restrictive of competition and not justified by reference to consumer protection or upholding of ethical standards. The US Supreme Court held in 1975 that the Sherman Act contained no exclusion for professions[7] and subsequently found offensive an agreement by a professional body for engineers not to compete on price before a client had selected between engineers for a project.[8] The rationale for the agreement was the danger of cost cutting, which, it was argued, would lead to inferior and perhaps dangerous design work. This was rejected on the basis that the risk of that result was small in comparison to the harmful effect of the absence of price competition:

> We may assume that competition is not entirely conducive to ethical behaviour but that is not a reason . . . for doing away with competition.[9]

The argument will be recognised as one made by many professions for many forms of self-regulation. In Australia, where the federal competition law had in the past not been applied to professions that were regulated at state level, the Hilmer Report (1993) recommended that that anomaly be removed by the enactment by each of the states of a competition law replicating the provisions of the federal law. It also recommended that where state law exempts any practice from competition law it should state explicitly that it is doing so. A report by the Australian Trade Practices Commission (1994) found that competition in legal services had been restricted by a combination of rules of the

---

[7]   *Goldfarb* v. *Virginia State Bar*, 421 US 773 (1975).

[8]   *National Society of Professional Engineers* v. *US*, 435 US 679 (1978).

[9]   *Ibid.*

professional bodies and statute. It recommended the removal of fee scales and of restrictions on some legal services being provided by non-lawyers. In Canada, the Ontario Supreme Court in 1988 found agreements by two law associations on fees and fee scales offensive and prohibited communications between practitioners on client fees. The Danish Competition Council (1991/92) undertook a study of the liberal professions and subsequently entered negotiations with professional associations to have changes made to rules they found restrictive of competition and not justified by the benefits attributed to them (*ibid.*). They found each one of the types of control described above to be potentially restrictive of competition. In Ireland, the Restrictive Practices Commission (RPC) undertook enquiries at the request of the then Minister into restrictions on conveyancing and advertising by solicitors (RPC, 1982), fixing of fees and advertising restrictions in accountancy (RPC, 1987a) and in engineering (RPC, 1987b), and a report on restrictive practices in the legal profession (FTC, 1990).

The significance of placing the self-regulation of a profession on a statutory basis is that it may, depending on the form of the institutionalisation, take it outside the scope of the general competition law. In Ireland, the Competition Act, 1991 applies to "decisions of associations of undertakings" and to agreements between undertakings. There is no exemption from the Act for professional services, so that the rules of professional bodies are subject to the Competition Act, except to the extent that they may have been replicated by or given the force of statute. Examples of statutory adoption of professional self-regulation would include solicitors,[10] accountants,[11] nurses,[12] medical doctors,[13] veterinary surgeons,[14] dentists,[15] engineers,[16] pharmacists[17]

---

[10] Solicitors Acts, 1954 to 1994.

[11] Royal Charter of Incorporation 1888 and Institute of Chartered Accountants in Ireland (Charter Amendment) Act, 1966.

[12] Nurses Act, 1985.

[13] Medical Practitioners Act, 1978.

[14] Veterinary Surgeons Acts, 1931, 1952, and 1960.

[15] Dentists Act, 1985.

[16] Institution of Civil Engineers of Ireland (Charter Amendment) Act, 1969.

and optometrists.[18] The level of statutory adoption differs from one profession to another. In some instances, all that is authorised is the existence of a professional body to carry out specific statutory functions such as the maintenance of a register of qualified persons, in which case other decisions of that body are not thereby made exempt from the Competition Act. In other cases, a statute may require or permit individual rules of a profession in such as way as to remove them from the scope of Sections 4 and 5 of the Act, whether they are anti-competitive or not. Other bodies — for example, accountants and engineers — are established by Charter and thereby given power to make by-laws, which are, variously, to be laid before the Oireachtas, or to be made with the consent of a Minister, or to be "allowed" by Government. The extent to which this may constitute delegated legislation, so as to take them outside the scope of the Competition Act, is a matter for statutory interpretation in each case.

Three different levels of involvement are looked at here, taking as examples the medical professions, then accountants, and then solicitors. The three medical professions — medicine, dentistry and veterinary science[19] — are dealt with by very similar legislation. In each case a council is created, which has the power and duty to create and maintain a register of qualified persons. The relevant Acts either make it a criminal offence to practise or offer to practise the profession or, in the case of medicine, to hold oneself out as a registered practitioner, unless one is registered. Thus, entry to the register is an absolute precondition to entry to the profession. The legislation also provides that no person may recover fees for medical or dental or veterinary attendance or advice unless they are registered, so that it is not possible for any person to choose to carry on business in these fields even where they do not hold themselves out as being a member of the profession or to be offering professional services.

---

[17] Pharmacy Acts, 1951 and 1962.

[18] Opticians Act, 1956.

[19] Veterinary Surgeons Acts, 1931, 1952, and 1960; Medical Practitioners Act, 1978; Dentists Act, 1985.

In each case, the legislation itself specifies qualifications, being specified degrees from specified Irish universities or colleges, (or where there is an obligation to recognise a qualification of an EU Member State, such a qualification) which entitle a person to registration. For doctors, it is also necessary to obtain a certificate of experience in a hospital approved by the council; and for each of the three, apart from provision for specific degrees, entry may be on the basis of training and education approved by the council. In each case, the council may refuse to register on the grounds of unfitness to practise, for doctors and dentists; and of "conduct disgraceful . . . in a professional respect" for vets. In any case of refusal to register there is a right of appeal to the High Court. The council of each profession has a responsibility to keep itself satisfied of the training and education provided by the bodies it recognises for purposes of registering their graduates. There are then duplicate provisions for doctors and dentists for further registration of specialisations, the training for which must also be approved by the council.

The legislation in a literal sense creates a barrier to entry to the three professions, although the rational reasons for having a barrier of some kind can immediately be seen. There is an obvious public interest in ensuring that the training of persons offering their services as doctors, dentists or vets is such as to ensure a level of competence. This might be seen as one of the lightest manifestations of statutory intervention into a market for professional services. However, in creating one body with responsibility for entry to the profession, the members of which are drawn from the profession itself, the danger inevitably is that that body has a powerful influence on entry by the way it exercises its statutory duties. Entry is conditional on obtaining one of the specified qualifications, and each council is responsible for satisfying itself that the qualifications offered are satisfactory. There is a numerical limit on the number of places available to study for any of those qualifications, set by the relevant universities. What is not possible to know is the extent to which each council could potentially influence a decision to increase, or not to increase, the number of places available for potential students. In *Association of Optometrists*,[20] the Competition Authority noted that:

> . . . [O]nly 20 new applicants are accepted each year by the DIT for the diploma in optometry. . . . [T]he number of places was said to be limited to 20 . . . because the College Authorities felt that 20 per year represented the number of optometrists required . . . . [I]f such a limit reflected a view of the Association on perceived requirements, the Authority would regard this as a serious restriction on competition.

Carlton and Perloff (1990) cite a study by Noether (1986) indicating that the increased supply of doctors in the United States between 1960 and 1981 (caused by changes in immigration laws, and in the control by professional associations), resulted in an average annual drop in income of $23,000 in 1981 prices. Control of entry by such a body is also subject to the effect described above, that where entry is conditional on the goodwill of incumbents, entrants to some extent are predisposed to accept the prevailing mores of those incumbents. For these three professions, the legislation does not deal with the other types of self-imposed restraints associated with self-regulation discussed above — that is, fee-setting and advertising. It is not proposed to explore here any non-statutory rules of these professions which may enter these areas, since these would come within the scope of the Competition Act, 1991.

The profession of accountancy is regulated in a more indirect manner than the mode of regulation considered above. Since use of the word "accountant" is not controlled by law, entry as such is not controlled. However, the Companies Acts provide that only persons recognised by the Minister, and members of bodies recognised by the Minister, may provide auditing services for the fulfilment of Companies Acts auditing obligations. The bodies which are so recognised by the Minister have *de facto* control of entry to a large and important area of practice of this profession. The bodies which are recognised for Companies Acts work each control entry to their own register of members. The Institute of Chartered Accountants of Ireland (ICAI) under its Charter of 1888 may make by-laws, which do not have effect until they have

---

[20]   Decision No. 16 of 29.4.93.

been submitted to and allowed by the Government. The Institute of Certified Public Accountants of Ireland (ICPA) and the Chartered Association of Certified Accountants (ACCA) are established under English statute or charter and their rules, in Ireland, may constitute no more than a contract between the institution and its members.[21] It seems clear that this area of work is of sufficient importance to new entrants to the profession of accountancy that the special statutory position of the three institutes gives a force to their contract with their members which it would not otherwise have. The rules of the ICAI have been held to be properly amenable to the remedies of judicial review on the basis of the public nature of the institute, but also on the basis that:

> . . . if . . . any . . . person wishes to be recognised by the Institute . . . [h]e must agree, inter alia, that the disciplinary committee has jurisdiction over him.[22]

A much more far-reaching form of statutory adoption or sponsoring of self-regulation is that displayed in the Solicitors Acts, 1954–1994. Section 5 of the 1954 Act provides for regulations made by the Society to be laid before each House of the Oireachtas. Some of the rules created by the profession are incorporated in the Act itself, as follows. Entry to the profession is in the first instance dependent on admission as an apprentice, for which the intending entrant must supply the Society with evidence of education, employment and character. The terms of apprenticeship, the education and attendance at training of an apprentice, are regulated by the Society, after which the admission of an apprentice to the register of solicitors, a precondition for practising, is subject to the apprentice satisfying the Society that he or she is "a fit and proper person to be admitted". It is a statutory requirement that a solicitor be three years in practice before setting up as a sole practitioner. The possibility of "incorporated practices" is created by the Act, but made dependent on the Society acting to initiate regulations for their establishment, until which time so-

---

[21] The English and Welsh body, and the Scottish body, whose members are eligible to do Irish Companies Act work, are not considered here.

[22] *Geoghan v. ICAI and AG*, unreported, Sup. Ct., Denham, J., 16.11.95.

licitors may not operate as limited companies, only as partnerships or sole traders. Similarly, the Society may initiate regulations for fee sharing between solicitors and non-solicitors, working
together in a partnership or agency relationship, but until that
should be initiated, solicitors may not form partnerships with
non-solicitors. The 1994 Act provides that the Society shall not
prohibit advertising by solicitors, save on specified statutory
grounds which include, inter alia, advertising which is in bad
taste, brings the profession into disrepute, reflects unfavourably
on other solicitors, is an unsolicited approach to any person with a
view to obtaining instructions in any legal matter, or is an asser-
tion of specialist knowledge superior to that of other solicitors.
This last is subject to exception where the advertiser has satisfied
the Society of their specialist knowledge. The effect is that many
possible forms of advertising are subject to the control of the advertiser's competitors, as represented by the Society. In the UK,
the Lord Chancellor (1989) indicated the view of the Government
of the day on restrictions on advertising as being that:

> . . . no further restraint is needed on the way information is
> given about the legal profession beyond the principles of the
> British Code of Advertising Practice . . . which are that adver-
> tising should be legal, decent, honest and truthful (para. 13.3).

The FTC Report (1990)[23] found that restrictions on any form of
advertising were "an extremely serious limitation upon competition". The Solicitors Acts provide that the Society will not prohibit
fee advertising for specific services, except that it may do so with
the consent of the Minister for Justice, where the Minister is satisfied that the regulations would be in the public interest. The
previous reports, by the National Prices Commission (1978) and
the RPC (1982), had both recommended the removal of restrictions on advertising as being an inhibition of price competition.
The FTC (1990) also recommended that restrictions on "cold calling" be removed, subject to control of content.

---

[23] The FTC Report dealt with both barristers and solicitors and found restrictive practices in both professions. In this context, the Report is only
considered insofar as it relates to the statutory adoption of the self-
regulation of solicitors.

The statutory scales of fees for solicitors, which are numerous and complex, are described in FTC (1990), where it is noted that in some important instances the scale fees regulate not the fee which a solicitor recovers from a client, but the fee which can be recovered as costs from an unsuccessful opposing party in litigation, which thus creates a most unusual market situation. For the normal fees payable by a client to a solicitor, the Report states that price competition is the most important feature of a free market economy, and that mandatory, maximum or minimum fee scales of any origin are harmful to that end. The extent to which the various different scale fees may be harmful to competition is explored very fully in the Report and is not further explored here. The National Prices Commission in 1976, and the Restrictive Practices Commission in 1982, had both reported that scale fees were unsatisfactory, in the first instance taking them as a given but as being set at levels too high and too low, resulting in cross subsidisation. In the second their operation was criticised, on the basis that the fee scale system "lent itself to a degree of price maintenance".

In a comprehensive survey of solicitors in every county in Ireland, taking both rural and urban samples in each county, Shinnick (1996) found that there was a very strong tendency in each county for conveyancing fees charged to be congregated closely around the scale fee for selling — one per cent plus £100. He suggests that the evidence on fee-setting behaviour indicates that either a high degree of price competition exists, or firms are using this scale fee as a collusively set floor.

Transport
For much of the history of the State, transport has been subject to high levels of regulation. In many areas such regulation was designed to favour particular activities — for example, railways as opposed to road transport. In others it was designed to foster and protect state-owned monopolies or particular interest groups. In some areas there have been moves toward deregulation over the past decade and the results have generally proved beneficial. Restrictions on competition in certain transport markets continue to impose significant costs on society.

Road Freight

Road freight was, until the mid-1980s, subject to considerable restrictions, not only in Ireland, but in many developed countries. The Road Transport Act (1933) restricted the operation of road freight for reward, other than in small areas adjoining the major towns and cities, to persons providing such services prior to the passage of the legislation. The Act also provided for the acquisition by railway companies of such hauliers, by compulsory purchase if necessary. The Act was specifically designed to restrict competition in order to protect the railways. The Minister for Industry and Commerce, Mr Lemass, stated that the aim was "to make it possible for the Great Southern Railway in its area and other railway companies in their areas to establish themselves in what is described as a monopoly position".[24] Such views were consistent with prevailing economic views. Conroy (1928: 70), for example, argued that:

> . . . it would not be inconsistent with the age of "trusts" and "combines" that all competition in the transport world should be eliminated. . . . Road transport should be merely used as a complement for rail transport, not as a substitute for it.

The number of independent road hauliers was reduced from 1,356 in 1933 to 886 by 1938 (Meenan, 1970: 161). In a submission to the Beddy Committee in 1956, CIE proposed that:

> . . . all commercial vehicles would be limited in their area of operation. Initially this limit was proposed at fifty miles for one year. The limit would be reduced each year until the full capacity of the railways is achieved (Barrett, 1990: 110).

Although this proposal was not accepted, the Transport Act, 1956 decreed that vehicle leasing was the equivalent of licensed haulage for hire or reward and was therefore subject to quantity licensing.

For the most part, firms simply chose to provide their own road transport services rather than rely on the railways. In 1964, 83 per cent of goods were transported by firms in their own vehicles (Barrett, 1990). Regulation imposed significant costs on the economy.

---

[24] Seanad debates, Vol. 16, Col. 979.

Own account operators could not transport goods for other firms for hire or reward. The effect of this was a greater volume of empty running than would have occurred if return loads could be carried for other firms (see Table 12.1). In 1980, 35 per cent of trucks surveyed were running empty, an increase of 4 per cent compared with 1964. The cost to industry of the restrictions was estimated as equivalent to 11 per cent of total freight costs in 1980 (Barrett, 1982).[25] In the UK, regulation was also found to have imposed substantial costs on society in the form of higher transport costs.[26] Short (1985) concluded that "it is not obvious that the system of economic regulation has brought benefits which justify its costs".

TABLE 12.1: PER CENT EMPTY RUNNING BY ROAD FREIGHT VEHICLES

	1964	*1980*
Own Account	30.4	35.6
Licensed Hauliers	39.9	34.6
Total	31.3	35.4

Source: CSO, *Road Freight Surveys*, 1964 and 1980.

Partial liberalisation of road freight began in 1971. Opposition from licence holders delayed full liberalisation for more than a decade. The Road Transport Act, 1986 provided for the replacement of existing carrier licences, restricted road freight licences and road freight certificates by a new Carriers' Licence. The new licences have no restrictions as to their area of operation, the type of goods carried and the number of vehicles which can be operated by a licence holder. The new licences were phased in over a two-year period with full liberalisation from 30 September 1988. The number of licensed hauliers increased from 766 in 1985 to 1,302 in 1988. The volume of goods carried by private hauliers increased from 18 million tonnes to 34 million tonnes over the same period.

---

[25] Barrett estimated total road freight costs in 1980 at £595 million which would imply that the excess cost of regulation amounted to £65 million in 1980 prices, equivalent to £151 million in 1995 prices.

[26] *Report of the Committee of Enquiry into the Road Haulage Industry* (1965): London: HMSO.

Fears that liberalisation might threaten safety by undermining hauliers' capacity to invest in new vehicles appear not to have been borne out. As Figure 12.1 illustrates, more than 40 per cent of goods vehicles on the road are less than five years old, with almost 80 per cent less than 10 years old. In contrast, only one per cent are more than 15 years old. Of course, safety concerns can be dealt with by qualitative regulations and do not require quantitative controls.[27]

FIGURE 12.1: AGE PROFILE OF GOODS VEHICLES (1992)

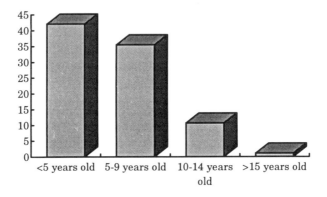

Source: Department of the Environment, 1992.

Buses

The Road Transport Act, 1932 prohibited the operation of scheduled road passenger services except under licence. As in the case of road freight, the legislation was designed to limit competition in order to protect the railways and by 1938 the railway companies had eliminated 1,098 independent bus services, 60 per cent of these being achieved by compulsory acquisition (Barrett, 1982). Licences cannot be obtained to operate on routes currently serviced by CIE or one of its subsidiaries. Indeed, Barrett (1990) pointed out that applications for licences were actually referred to

---

[27] Goods vehicles are subject to checks for road worthiness. In 1992 more than 42,000 goods vehicles, equivalent to 29 per cent of the total registered, were subject to testing. Of these 32 per cent passed, while a further 52 per cent passed, subject to having certain defects rectified (Department of the Environment, 1992).

CIE, thus giving them the benefit of competitors' market research. The absence of competition has had a negative impact. The National Prices Commission found that licensed provincial bus operators generally charged lower fares, in some cases much lower, than CIE (NPC, 1972a: 27). Table 12.2 shows that, in the case of CIE bus subsidiaries, average receipts per passenger increased by almost 40 per cent more than the rate of inflation over the 1982–93 period, while passenger numbers remained static. Barrett (1990) reported that in 1982 the CIE Expressway fare was 82 per cent higher than that charged by the Midland Bus Company on the Athlone–Mullingar route. Since the early 1980s, private bus operators have emerged to provide growing competition for Bus Éireann and Iarnród Éireann on long distance services. Such services appear to have taken advantage of a legal loophole. Barrett (1990) noted that there were daily private bus services from most regions to Dublin. Jakee and Allen (1995) estimated that "rent seeking" in the case of CIE intercity and rural bus routes cost £14.4 million in 1986.

TABLE 12.2: STATISTICS ON CIE BUS SERVICES

	Passengers (000)	Average Receipts (pence)
Dublin — 1982	162,940	0.29
Dublin — 1993	165,694	0.54
% Real Change		39.1%
Other Cities — 1982	22,759	0.31
Other Cities — 1993	20,957	0.55
% Real Change		32.6%
Long Distance — 1982	45,036	0.69
Long Distance — 1993	44,618	1.28
% Real Change		38.6%

Source: CSO, Statistical Abstract, various issues.

In contrast to long-distance routes, there is no competition on bus routes in urban areas. UK experience of liberalisation in urban areas shows that the results have been somewhat mixed. Companies have frequently adjusted their schedules to match those of competitors, resulting in a situation where there was widespread confusion among consumers regarding service schedules. Kilvington (1985) concluded that competition for the market had proved better than competition in the market. Competition for a market can be achieved by means of tendering for exclusive licences to operate on a particular route for a period of time. This form of competition for the market was advocated by Demsetz (1968). The National Planning Board (1984) argued that such tendering should be used in the case of loss-making routes in order to ensure that such services are provided at the lowest possible cost to the Exchequer. It is frequently argued that without restrictions on competition, new entrants would engage in cream skimming and leave the loss-making uneconomic routes. Such claims are not borne out by the evidence. Existing licensed private bus operators, which are mainly small, operate largely on remote rural routes in which CIE has chosen not to operate. Barrett (1990) pointed out that CIE has never identified which routes are loss making.

Railways

As noted above, many of the regulations applying to road transport were designed to protect the railways. In this regard, they have proven to be singularly unsuccessful. As already noted, in spite of restrictions on road freight, many firms opted to operate their own truck fleets. Similarly in the passenger market, the railways have over time steadily lost out to buses. During the debate on the Transport Act, 1944, Seán Lemass criticised the failure of Great Southern Railways to provide satisfactory levels of service "despite the quasi-monopoly which was created for them by legislation".[28] In spite of the decision to bring the railways under State ownership, the position has not improved greatly in the intervening half century. Mainline railway services have recorded continued deficits. Indeed, the bulk of Government funding to CIE has been used to finance losses on the mainline rail network.

Statutory restrictions designed to protect the railway network against competition from road-based transport have proven wholly ineffective. Ongoing state subsidies to the railways further distort competition. To the extent that the continued payment of

---

[28] Dáil Debates, Vol. 72, Col. 118.

subsidies to Iarnród Éireann is based on wider social and environmental policy considerations, it involves considerations that are outside the scope of the present book. Though the railway network is a natural monopoly, competition in actual railway services is possible. Such competition could occur by allowing new entrants to run services on the existing rail network subject to their being charged for such use.[29] In practice, it would probably be more realistic to introduce competition for the market by effectively awarding franchises to operate services on particular routes on a tender basis.[30] Such competition could reduce the cost of the State subvention to the railways since competition for such franchises would ensure that services are operated as efficiently as possible. In contrast to the situation in the UK, it would appear that the size of the country would militate against having competition for individual services on most routes.

Taxis

Taxis play an important role in urban public transport in most OECD countries. Traditionally, there has been a distinction between taxis that ply for hire in the street or wait at taxi stands within the licensed taximeter areas,[31] and private hire vehicles (referred to in Ireland as hackneys), which are generally pre-booked for specific journeys. The justification for regulations is based ostensibly at least on consumer protection grounds. A Government report on the taxi market, for example, argued that prior to tightening of licensing regulations in 1978, the quality of service was sub-standard with widespread abuse and overcharging the norm, but it failed to show that the position had improved as a result of regulation (Report of the Inter-Departmental Committee, 1994). The report also argued that, in a deregulated market,

---

[29] The question of introducing competition in sectors where the network constitutes a natural monopoly is an issue that is considered at greater length in the following chapter.

[30] For a more detailed discussion of allocating franchises to operate services as a means of organising competition for a market, see Demsetz (1968).

[31] There were four designated taximeter areas (Dublin, Cork, Galway and Limerick) prior to October 1991. A further 12 areas were designated taximeter areas in October 1991.

operators may seek to maximise income from individual hirings, leading to single hires and hirings for journeys deemed uneconomic being refused. In reality, refusal of uneconomic journeys or multiple hirings are features of a system where supply is inadequate since suppliers can pick and choose. The Report concluded that price competition was not possible as individual operators could effectively charge what they want for individual journeys, leading to abuses such as excessive charging with "visitors arriving at airports being particularly vulnerable". Taxi services throughout the world (even where there are price controls) are notorious for overcharging visitors coming from airports.

In 1978, the relevant local authority was given responsibility for deciding on the number of taxi licences (plates) to be issued in taximeter areas. No new taxi licences were issued in the four old taximeter areas between 1979 and 1991. During the 1990/91 Christmas period there were widespread complaints that taxi services in Dublin were inadequate. This led to the establishment of an Interdepartmental Review Group (IRG) by the Minister for the Environment. It found that:

> ... the failure to increase numbers in line with demand has led to problems with the adequacy of the service provided by taxis in a number of areas especially at peak periods and in turn was a primary factor in the development of the present unstable market in those areas i.e. the development of organised private hire operations. It has also led to high monetary values being placed on taxi licences in all areas (*ibid.*, para. 5.19).

Massey (1994) reported that there were significant changes in population, particularly in the Dublin region, over this period, which would have justified an increase in the number of taxi licences. A hundred new taxi licences were issued for Dublin in October 1991. No further licences have been issued. A more recent survey by Dublin Corporation again concluded that the level of taxi services was inadequate. A clear indication that taxi numbers are still totally inadequate is the high prices paid for the transfer of existing taxi licences, which reportedly change hands for as much as £70,000. A decision by Dublin Corporation to issue 200 new taxi licences in early 1996 provoked a wave of protests from incumbents and the decision was subsequently reversed.

The failure to increase taxi numbers has resulted in an on-going shortage of taxis at peak times and has led to increased friction between taxi and hackney drivers, as the latter have sought to take advantage of the shortage in taxi numbers by offering competing services. Legally, hackneys cannot ply for hire, operate from taxi ranks or use telephones or radios in vehicles to initiate or facilitate a hire while the vehicle is in a public place. In practice, many hackneys appear to operate freely in a number of taximeter areas in direct competition with taxis. The hire is initiated by way of either a personal or telephone call to the base, while the vehicle remains parked on private property close by. Taxis and hackneys are in direct competition with each other, indicating that it may be time to abolish the distinction between them. The grounds for maintaining the distinction appear to be based on the quite different role of the traditional rural hackney.

The high price for taxi plates indicates that the business is divided up between a smaller number of suppliers than would be the case in a more competitive environment. In effect, taxi services are rationed under such a regime and this manifests itself in consumers having to spend a long time waiting and, on occasion, being unable to obtain a taxi. It may be that individuals in the taxi trade are able to secure some share of the monopoly profits to be earned as a result of the restrictions on competition. It seems likely, however, that most of the gains would accrue to those individuals selling plates who have seen the capital value of the plates rise over time as demand for taxi services exceeded supply. Indeed, a major bone of contention among taxi operators is that individuals have made large amounts of money selling their taxi plates and have promptly re-entered the market as hackney operators. Ultimately the consumer bears the high cost of taxi plates in some form, as such outlays must be recouped somehow. A study commissioned by the US Department of Transportation (1984) concluded that the cost of restraints on new entry and regulations which prevented fare discounting in the US amounted to nearly $800 million annually and the loss of 38,000 jobs in the taxi industry. The US Federal Trade Commission (1989) estimated the costs of restrictions on taxi numbers on the basis of the interest costs incurred arising from the capital outlay involved in acquiring a taxi plate. Adopting a similar approach, and assuming an interest rate of 10 per cent, implies that a profit stream of £7,000 per annum would be required to cover the interest costs of the purchase of a taxi plate for £70,000. Given that there are roughly 2,000 licensed taxis in Dublin, this suggests that the total excess cost to Dublin consumers caused by restrictions on taxi numbers amounts to £14 million per annum.

US studies also indicate that the brunt of the costs of taxi regulation is borne by the elderly and less well-off. One study found that 70 per cent of elderly respondents reported "extreme distress" at the length of wait for a taxi sent by radio dispatch, 27 per cent had been refused service by a dispatcher or cab-driver, and 44 per cent reported that after waiting 30 minutes or more, the cab had failed to show-up. A survey in Seattle found that 25 per cent of total taxi trips were accounted for by financially disadvantaged groups. These findings were supported by more detailed studies which found that the inappropriately high fares resulting from regulation imposed a disproportionate burden on low-income people.

The removal of quantitative limits on taxi numbers would provide consumers with some of the benefits of a more competitive environment — that is, greater availability of taxis, reduced waiting time and better quality of service. As the present restrictions appear to have produced a situation where suppliers enjoy monopoly profits, abolishing restrictions would probably attract large numbers of new entrants into the business. This could produce a situation of excess supply in the short term. Rather than abolishing quantitative limits overnight, it might be preferable to increase them steadily, with the ultimate aim of eliminating them. To begin with, the distinction between taxis and private-hire vehicles in urban areas could be abolished. The number of licences could be increased steadily, say by 10 per cent per year, with quantitative limits being removed altogether after a period of, say, seven years.[32] It is important to stress that removing quantitative

---

[32] New licences could be allocated by tender, subject to applicants meeting the quality requirements. A tender system would allow the authorities to capture some of the capital value of the monopoly profits arising from quantitative restrictions. It must be expected, however, that a steady increase in licence numbers, together with proposals to eliminate quantitative restrictions entirely, would reduce the capital value of licences.

controls does not mean abandoning qualitative controls. Such controls would have to be retained for public safety and other reasons. Existing provisions for random inspection of vehicles would have to be maintained. To make such measures effective, it would be necessary to impose stiff penalties in the form of fines and/or suspension of taxi licences and to devote sufficient resources to such checks, so that they represent an adequate deterrent.

The phasing out of quantitative controls may be argued to be unfair on those individuals and firms who have spent large sums to acquire taxi plates under the existing regulations. People were prepared to pay high prices on the basis that fares would be sufficiently high to recoup such costs and in the expectation that the capital value of plates would continue to rise. In effect, this is a form of speculation based on the individual's assessment of the likely future income stream and/or capital gain arising from ownership of an asset, in this case a taxi plate. It is hard to see why public policy should concern itself with protecting those engaged in speculative activity from making a loss. The high price of plates stems from a restriction on competition and thus is not justified.

Taxi fares are one of the very few areas where price controls still exist. In an environment where the number of taxis is limited, price controls are probably necessary to protect consumers. The removal of numerical limits would produce a situation where price competition could operate effectively in the taxi market. The removal of price controls would have to be delayed until taxi numbers were increased significantly. Otherwise the removal of controls could be expected to result in a considerable increase in fares. Taxis could be required to display their fares, allowing consumers to shop around when hiring a taxi from a rank and seek to attract customers by advertising their charges, thus providing consumers with the information necessary to make choices.[33] A

---

[33] Where space was available, ranks might be redesigned to allow separate ranks for different taxi groups. Such a system would be particularly desirable at places such as airports, where taxi services are important. Taxi organisations could then advertise within the precincts of the airport and consumers could then choose which taxi rank they wished to use on the basis of price comparisons.

more competitive market may be expected to result in the development of new services. The demand for taxi services could be expected to increase in an environment where prices were lower and supply was more plentiful, resulting in more jobs at little cost to the State. It would also lead to some reduction in the use of private cars and would thus have a favourable impact on traffic congestion.

Taxi services have tended to be heavily regulated in most OECD countries. There have been some significant changes in this respect in recent years, however. In Sweden, the number of licences is no longer limited, licence holders are no longer restricted in their areas of operation and prices are no longer regulated but may be fixed freely by individual operators who must make a schedule of fares available to customers. An examination by the competition authority after 18 months found that prices had initially increased sharply although this has since been partly reversed (Swedish Competition Authority). The number of taxi operators increased by 26 per cent between 1989 and 1991. There was also an increase in the number of taxi booking offices and undertakings. Where new companies were established there was a noticeable increase in competition between undertakings. At least a dozen US cities have deregulated aspects of the taxi trade, primarily by opening up entry, accompanied, in most cases, by some deregulation of fares. In Seattle, deregulation was found to have resulted in about 200 additional jobs, and fares were estimated to be 15 per cent lower than under a regulated regime. In San Diego, the average waiting time for radio-dispatched cabs declined by 20 per cent. Waiting times were also found to have fallen significantly in Milwaukee, Santa Barbara and Seattle. Virtually all cities which had changed to open entry experienced an increase in the number of firms in the taxi industry and a decrease in the market shares of the largest firms. Vehicle quality also increased in a number of cities (OECD, 1992). Taxi services were deregulated in New Zealand in the latter part of 1989. One year later, increased competition had occurred in the three main urban centres — namely, Auckland, Wellington and Christchurch, which between them account for almost half of New Zealand's population. Profitability had declined, while fares had remained constant or declined in real terms. Service standards had generally increased with a modernisation of fleets, increased vetting and monitoring of drivers, while consumers were provided with more information and the response time to telephone call-outs had declined (Ministry of Transport, 1991).

Airline Services

Up to the mid-1980s competition in airline services to and from Ireland was restricted. Such restrictions were common worldwide. In many European countries, airlines have traditionally been state owned so that anti-competitive measures were caused, in part at least, by a desire by Governments to protect state-owned airlines. In the US, there has been a considerable liberalisation of airline services since the late 1970s. The decision to permit greater competition in the US was to a large extent based on contestability theory. Subsequent experience suggests that airline services are not in fact contestable (Bailey and Baumol, 1984). Following liberalisation many new entry barriers have been created. These include:

- Control of hub airports

- Control of ground handling

- Control of computer reservation systems

- Geographical price discrimination, and

- Anti-competitive mergers.

Such developments do not necessarily imply that the introduction of competition has been harmful. Rather they show that liberalisation needs to be accompanied by active enforcement of competition rules to prevent anti-competitive behaviour by dominant incumbent airlines.

In Europe generally, liberalisation has been far more limited. There has been a major liberalisation in respect of routes between Ireland and Britain, with far less progress towards opening up competition on European routes. Competition on air routes between Ireland and the UK has produced considerable benefits. Barrett (1990) reported that air fares had fallen by as much as 65 per cent in the case of unrestricted fares. This is in contrast with the experience during the 1980–85 period when the CAA found that fares on the Dublin–London route had increased by 75 per cent in real terms (*ibid.*). Lower airfares resulted in a dramatic increase in passenger traffic, in contrast to the declines recorded prior to 1986 (see Figure 12.2). Passenger movements in both directions more than doubled between 1986 and 1994.

FIGURE 12.2: DIRECT AIR PASSENGER MOVEMENTS (000)

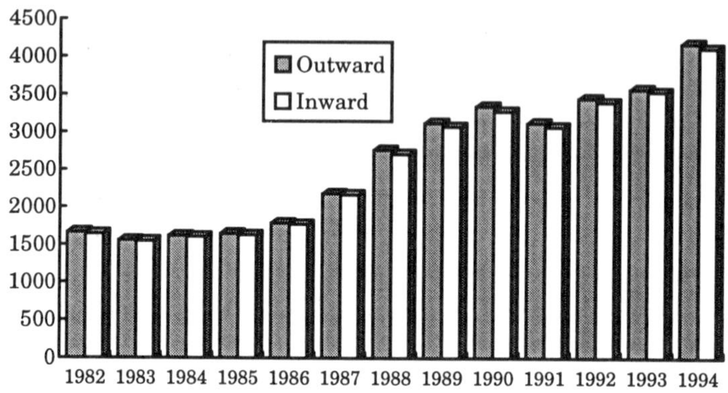

Source: CSO, Statistical Abstract, various issues.

Distribution — Public Houses

Regulation of public houses, and indeed the sale of alcoholic drink in general, is apparently based largely on social grounds. Specifically, measures to restrict the number of outlets permitted to sell alcoholic drink for consumption either on or off the premises and to restrict the hours during which it may be sold are designed to control the consumption of alcoholic drink. Not surprisingly, they have proven to be a very ineffective means of achieving that end. They do, however, restrict competition to an appreciable extent and may have facilitated collusive behaviour in the trade. The licensing laws effectively prevent any increase in the total number of licensed public houses on the level pertaining at the turn of the century. The number of licences in urban areas cannot be increased relative to the 1901 level. In rural areas a new licence can only be obtained when two existing licences are extinguished. In addition, it must be shown that a licence for a new premises would not be unreasonably detrimental to the business of an existing premises in the neighbourhood, while no application will be allowed if the new premises are less than one mile, measured by the shortest public thoroughfare, from premises which were first licensed on or before 4 July 1960.

One of the features of applications for "new" licences — that is, existing licences attaching to new premises — under the provisions for moving or extinguishing licences, is the use of the objections process by competing publicans. It is said not to be the purpose of the licensing applications to determine the effect of the licence on competition:

> The object of the (Acts) was to safeguard the public interest by preventing a proliferation of licensed premises . . . and not to shelter existing publicans from competition. . . . To decide that a licence ought not to be granted because the competition it would offer to existing licences would be economically disadvantageous to the holders of those licences is not a ground which is contemplated by the code.[34]

Nonetheless, it is the case that competitors can and do object, if not on the grounds ruled out above, then on other grounds which are intended for the public interest generally. The objection mechanism does provide an obstacle for incumbents to put in the way of an intending new entrant, and they are recognised as having the right to use that weapon by being recognised as a category of competent objectors in their own right. The licensing legislation for "new" on and off licences (in the sense of licences attached to new or different premises, but replacing existing licences which are extinguished) specifies categories of competent objector. Competitors are recognised as coming within the category of "any person who would be affected by the decision to grant a licence".[35] Thus competitors may challenge the new applicant on any matter that is required to be proved in the application, which could be the fitness of the premises, the fitness of the applicant or any other matter.

---

[34] *Re Power Supermarkets Ltd.* (1988) IR 206.

[35] *Jaggers Restaurant Ltd.* v. *Ahearne* (1988) IR 308.

The regulations have resulted in a number of serious anomalies. For example, there are considerable variations in the ratio of public houses to population between different areas of the country. The requirement that two licences must be extinguished for the grant of a new licence in rural areas has created an unearned property right for licence holders. This may cause uneconomic outlets to remain open in order to preserve the licence with a view to its future sale. In urban areas it has given rise to the phenomenon of the development of large-scale premises complete with extensive car-parking facilities, which rely on drawing custom from a wide area. Table 12.3 shows that the average size of public houses in Dublin is more than double the average for the State. Given the original intention of the legislation to control or limit drinking, it would seem an unintended and undesirable effect for urban centres of population that it should cause people to drive in order to reach public houses.

TABLE 12.3: AVERAGE SIZE OF PUBLIC HOUSES IN 1988 (SQUARE FEET)

Dublin	1,881
Rest of Leinster	1,035
Munster	748
Connacht	757
Ulster	745
State	936

Source: CSO; Census of Services (1988).

A consultants' report for the National Prices Commission (NPC) found that the licensing system constrained competition and facilitated higher prices. Commenting on the consultants' report, the NPC concluded that:

> Competition is inhibited by the present system, and property rights (in licences) with a sale value are created that have no obvious justification. It is not apparent that the system reduces the total amount of drinking as distinct from affecting detailed drinking habits (NPC, 1972b).

In a subsequent report, the RPC was also critical of the licensing system, finding that it restricted competition, resulted in a serious distortion in the structure of the trade and tended to increase operating costs and prices (RPC, 1977). Some evidence that the restrictions on competition have resulted in some amount of monopoly profits can be seen by looking at trends in gross margins, expressed as a percentage of turnover. Figure 12.3 indicates that public house gross margins have increased from 19.7 per cent of turnover in 1971 to almost 37 per cent in 1991. Fingleton (1995) found that the price of stout in on-licence premises increased by about 1.6 per cent per annum in real terms between 1986 and 1994, while packaged stout sold in off-licences fell by 1.8 per cent per year in real terms over the same period.

FIGURE 12.3: PUBLIC HOUSE GROSS MARGINS AS PER CENT OF TURNOVER

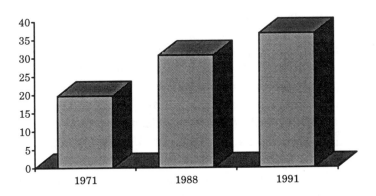

Source: RPC (1977) and CSO (1988 and 1991).

The RPC (1965) found that collective arrangements, involving retail prices through the issue of price lists by local vintners' associations, were widespread. It also found that such price lists were discussed at meetings of the committees of management or, in some cases, at meetings of the members. "The understanding was that even where some members disagreed with the proposed list prices, all would undertake to observe them" (RPC, 1977: 60). Following publication of the Report, the Minister introduced a Restrictive Practices Order prohibiting a retail trade association from "deciding, recommending to retailers for adoption, or proposing for adoption by retailers, the retail selling price of intoxicating liquor or non-alcoholic beverages sold in or from bottles or cans." Subsequent enquiries by the RPC concluded that apart from inducing a more circumspect approach by the parties involved, the Order appeared to have little effect (*ibid.*: 62). Following an extensive investigation between August 1975 and October 1976, the Examiner of Restrictive Practices concluded that the Order was being breached in nine towns. The *Irish Independent* reported in September 1976 that:

> The price of the pint and the half-pint go up 1p in Dublin on Friday, the city's publicans decided last night. . . .
>
> At their meeting the publicans decided on the move to help them to meet spiralling wage costs. . . . However a spokesman for the Publicans Association said last night that the new increase would only increase their take by 2 per cent (*Irish Independent*, 15 September 1976).

More recently, there have been similar reports of publicans "agreeing" on price increases. In 1994, for example, following similar reports, the Minister for Enterprise and Employment requested the Director of Consumer Affairs to investigate whether there had been a breach of the Competition Act. In the autumn of 1995 publicans were once more reported to have "agreed" to increase prices (*Evening Herald*, 8 August 1995). Newspaper reports do not of course establish that publicans have engaged in collusive behaviour. The licensing system, however, may facilitate such behaviour by preventing the undermining of any cartel-type arrangement by new entrants.

Financial Services
In the mid-1980s it was argued that Ireland had one of the most heavily regulated banking systems of any developed economy and that competition in the financial services market was seriously distorted as a result (DKM, 1984). These views were echoed by Kinsella who observed that:

> We are saddled with a regulatory regime that is outdated, inefficient, discriminatory and one which, ironically, actually impedes innovation and competition (Kinsella, 1988: 16).

As noted in Chapter 3, the financial sector traditionally consisted of different types of institution, each of which was legally confined to particular activities. The traditional distinctions between different types of financial institution have become increasingly blurred, while many regulatory distortions have been removed, resulting in increased competition in the various financial services markets. Again, as noted previously, both the associated banks and major building societies operated cartel arrangements in the past with official sanction. Interest on building society deposits was given favourable tax treatment up to 1986 as a means of assisting new-home buyers. This placed other financial institutions at a severe disadvantage in attracting deposits. Massey (1984) showed how banks would have had to offer a significantly higher gross interest rate to provide the same after-tax return as building society deposits. As a result, societies were also effectively insulated against competition in mortgage lending. Thom (1984) argued that the result was that building society depositors effectively subsidised mortgage holders. Kinsella (1992) found that tax-based distortions undermined the loan-generating capacity of the banks.

Credit guidelines were first imposed in 1965 as a means of curtailing growth in the associated banks' lending to the private sector and to the Government and were subsequently extended in 1970 to cover non-associated bank total lending.[36] Credit guidelines were introduced in an attempt to curb inflation, although economic theory argues that in a small open economy with a fixed exchange rate link to a larger economy, inflation will be largely externally determined so that domestic monetary policy will have little impact on inflation. The decision to join the EMS in 1979 indicated official acceptance of this view. Credit guidelines, however, constrain the efficient bank to expand at the same rate as the inefficient bank. The Central Bank had long recognised the adverse effects of credit guidelines on competition.

> Direct limits on bank lending . . . if pursued for long periods of time, hamper competition between banks and lead to inequities and possible misallocation of scarce resources. They also en-

---

[36] Excluding instalment credit.

courage attempts to circumvent the ceilings, thereby leading to pressures to extend the scope of the quantitative restrictions (Central Bank of Ireland, 1971: 32).

The adverse effect on competition was one of the reasons advanced by the Central Bank for temporarily abandoning credit guidelines in 1973 (Leddin and Walsh, 1990). Again in 1980, the Governor of the Central Bank stated that:

> They (credit guidelines) . . . severely inhibit competition among banks by limiting the growth of the more efficient banks to the same rate as the less efficient . . . (and) entail a large element of credit rationing which is in itself inefficient . . . if circumstances so permitted, the Bank would prefer to administer monetary growth by influencing bank liquidity (Murray, 1980: 115).

Credit guidelines kept interest rates below market-clearing levels, leading to excess demand for credit, thus forcing banks to respond by rationing credit. The net result of rationing was that banks financed low-productivity projects at the expense of high-productivity ones. In the absence of credit guidelines, the price mechanism, in the form of the interest rate, is the means by which available credit is rationed and means that the most profitable projects will be financed.

The non-uniform application of liquidity ratios[37] discriminated most heavily against the clearing banks, thereby diverting business towards less regulated or unregulated institutions (DKM, 1984). The tendency for ratios to result in this form of disintermediation is widely recognised. As with credit guidelines, differing liquidity ratios mean that efficiency ceases to determine which institutions will be successful. By aiding less efficient institutions, regulations reduce overall economic welfare. It was estimated that the primary liquidity ratio cost the licensed banks £20 million annually (Walsh, 1987: 31). Liquidity ratios are usually justified on prudential grounds — that is, as preventing banking failures. The Reserve Bank of New Zealand (1986: 94) noted, however, that:

---

[37] Such ratios refer to the proportion of their assets which financial institutions must hold on deposit with the Central Bank.

> . . . the compulsory holding in their portfolios of a substantial proportion of Government securities is not an appropriate means of encouraging sound prudential management for a number of reasons.

There has been a widespread liberalisation of the financial sector since 1984. The establishment of a more market-oriented mechanism for setting interest rates was quickly followed by the break-up of the associated bank cartel. Rates for large commercial borrowers are now determined between the banks and their customers "on a fully competitive and deregulated basis" (Central Bank 1991: 18). The differences in the tax treatment of deposit interest between banks and building societies was eliminated with the introduction in the 1986 Budget of Deposit Interest Retention Tax (DIRT), which applied equally to both types of institution. The prolonged domestic recession of the 1980s led to a sharp downturn in private-sector credit demand, effectively rendering the credit guidelines redundant. There has also been a significant relaxation of the restrictions on the activities in which financial institutions are permitted to engage. The Building Societies Act, 1989, for example, allows societies to engage in unsecured lending up to certain limits, to provide foreign exchange and a variety of other services, subject to Central Bank approval. The restrictions on non-government lending by the TSB have also been relaxed. The operating brief of the ACC and ICC has also changed, enabling them to provide a wider range of banking services. Competition has also come from non-financial institutions which have begun offering some financial services. The introduction of store credit cards by major retail outlets is one example of this. McGowan (1986b) reported that larger companies had begun to engage in lending activities, citing this as possibly heralding the development of a domestic commercial paper market.

While technological developments undoubtedly played a major role in the deregulation process, changes in attitude with regard to State intervention and a growing awareness of the adverse consequences of such intervention also played a part. There was a degree to which financial deregulation was an idea whose time had come, as reflected by the fact that the 1980s saw financial deregulation in virtually all developed economies. The increasingly global nature of financial markets made it extremely difficult for a small open economy like Ireland's to swim against what was virtually a worldwide tide in favour of deregulation. The gradual dismantling of Irish exchange controls was prompted largely by the need to prepare for the single market, as was the reduction, in late 1991, of the primary liquidity ratio for licensed banks.

The introduction of uniform tax treatment of interest paid by banks and building societies undermined the societies' ability to keep deposit interest rates low. The result is that, while for most of the period up to the mid-1980s mortgage interest rates were below wholesale interest rates, such as the one-month inter-bank rate, this position has now been reversed, making it possible for institutions to fund mortgage lending on the wholesale market. As a result, the associated banks and, more recently, specialist mortgage lending agencies have entered the market, funding their activities on the wholesale money market. The cartel between the largest societies broke up in the face of the increased competition in the deposit and lending markets. As noted in Chapter 3, these changes greatly increased the level of competition in the home mortgage market. As mentioned earlier, building societies have begun to engage in unsecured lending, while restrictions on personal and corporate lending by the TSB have also been eased. Building societies have also begun to compete more actively in the wholesale deposit market and to offer credit card services, while the largest society has announced plans to establish a leasing subsidiary. The tendency for financial institutions to compete across a broader range of products has significantly increased consumer choice. Moves into new areas of business entail some risk, however, a point that is considered below.

Increased competition should force financial institutions to unbundle their products and introduce explicit charges for identifiably separate services, thus increasing allocative efficiency. In particular, it should eliminate cross subsidisation of certain services — for example, money transmission from net interest margins. In a more competitive environment, as Ackland and Harper (1990) point out, institutions have an incentive to cut their net interest margins and introduce fees and charges, as this would enable them to expand their borrowing and lending activities, eliminating profit haemorrhage through overuse of under priced ancillary services. Figure 12.4 shows that net interest income as a proportion of total income of the big two banking groups has fallen by over 10 per cent since 1987. Increases in bank charges, along with the introduction of new charges for what were regarded as free services, has, inevitably, met with some consumer resistance. Milbourne (1990) argues that banks themselves may be somewhat reluctant to introduce fees and charges on a comprehensive basis because of the odium likely to be borne by the first bank to make a substantial move in this direction. As a result, he argues, the banks (and society) may be locked into a suboptimal Nash equilibrium, with inappropriately-priced financial services and net interest margins that are too wide. In Ireland, concern about increased bank charges prompted legislation which may discourage such increases.

FIGURE 12.4: NET INTEREST INCOME AS PER CENT OF BANK'S TOTAL INCOME

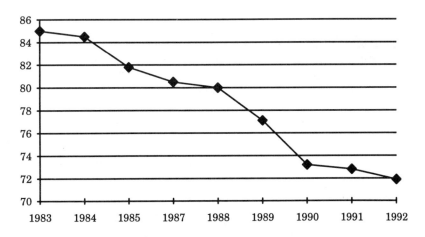

Source: Annual Reports, AIB Bank and Bank of Ireland.

The Consumer Credit Act, 1995 requires that bank charges must be approved by the Director of Consumer Affairs and imposes a charge of £25,000 for each application for an increase in fees or the introduction of new charges. The rationale for such a high fee is that it is designed to cover the costs of assessing such requests. Increased competition would lead to reduced net interest margins

and consequent increases in fees and charges. It is important that
the Act should not prevent charges from being set at efficient levels,
since otherwise cross-subsidisation would continue and net interest margins would be higher than would otherwise be the case.

Both McGowan (1986b) and Walsh (1988) argue that Irish institutions had in the past been slow to develop new products. Increased competition should produce dynamic efficiency gains in
the form of product innovation. The introduction of ATMs, over-
the-counter sales of shares and insurance products, banking by
telephone are all examples of innovation by institutions to
changing market conditions or dynamic efficiency gains in response to increased competition. It is extremely difficult to establish whether increased competition has resulted in improved levels of service quality. Moves by the associated banks to extend
opening hours are one indication of how competition has increased the pressure on institutions to improve service quality.
Commenting on the effects of deregulation on the quality of
banking services in Australia, Ackland and Harper (1990: 24) argue that:

> The effect of deregulation on loan business is much more likely
> to obtain the approval of the average bank customer. The
> change in the attitude of bank managers to loan requests fol-
> lowing deregulation is truly remarkable.

They also found that increased competition reduced bank profitability in Australia, a result supported by Leung (1989). Spencer
and Carey (1988) report similar results for New Zealand. Llewellyn (1986) found that building society profitability in the UK declined because of increased competition which followed deregulation there. Walsh (1987) argues that increased competition had reduced the profitability of traditional banking activities in Ireland.

It was argued in Chapter 3 that there was strong competition
in many financial service markets. Small firms have frequently
been critical of the banks, and it may be that competition is less
strong in this segment of the market, enabling banks to charge
higher rates to such borrowers. Ackland and Harper (1990) reported similar experiences following financial deregulation in
Australia, with margins narrowing on larger commercial loans
but widening on smaller loans. In the UK, increased competition

in the early 1980s was concentrated in the personal sector because of competition from building societies providing banking services and in the larger corporate sector where firms borrowed on the wholesale markets. Competition in the small business sector was less intense. Complaints that this lack of competition in the small business sector had led to UK banks overcharging small firms were not, however, borne out by a Government inquiry initiated in response to such complaints.

Contrary to oft-expressed claims that competition leads to job losses, the experience of the financial sector is that deregulation and increased competition has resulted in increased employment (see Table 12.4). Building society employment increased by almost 40 per cent, while employment in banks increased by 11 per cent between 1988 and 1994. This is consistent with the view that increased competition, by lowering prices, will result in increased demand and this should in turn generate an increase in employment. The performance of the financial sector in recent years is consistent with such predictions and tends to contradict arguments that competition harms employment.

TABLE 12:4 EMPLOYMENT IN BANKS AND BUILDING SOCIETIES

	1988	*1994*	*% Change*
Banks	20,575	22,925	+11.4
Building Societies	1,975	2,750	+39.2
Total	22,550	25,675	+13.9

Source: CSO, Irish Statistical Bulletin, various issues.

Leung (1989) notes that increased competition in the financial sector carries with it greater risks of default and bankruptcies. It has been claimed that financial deregulation in countries such as the US, UK, Australia, Canada and New Zealand allowed the growth of credit to "explode" in an unseemly fashion, resulting in an increase in the indebtedness of firms and individuals to dangerous levels (see, for example, Lawson, 1992; and Ackland and Harper, 1990). Lawson argues that the growth in borrowing which occurred in these countries was a once-off adjustment to deregulation. Increased loan defaults following liberalisation may reflect poor lending decisions by financial institutions. Kaufman (1986) argues that the great majority of failures in the US were "due to the old-fashioned reasons of fraud and excessive loan concentration" rather than deregulation. Poor lending decisions may be regarded as part of the learning process involved in adjusting to a deregulated regime. There have been few indications to date of similar problems emerging in Ireland. Some of the larger Irish banking groups have already had some rather painful experiences in overseas markets. Ruane (1987: 26) warns that:

> In the unsecured lending area in particular the skills and experience needed will be very critical and will probably be acquired outside the (building society) movement.

Some Conclusions

Government-imposed regulations apply to many sectors of the economy. In some areas regulations have been deliberately designed to restrict competition, based on a view that competition in particular sectors is harmful. Frequently, however, such views are not supported by the evidence. More often, regulations are designed to achieve other objectives, and restrictions on competition may be an unintended side effect. Restrictions on competition arising from regulations impose substantial costs on the economy and have adverse effects on the international competitiveness of Irish business. In important sectors such as road freight, airlines and financial services, liberalisation has produced substantial benefits. The fact that regulations restrict competition, however, benefits particular groups who have a vested interest in the retention of such regulations, long after the original rationale for such regulations has ceased to apply.

Government regulation is likely to remain an important feature of the economy, and indeed regulation is frequently necessary to protect consumers, public health and safety and the environment, to give just a few examples. It is important to recognise, however, that regulations which restrict competition have harmful effects. In the past, all too frequently the harmful consequences of particular regulatory measures were not fully taken into account. Nor is there any formal mechanism to assess whether any particular regulations have outlived their usefulness or to evaluate whether regulatory objectives could be achieved with less harmful effects on competition. In many OECD countries, competition authorities are permitted to express views regarding the competition implications of regulation and legislation. The FTC (1991a) recommended that the Competition Authority should be given such a role but this was not given effect in the Competition Act. The Hilmer Committee review of competition legislation in Australia concluded that, when considering the desirability of reforming particular regulations, the onus of proof should be reversed, making it necessary to justify continued regulatory restrictions on competition. It concluded that:

> A mechanism to facilitate the reform of government regulation that unjustifiably restricts competition should be a central plank of national competition policy. The starting point should be acceptance by all governments of the principle that there should be no regulatory restrictions on competition unless clearly demonstrated to be in the public interest (Hilmer, 1993: 205).

In 1995, the Commonwealth and State Governments signed an agreement committing them to review all existing regulations by the year 2000. It is somewhat anomalous that regulatory provisions in many sectors may be just as harmful as anti-competitive practices by private-sector firms and yet are not subject to detailed scrutiny. Restrictions on competition because of regulations impose costs on the economy and have an adverse impact on the international competitiveness of industry. In such circumstances, there is a need for a detailed review of regulations in order to establish (a) whether the cost of restrictions on competition is clearly outweighed by their benefits, and (b) whether the desirable objectives of regulation could be achieved in a less restrictive fashion.

13

COMPETITION IN ENERGY AND TELECOMMUNICATIONS[1]

Throughout the world the electricity, gas and telecommunications industries[2] have undergone dramatic changes over the past 20 years. These changes have involved a major re-appraisal of the role of government regulation in such industries, with greater emphasis being placed on promoting competition. Historically in Ireland the public utility industries were public-sector monopolies. This position is changing because of a combination of technological developments, EU legislation requiring Member States to liberalise such industries, and a growing realisation domestically that greater competition in these industries may be beneficial to the economy at large. The present chapter analyses the implications of such changes.

The Energy and Telecommunications Sectors in Ireland
Background

Bord Gáis Éireann (BGE), the Electricity Supply Board (ESB) and Telecom Éireann are State companies engaged respectively in the provision of gas, electricity and telecommunications services throughout the State. Summary statistics for all three are set out in Table 13.1. The government response to the natural monopoly aspect of the transmission network in these industries was to extend the monopoly into the downstream supply markets, thereby establishing vertically-integrated monopoly public-utility operators.

---

[1] For a more detailed analysis of competition and regulatory issues pertaining to public sector monopolies, see Massey and O'Hare (1996).

[2] These industries are collectively referred to as public utilities throughout this chapter. Generally the term public utilities includes water supply and sewage services as well as gas, electricity and telecommunications. The present chapter is not concerned with water supply and sewage services.

This pattern was common in many European countries in contrast to the United States where private ownership of such industries was the norm, with the natural monopoly problem being dealt with by means of regulatory controls.

TABLE 13.1: SUMMARY STATISTICS FOR IRISH PUBLIC UTILITIES (1994)

	BGE	*ESB*	*Telecom*
Turnover £m	217	977	979
Profit (Loss) £m	45	(19)	80
Employment	788	10,966	12,332

Notes: The figures for Telecom relate to the year ending 31.3.1995.

Source: Annual Reports.

The public-utility industries, while differing in a number of respects, share certain common features. As pointed out in Chapter 2, natural monopolies arise where economies of scale are such that efficiency is maximised by having a single producer of the product in question. Public utilities have traditionally been viewed as classic examples of natural monopolies, although only certain parts of them constitute a genuine natural monopoly, while other activities are at least potentially competitive. In the case of electricity, the transmission line network which makes up the national grid and the local distribution network are natural monopolies since it would be highly inefficient for competing firms to duplicate such facilities.[3] Similarly, the gas pipeline network also constitutes a natural monopoly. Historically, the local telecommunications network was regarded as a natural monopoly, although the position here is less clear cut, a point considered below.

While the transmission and distribution systems involve a high level of sunk costs, the marginal cost of providing services over the network is often quite low, and in some instances may be virtually zero. For this reason, two-part tariffs which split charges into a fixed charge for access to the service, combined with a variable charge based on consumption, are commonly employed in utility

---

[3]   While local distribution networks are natural monopolies, this does not preclude having several regional distribution networks owned separately.

industries. Fixed — that is, rental — charges are significant for telephone services but relatively low in the case of gas and electricity. Such tariffs can enable price for consumption to be set at the level of marginal cost in order to increase allocative efficiency, with the fixed charge being set at the level necessary to recoup the fixed costs.[4]

A second feature of utilities is that demand fluctuates systematically during the course of each day, week and year. For example, business demand for gas, electricity and telephone services is concentrated during working hours, while domestic users consume more outside working hours. Similarly, demand for gas and electricity is greater in winter than in summer. The bulk of the cost involved with catering for peak demand is the fixed cost of installing sufficient capacity to cope with such demand. Higher prices for peak use — "peak-load pricing" — are commonly applied in utility industries to discourage costly peak-time usage and to meet the higher cost of providing such services (for a more detailed analysis of peak-load pricing see, Berg and Tschirhart, 1988). Demand may also fluctuate randomly in a way that is unpredictable, so that demand for electricity and gas will be higher on a particularly cold winter's night than on the average winter's night. This poses problems because capacity is fixed and electricity and telecommunications output is largely non-storable.[5] A trade-off is required between installing enough capacity to meet the average peak, which will be insufficient to deal with unusual peaks, and installing enough capacity to meet all conceivable levels of demand, thereby incurring much higher construction costs.

In the case of electricity, the capacity problem could be alleviated if there were scope for imports, which is possible following the restoration of the inter-connector to Northern Ireland. In the case of both gas and electricity, the trade-off between installing sufficient capacity to meet any conceivable level of demand and the cost of failures arising from inadequate capacity can be resolved through

---

[4] As noted in Chapter 2, two-part tariffs are a form of price discrimination.

[5] Night storage heaters, however, use off-peak power to produce heat at other times, while fax transmissions can be stored. Such considerations do not apply in the case of gas which can be stored.

differential pricing. Thus industrial users can be offered a choice between a high price with supply guaranteed and a lower price with some risk that if demand exceeds capacity their supply will be cut off. The higher guaranteed supply price means that consumers who value the service most will choose this option. Customers who are only prepared to pay the lower interruptible price, because they place a lower value on having a guaranteed supply, will be the first to be cut off if supplies are inadequate to meet demand. Such a system of firm and interruptible tariffs is operated by British Gas, for example.

Electricity

The production and supply of electricity to final consumers is a highly complex, integrated process which can be broken down into four stages, as follows:

1. Generation

2. Transmission

3. Distribution

4. Sale to individual customers.

The first and last of these activities is potentially competitive. Both transmission and distribution involve high sunk costs and are natural monopolies.[6] Total ESB investment in the distribution system between 1988 and 1994, for example, amounted to £516 million. Currently the ESB is the only entity that may sell electricity within the State and it owns virtually all of the generating plant along with the transmission and distribution network. Electricity is costly to transport and a proportion is lost in the course of transmission. Transmission losses increase with the level of use of the system and with distance. The situation is further complicated because supply is subject to unpredictable outages. Balance

---

[6] By transmission we mean the high-voltage nationwide network of lines which carry power from the generating stations. Distribution involves taking power from the high-voltage transmission network, reducing voltage by means of transformers to levels suitable for industrial and domestic usage and then supplying power to individual homes and business premises by means of the lower voltage local-line network.

between supply and demand must be maintained constantly throughout the system. Otherwise, non-localised power outages or blackouts will occur. The need to maintain constant balance between supply and demand requires very close co-ordination between generation and transmission and is a major reason why these two activities have traditionally been vertically integrated. Installed generating capacity has to exceed demand. Plant has to be up and ready to supply to cope with any sudden surge in demand or plant failure. This is referred to as "spinning reserve". In addition to the requirement that some stations be run in order to meet spinning reserve requirements, start-up costs mean that it may be cheaper to keep stations running even when they are not producing, rather than shutting them down and starting them up again. Electricity systems generally use a mixture of different plant types with a diversity of fuels. Very small generating units have traditionally been regarded as inefficient, with estimates that capacity of around 400 MW was the minimum efficient scale for fossil fuel generating plants (Armstrong et al., 1994). Technological changes, however, mean that small-scale generating plant may be efficient and could become more common in the future.

Gas

The natural gas industry is similar in many respects to electricity. Natural gas production involves the extraction and pumping ashore of natural gas from gas fields located offshore.[7] It is then transmitted via the gas pipeline and distributed to individual users. Production is potentially competitive and indeed the extraction and piping ashore of gas is carried out by private-sector exploration companies. All natural gas extracted offshore must, however, be sold to BGE for resale. BGE also controls the national gas grid (transmission network), and during the 1980s it acquired control of all of the old town gas companies, giving it control of the local distribution networks. The gas pipeline is confined to the south and east of the country and it is estimated that only one-third of households are within the pipeline network (BGE, 1994). The

---

[7]   Seventy-eight per cent of the reserves in the Kinsale Head and Ballycotton fields had been depleted by the end of 1994 and it is estimated that the fields will be exhausted by the turn of the century (BGE, 1994).

completion of an interconnector linking Ireland to the UK gas network means that natural gas can be imported from other European
countries, thus ensuring continuity of supply in the absence of any
further offshore discoveries. The interconnector could allow competition as large customers could purchase from overseas suppliers.

The pattern of BGE gas sales and revenues is shown in Figure
13.1. In volume terms, more than 40 per cent of natural gas in
1994 was supplied to the ESB for electricity generation. A further 23 per cent was provided to Nitrigin Éireann Teoranta
(NET), a State-owned company engaged in fertiliser production,
in a joint venture with a subsidiary of ICI.

FIGURE 13.1: PER CENT DISTRIBUTION OF GAS SALES AND REVENUE

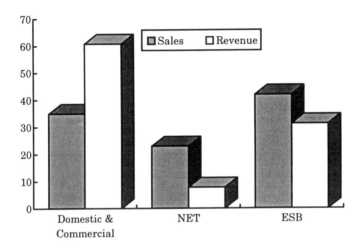

Source: BGE, Annual Report, 1994.

The balance went to the household, industrial and commercial
sectors.[8] Gas is supplied to ESB and NET at prices that are well
below market rates. Revenues from sales to NET represented just
£17 million out of total sales revenue of £217 million, or less than
8 per cent of BGE revenue. Households, along with industrial and
commercial users, contributed almost two-thirds of BGE revenues.

---

[8]   Households accounted for only 11 per cent of sales in volume terms in
       1994.

Telecommunications

Telecommunications services now extend far beyond basic voice telephony, as the distinctions between telecommunications, broadcasting and computer services are becoming increasingly blurred as a result of technological changes. In considering the sector, it may be useful to distinguish between the actual telephone network and the services provided over the network, while recognising that the distinction between these concepts is not always clear-cut. The telecommunications network connects users by means of a combination of exchanges and transmission links. Subscribers are connected to local exchanges by means of a "local loop". These are in turn linked to trunk or long-distance exchanges and ultimately to international networks. In practice, local exchanges may be connected to more than one main exchange, thus providing several possible routes for any long-distance call. The capacity of telecom networks has been greatly expanded by the introduction of fibre optic cables in place of the traditional copper wires. For example, a single fibre thinner than a human hair can carry 30,000 simultaneous telephone conversations (*The Economist*, 30 September 1995). While installation costs for fibre optic and traditional cables are similar, the maintenance costs of the former are far lower. The introduction of fibre optic cables has also dramatically reduced the long-run marginal cost of long-distance calls. The increased capacity of fibre optic cables, combined with the growing complexity of exchanges which now use electronic switching equipment, has also greatly extended the possible range of services that can be provided over the network. Digital transmission has replaced traditional analogue signals leading to a growing convergence between telecommunications and computing technology. By 1993, digital exchanges accounted for 66 per cent of Telecom's capacity, while 70 per cent of the transmission network consisted of fibre optic cables (Hall, 1993). As Figure 13.2 illustrates, labour productivity in Telecom, in terms of main lines per employee, in 1990 was the lowest in the OECD. Although Telecom had increased the number of lines per employee by 34 per cent from 73 to 98 between 1990 and March 1995, this still only put it ahead of the 1990 figure for Australia, New Zealand and Turkey. In contrast, the number of lines per employee in Telecom New Zealand increased from 86 to 214 between 1990 and 1994 (Treasury and Ministry of Commerce, 1995).

FIGURE 13.2: MAIN TELEPHONE LINES PER EMPLOYEE (1990)

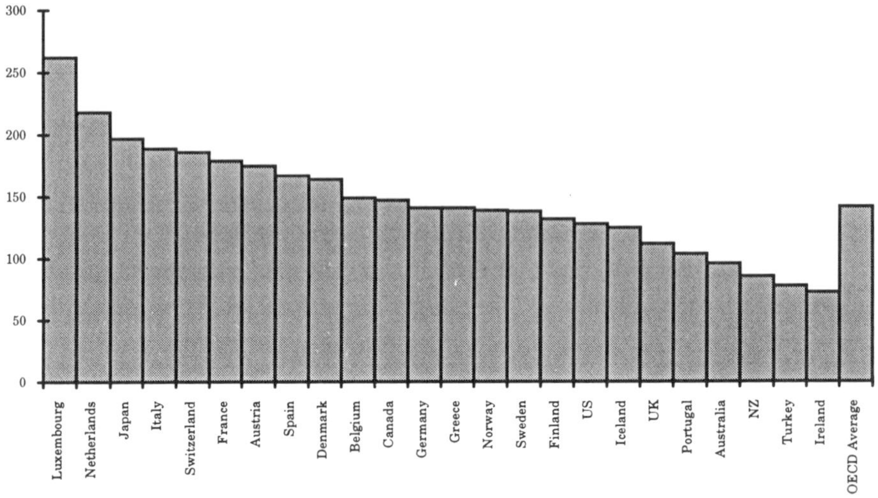

Source: OECD (1993b).

At local level, cable television companies have emerged as significant competitors to public telecom operators (PTOs) in countries such as the US and the UK. The coaxial cable normally used for cable networks provides much more bandwidth than the copper wires traditionally used in telephone networks. In many countries cable companies have been installing fibre optic cables and providing telephone services over their networks. Ireland already has a well-established cable network covering all of the major urban areas, although each cable operator has a statutory monopoly in its allotted territory. Currently Telecom is the majority shareholder in Cablelink, which provides cable services in Dublin, Galway and Waterford. Cablelink was estimated to enjoy a profit of £17 per subscriber in 1995.

Increasing Competition

The Scope for Increased Competition

Experience of liberalisation of energy and telecommunications markets elsewhere shows that competition has resulted in increased efficiency, lower prices and improved quality and range of services to consumers. OFTEL (1994) reported that telephone charges in the UK fell by 35 per cent in real terms in the decade after 1984, in spite of the fact that, initially, competition was limited by the government decision to allow only one new entrant to the industry, thereby establishing a duopoly. In the US, the break-up of the AT&T telephone monopoly following a lengthy antitrust case resulted in residential long-distance telephone charges falling by 50 per cent in real terms between 1984 and 1994 without unduly compromising universal services (Bingaman, 1995). Increased competition in US telecommunications hastened the deployment of fibre optic technology and spurred an increase in technological innovation (US Department of Justice, 1994). In New Zealand, liberalisation resulted in falls in both household and business charges.[9] It was also accompanied by a major investment programme which has meant that 98 per cent of lines are now connected to digital switches. Competition in telecommunications was also found to have yielded substantial benefits to users and PTOs in Australia and Japan (OECD, 1995). In the case of electricity in the UK, large customers' bills have fallen by 10 per cent on average in real terms, while prices to smaller customers are down by 4.5 per cent (Green, 1995). Henney (1994) also found that liberalisation of the electricity industry in the UK, while suffering from certain shortcomings, nevertheless represented an improvement on the previous regime where generation was confined to a monopoly producer. (For a more detailed review of the benefits from introducing competition in public-utility industries, see OECD, 1992).

Competition could be introduced in electricity by permitting suppliers other than the ESB to sell directly to users. At the time of going to press, EU ministers have agreed proposals which would allow competition in respect of a significant part of the market. It appears that competition will be introduced in respect of industrial users from 1998. Minister Michael Lowry has announced that an independent power procurer would be established. It would be

---

[9] Estimates for a basket of services showed that between 1990 and 1994, residential charges fell by more than 4 per cent while business charges fell by 11 per cent (Treasury — Ministry of Commerce, 1995).

responsible for purchasing electricity from all suppliers and re-selling it to users. The alternative would be to establish a wholesale electricity market where suppliers and consumers can purchase and sell electricity. Wholesale electricity pools now operate in some 50 countries. Either alternative could be combined with allowing industrial users to negotiate directly with individual producers for electricity supplies. In the case of natural gas supply competition is also possible by allowing overseas suppliers to supply customers in Ireland by using the interconnector link with the UK. The Energy (Miscellaneous Provisions) Act, 1995 in fact allows single customers taking in excess of 25m cubic metres per annum at a single premises to purchase gas from UK suppliers using the interconnector. According to the Chairman of BGE, the number of Irish customers in that category is small. At present, disputes over access charges fall to be resolved by the Minister (see below).

There has been some liberalising of parts of the telecommunications market, partly as a result of pressure from the EU Commission and partly because of technological developments. Telecom is exposed to competition in international markets from domestic suppliers using leased lines and from overseas call-back services. Leased lines are also being used to introduce competition on internal long-distance calls. A licence has been awarded to a second mobile operator. Competition in local services is also theoretically possible given the high level of penetration of cable systems in all major urban areas.

Possible Difficulties

While liberalisation or deregulation of the public utility industries would make competition possible, at least in theory, it has to be recognised that, of itself, it would not necessarily result in competition emerging. As the transmission and distribution networks for electricity and gas constitute natural monopolies, it would be necessary to allow private producers access to the transmission and distribution networks. Incumbent operators, however, have a strong incentive to deny competitors such access or to impose excessively high charges for access to prevent competition. Ergas (1995) observed that:

> Even if it were in the incumbent owner's interest to allow competing entry because its owner's losses from increased competition in the downstream market would be outweighed by gains from access revenues and enhanced internal efficiency, principal–agent problems may still lead the firm's managers to refuse to deal. Particularly in public enterprises with a long history of public ownership, managers may be output or employment maximisers, more interested in retaining market share than in increasing shareholder value. Being risk-averse, the incumbent's managers may weigh the certain loss of a "quiet life" far more heavily than the uncertain gains they could secure from operating in a competitive environment. . . . As a result, the firm's managers may stall or obstruct access by the entrant even when such access would have been granted by the facility's owners (Ergas, 1995: 6).

Stern (1992) claims that incumbent firms in the gas industry throughout Europe deliberately exaggerated the problems and advanced obscure technological arguments to block proposals that EU Member States grant gas suppliers from other states access to their networks. In the UK it took almost four years of negotiations to secure agreement on the question of access charges permitting Mercury to enter the market in competition with British Telecom. Similarly, in New Zealand disputes between Telecom New Zealand and Clear Communications relating to access charges for the local loop were only resolved after a long drawn-out court battle which was ultimately decided by the Privy Council in London. Interconnection charges in respect of a number of other services were agreed, however.

Technological changes mean that local telephone networks may no longer constitute a natural monopoly. In New Zealand, for example, one new entrant has constructed networks in the major cities. Similarly, cable TV networks can be used to provide telephone services, and in the UK many cable operators have installed local networks. Any new entrant wishing to compete in the market would still need access to the existing Telecom network because potential subscribers to any alternative telephone network will want to be able to make calls to existing network subscribers. Unless they could have such access, there would be no incentive for any consumers to subscribe to any new network so that denial of such access would effectively prevent a competing service from getting off the ground. Consequently, even though the local network may not be a natural monopoly, access to the existing network is still vital for entry to the market.

A second problem arises because the existing State companies have a dominant position and this is unlikely to change in the short term. Purchases of electricity by the ESB from small suppliers amounted to only 0.2 per cent of sent out load in 1992. Admittedly there are some large industrial concerns in the State which generate their own electricity. Realistically, this is still likely to represent only a very small proportion of total electricity demand. Consequently, the ESB is likely to remain the major electricity generator for the foreseeable future. Over time this could change if liberalisation attracted more private investment into electricity generation. In the case of telecommunications, competition in the market for local calls may remain rather limited for some time, unless Telecom is required to dispose of its shareholding in Cablelink. The impact on incumbent behaviour of the threat of new entry should not be entirely discounted. Massey and O'Hare (1996), for example, note that the threat of entry appeared to have a significant effect in the New Zealand electricity market. There are limits to the effectiveness of potential competition if none actually materialises.

A third difficulty often raised in the context of proposals to introduce competition into the utility industries is the threat of "cream-skimming". This arises because the incumbent state firms are required to provide some services on terms that make it uneconomic to do so. Rural customers, for example, do not bear the full cost of being linked to the network. Instead, other customers may pay more than the true cost of having services provided, thereby cross-subsidising those consumers who do not pay the full cost of the service. In such circumstances the removal of restrictions on entry may cause new entrants to concentrate on those segments of the market where the costs of providing services are lowest and where they will be able to undercut the price of the incumbent firm, since they do not have to cross-subsidise operations elsewhere. This raises the question of whether charges for access to the transmission and distribution networks should in some way reflect the costs of the provision of uneconomic services in order to prevent "cream-skimming". This point needs to be treated with some degree of caution, however.

Some Practical Difficulties

Theoretical Issues

Some form of regulatory regime is needed because the incumbent firm (a) may abuse its market power by charging excessively high prices for its output and (b) because it might set prices for network access in a way that is designed to hinder its competitors. (It may also be true that new entrants will want to obtain access for as low a price as possible). The regulatory problem can be viewed as a form of principal–agent relationship where the regulator is the principal and the regulated firm is the agent. Principal–agency theory recognises the existence of information asymmetries between the principal and the agent. It also recognises that agents face incentives to act in their own best interests rather than those of the principal. This requires that the principal devise a set of rules that will provide the agent with an incentive to operate in the principal's interests. This, however, is easier said than done. We now consider some general principles that are common to setting both output and interconnection charges, before considering each of these individually.

Orthodox economic theory argues that efficiency is maximised where price equals marginal cost. In public-utility industries economies of scale mean that marginal cost is less than average cost. Setting price at the level of marginal cost will result in losses for the regulated firm. The first best solution to the problem would be to set prices equal to marginal costs, in order to maximise allocative efficiency, and for the government to compensate the incumbent firm by payment of a direct subsidy. As Stiglitz (1990) points out, however, such a policy ignores the question of how the revenues to pay such a subsidy are to be raised and assumes, in particular, that there are no distortions associated with raising such revenue. It also requires that the government know the magnitude of the subsidy required to make the firm viable.

The second best solution to such problems is to require the firm to operate at the intersection of its demand curve and its average cost curve. At this point, the firm simply breaks even. The picture becomes even more complicated for multi-product firms like public utilities. Where there are differences in the elasticity of demand for the different outputs of the firm, price discrimination may result in a more efficient outcome than would otherwise occur because it results in higher output than would arise under the monopoly price. One mechanism for setting prices based on this approach is Ramsay pricing, which approximates what a profit-maximising monopolist would tend to do naturally but constrains the total amount of revenue accruing to the monopolist. Ramsay prices operate on the basis that mark-ups should be lower for those products with high price elasticities of demand and higher for those where demand is relatively inelastic.[10] The rationale for this is that the distortions arising from the need to set price above marginal cost will be minimised if the mark-ups lead to approximately the same proportionate reductions in demand for different services, since this will result in a smaller contraction of output and smaller deadweight losses than might otherwise occur. Ramsay prices suffer from a number of deficiencies, however. They require that the regulator possess enormous amounts of information regarding demand elasticities in different markets and firms' costs. Armstrong et al. (1994) point out that Ramsay prices are rarely used in practice and were not applied in the case of Electricité de France even when Boiteaux — a pioneer of the concept of Ramsay pricing — was in charge of that company. Ramsay prices also require that different customers be charged different prices for the same product and this may not prove acceptable politically. Baumol and Sidak (1994) point out that it is not clear that Ramsay prices calculated *ex ante* will necessarily maximise economic efficiency, particularly in the case of telecommunications.

---

[10] Ramsay pricing states that the regulator of a natural monopoly should set prices such that, in any given market segment i

$$((P_i - MC_i)/P_i) = R(1/e_i), \quad 0 < R < 1 \dots\dots\dots\dots\dots (1)$$

where e_i is the price elasticity of demand for the market segment i and R is the Ramsay number and P and MC are price and marginal cost respectively. Effectively, it involves limiting the degree of mark-up over marginal costs.

Regulating Output Prices

Forcing dominant suppliers to charge very low prices might benefit consumers in the short term but it may inhibit entry by new suppliers, thus preventing the development of competition to the long-term detriment of consumers. National Utility Services (NUS) (1995) found that the development of competition in UK telecoms had been stifled by the price-cap regime which operates there. If adequate competition does not develop, it may cause prices to rise in the longer term. The sunk-cost nature of investment in public utilities raises other problems. Once the regulated firm has invested in new capacity, a price that is sufficient to cover variable costs is sufficient to cause it to continue supplying services. The risk that the regulator may set prices *ex post* which are too low to cover the fixed costs of necessary investment may actually deter the firm from undertaking such investment *ex ante*. This raises problems of commitment and the credibility of the regulator. To avoid this problem many regulatory regimes require that the regulator allow firms to earn a "fair" rate of return on capital. While such a guarantee provides an incentive for firms to engage in a high level of investment, it suffers from certain drawbacks because it means that unnecessary or inefficient projects should be rewarded as much as efficient ones. In the US, judicial precedents have established that regulators are only required to allow a fair return on capital that is "used and useful" (Armstrong et al., 1994). In the UK regulators are obliged to ensure that the regulated firm can finance its operations. Nevertheless, the scope afforded to regulators under the UK regime permits regulators to alter the rules of the game after firms have borne the "sunk costs" of investment. This reduces the incentive to invest and raises capital costs. The importance of regulator credibility was highlighted by the decision of the electricity regulator in the UK in early 1995 to implement a full-scale pricing review less than a year after agreeing a price-cap with the electricity companies and within days of the Government selling its shares in the two electricity generating companies. To some extent this move damaged the credibility of the entire regulatory system in the UK.

The problem of setting prices would be greatly simplified if the regulator had sufficient information to set prices at their optimal level. It is now widely recognised in the literature that information asymmetries between the regulator and the regulated firm make effective regulation very difficult. The more information the regulator possesses, the more effective regulatory decisions are likely to be. Information is not costless, however, and the regulator will have to choose between the cost of acquiring additional information and the benefit to be obtained from more efficient regulation. The information asymmetry problem can be eased by setting price-fixing rules that provide incentives for firms to reveal information about their operations. Of course, because regulation is a dynamic rather than a static process, firms will know that it is in their interests to provide misleading signals to the regulator in the hope of producing a more beneficial regulatory regime in the future. The announcement of a full-scale review of electricity prices in the UK in early 1995 was prompted by a belief that the electricity companies had misled the Regulator.

Several forms of output price regulation have been used in practice. Indeed, the ESB could already be said to operate under a form of output price regulation since, as noted, it is obliged by statute to operate on a break-even basis. Such rules provide no incentive at all to control costs. In addition, the ESB has also evaded this constraint by effectively adopting in its accounts a system of double depreciation.

Bailey (1986) describes how, up to 1949, under an arrangement known as the sliding scale, dividends paid by UK gas companies to their shareholders could not exceed 10 per cent of their capital unless their prices fell. If prices rose, dividends had to be reduced. An alternative, known as co-partnership, provided that increases in profits caused by a fall in prices were to be split between the workforce and the shareholders, thus providing a direct incentive to efficiency. Burns et al. (1995) called for the re-introduction of sliding-scale regulation in the UK in place of price-cap regulation, and Offer (1995) included sliding-scale regulation as an option for regulating national-grid transmission prices. Burns et al. (1995) found that, although price-cap regulation works well in ensuring technical and allocative efficiency, various factors can result in profits being either very high or very low. Such outcomes can arise where the regulator is weak or ill-informed or overly aggressive, or if the company is subject to unexpected shocks in the interval between regulatory reviews.

Sliding-scale regulation avoids the need to forecast inflation. Dividend sliding-scale regulation operates on the basis that dividends can only increase beyond a certain level provided that prices throughout the year have been below a certain level.[11] If at the end of the year the firm wished to pay a dividend which was above the standard dividend, even though its price had not been below the standard price, the regulator would oblige it to make an end of year rebate to its customers, the size of which would be determined by the profit-sharing parameter. The scheme operates on the premise that the firm's objective will be to maximise profits even though some of the benefits of doing so will accrue to customers. As Burns et al. (1995) point out, however, the level at which the profit-sharing parameter is set may have implications for the regulated firm's behaviour, since the incentive effects of a regime which embodies a 90:10 share-out in favour of the customer is likely to differ from one that offers a 90:10 share-out in favour of shareholders. For a dividend sliding-scale regime to be effective, the regulator needs to ensure that the regulated firm does not manage to evade regulatory controls by paying dividends to shareholders in other ways. An alternative to the dividend sliding-scale regime is a price-related profits levy under which it is the firm's profits, rather than dividends, that are conditional on its pricing behaviour. Burns et al. (1995) show that such a regime will produce the same results as a dividend sliding scale. Again, the regulator in such a regime needs to ensure that the firm does not manipulate its profits by changing its accounting procedures in respect of depreciation and bad debts. A more fundamental problem in the existing Irish context is that the ESB, BGE and Telecom are all state owned so that regulatory regimes that focus on dividends or profits are unlikely to prove very effective.

Rate-of-return controls have been extensively used in the

---

[11] Formally such a constraint can be expressed in the form:

$$(l_A - l_s) < ((P_S - P_A)/P_S).a \dots\dots\dots\dots\dots\dots (2).$$

where l_A and l_s represent actual and expected dividend yield respectively, P_A and P_S are actual and standard price and a is the profit-sharing parameter.

United States over a long period. Essentially, controls in this form set limits on the profits that a regulated firm may earn. Once the rate of return is set, the firm can raise prices to offset any increase in costs, so there is little incentive to minimise costs. Rate-of-return regulation encourages excessive or so-called "gold plating" investment because increasing the capital base increases allowable profits — the so-called Averch-Johnson effect. In the case of a multi-product firm selling some outputs on competitive markets, such regulation may lead to pricing below marginal costs in those markets as a means of inflating the rate base. Regulation of this type provides little incentive for firms to worry about X-efficiency. In practice, rate-of-return regulation is based on past performance, giving rise to "regulatory lag". The existence of regulatory lag means that there is some incentive to reduce costs since the firm will enjoy a short-term benefit from doing so, at least until the next regulatory review. Rate-of-return regulation also requires that the regulator possess substantial information about cost and demand. There is also the thorny issue of deciding on an appropriate rate of return. The US system is characterised by lengthy legal disputes between the regulators and the regulated firms on the issue of the rate of return to be allowed.

Because of doubts about the efficacy of rate-of-return regulation, the UK Government commissioned a study of all options for regulating British Telecom before its privatisation in 1983. Littlechild (1983) advocated a form of price-capping regulation which he claimed was superior to rate-of-return regulation in terms of restraining monopoly power, promoting competition, reducing X-inefficiency, and providing incentives for cost reductions. It was also claimed that such regulation would be simpler to operate and less vulnerable to producer capture. As a result, price-capping was applied to British Telecom and has since been applied to a number of other privatised utilities in the UK. In the US, price-capping has replaced rate-of-return regulations in the case of telecommunications.

The price cap applied to British Telecom and a number of other utilities in the UK has generally involved setting the maximum rate of price increase as some amount less than the increase in the general level of consumer prices — the so-called RPI–X formula where X represents a target for efficiency gains by the firm.[12] The retail price index was chosen in preference to any industry-specific price index since the latter could be manipulated by the regulated firm. It also provides clear and easily understood signals to consumers. It was argued that this system would give the regulated firm an incentive to achieve productive efficiency and would promote innovation because cost reductions greater than X would be reflected in higher profits for the firm. Such a regime was also claimed to be simpler to operate since there was no need to measure the asset base or rates of return, cost allocation between competitive and monopolistic parts of the firm was unnecessary, and future movements of costs and demand did not have to be forecast.[13]

Pure price-cap regulation would not permit any degree of cost pass-through. In practice, in the UK, cost pass-through is permitted in respect of a relatively large part of the regulated firm's total costs, to protect the firm against increases in costs that are outside its control, while allowing consumers to benefit from downward movements in costs before the next review (Armstrong et al., 1994). The regulator has two main alternatives to permitting costs to be passed through: either to set a higher price cap to compensate the firm for the risk of higher profit volatility, or to

---

[12] The RPI is the retail price index. The equivalent measure in Ireland is the consumer price index (CPI).

[13] Two different forms of price-capping have been applied. The first known as the "tariff basket method" has been used in the case of British Telecom and the water companies. This type of price cap requires that the weighted average of price increases of the products included in the basket should not exceed the RPI-X price cap. This method can be used whether products are commensurable or not. The second method is known as average revenue regulation and has been used in the case of gas and electricity. This mechanism can only be applied where the products supplied by the regulated firm are commensurable, which is the case for gas and electricity where output can be measured on the basis of therms or kilowatt hours. Under this system, the regulated firm proposes price changes and predicts the total revenue and output given the new prices. Predicted average revenue is only permitted to grow by RPI-X. Since the firm faces an obvious incentive to act strategically in making its forecasts a clawback factor is included to clawback any gains or losses from forecasting errors.

increase the frequency of regulatory reviews.

Setting price caps in respect of a basket of products simplifies the task of the regulator. It also has certain other advantages. Flexibility will allow the firm to increase profits and, if the price cap ensures that consumers as a whole are not worse off as a result, the net result is increased social welfare. Flexibility also enables the firm to alter relative prices in response to changes in costs and to unwind cross-subsidies that may exist. Complete freedom to vary prices could also permit anti-competitive behaviour by the firm, since it might attempt to reduce prices in competitive markets and engage in predatory pricing, while financing this behaviour through higher prices in markets where competition is limited. The longer the lag between price cap reviews, the greater the incentive for productive efficiency, since it increases the benefit to the firm arising from any cost reductions. Long lags, however, might adversely affect allocative efficiency. There is obviously some trade-off between these two objectives. Price caps suffer from an obvious defect in that they provide no incentive for the firm to provide a good quality service. In fact, the firm has an incentive to under-invest in quality. Consequently, price-capping also requires that the quality of services be regulated.

In order to determine the appropriate X factor, regulators in the UK have taken into account a variety of factors such as the value of existing assets, the cost of capital, expected rates of growth of productivity and demand and the progress of competition. One of the alleged benefits of price caps was that they reduced the regulatory burden since they did not require the measurement of capital or rates of return. As Armstrong et al. (1994) point out, regulators concerned with allocative efficiency must take such factors into account. Estimating the cost of capital and the value of the regulated firm's asset base is an extremely complex task. Clearly, problems arise here because of the existence of information asymmetries. The whole process is therefore a highly complex one and far more difficult than originally envisaged.

There has been a tendency over time in the UK to increase the range of regulated products. Armstrong et al. (*ibid.*) point out how, in the case of BT, international calls, leased lines and connection charges were added to the basket of regulated services, increasing the proportion of Telecom's business (in terms of revenue) which was regulated, from 50 per cent in 1984 to 70 per cent.[14] Commenting on the experience of British Gas, Spring (1993) found that "regulatory intervention has spread from the tariff segment to all aspects of the business and become increasingly intrusive". Price caps have tended to become tighter, while regulators have tended to become more closely involved in actively trying to influence firms' decisions on the level and structure of prices, rather than simply checking that licence conditions are being adhered to. It has, in effect, become more like "rate-of-return" regulation over time. Littlechild (1986) conceded that "rate-of-return considerations are necessarily implicit in setting and resetting X". The UK regime originally avoided much of the lengthy legal disputes characteristic of the US regime. Instead, price caps and other licensing obligations were resolved by negotiations between the regulators and regulated firms. It has been established that the regulator's decisions may be challenged in the courts. The Director General of OFTEL stated that it was having to deal with an increasing number of legal issues and that it had had to double its legal staff (*Financial Times*, 10 February 1995).

Price-cap regulation has not proved to be as successful as originally predicted. Lynk (1993) found evidence that BT continued to earn above-normal profits in spite of price-capping. Burns and Weyman-Jones (1994) found that few of the regional electricity distribution companies (RECs) had significantly improved their productivity following privatisation, although price caps supposedly offer firms the incentive to beat the cap and maximise profits. The decision by the electricity regulator to undertake a full-scale price review in 1995, less than a year after establishing new price caps, because the regulated firms' financial performance was much better than previously envisaged, also raises some very serious questions about the system. A number of studies of utility regulation indicate that the individual regulators have had a crucial influence on its overall efficacy (see, for example, Foster, 1993). The fact that success is more dependent on the individual

---

[14] In 1996, the telecom regulator announced that the range of BT services subject to price-cap controls would be reduced in the context of adopting a rule prohibiting anti-competitive behaviour.

regulator than on the regime itself again raises serious questions about the regime. More importantly, all of the output price regulatory regimes considered here are designed to regulate output prices of privately-owned firms. They assume that such firms will act as profit maximisers. Thus, price-cap regulations operate on the assumption that the firm will endeavour to minimise costs, thereby providing information to the regulator about the scope for efficiency gains which can be used in future price-cap reviews. It is not at all clear that such a regime would represent a solution in an Irish context where the regulated firms continue in State ownership. Specifically, it would appear that such firms would not have the same incentive to minimise costs and maximise profits subject to the price cap. If one argues that competition will pressurise them to cut costs, this begs the question: if competition is adequate to ensure such an outcome, why regulate?

Setting Access Charges

When the network operator is part of a vertically-integrated firm which is also competing in the provision of services over the network, it has obvious incentives to provide access to its competitors on less favourable terms. Such unfavourable terms may relate not only to price but to quality of service and a number of other factors. Ensuring that this does not happen requires that the regulator possess highly detailed information about the operations of the incumbent firm and be prepared to undertake extensive monitoring of its activities. This is both complex and expensive. If the regulator fails to detect and prevent such behaviour, many of the benefits from competition will be lost.

Once the incumbent firm has met the fixed cost of establishing a transmission network, the marginal cost of providing services is extremely low. Setting access charges at marginal cost means that the network owner will not receive any contribution towards the fixed cost of the network. Since the incumbent will have to recoup such costs from customers of its services, access charges based on marginal cost would also allow rival operators to undercut the network owner's prices, resulting in "cream-skimming". The Minister for Transport, Energy and Communications had indicated that access charges would have to reflect the cost of providing universal services (Dáil Debates, 21 February 1995). It is extremely difficult for a regulator to establish the true level of such costs, and incumbent firms have an incentive to overstate them.

A considerable amount of work has been undertaken into establishing how access charges for connection to networks should be determined. Willig (1979) considered the question of access charges in respect of telecommunications, while Baumol (1983) also analysed this question in respect of access to the railroad network. The rule proposed in those studies has become known as the efficient component pricing rule (ECPR) and it is discussed further in Baumol and Sidak (1994). The ECPR recognises that each unit of access supplied to a competitor represents a unit of sales lost by the incumbent and, according to this rule, the access price should be equal to the marginal cost of access plus the profit loss suffered by the incumbent from the loss of that unit of sales. It is a form of marginal cost pricing that includes the opportunity cost to the incumbent of granting access to a competitor. The inclusion of opportunity costs is designed to provide a contribution towards fixed costs and, at the same time, to prevent inefficient entry and "cream-skimming" by ensuring that rivals take custom from the vertically-integrated firm if, and only if, they are more efficient in producing the final product. The ECPR ensures efficient production and, provided that entry conditions are not otherwise distorted, it will result in efficient entry.[15]

---

[15] To illustrate how the ECPR operates, let us suppose that the incumbent firm produces an essential input to services in the downstream market at a constant marginal cost of 2p. Now assume that the firm also has a downstream subsidiary which converts the input into a final product at an additional constant marginal cost of 3p. If the final product sells at a price of, say, 10p, the incumbent enjoys profits of 5p per unit sold. A new entrant wishing to enter the downstream market must purchase the essential input from the incumbent firm. How much should it pay the incumbent? According to the ECPR, if every unit sold by the new entrant results in a loss of sales to the incumbent, then the price should be the 2p marginal cost of production of the essential input, plus 5p in profits foregone, giving a total charge of 7p. Only new entrants with marginal costs equal to or less than 3p, which is the marginal cost to the incumbent of converting the input into the final product, will be able to enter the market profitably — less efficient firms will not be able to enter. It is assumed that the marginal cost includes normal profit so that the 5p profits that the incumbent enjoys on each unit sold constitute monopoly profits.

The ECPR, however, suffers from a number of shortcomings which raise considerable doubts about its usefulness for setting access charges. OFTEL (1994) argued that for public utilities which are characterised by economies of scale and sunk costs, it would be difficult for a new entrant to achieve the same or lower costs than the incumbent initially and thus, under the ECPR, it would not be able to enter the market. It has also pointed out that in its simplest form the ECPR would mean that competitors could end up contributing to the incumbent's inefficiency as the opportunity cost to the incumbent includes its monopoly profits. Baumol and Sidak (1994) argue that this will only be true where final product prices are not subject to regulatory control, indicating that the ECPR can only be used where prices in the downstream market are also regulated. More importantly, however, in order for the ECPR to operate as an optimal pricing rule it is necessary that other regulated prices be set optimally too. If regulated output prices involve some degree of cross-subsidisation, there will still be some incentive for new entrants to "cream-skim" and only enter the higher revenue markets. OFTEL concluded that the rule was too restrictive and, while it may yield short-term benefits by discouraging inefficient entry, the ECPR would deter new entrants who might prove more competitive in the long run, and it was therefore too restrictive if the major objective of policy was to move towards a competitive market. Dews (1995) advanced similar criticisms, arguing that, in the longer term, competition would deliver a more efficient industry with lower costs to consumers. She also argued that the rule was flawed since it required that lower prices from the new entrant could only be sourced from efficiency savings and cost reductions, rather than squeezing retail margins.

Various alternative mechanisms for setting access charges have been proposed by economists including:

Now if final output prices are regulated, the regulator should set prices at a level that would eliminate any monopoly profits, i.e. 5p. In that case, the access price is 2p. Suppose now that the incumbent firm has to discharge certain social functions which impose an additional cost of 1p per unit. In that case the access price should be set at 3p, i.e. 2p + 1p. Thus, the ECPR will take account of such social obligations.

1. Setting prices at short-run or long-run marginal cost

2. Setting prices at long-run average incremental cost

3. Ramsay Pricing

4. Two-part charges — for example, a high "fixed" charge with a low "usage" charge

5. Peak-load pricing

6. Revenue-capping rules.

A number of these options, however, also suffer from some serious deficiencies. As noted above, pricing at short-run marginal cost will not provide sufficient revenue to cover total costs. Ramsay prices are difficult to estimate and rarely used in practice. Using long-run average incremental costs is a particularly favoured pricing rule in telecommunications (OFTEL, 1995). All access-pricing rules involve difficult and detailed economic analysis. Setting prices wrongly is likely to have significant adverse consequences. "There simply do not exist 'bright line' rules to determine what constitutes an appropriate access price across all industries and situations" (Treasury and Ministry of Commerce, 1995: 54).

Promoting Greater Competition
The implications of the previous sections are that regulating public-utility industries is a highly complex task. Setting output prices and access charges requires that the regulator possess detailed information regarding the business concerned. However, the regulator must rely on the regulated firm to provide the necessary information. The existence of information asymmetries greatly complicates the regulator's task. International experience shows that sector-specific regulatory regimes are particularly vulnerable to capture. In the US, regulation of the electricity industry was found to have no discernible effect on the industry's behaviour (Stigler and Friedland, 1962). Similarly, in the case of telecommunications, the break-up of AT&T and the competition that ensued as a result were far more beneficial than regulation. Armstrong et al. (1994) describe as a missed opportunity the decision initially to limit competition in telecommunications in the UK.

The main lesson, therefore, is that regulation is no substitute for competition.

Horizontal Issues

One very effective way to foster competition in the electricity industry would be to restrict investment in new generating capacity to firms other than the ESB, at least until the ESB's share of the market had been reduced below a certain level. The target could be set at a level that would expose the ESB to a significant degree of competition. The proposals recently announced by the Minister for Transport, Energy and Communications would allow only a small number of consumers to purchase electricity directly. It is not clear why this option should not be afforded to a wider number of customers. Competition could also be increased by allowing consumers to purchase electricity from suppliers located outside the State. Effectively, in the short term this means allowing users to purchase supplies from generators in Northern Ireland. Access would have to be granted to the inter-connector on the same basis as for the rest of the transmission system. Such proposals would lead to greater competition in electricity supply in the medium to long term.

The only way to achieve a greater degree of competition in the short term would be actually to break up the ESB's generating activities into several competing generation companies. In practice, a horizontal break-up of the ESB's generating capacity would encounter several difficulties. ESB generation is dominated by a small number of stations whose production costs vary quite considerably. Moneypoint accounted for more than 40 per cent of total electricity generation in 1992. The next three stations, in terms of units generated, accounted for a further 32 per cent of total generation. Given that peak demand for electricity in 1992 was 2,700 MW, if it were true that 400 MW was the minimum efficient size for a fossil fuel station, this would imply that seven stations of that size would be sufficient to meet the nation's electricity requirements. Thus, as Fitzgerald and Johnston (1995) have argued, even a horizontal break-up of the ESB generating network may result in only a limited degree of competition in the market. Technological developments which may make smaller power plants viable may alter the position considerably, although unless competition is permitted, the potential of such plants may not be fully realised. Any possible break-up is made more difficult by the fact that generating costs vary greatly between plants so that it would be difficult to split the ESB generation system up into two or three similarly sized units with roughly equivalent cost structures. Fitzgerald and Johnson (1995) proposed that some ESB power stations could be franchised out.

The position in telecommunications is quite different. Competition already exists in the market for international calls and in the market for inland long-distance services. New entrants in this sector may well be tempted to enter into arrangements with companies such as the ESB, Iarnród Éireann and possibly Bord na Móna, which already possess much of the necessary physical infrastructure and/or have the necessary rights of way for such infrastructure. Competition in local services could be provided by cable TV networks which are well established in all the main urban areas. Massey and O'Hare (1996) argued that, in order to promote competition in the market for local telephone services Telecom would have to be obliged to divest itself of its Cablelink shareholding. In a major report on industrial policy, Forfás (1996) also recommended that Telecom be required to sell its shareholding in Cablelink. If the cable system were used to provide telephone services, this could also lead to lower cable subscription rates, given that economies of scope would result from supplying both telephone and cable services over the network.

Vertical Issues

It was argued that the question of determining access charges was made far more difficult where the network operator also competed in downstream markets. One solution, advocated by Forfás (1996), would be to break up incumbent firms vertically, by establishing separate companies for the operation of the transmission and distribution systems. Armstrong et al. (1994) have argued that deciding whether or not to separate vertically-integrated monopolies was possibly the most important question for structure regulation. Experience in other countries indicates that it is not essential that the transmission and distribution systems be owned by the same organisation. Indeed, in many instances, liberalisation of utility industries was accompanied by the break-up of vertically-integrated incumbent firms. This was the route followed, for example, in the case of electricity in England and Wales. In New Zealand, the separation of the national grid into a separate independent firm was seen as essential for the introduction of competition into the electricity market (Electricity Task Force, 1989). Such a split-up had the added advantage that it reduced the need for detailed regulation of access charges (Trans.-Power Establishment Board, 1991). In the US, AT&T's vertically-integrated monopoly in telecommunications was broken up as a result of a landmark antitrust case. This resulted in the separation of AT&T's business in the competitive long-distance market from the local networks. Mulgan and Briscoe (1995) advocated the vertical break-up of the UK telecommunications sector.

There are benefits from vertical separation of the transmission and distribution networks, at least in the case of electricity and gas. Vertical separation of networks reduces some of the problems associated with regulating such activities, since independent operators of transmission and distribution systems do not have the same incentive as a vertically-integrated firm to discriminate against new firms providing services in competition with the incumbent over their networks. Armstrong et al. (1994) point out that partial separation involving the establishment of separate subsidiaries with separate accounts may or may not be able to ease the problem of regulating access charges of a vertically-integrated firm. Local distribution networks also constitute natural monopolies. In the event of vertical separation, there is the possibility of establishing several local distribution companies for different parts of the country, which would allow the possibility of yardstick competition since the regulator could compare the performance of the different distributors. Yardstick competition represents a useful means for overcoming the problem of information asymmetries between the regulator and regulated firms. Scott and Convery (1990) argue that separating the transmission and distribution systems from production in the case of gas and electricity has the advantage that it is designed to allow and indeed encourage competition. As against this, if there are significant economies of scope arising from vertical integration, these will be lost in the event of a vertical split. In New Zealand, the Electricity Task Force (1989) concluded that the benefits from vertical separation outweighed the costs. Landon (1983), however, observed that the costs of vertical separation in such circumstances could be quite high. Kaserman and Mayo (1991) estimated that armslength contracts between generators and suppliers added almost 12 per cent to US electricity prices, compared to vertically-integrated production.

Incumbent Advantages

The basic advantage of any statutory monopoly is that it has been given the opportunity to establish itself in the absence of competition. The three utilities being considered here have all had the benefit of this statutory protection and, for their physical networks, have had powers to compulsorily purchase land or easements. They also have miscellaneous statutory powers, privileges and protections of varying importance.

Electricity

The ESB was established by the Electricity Supply Board Act, 1927 and it has a statutory monopoly of generation, transmission, distribution and sale to the public.[16] Originally, electrical generation had been owned privately, but existing operations were acquired successively by the ESB. The Board has power to make orders affecting, and to issue permits to, any new "permitted undertakings" to generate, distribute or supply, so that no new entry into generating has been able to occur, or grow, without the consent of the ESB. It has had the benefit of compulsory purchase powers, and the right to enter on lands in specified circumstances in pursuance of the job of building and maintaining the network.[17] If it were a given that the transmission and distribution network was a true natural monopoly, these privileges would not be

---

[16]   1927 Act, ss. 35, 37, 61.

[17]   1927, ss. 20, 45, 51 and 53 as amended.

enormously relevant to the areas in which competition is possible
— generation and retail sale. However, independent producers
would be free under EU draft legislation to construct direct lines
to their large customers.

The status of the ESB as a State company is marked by statutory privileges: the power to make delegated legislation in respect,
for example, of trespassing at generating stations, and the
transmission and distribution system;[18] the creation of criminal
offences of abstracting electricity or of discharging corrosive matter into water where it can enter a generating station owned by
the ESB.[19] *Vis-à-vis* its customers, the Board may enter any
premises to which electricity is supplied to check meters.[20] Some
of these privileges could be reproduced by way of contractual
provision by any competing supplier. Even where they cannot,
they may not be a benefit of any commercial significance. However, there may be an intangible benefit to any company that is
identified in the eyes of its customers by such statutory indicia, as
the "real" or State-endorsed provider, particularly in the retail
sector.

Gas

BGE was set up by the Gas Act, 1976, which provides that all gas
landed in the State or got within the jurisdiction of the State by a
licensee under an exploration licence shall be offered for sale to
BGE on reasonable terms.[21] Not unlike the ESB's situation, BGE
is not given statutory protection for all its areas of operation, but
has a *de facto* monopoly resulting from the statutory protection it
does have. The Board may make use of acquisition orders to lay
pipeline over or under land. No other person may lay a pipeline
without the consent of the Minister for Transport, Energy and
Communications.[22] The Minister may, with the agreement of the

---

[18] 1927, s. 33.

[19] 1945, s. 42.

[20] 1927, s. 25.

[21] s. 37.

[22] s. 40.

Minister for Finance, give BGE general directions on pricing policy but does not have power in relation to a price to be charged in a particular case.[23]

Telecommunications

Bord Telecom was established as a statutory company by the Postal and Telecommunications Services Act, 1983. Its statutory monopoly includes, apart from voice telephony, telex, mobile radio telephony (one other operator has been licensed in this area), paging and satellite services. It does not include cable television, which is regulated by the Wireless Telegraphy Acts, 1927–1972, or radio and television broadcasting. Telecom's role as a shareholder in Cablelink, the cable network owner, does not carry with it its statutory privileges in respect of its telecommunications functions. The exceptions to Telecom's monopoly are for limited applications which are mainly not of commercial importance;[24] internal telecom systems within private homes, or within one building or between employees of one business, for internal use. Telecom is given some miscellaneous statutory privileges, applicable to all its services: it is immune from tort or contract liability for various failures or delays of the system;[25] it is a criminal offence wilfully to cause Telecom to suffer loss in respect of a rental, fee or charge.[26] As in the gas and electricity sectors, these may be anomalous in a competitive retail market.

The Sector-specific EU legislation

The existing and proposed sector-specific legislation affecting the three utilities shows some common threads. The EU legislation will require barriers to new entry to be removed, encourage access to networks to take place on a commercially negotiated basis, and allow for and perhaps require the funding of a universal service obligation, the minimum content of which will be prescribed from competitors within the sector. It will require Member States to

---

[23] s. 11.

[24] 1983, s. 87 (3).

[25] 1983, s. 88.

[26] 1983, s. 99.

put in place a body or bodies as the regulator of specified questions of licensing and dispute resolution. It does not provide for the control of output pricing.

Electricity

The Commission issued a draft directive in 1993[27] based on the principle of Third-Party Access. The net question which has been most problematic for Member States was whether liberalisation would be by way of permitting Third-Party Access to the grid, or by way of appointing a Single Buyer. The Commission reported[28] in 1995 to say that it would be possible for Member States to proceed by way of a Single Buyer regime if, and only if, the type of Single Buyer put in place by a Member State complied with criteria which the Commission then defined. These are, inter alia, that:

- Large customers would be able to negotiate directly with independent producers and importers, including agreeing price.

- The Single Buyer would act as a transparent mechanism for the transport of electricity bought by such direct negotiation.

- The Single Buyer would be obliged to buy all electricity offered.

- Distributors, as well as large customers, would be eligible to buy from the Single Buyer.

Under the 1996 draft directive,[29] as agreed by the Council of Ministers, Member States could choose to proceed by way of either Single Buyer or Third-Party Access. The networks to which access would be granted are the transmission and distribution grids. The third parties to whom it is proposed to give access are specified as being generation and transmission companies inside or outside the territory who wish to supply distribution companies or large industrial customers or their own establishments. This presupposes the absence of national bans on the import of

---

[27]   COM (93) 643, OJ C123 4.5.94.

[28]   COM (95) 80/5 of 15.3.95.

[29]   SN 3312/96 (ENER), 21.6.96.

electricity.[30] Third-Party access where chosen would be given on a negotiated basis, with Member States providing a dispute resolution mechanism. The Single Buyer, where that is chosen, would have to buy electricity at the request of users who have made contracts with qualified sellers, inside or outside the State; and where buying for transmission to a specific user, give access to the grid on the basis of a published and transparent tariff for transmission. This had been a minimum requirement of the Commission Working Paper.[31]

The 1996 draft directive, apart from modes of access to the grid, proposes unbundling of the vertically-integrated companies and opening up of the construction of generating and transmission capacity. The "unbundling" provisions would require the separation of accounts for production, transmission and distribution activities and, in the case of vertically-integrated companies such as the ESB, administrative independence of the grid operator from the other activities. What is proposed in relation to the construction of generating capacity is that there be either (a) non-discriminatory authorisation procedures, or (b) competitive tendering organised by an independent regulatory body. The liberalisation of construction and operation of generating capacity would require some institution to oversee the commissioning of that capacity. The Commission states that the proper person to have oversight of the issue of commissioning production capacity is a public body independent of the grid operator. At the time of the announcement of Minister Lowry's choice of the Single Buyer system, it was reported that parts of this function would be reserved still to Government. The question as to whether it is possible for a Minister, who also gives commercial directions to the ESB as shareholder, to operate the non-discriminatory licensing procedure is explored below.

Member States may "decide not to apply" the provisions of the directive in relation to generation, and access to the grid "insofar as [they] would obstruct the performance . . . of the obligations

---

[30] The Commission has brought Article 169 actions against all the Member States, including Ireland in respect of their import and export bans.

[31] COM(95)80/5.

imposed on electricity undertakings in the general economic interest". It remains to be seen how extensive this exemption might be.

Gas

The Commission has advanced on the basis that liberalisation of the energy market would proceed with electricity first and then gas. The legislation before the Council in respect of gas is a draft directive[32] parallel to that currently being considered in respect of electricity, the basic provisions of which are as follows.

Natural gas undertakings shall be operated on commercial principles. (This mirrors a similar provision for electricity undertakings, and both provisions are subject to the imposition of a public service obligation.) Licences shall be granted for the building and operation of gas facilities, storage, transmission and distribution on qualitative and not quantitative grounds. Licence conditions shall be published, objective and non-discriminatory, and concern safety and environmental considerations, and the capability of undertakings. Transmission companies — those owning the transmission grid — "shall conclude all agreements necessary" with other transmission companies "to enable a user . . . to use the interconnected system". Costs of all transmission and distribution companies must be unbundled. Member States shall take all necessary steps to allow commercial agreements to be negotiated between suppliers, large industrial customers and distribution companies, and to provide a dispute resolution mechanism. Member States shall ensure that producers and customers are free to sell and buy gas by means of a direct line.

Telecommunications

The Telecom area of privilege has been successively eroded by EU legislation. The Terminal Equipment Directive[33] required the removal of statutory privileges in supply of terminal equipment and required licensing to be subject only to specified qualitative criteria. Telecom had previously had the benefit of one of the limited number of licences issued by the Minister under section 111(2) of

---

[32] COM(93) 643 final, COD 385.

[33] 88/301/EEC.

the 1983 Act. The Services Directive, 1990[34] required that services, other than the public provision of voice telephony be opened to all comers, subject only to specified, qualitative, licensing criteria. This did not apply to mobile radio telephony, paging or satellite services, but it opened the market for the provision of value-added services (VAS) of handling and storing voice telephony, such as voice mail systems, and voice and data services for internal use in businesses and closed user groups — bank or airline reservation dedicated lines, for example. These are still licensed by the Minister under s.111 of the 1983 Act, but there is no quantitative criterion. In practice, applicants are required to declare that they will not provide voice telephony, and that they will use the public network. SI 328 of 1994 obliges a National Regulatory Authority (NRA) to publish details of licensing and declaration requirements, and conditions for the attachment of terminal equipment to leased lines. Directive 96/19EC requires liberalisation of voice telephony by 1 January 1998.[35] It also requires Member States to remove, by 1 July 1996, all regulatory restrictions on the establishment of networks for closed user groups, and the use of existing infrastructure for services already liberalised.

Access Pricing. Neither terminal equipment nor VAS provision raises issues of access pricing, or output pricing. The Leased Lines Directive,[36] however, obliges Telecom to provide to applicants a minimum set of leased lines for use or resale. The directive requires the cost of lines to be "cost oriented". Access to the incumbent's network is also necessary, and the original Open Network Provision Directive[37] lays down "guiding principles" and "essential requirements" for ONP conditions of access. These are, principally, that the conditions for interconnection must be objective, transparent and published; they must guarantee equality of access and

---

[34]   90/388/EEC of 28.6.90.

[35]   Ireland has requested a derogation until 2000 in respect of voice telephony, infrastructure, and mobile interconnection. At the time of going to press, the Commission has not decided on the request.

[36]   Council Directive 92/44/EEC of 5.6.92.

[37]   90/387/EEC of 28.6.90.

they must be non-discriminatory. Only reasons based on security of the network, maintenance of the network integrity, protection of data and the interoperability of services should be applied to limit access to networks or services. For leased lines, the Minister for Transport Energy and Communications is again designated the NRA to "decide on . . . disputes between (Telecom Éireann) and users in matters relating to any refusal to provide leased lines, or the interruption of the provisions to provide leased lines".

The Directive requiring the opening up of voice telephony by 1998 and the licensing of new entrants,[38] requires the removal of all barriers to new entrants. The new ONP Directive[39] specifies the principles to be applied by Member States in "interconnection, with regard to . . . universal service and interoperability" applying the principles of Open Network Provision. Member States are required to remove any obstacle to the free commercial negotiation of interconnection. It also places a direct obligation on operators of the public network, and public telecommunications services, to provide interconnection. The cost of interconnection may include an element, added by the Member State, of a charge for the provision of the universal service obligation, which must be calculated in a transparent way. The directive goes further than the original ONP Directive in providing that charges "promote economic efficiency and sustainable market entry" and that they "normally" include "re-imbursement of one-time costs of interconnection" and usage charges, which may be capacity-based charges, and/or traffic related charges.

Universal Service Obligation. The Services Directive[40] takes as given that the "task" (in the Article 90 sense) assigned to the national PTOs is the provision of the universal network. It is also assumed that the universal service obligation (USO) should be financed by cross-subsidisation from within the sector. The subsequent ONP Directive[41] takes the present minimum content

---

[38] Directive 96/19EC.

[39] Directive 95/62 EC.

[40] 90/388/EEC of 28.6.90.

[41] 95/62 EC.

of a USO as being connection to a network for basic voice telephony, emergency services, and public call boxes. It also appears that Member States will be free to increase that minimum content, and require competitors to fund it, subject to doing so in a transparent fashion. Council Resolution 94/C/48/01[42] on universal services principles in the telecommunications sector states, inter alia, that "the concept of universal service must evolve to keep pace with advances in technology, market development and changes in user demand". This reflects the general EU approach that the content of the universal service obligation will and should increase.

The Director General of Competition for the European Commission has indicated (Schaub, 1996), in the context of telecoms, that where Member States fail to meet the deadlines for liberalisation, the policy of the Commission will be to take proceedings immediately on expiry of those deadlines. Hocepied (European Commission 1996: 17) points out, in respect of the telecoms directives:

> According to the case-law of the Court of Justice, provisions of the Directives have direct effect where they are complete and precise . . . . The relevant undertakings may thus proceed, so long as they comply with all other relevant rules, to apply these rights acknowledged in the Directive [to establish infrastructure, and use existing alternative infrastructure for closed user groups] without having to wait for national measures implementing the Directive. . . . [A]s regards provisions of the Directives requiring further national implementation measures, the Court of Justice confirmed in its judgment of 5 March 1996 (*Brasserie du Pecheur de Schiltighem*) that the national governments were liable for damages to compensate companies in case of infringement of Treaty provisions conferring rights on the latter.
>
> The case law is as a matter of fact probably more effective to ensure full compliance with the Directives than the infringement procedure provided for in Article 169 of the Treaty . . . .

The Treaty Rules

The Treaty Rules are not suspended in respect of the three sectors under consideration merely by virtue of the fact that sector-

---

[42] OJ 16.2.94.

specific legislation is in place. In principle, a number of remedies are provided by the general competition rules to intending entrants who find their entry blocked, or any entrant who finds their progress blocked. The nature of the blockage may be anti-competitive behaviour by a State firm or firms, or domestic legislation or the absence of domestic legislation — that is, the failure to implement changes required by the sector-specific legislation. The State firms do not have a blanket immunity from action under Articles 85 and 86 for any anti-competitive agreements, or abuse of a dominant position. What is provided by Article 90(2) is that undertakings "entrusted with . . . services of general economic interest or . . . a revenue producing monopoly" are subject to Articles 85 and 86 insofar as the competition rules do not obstruct the performance of the tasks entrusted to them. The ESB, BGE and Telecom are such undertakings, but it is not necessarily the case that all services supplied by them are services "of general economic interest". The importance of this in relation to the State utilities is that it is a feature peculiar to vertically integrated monopolies that a dominant position in one market may allow them to abuse, or maintain, a dominant position in another. Articles 85 and 86 are directed to the independent commercial behaviour of undertakings. The situation in State companies where anti-competitive effects result not from the behaviour of the company but from the actions or directions of the State can be addressed not under 85 and 86, but by Article 90(1). The ESB, BGE and Telecom again come within the definition of "public undertakings, and undertakings to which Member States grant special or exclusive rights" and the State's obligation therefore is that it "shall not enact or maintain in force any measure contrary to the rules contained in this Treaty, in particular . . . Articles 85 to 94". It is established that the mere grant or existence of exclusive rights is capable of amounting to a restriction on competition[43] or an abuse of a dominant position.[44] The position of the Commission in the past has been that the grant of exclusive rights in respect of voice telephony was justified in order to cross-subsidise the fulfilment

[43] Commission Telecommunications Equipment Directive 88/301.

[44] *Höfner and Elser* v. *Macrotron*, Case 41/90 I ECR [1991] 1979.

of the universal service obligation on PTOs, and the Court of Justice has taken the same view in respect of exclusive rights in postal services in *Corbeau*.[45] However, that view of the Commission has now been overtaken by the sector-specific provision for the telecoms sector, which is based on universal service being funded in a variety of ways other than cross-subsidisation within one undertaking. It is not possible to know to what extent the Court of Justice would still take the same view as that taken in *Corbeau*.[46]

Actions in respect of a breach of Article 90 may also be brought by private litigants in the Irish courts. The *Francovich* case[47] established that there must be a remedy, if necessary in damages, in private action against a Member State for the failure to implement a directive. It would not be an extraordinary extension of *Francovich* to suggest that there is an action for damages in the Irish Courts for breach of Article 90(1). The remedy of damages for breach of Article 90(1) was sought in *O'Neill v. Minister for Agriculture*[48] and, while the plaintiff was not successful on the merits, it appears from the judgment that no issue was taken by the State on this specific point. Having considered the possibility of litigation, there are, of course, important reasons why new entrants to a State-regulated sector would not wish to effect a forced entry.

Article 37 applies the free movement of goods provisions to State monopolies of a commercial character. The obligation on Member States is progressively to adjust such monopolies to the goal that there be "no discrimination regarding the conditions under which goods are procured and marketed . . . between nationals of Member States". Articles 37(1) and 37(2), as noted in Chapter 4, can be invoked before the Irish courts. The Article applies to electricity and gas which have been deemed to be "goods" for the purpose of the Article and the Article is the basis for the Commission's Article 169 actions against the Member States, including Ireland, in respect of import bans for gas and electricity.

---

[45] *Procureur du Roi* v. *Corbeau*, Case C 320/91 1 ECR [1993] 3283.

[46] Op. cit.

[47] *Francovich and Bonifaci* v. *Italy*, Joined Cases C 6/90 and 9/90; 1 ECR [1991] 5357

[48] High Court, Budd, J., 5.7.95

Institutional Aspects of Regulation

In Ireland there is an EU obligation to provide an institution, or institutions, to perform tasks specified in the existing and proposed legislation for the three utilities considered here. The nature of the institution(s) is not prescribed. The tasks would be:

- Licensing (of voice telephony services, mobile telephony and construction of electricity generating capacity)

- Dispute resolution (interconnection charges to the fixed and mobile telephone network; access to the electricity transmission and distribution grid; access to the gas transmission and distribution pipelines; any other issues arising in relation to the operation of the gas or electricity grids)

- Some miscellaneous other tasks, such as terminal equipment-type approval, and the "encouragement" of the sharing of telephone network facilities.

The institution(s) granting licences for services in any of the sectors would have to be competent to establish and administer criteria for maintenance of integrity of the network; security of supply; interoperability; in the case of telecommunications, allocation of frequencies and protection of data; and, in the case of electricity, inter alia, protection of the environment and land use. The institution(s) performing the dispute resolution functions for access pricing would have to be competent to establish "real" costs for elements of the access provided by the vertically-integrated monopoly, but ultimately, if necessary, to set the access price. The ONP Directive establishing a compulsory range of formulae for access prices does not determine what will ultimately have to be a policy choice.[49] There are other tasks which are more policy-making than rule-making, such as determining the extent of a universal service obligation, and tasks which are not imposed by the EU, such as output pricing, which might properly be allocated to the institution(s) dealing with the above.

It is important to state that literal compliance with EU requirements would fall short of providing an institution with

---

[49]   COM (95) 379 final.

overall responsibility for promoting competition in the sector or sectors being regulated. There are immediate criteria for the performance of the above tasks which involve satisfying the needs of different interest groups, as well as operating in the public interest. Thus, for dispute resolution it should obviously provide decisions that resolve the instant dispute, are timely and are credible to all parties. This last is not a matter of reaching decisions that are liked by all parties, but of ensuring that decisions meet criteria of internal consistency, and the decision-making process is seen to be procedurally fair. For licensing, one criterion would be that the system be sufficiently certain not to discourage potential entrants. However, the overriding criterion for all tasks should be that the regime chosen is genuinely effective in promoting competition.

In Ireland, State monopolies have been subject to informal control from the Minister who is also the shareholder. This would be simply unacceptable to fulfil the EU requirements for provision of a regulatory institution, both on general principles[50] and as specifically provided for in directive 96/19 on voice telephony. This does not preclude Ministerial control, but it does preclude control by the Minister who is the shareholder in the incumbent operator. There is also a specific problem for a Government department or departments using officials who are potentially transferable between the functions of regulating competition in a sector such as electricity or telecom, and making commercial policy decisions for the State company or companies in that sector.[51]

The dispute resolution mechanism provided in this State in fulfilment of the requirements of the EU Services Directive and Leased Lines Directive is the Minister for Transport, Energy and Communications. The net issue on which the Department is potentially required to arbitrate, that of access charges, is one on which there has been no statement of policy by the Minister or

---

[50] *France v. Commission* [1991] 1 ECR 1223.

[51] *Samenwerkende NV* v. *Commission* C 36/92 (1994) I ECR (not appropriate for Ministry officials in their capacity as a national competition authority to receive from the Commission documents of commercial relevance to one firm, where within the same Ministry, commercial decisions were taken in respect of the state company which was one of its competitors).

the Government, and there has been no public discussion of or input into the principles to be applied. There is an appeal from the decisions of the NRA to the District Court, which appears inappropriate to the issues involved in access pricing. The Energy (Miscellaneous Provisions) Act, 1995 also makes the Minister responsible for resolving disputes over access charges for the gas interconnector.

As stated above, the conflict of interest issues do not preclude regulation by a Minister other than the Minister who is a shareholder in the relevant State utility. Having a Ministerial regulator may initially avoid having to draw a line between policy issues and administrative issues. The disadvantage of not drawing that line is that all regulatory decisions and actions remain subject to direct lobbying of the relevant politician by the affected persons. Secondly, there is an added fear where the regulator is a Minister, which is that regulation will be too directly a vehicle for "ideology and political opportunism" (Foster, 1994). Thirdly, Ministerial controls at present are perceived to lack the transparency essential to effective regulation, perhaps because they have rarely been accompanied by a duty to give or publish reasons.

In *Carrigaline*,[52] a community-based, non-profit-making television UHF (ultra high frequency) re-diffusion system sought injunctions restraining the Minister from prosecuting it for operating without a licence, and a mandatory injunction requiring the Minister to consider its application for a licence. It succeeded on the basis, *inter alia*, that the Minister in exercising his discretion to license re-diffusion systems had not made explicit to the would-be licensees the technical argument forming the basis of his preference for another distribution system. It is very clear that in operating any regulatory system a Minister, or any regulator, cannot rely on the scarcity of their resources to limit the type of decision they make. It will be necessary for any regulator to be funded to the point, not necessarily of themselves making all the arguments for and against every option under consideration, but of being able to tell every party affected the arguments they need to meet.

---

[52] High Court, unreported, Keane J., 10.11.95.

The Institutional Options

The options for any regulatory regime include (a) sectoral regulators, and (b) a general regulator with responsibility for the entire economy — that is, the national competition authority, the courts, a Minister, or any combination of two or more. At the time of writing, it appears that the Government's preferred option is that of a sector-specific regulator for telecommunications, to be followed by a sector-specific regulator for electricity and possibly in the future other utilities within one institution.

The substantive law used to regulate the utilities may be self-contained, sector-specific law; or it may be the law of general application to the entire economy; or it may be a combination of the two, as where it is provided that the sector-specific rules do not preclude the application of the general law. Any regulatory regime has to be credible and acceptable to incumbents, entrants and customers, which in these sectors are ultimately the public at large.

Sector-specific Regulator

The decision to have a sector-specific regulator is one that typically goes hand in hand with the decision to have sector-specific rules. If the rules being applied are the general competition law, there will typically already be an institution in place — a national competition authority and/or access to a court system — to apply those general rules. If sector-specific rules are considered to be needed, then, typically, that will form part of a regime in which sector-specific expertise is accumulated in one institution which is dedicated to the sector. For access pricing, output pricing, administering a universal service obligation and licensing, it is clear that sector-specific expertise is required. It is not as immediately obvious, but it is the case, that expertise in applying wider general principles of competition regulation is necessary. The perceived advantage of sector-specific regulators is that they are designed to have expertise in the industry being regulated. All regulatory institutions are in danger of lack of information *vis-à-vis* the regulated firms, but sector-specific regulators can potentially be staffed with expertise in the industry. They can also deal with continuing day-to-day matters where that level of regulatory availability is required.

A major disadvantage of sector-specific regulators is that they are prone to regulatory capture, and this is more likely if specialist expertise must perforce to some extent be recruited from the monopolist itself, or from State officials who have, prior to the introduction of competition, had responsibility for the State company. Regulatory capture arises because regulators tend to identify over time with the regulated industry and end up defending it rather than policing it. Indeed, Stigler (1975: 115) argued that: "as a rule regulation is acquired by the industry and is designed and operated primarily for its benefit." There are some indications that the composition of any regulatory agency is important for the prevention of regulatory capture. A second problem is that, once established, regulatory bodies tend to perpetuate and enlarge their activities. The countercheck of a regulatory institution based more widely than the relevant industry is some guard against the danger of capture. This is not incompatible with focusing expertise necessary for this sector in one office, while simultaneously making that office part of a wider structure. The wider structure can be provided by the existing competition institutions; to a lesser extent by the type of general public utilities office which has been proposed; or by another institution such as the courts. It is notable that in some countries the role of sector-specific regulators has been reduced or even abolished and responsibility transferred to an overall competition agency.

Broad Spectrum Regulator

A regulatory body which is responsible for all sectors of the economy, such as in Ireland the Competition Authority, is also typically associated with applying a general law, rather than detailed sectoral rules. For the purposes of regulating the former monopoly markets of the State utilities, the advantages and disadvantages of a broad spectrum regulator are rather the mirror image of those of the sector-specific regulator. A general purpose body set up as such will not, without special provision, have the sectoral expertise to apply detailed sectoral rules. The corollary of this is that unlike a sector-specific regulator it will, in theory, have the benefit of a concentration of economic and legal expertise and experience. This type of interaction is used in Finland, on a basis of informal requests for views, which has reportedly worked well but is about to change, with more of the responsibility being returned to the general competition authority. One perceived advantage of a general competition authority is that it has a broader economy-wide perspective. Similarly, such an agency, where there is a collective responsibility for decisions about a sector, is to that extent less likely to be subject to, or be perceived to be subject to, regulatory capture.

The Courts

More even than a broad spectrum regulator, the courts are not typically used to apply sector-specific rules, but rather the general rules. That can be either as the sole form of regulation, as in New Zealand, or it can be in combination with any of the other institutions discussed here. The sector-specific tasks prescribed by EU legislation might theoretically be carried out using the Courts as the sole regulator, although it could be expected to be too unwieldy in practice. A court cannot be used as a policy-maker. It also cannot be used as a day-to-day resource where that level of availability of the regulator is required. Courts will not in the normal course of events be staffed by experts in the relevant sector and that gap would then have to be bridged by expert evidence. The court's function is to resolve a dispute between the parties on facts before it, which does not necessarily create general rules for the convenience of other competitors in the market.

> It is a regrettable fact that the decision of this appeal will only decide whether, in the past, Telecom has abused its dominant market position. It will not decide whether Clear's past stance in negotiations was reasonable, let alone fix the terms for inter-connection.[53]

Posner (1977), on the other hand, has argued that the courts are a mechanism superior to regulatory agencies, firstly, because courts are not easily subject to regulatory capture, and secondly, because the injured parties in any abuse of dominance situation are in a better situation than any regulator to know when their interests

---

[53] *Telecom Corporation of New Zealand Ltd.* v. *Clear Communications Ltd.*, PC 21/94 of 19.10.94.

are harmed and to prosecute those interests by litigation.

> We do not believe that the courts will do an especially good job in
> dealing with this issue — distinguishing predatory behaviour
> from ordinary competitive actions is not easy . . . — but only that
> the problem will be no more difficult in the telecommunications
> industry than elsewhere (Besen and Woodbury, 1983).

Two other criticisms of the courts are delay and rigidity. A competitor (and this might be either the incumbent or the new entrant) can deploy litigation as a delaying tactic by litigating every
issue in sequence. Also, once an issue of principle is decided, at a
Supreme Court level, it is in place until such time as the Court
either reverses itself or is overtaken by legislation. This may result in an issue that arises in the context of one sector being dealt
with in a way that is binding for all regulated utilities. Arguably,
this is also true of a general regulatory body, where the view of
the body on an issue of general principle may not change until the
personnel of that body is changed. Any decision of a court suc-
ceeds insofar as it resolves the issue as between the parties and,
as in the *Clear* case,[54] permits access to begin. In an area where
there is not one right answer plainly apparent to such questions
as the level of access charges, arguably any machinery chosen to
arrive at a determination will be open to the criticism of having
failed to find the right answer.

Sector-specific Rules

The decision to have sector-specific rules, like a decision to have a
sector-specific regulator, reflects a view that there are problems
peculiar to monopoly utilities which require some form of treatment beyond the normal competition regime.[55] One of the fore-
most problems is that they are monopolies and, typically, heavily
vertically integrated. A general prohibition competition law, like
the Competition Act or Article 85 and 86 of the Rome Treaty, provides for agreements, or abuses, which restrict competition, but it

---

[54] Op. cit.

[55] Obviously, sector-specific rules can be applied either by a sector-specific
regulator or by a body with responsibility for applying the general competition rules.

does not provide a detailed guide to altering an existing market structure. The function of the sector-specific regulators in the UK has been described as being to "act as a substitute for competition, at least until competition emerged" (Whish, 1993). This is not wrong as such, but there is a danger with this approach, which is that it can become fixed in stone and become an obstacle to the sector moving towards true open competition. Full competition should, arguably, include being subject to the same competition rules as other sectors. A serious issue to be addressed is whether the creation of different rules for a sector could operate as a block to the emergence of a natural market. A first concern should be that the existence of different rules should not itself cause a distortion of the emerging market. This is recognised in different ways in different countries. The extreme example is the New Zealand decision to make whatever structural changes were thought necessary and then leave the field open to the competitors and the general law. A less extreme approach is that adopted by Finland and Australia, where, having had a detailed sectoral regulation for telecommunications, they are now, as they had planned, rolling back the sectoral regulation and leaving more functions to the general competition authority. Where a time limit is placed on the sector-specific regime, this operates to some extent to inhibit the danger, inherent in any regulator, of perpetuating its own existence.

For Ireland, the EU obligations in the utilities sector require something more than the existing Competition Acts. It is possible, in theory to take the approach that a mechanism could be provided by recourse to the courts or other body to apply the general principle set down in Section 5 of the Competition Act, 1991, and Article 86 of the Treaty and elaborated in the case law discussed above. However, specific provisions such as the obligation to "encourage" facility sharing in telecommunications go beyond the general principles of the Competition Act and the Treaty.

In the case of telecommunications, sector-specific rules face a further problem because technological change means that the extent of the natural monopoly, which is the area that, from an economics perspective, needs to be regulated, is constantly changing, thus threatening to render sector-specific rules obsolete. Australia's telecom regulator has indicated that regulatory provisions may have a life span of two years or less. The UK experience of having only sector-specific rules has been that OFTEL, for example, has expressed concern that it is not possible under the present Telecommunications Act to provide a general condition forbidding anti-competitive behaviour or abuse of dominant position. This point is considered below.

General Rules

Following liberalisation of electricity and telecommunications, the New Zealand authorities specifically rejected the idea of establishing specific industry regulators and decided instead that the problem of abusive behaviour should be dealt with under the Commerce Act, 1986. The Treasury argued that:

> . . . officials consider, and Ministers have agreed that this sort of problem is best dealt with through general competition policies and rules including provisions within the Commerce Act. We would not agree with the contention that special legislation may be required. The introduction of special legislation would imply an ad-hoc approach to regulation of the Electricity Corporation and the electricity industry that is inconsistent with the general thrust of policies agreed to for SOEs. In particular, corporation or industry specific legislation can, as history has demonstrated, create major distortions in the economy which lead to the inefficient use of resources (Spicer et al., 1991: 107).

Poland has also chosen the option of simply removing the statutory privileges of the State utilities, leaving them subject to the application of the general competition legislation. This option was chosen despite, or indeed perhaps because of, the disproportionate level of vertically-integrated monopolies in the Polish economy. The Anti-Monopoly Office found the access pricing of the incumbent telecommunications operator to be an abuse of its dominant position.[56] The problems which are identified in using a general law to deal with the specific areas of access pricing, universal service obligation, and output pricing are uncertainty, and delay,

---

[56] It was found to be cross-subsidising its long distance tariff to customers by its charges to competitors for local access.

pending determination by the relevant institution of the application of the general principle to the fact situation.

Interaction between Institutions

In a number of countries (Sweden, Australia, Germany, Finland, Canada and the US), utility sectoral regulators operate alongside the antitrust laws. The potential interaction between a sector-specific regulator and a general body, which might be either the courts or a competition authority, is by way of a division of responsibility for issues, rather than industry sectors. The interface is effectively the same as that between sector-specific rules and a general competition law. The interaction of the Finnish system was already described above. The Canadian interface between sector-specific and general rules is what is called the regulated area defence: where behaviour that ousts the jurisdiction of the general rule is required or explicitly permitted by detailed sectoral rules. By contrast, the US courts have repeatedly and consistently rejected claims that activities approved by regulatory agencies as essential to comply with the regulatory rules were immune to challenge under the antitrust statutes. Both regimes, however, are successful in that they have a white-line distinction between the two types of institution, which is sufficient to prevent duplication of jurisdiction. It would appear to be extremely difficult to frame sector-specific rules *ex ante* to deal with all possible forms of anti-competitive behaviour. Rather than attempting such an exercise, it would appear preferable that such behaviour would be subject to the general competition rules leaving specific matters such as access pricing to be dealt with by a sector-specific agency. A regime that combines sector-specific rules with general competition rules would appear to have the benefit of maximising the strengths and minimising the weaknesses of each type of regime.

Some Misconceptions

Although it is sometimes claimed that the introduction of competition would have an adverse effect on employment in the public-utility industries, the reality, as noted in Chapter 1, is that competition has a positive effect on employment. Schaub (1996: 17) notes:

In those countries in the EU and around the world with the longest experience of liberalisation, it is also evident that telecoms employment in new service suppliers offsets jobs shed by incumbent PTOs as they take on the productivity gains of new technology.

It is sometimes suggested that, in the case of electricity at least, competition would not represent an efficient outcome in an economy as small as Ireland's. Claims that competition would not be efficient in small countries ignores the fact that many small countries such as New Zealand, Finland and Sweden have permitted or intend to permit greater competition in utilities.

> International experience has shown that electricity systems that are regulated, state managed or controlled, and/or non-competitive do not deliver electricity or security of supply at the lowest possible cost and price to consumers. Such systems are also economically inefficient (Wholesale Electricity Market Development Group, 1994: 15).

Another criticism advanced in respect of liberalisation is that it would permit "cream-skimming" and undermine universal service provision. It is worth noting in this context that the level of telephone penetration in Ireland, which is perhaps one measure of universal service provision, is low by developed-country standards (see Figure 13.3). Armstrong et al. (1994) point out that the danger of cream-skimming can be exaggerated and that restricting competition is not the only way to deal with this problem where it arises. In addition, the incumbent operator has an incentive to overstate the cost of social obligations where it is allowed to recoup them in access charges from other suppliers. OFTEL (1994) reported that the cost of the universal service obligation was lower than previously thought. Similarly, while Telecom Australia estimated the cost of its social obligations at A$850 million, an independent study estimated them at A$250 million.

> At the same time there is no evidence to indicate that infrastructure competition has had a negative impact on the provision of telephone services. Despite the fact that a number of PTOs in monopoly markets have argued this case they have not been able to provide persuasive evidence in support of their

position. Instead there is growing awareness that competition can be applied to improve and enhance universal service through direct service provision and transparent financial contributions from new operators; applying price discipline to incumbent PTOs; stimulating market growth; and introducing new technologies, flexible pricing and innovative services. Moreover it is often overlooked that increased efficiency in incumbent PTOs, stimulated by competition, is a major factor in bringing down the cost of delivering universal service (OECD, 1995: 5).

The above study found that in the UK the entry of cable TV companies to the telephone market meant that some households which had previously been unable to afford a telephone were able to obtain one. This represents a good example of how competition has enhanced universal service provision.

FIGURE 13.3: MAIN TELEPHONE LINES PER 100 INHABITANTS, 1993

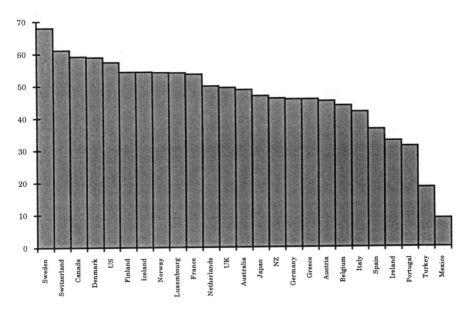

Source: Rey (1995).

Some Conclusions

There is considerable scope for increased competition in public utilities to the benefit of consumers and the economy at large. Competition requires the government to face up to the essential contradiction involved in the present policy, whereby state utility companies are required to attempt simultaneously to operate on a commercial basis and to discharge a number of non-commercial obligations for social reasons. If the Government wants a state enterprise to supply goods and services on a non-commercial basis, it should enter into a formal agreement with the relevant company and pay for the provision of such services.

Liberalisation will leave a number of other important issues to be resolved. Incumbent firms are likely to remain dominant and they will be able to abuse that dominance in respect of both their customers and their rivals who will need to gain access to the incumbent's distribution network in order to compete, raising questions as to what sort of measures need to be put in place to deal with such behaviour. In some respects, EU policy has defined the type of measures to be adopted, while in others there is still a considerable range of policy options available. Regulation, however, is not a substitute for, and will not deliver the benefits which can accrue from, competition. In fact, as noted in Chapter 12, certain forms of regulation may even hinder the development of competition. Regulating public utilities poses a number of complex problems. As Schick (1993) observed, "the task of supervising national, centralised monopolies appears one that most economists would wish only on their worst enemies". The appropriate objective for regulation is to prevent anti-competitive behaviour but otherwise to allow competition, rather than attempt to manage the market. Such an objective can best be achieved by sector-specific rules to deal with specific issues such as interconnection charges, operating in tandem with general competition law.

Schaub (1996) states:

> Liberalisation (lifting restrictions) certainly implies a burst of regulatory activity, including strong pro-competition rules. A key question is whether the latter needs to be telecoms specific or not. Under conditions of market convergence between telecoms,

media, information and broadcasting, it would seem unwise to make rigid regulations based on outdated sectoral divides. Some say the answer is to promote regulatory integration. However, the longer term solution is clearly increasing reliance on general competition rules. In the shorter term, more focused and "ex-ante" guidelines are needed. In any case improved co-operation and coordination between regulatory authorities and competition authorities is essential.

14

CONCLUSIONS

Historically, there has been little political enthusiasm for competition policy in Ireland. As noted in Chapter 5, the then Government adopted a rather cautious approach when competition legislation was first introduced in 1953, to the extent that its application was limited primarily to goods with various services being gradually added over time, so that it took over 30 years before the legislation was applicable to virtually every sector of the economy. This slow rate of progress occurred in spite of numerous calls for the adoption of a more effective competition policy. As early as the 1960s, the National Industrial Economic Council advocated that the scope and coverage of the existing legislation should be extended. The cautious official approach is reflected also in the fact that, although the adoption of a prohibition-based system of competition law was first advocated in an official report in 1977, it took 14 years for such legislation to be enacted. Even then, its impact was greatly limited by the decision not to have any active State enforcement of the Act. Nor is this the only indication of a lack of political enthusiasm for an active competition policy. As noted in Chapter 12, various governments over the years have implemented measures that seriously restrict competition, and indeed it is clear that, on occasion, this was the primary intention. State companies have been given monopoly rights in key sectors of the economy.

In part, this approach reflects the fact that competition was not regarded in the past as a major issue for economic policy. The focus of much of the economic debate in Ireland over recent decades has been on macroeconomic policy areas such as monetary, fiscal and exchange rate policies. With one or two notable exceptions, little attention has focused on microeconomic issues. It is true that there have been frequent criticisms of the performance of various State-owned monopolies, accompanied by calls to end such monopoly privileges. By and large, however, until quite recently little attention had been paid to the important role that an active competition policy can play in achieving macroeconomic policy objectives such as higher growth and employment. This position has changed considerably as is evidenced, for example, by the Culliton Report, which emphasised the importance of competition in improving economic performance and employment prospects.

Cultural Attitudes

Admittedly the Irish approach is by no means unique. As pointed out in Chapter 1, UK governments have been less than wholehearted supporters of the idea of a strong competition policy. To take a very different example, Martin Wolf, writing in the *Financial Times* of his experience as a senior economist in the Indian Division of the World Bank, described how, when he asked one of his colleagues if they would favour granting manufacturing licences to new entrants who could produce particular goods cheaper than incumbent firms, was greeted with surprise at the idea that the ability to produce a product more cheaply would justify permitting entry. In many respects, the approach to competition in Ireland has not been all that different and reflects the fact that, in some respects, the country lacks a strong pro-competition culture. Most readers will recognise intuitively that there is some level of popular resistance to the belief that competition will be beneficial. One expression of this belief is the persistence of the view that the duty of the Government of the day where any company looks to be in danger is always to leap to the rescue. The main content of the public debate on those occasions is not whether the Government should provide the money, but how much it should provide. While it can be seen why there would be public empathy with individuals who will be in personal difficulties if they lose a job, there is rarely public discussion of the question as to why these particular jobs should be bought and those particular people kept in employment. Firms do not all succeed and firms that succeed do not all stay successful perpetually. They can become inefficient, or they may make mistakes about the products or services they can sell to the public, or the price at which they can sell them. It is only the possibility of having to face the consequences of failure that forces firms to operate efficiently, which is the only effective way to protect jobs in the longer term. The economic theory is that the failure of a firm frees resources such as capital, labour and materials which will then be put to more productive use. The popular sceptical belief is that once jobs disappear they are permanently lost, and nothing in particular will replace them, so keeping the semblance of a job alive on a subsidy is better than the nothing that is the alternative. Guiomard (1995) follows the roots of this cultural pessimism through Ireland's colonial experience finding that "'anti-market economics cuts with the grain of Irish opinion". He also identifies "a very anti-intellectual and uncritical culture". Jakee and Allen (1995) observe:

> . . . we conclude that Ireland's lacklustre showing has much to do with its vast array of economic restrictions and the rather one-sided intellectual framework that keeps these restrictions in place. To our knowledge, this intellectual — and public — aversion to markets has not been examined before in the context of Ireland's poor economic achievements.

The late John Kelly, TD, perhaps more kindly, speaking of a lack of entrepreneurial spirit said:

> Very rarely will it be an Irish person who sees an opportunity . . . and makes the most of it. This is not because we are worse than anybody else or are defective in any way but rather because we are not trained or encouraged to think like that . . . [1]

The Case for Competition Restated

The strong antipathy to competition which is so pervasive in Ireland means that there is a need to press the case in its favour. As the Fair Trade Commission noted in its *Study on Competition Law*:

> One of the most potent forces in ensuring competitive markets may be an educated public opinion. There is a need to publicise the benefits of free and competitive markets so that a climate exists where those who are breaking competition laws are seen to deserve their punishment (FTC, 1991a, para. 14.22).

At various stages in this book, examples have been offered of ways in which competition has a positive effect on economic welfare. There is a multitude of evidence for all types of business and from

---

[1]   Dáil Debates, 2.2.89.

countries across the world which shows that competition leads to higher levels of output and employment while, in the large majority of cases, restrictions on competition are harmful. In Chapter 1, it was noted that the cost of restrictions on competition in the Irish economy were substantial, amounting to at least £300 million. Some might argue that the economy appears to be growing quite strongly anyway and there is no need to disturb the status quo in order to generate even higher growth. Suffice it to say that restrictions on competition exclude a significant proportion of Irish society from sharing fully in the benefits of such growth.

In recent years numerous reports have stressed the need for stronger measures to eliminate restrictions on competition, precisely in order to promote greater employment opportunities. The National Economic and Social Forum, commenting on arguments that various restrictions on competition had an adverse effect on employment, noted, for example, that:

> Recent work undertaken, both internationally and in this country, has highlighted the potential significance of these issues for employment in the services sector. For example, a study by McKinsey & Company, Inc. found that product market restrictions (i.e. absence of competition) were probably more important than labour market restrictions in explaining why job creation in Europe was below that in the US, particularly in the services and construction sectors (NESF, 1995, para. 4.17).

It is frequently argued that greater encouragement must be given to small business in Ireland. Less bureaucratic interference, tax incentives, reduced borrowing costs, and employment subsidies are all regularly advanced as means of supporting the development of the small business sector. A strong competition policy is rarely included in such lists, yet in reality it has an important role to play.

> The climate for new-business formation in New Zealand is inadequate. This is a very serious matter for New Zealand, since new-business formation is integral to the process of upgrading the economy. Legislated monopolies, state-owned enterprises and private oligopolies dominate many of the areas of the New Zealand economy that could be fertile ground for new companies. New entry is prohibited or blocked in large sectors of the economy. Government can contribute to the climate for new business in a number of ways. New-business formation can not flourish without a strong commitment to competition (Crocombe et al., 1991: 177).

Substitute Ireland for New Zealand and the observation remains equally valid.

Towards a More Effective Competition Policy

Fortunately there are some positive indications that things are moving in the right direction. The case for more effective State enforcement of the Competition Act, 1991 has been accepted as evidenced by the passage of the Competition (Amendment) Act. The 1996 Act, which allows the Competition Authority to investigate and prosecute breaches of competition law, represents a positive move. It will take some years to see how effective it will prove to be in tackling anti-competitive behaviour. General competition legislation of itself is necessarily only one component in an effective overall competition policy. There are limits to what legislation of the type enshrined in the Irish Acts can achieve in terms of preserving competitive markets. In particular, as was argued in Chapter 8, overseas experience shows that a prohibition on abuse of dominance along the lines contained in Section 5 is likely to be insufficient of itself to deal with all of the problems that can arise from such behaviour. In a small number of instances, the break-up of the dominant firm may well be the most appropriate remedy. While such a provision exists under Section 14 of the Act, it is not clear in what circumstances it might be invoked. Given the limitations inherent in Section 5, measures to prevent the establishment of a dominant position by means of a merger or takeover remain an essential weapon in the overall competition policy armoury. It is therefore important that mergers policy gives due weight to competition considerations, while recognising that, on occasion, other policy considerations must also be taken into account.

The State intervenes in markets, as discussed in Chapter 12, for a variety of reasons; some valid, some less so. Even where it is correct in intervening, the form of intervention chosen may have harmful effects on competition. A broader competition policy must encompass those restrictions on competition which arise as an unintended and unnecessary result of regulation. The result of State intervention in a market can be as harmful to competition, and more so, than the deliberate actions of a firm or a cartel setting out to that end. It merits questioning not only the form of regulation, but in each case the need for regulation in the first place. In practical terms, there is a role for an advocate of competition to make an input into the framing of any legislation that might have a market impact. There is also the wider task of reviewing existing legislation, with the specific intention of rolling back unnecessary restrictions on competition. This point has been recognised.

> By end 1993 the Department of Enterprise and Employment should have brought forward a programme of proposals to increase the efficiency and operation of market forces through the relaxation of controls, restrictions, licences and other limitations, whether official or private, that operate to restrict entry of suitably qualified people or firms into trades, professions and services (*Employment through Enterprise*: 43).

In the case of the major public-utility industries such as gas, electricity and telecommunications which, until now, have largely been cocooned from competition, the opportunity now exists to reap substantial benefits from liberalisation and allowing other suppliers to compete in such markets. It is important that the benefits which can accrue to the economy from such competition are not lost by attempts to hinder its development. In this respect it is important that any new regulatory regime for such industries is designed with the aim of promoting competition to the greatest extent possible in order to maximise the benefits to the national economy. Indeed, given the pace of technological change in such sectors, attempts to limit competition are likely to prove both misguided and futile and leave the incumbent firms they are designed to protect in a position where they are ultimately unable to compete.

The Way Ahead
Competition policy in Ireland is not shaped in a vacuum. For over 20 years now Irish firms have been subject to EU competition law whenever their activities involved inter-state trade. More recently, legislative developments in Brussels have been an important factor in moves to introduce competition into public-utility industries. The European Commission is anxious to devolve responsibility for the implementation of Articles 85 and 86 to the national

competition authorities of the Member States. Indeed, such proposals are already quite far advanced. Some Member States, although not all, have advocated the establishment of an independent EU competition agency, and such proposals are at a much
earlier stage. As noted in Chapter 4, the conclusion of the Uruguay Round GATT agreement, which removed many State-
imposed restrictions on international trade, means that the focus
of attention is now turning to private impediments to trade such
as cartels or abuses of market power by dominant firms in individual markets. The potential of such behaviour to give rise to international trade disputes means that consideration is now being
given to devising a mechanism for resolving such issues. Of
course, this is not to say that some form of agreed international
competition rules are likely to be implemented in the foreseeable
future. Nevertheless, it signals some level of recognition by governments that there is an issue of competition policy to be resolved.

In the years ahead, competition policy is likely to grow in importance. It largely remains to be seen how the complex economic
arguments that frequently arise on competition issues will be
applied within a legal framework. Policy will undoubtedly continue to develop, reflecting the ongoing and vigorous evolution of
ideas which characterises this field of law and economics. An effective competition policy can be expected to produce tangible
economic benefits for the community at large.

> The only ones who should fear competition are the inefficient
> and those who conspire to deprive the consumer of the benefits
> to which he is entitled.[2]

---

[2] D. O'Malley, Dáil Debates, 30.4.91, col. 1492.

BIBLIOGRAPHY

Ackland, R. and Harper, I. (1990): *Financial Deregulation in Australia: Boon or Bane?*, New Zealand Association of Economists, *mimeo*.

Adams, W. and Brock, J.W. (1994): "Revitalising a Structural Antitrust Policy", *Antitrust Bulletin*, 39(1) (Spring): 235–73.

Addanki, S. (1995): "The DOJ's Draft Intellectual Property Guidelines: An Economist's First Look", *European Competition Law Review*, 4: 220–24.

Ahdar, R. (1991): "American Antitrust in New Zealand", *Antitrust Bulletin*, 36(1) (Spring): 217–48.

Allen, W. and Curwen, P. (1991): *Competition and Choice in the Publishing Industry*, London: Institute for Economic Affairs.

Areeda, P. and Turner, D.F. (1975): "Predatory Pricing and Related Issues under Section 2 of the Sherman Act", *Harvard Law Review*, 88: 697–733.

Armstrong, M., Cowan, S. and Vickers, J. (1994): *Regulatory Reform: Economic Analysis and the British Experience*, Cambridge, MA: MIT Press.

Arndt, H.W. (1944): *The Economic Lessons of the Nineteen-Thirties*, Oxford: Oxford University Press.

Audretsch, D. (1988): "Divergent Views in Antitrust Economics", *Antitrust Bulletin*, 33 (Spring): 135–60.

Australian Price Surveillance Authority (1989): Report No. 25 *Inquiry into Book Prices Final Report*, 19 December.

Australian Trade Practices Commission (1990): "Background Paper on Section 46 of the Australian Trade Practices Act 1974", in *European Community Law Review*, (4): 147–78.

Bain, J. (1956): *Barriers to New Competition*, Cambridge: Harvard University Press.

Bailey, E. and Baumol, W. (1984): "Deregulation and the Theory of Contestable Markets", *Yale Journal of Regulation*, 1(2): 111–37.

Bailey, R. (1986): "Gas Privatization and the Energy Strategy", *National Westminster Bank Review,* August: 2–12.

Baker, D.I. and Baker, B.G. (1983): "Antitrust and Communications Deregulation", *Antitrust Bulletin,* 28(1) (Spring): 1–38.

Baldrige, R. (1985): "Rx for Export Woes: Antitrust Relief", *Wall Street Journal,* 15 October.

Barrett, S. (1982): *Transport Policy in Ireland,* Dublin, Irish Management Institute.

Barrett, S. (1990): "Transport Deregulation and Privatisation" in Convery, F. and McDowell, M. (eds.), *Privatisation: Issues of Principle and Implementation in Ireland,* Dublin: Gill and Macmillan.

Baumol, W.J. (1983): "Some Subtle Pricing Issues in Railroad Regulation", *International Journal of Transport Economics,* 10: 341–55.

Baumol, W.J. (1992): "Horizontal Collusion and Innovation" *Economic Journal,* 102 (January): 129–37

Baumol, W.J., Panzar, J.C. and Willig, R.D. (1982): *Contestable Markets and the Theory of Industry Structure,* San Diego: San Diego University Press.

Baumol, W.J. and Sidak, J.G. (1994): *Toward Competition in Local Telephony,* Cambridge, MA: MIT Press.

Baumol, W.J. and Willig, R.D. (1986): "Contestability: Developments Since the Book", in Morris, D.J., Sinclair, P.J.N., Slater, M.D.E. and Vickers, J.S. (eds.), *Strategic Behaviour and Industrial Competition,* Oxford: Clarendon Press.

Beath, J., Katsoulacos, Y. and Ulph, D. (1994): "Strategic R&D and Innovation" in Cable, J.(ed.), *Current Issues in Industrial Economics,* London: Macmillan.

Bellamy, C.W. and Child, G. (1993): *Common Market Law of Competition.* London: Sweet and Maxwell.

Bennion, F.A.R. (1992): *Statutory Interpretation,* London: Butterworths.

Berg, S.V. and Tschirhart, J. (1988): *Natural Monopoly Regulation,* Cambridge: Cambridge University Press.

Bertrand, J. (1883): book review of "Theorie Mathématique de la Richesse Sociale", *Journal des Savants,* 67: 499–508.

Besen, S.M. and Woodbury, J.R. (1983): "Regulation, Deregulation and Antitrust in the Telecommunications Industry", *Antitrust Bulletin*, 28(1) (Spring): 39–68.

Bingaman, A. (1995): Statement before the Committee on Commerce, United States Senate Concerning Telecommunications Reform Legislation, 2 March.

Blair, R.D. (1985): "A Suggestion for Improved Antitrust Enforcement", *Antitrust Bulletin,* 30(2) (Summer): 433–56.

Blinder, A. (1987): *Hard Heads and Soft Hearts: Tough Minded Economics for a Just Society,* Reading, MA: Addison Wesley.

Bok, D.C. (1960): "Section 7 of the Clayton Act and the Merging of Law and Economics", *Harvard Law Review*, 74: 291–350.

Bord Gáis, various years: *Annual Reports.*

Bork, R.H. (1978): *The Antitrust Paradox: A Policy at War with Itself*, New York: Basic Books.

Bos, P., Stuyck, J. and Wytinck, P. (1992): *Concentration Control in the EC*, London: Graham and Trotman.

Brady, U. (1994): "An Economic Evaluation of Irish Competition Policy" in McNulty, P. (ed.), *Perspectives on Policy Issues: Ireland and the European Community*, Belfast: Centre in Economics and Law, University of Ulster at Jordanstown.

Breit, W. and Elzinga, K. (1989): *The Antitrust Casebook: Milestones in Economic Regulation,* New York: Dryden.

Bristow, J. (1985): "State Sponsored Bodies" in Litton, F. (ed.), *Unequal Achievement: The Irish Experience,* Dublin: Institute of Public Administration.

Bruton, R. (1995): Press release by Minister Richard Bruton, dated 2 March 1995.

Building on Reality 1985–1987 (1984): Dublin: Stationery Office, Pl. 2648.

Burke, T., Genn-Bash, A. and Haines, B. (1991): *Competition in Theory and Practice,* London: Routledge.

Burns, P. and Weyman-Jones, T.G. (1994): *The Performance of the Electricity Distribution Business — England and Wales, 1971–1993*, London: Chartered Institute of Public Finance and Accountancy.

Burns, P., Turvey, R. and Weyman-Jones, T.G. (1995): *Sliding Scale Regulation of Monopoly Enterprises,* London: Chartered Institute of Public Finance and Accountancy.

Business and Finance (1995): "The Top 1000 Companies", 26 January 1995.

Cable, J.R. (1986): "Industry" in Artis, M.J. (ed.), *The UK Economy,* London: Weidenfeld and Nicholson.

Cable, J.R. (1994): "Introduction and Overview: Recent Developments in Industrial Economics", in Cable, J. (ed.), *Current Issues in Industrial Economics,* Basingstoke: Macmillan.

Callanan, F. (1991): "Authority's Edict on Employee Restraints is Highly Tendentious", *Competition,* 1: 274.

Carlton, D. and Perloff, J. (1990): *Modern Industrial Organisation,* London: Scott, Foresman/Little, Brown.

Caves, R.E. (1968): *Britain's Economic Prospects*, London: Allen and Unwin.

Central Bank of Ireland, *Quarterly Bulletin,* various issues.

Central Statistics Office, *Annual Services Inquiry, 1991,* Dublin: Stationery Office.

Central Statistics Office, *Census of Industrial Production,* various years, Dublin: Stationery Office.

Central Statistics Office, *Census of Services, 1988*, Dublin: Stationery Office.

Central Statistics Office, *Statistical Abstract,* various years, Dublin: Stationery Office.

Central Statistics Office, *Statistical Bulletin,* various issues, Dublin: Stationery Office.

Chamberlin, E.H. (1933): *The Theory of Monopolistic Competition,* Harvard.

Chard, J.D. (1980): "The Economics of Exclusive Distributorship Arrangements with Special Reference to EEC Competition Policy", *Antitrust Bulletin,* 25(2) (Summer): 405–36.

Clarke, J.M. (1940): Toward a Concept of Workable Competition, *American Economic Review,* 30 (June): 241–56.

Clarke, R. (1985): *Industrial Economics,* Oxford: Blackwell.

Coase, R.H. (1937): The Nature of the Firm, *Economica,* 4: 386–405.

Competition Act, 1991, Dublin: Stationery Office.

Competition Authority, various years: *Annual Report,* Dublin: Stationery Office.

Competition Authority (1992): *Report of investigation of the proposal whereby Independent Newspapers plc would increase its shareholdings in the Tribune Group from 29.9% to a possible 53.09%,* Dublin: Stationery Office.

Competition Authority (1995): *Interim Report of Study of the Newspaper Industry,* Dublin: Department of Enterprise and Employment.

Conroy, J.C. (1928): *A History of the Railways in Ireland,* Dublin: Longman Green.

Cournot, A.A. (1838): *Researches into the Mathematical Principles of the Theory of Wealth,* translated by N.T. Bacon (1927), New York: Macmillan.

Craswell, R. and Fratrik, C. (1986): "Predatory Price Theory Applied: The Case of Supermarkets vs. Warehouse Stores, *Case Western Reserve Law Review,* 36(1).

Crocombe, G.T., Enright, M.J. and Porter, M.E. (1991): *Upgrading New Zealand's Competitive Advantage,* Auckland, NZ: Oxford University Press.

Culliton, J. (1992): *A Time for Change: Industrial Policy for the 1990s,* Report of the Industrial Policy Review Group, Dublin: Stationery Office.

Danish Competition Council (1992): *Annual Report, 1991/92.*

Demsetz, H. (1968): "Competition for a Market: Why Regulate Utilities?", *Journal of Law and Economics,* 11 (April): 55–65.

Department of the Environment, *Annual Bulletin of Housing Statistics,* various issues, Dublin: Stationery Office.

Dews, S. (1995): "Baumol-Willig Rules — No Way", *Australian Communications,* March: 65–6.

Dick, R.P. (1994): *Antitrust Enforcement and Vertical Restraints,* US Department of Justice, Antitrust Division, *mimeo.*

Director of Consumer Affairs (DCA), *Annual Reports,* various years.

DKM (1984): *The Control of Banking in the Republic of Ireland,* DKM, Dublin.

Douglas, R.O. (1993): *Unfinished Business,* Auckland, NZ: Random House.

Dym, H. and Sussman, R.M. (1983): "Antitrust and Electricity Utility Regulation", *Antitrust Bulletin*, 28(1), (Spring): 69–100.

Edgeworth, F.Y. (1897): "The Pure Theory of Monopoly" in Edgeworth, F.Y. (ed.), *Papers Relating to Political Economy*, London: Macmillan.

Electricity Task Force (1989): *Structure, Regulation and Ownership of the Electricity Industry,* Wellington, NZ: Government Printer.

Ellig, J. (1992): Untwisting the Strands of Chicago Antitrust, *Antitrust Bulletin,* 37(4) (Winter): 863–79.

Employment through Enterprise: The Response of the Government to the Moriarty Task Force on the Implementation of the Culliton Report (1993): Dublin: Stationery Office,

Ergas, H. (1995): *Access and Interconnection in Public Utilities*, Centre for Research in Network Economics and Communications, University of Auckland, *mimeo.*

ESB, various years, Annual Reports.

European Commission (1980): *Xth Report on Competition Policy*, Brussels: EU Commission.

European Commission (1989): *Competition Law in the European Communities*, Volumes 1 and 2, Brussels: EU Commission.

European Commission (1989): *(EEC) No. 4064/89 of 21 December 1989 on the Control of Concentrations between Undertakings*, OJ L257/13, Brussels.

European Commission (1995): *Competition Policy Newsletter*, 1(5) (Summer), Brussels.

European Commission (1996): *Competition Policy Newsletter*, 2(1) (Spring), Brussels.

Fairburn, J. and Kay, J.A. (eds.) (1989): *Mergers and Merger Policy,* Oxford: Oxford University Press.

Fair Trade Commission (FTC) (1956): *Report of Enquiry into the Conditions which Obtain in Regard to the Supply and Distribution of Grocery Goods and Provisions,* Pr. 3722, Dublin: Stationery Office.

Fair Trade Commission (FTC) (1972): *Report of Enquiry into the Conditions which Obtain in Regard to the Supply and Distribution of Grocery Goods for Human Consumption,* Prl. 2517, Dublin: Stationery Office.

Fair Trade Commission (FTC) (1990): *Report of Study into Restrictive Practices in the Legal Profession,* Dublin: Stationery Office.

Fair Trade Commission (FTC) (1991a): *Study of Competition Law,* Dublin: Stationery Office.

Fair Trade Commission (FTC) (1991b): *Report of Review of Restrictive Practices (Groceries) Order, 1987,* Dublin: Stationery Office.

Fair Trade Commission (FTC) (1991c): *EEC Policy on Competition — A Guide for Irish Business,* 4th ed., Dublin: Stationery Office, Pl 8783.

Fair Trade Commission (FTC) (1992): *A Guide to Irish Legislation on Competition,* PL. 9199, Dublin: Stationery Office.

Ferrands, C. and Totterdill, P. (1993): "A Rationale for an Appropriate Level of Regulation in the European Community", in Sugden, R. (ed.), *Industrial Economic Regulation: A Framework and Exploration,* London: Routledge.

Fingleton, J. (1995): "Competition and Efficiency in the Services Sector" in O'Hagan, J. (ed.), *The Irish Economy: Policy and Performance,* London: Macmillan.

Fitzgerald, J. and Johnston, J. (1995): *Restructuring Irish Energy Utilities,* ESRI, *mimeo.*

Fogt, H.W. and Gotts, I.K. (1995): "US Technology Licensing Arrangements: Do New Enforcement Guidelines in the United States Mirror Developments in the European Community?", 4 *European Community Law Review*: 215

Folsom, R.H. (1990): "State Antitrust Remedies: Lessons from the Laboratories", *Antitrust Bulletin,* 35(4) (Winter): 941–83.

Foreman-Peck, J. (1983): *A History of the World Economy: International Economic Relations Since 1850,* Brighton: Wheatsheaf Books.

Forfás (1996): *Shaping Our Future — A Strategy for Enterprise in Ireland in the 21st Century,* Dublin: Forfás.

Foster, C.D. (1993): *Privatisation, Public Ownership and the Regulation of Natural Monopoly,* Blackwell: Oxford.

Foster, C.D (1994): *Natural Justice and the Process of Natural Monopoly Regulation,* London: Chartered Institute of Public Finance and Accountancy.

Galbraith, J.K. (1970): "Economics in the Industrial State: Science and Sedative", *American Economic Review,* Papers and Proceedings of the 82nd annual meeting of the American Economics Association: 469–78.

Galbraith, J.K. (1987): *A History of Economics: The Past as the Present*, London: Penguin.

Gavil, A.I. (1994): "Attitudinal Discretion and the Prospects for Reinvigorating Antitrust: A Look at the New Federal Rules", *Antitrust Bulletin,* 39(1) (Spring): 27–57.

George, K. and Jacquemin, A. (1992): "Dominant Firms and Mergers", *Economic Journal,* 102 (January): 148–57.

Geroski, P.A. (1994): "Entry and Market Share Mobility" in Cable, J. (ed.), *Current Issues in Industrial Economics*, London: Macmillan.

Geroski, P.A. and Jacquemin, A. (1985): "Industrial Change, Barriers to Mobility and European Industrial Policy, *Economic Policy,* 1(November): 169–218.

Green, R. (1995): *Competition in the British Electricity Industry*, Economic and Social Research Institute, *mimeo.*

Guiomard, C. (1995): *The Irish Disease and How to Cure It*, Dublin: Oak Tree Press.

Hall, E.G. (1993): *The Electronic Age: Telecommunications in Ireland*, Dublin, Oak Tree Press.

Hardach, K. (1975): "Germany 1914–1970" in Cipolla, C.M. (ed.), *The Fontana Economic History of Europe*, 6(1): 180–265, Glasgow, Collins/Fontana,

Hawke, B. and Huser, H. (1993): "A Bright Line Shareholding Test to End the Nightmare under the EEC Merger Regulation." *CMLR,* 30, 1155–1183.

Hayek, F. (1957): *Individualism and Economic Order*, London: Routledge and Keegan Paul.

Henney, A. (1994): *A Study of the Privatisation of the Electricity Supply Industry in England and Wales*, London: EEE Ltd.

Hicks, J.R. (1935): "Annual Survey of Economic Theory: The Theory of Monopoly", *Econometrica,* 3 (January): 1–20.

Hilmer, F.G. (1993): *National Competition Policy: Report by the Independent Committee of Inquiry*, Canberra: Australian Government Publishing Service.

Hocepied, C. (1996): "Telecoms Sector Soon Fully Open to Competition: The Central Role of the European Commission", *EU Commission Competition Policy Newsletter,* 2(1) (Spring): 13–17.

Hogan, G. (1989): "The Need for a New Domestic Competition Law", *Irish Banking Review* (Winter): 34–44.

Hogan, G. and Morgan, D.G. (1991): *Administrative Law in Ireland*, London: Sweet and Maxwell.

Horowitz, I. (1981): "Market Definition in Antitrust Analysis: A Regression-based Approach", *Southern Economics Journal*, 48 (January): 1–16.

Hopper, W.J. and Sharpe, T.A.E. (1983): "Competition Policy of the European Communities", *The Three Banks Review*, 140: 38–45, Royal Bank of Scotland Group.

Howe, M. (1995): *Mergers: A Fix it First Approach*, OFT, *mimeo.*

IPA (1994): *IPA Yearbook,* Dublin, Institute of Public Administration.

Jakee, K. and Allen, L. (1995): "Destructive Competition or Competition Destroyed? A History of Irish Transportation Legislation in light of Regulatory Theory, Economic Performance and Economic Rhetoric", Irish Economics Association*, mimeo.*

Jakobsen, E.L. (1984): *Report of the Inquiry into Electricity Prices,* Department of Energy, Dublin: Stationery Office.

Jorberg, L. (1975): "The Industrial Revolution in the Nordic Countries", in Cipolla, C.M. (ed.), *The Fontana Economic History of Europe,* 4(2): 375–485, Glasgow: Collins/Fontana.

Kaserman, D. and Mayo, J. (1991): "The Measurement of Vertical Economies and the Efficient Structure of the Electric Utility Business", *Journal of Industrial Economics,* 39: 483–502.

Kaufman, G.G. (1986): "Banking Deregulation in the United States, *Irish Banking Review*, (Autumn): 66–87.

Kay, J.A. and Thompson, D.J. (1986): "Privatisation: A Policy in Search of a Rationale", *Economic Journal,* 96 (March): 18–32.

Kennedy, K.A. (1960): *Competition and the Fair Trade Commission*, unpublished MA thesis, University College Dublin.

Kennedy, K.A. and Bruton, R. (1975): *The Irish Economy*, Studies, No. 10, Brussels: EC Commission.

Kilvington, R.P. (1985): *Lessons of the 1980 Transport Act,* Oxford, Transport Studies Unit, *mimeo.*

Kingston, W. (1987): "A Patent System to Suit Ireland?", *Irish Banking Review*, (Autumn): 21–30

Kinsella, R.P. (1988): Financial Regulation: A New Approach, *Irish Banking Review*, (Spring): 3–21.

Kinsella, R.P. (1992): *The Medium Term Development of Indigenous Industry: The Role of the Financial Sector,* A Report to the Industrial Policy Review Group, Dublin: Stationery Office.

Korah, V. (1990a): *An Introductory Guide to EEC Competition Law and Practice*, Oxford: ESC publishing.

Korah, V. (1990b) "From Legal Form Toward Economic Efficiency — Article 85(1) of the EEC Treaty in Contrast to US Antitrust.", *Antitrust Bulletin* 35(4) (Winter): 1,009–34.

Korah, V. (1994): "Articles 90 and 86 of the EEC Treaty", Conference of Irish Society for European Law, 2 July, *mimeo*.

Kramer, V.H. (1991): "Legislating Fair Trade by Foul Means (1937–1939)", *Antitrust Bulletin,* 36(1) (Spring): 81–90.

Krugmann, P. (1994): *Peddling Prosperity: Economic Sense and Nonsense in the Age of Diminished Expectations,* New York: Norton.

Lande, R. (1994): "Beyond Chicago: Will Activist Antitrust Arise Again?", *Antitrust Bulletin,* 39(1), (Spring): 1–16.

Landon, J.H. (1983): "Theories of Vertical Integration and their Application to the Electric Utility Industry", *Antitrust Bulletin,* 28(1), (Spring): 101–30.

Langenfeld, J.A. and Morris, J.R. (1991): "Analyzing Agreements Among Competitors: What Does the Future Hold", *Antitrust Bulletin,* 36(3) (Fall): 651–79.

Lawson, N. (1992): "Side Effects of Deregulation", *Financial Times,* 27 January.

Leibenstein, H. (1966): "Allocative Efficiency vs. X-Inefficiency", *American Economic Review,* 56: 392–415.

Leddin, A. and Walsh, B.M. (1990): *The Macroeconomy of Ireland,* Dublin: Gill and Macmillan.

Leung, S. (1989): *Financial Liberalization in Australia and New Zealand,* Australian National University, Centre for Economic Policy Research, Canberra, Discussion Paper No. 208.

Littlechild, S.C. (1983): *Regulation of British Telecommunications Profitability*, London: HMSO.

Littlechild, S.C (1986): *Economic Regulation of Privatised Water Authorities*, London: HMSO.

Llewellyn, D.T. (1986): Financial Deregulation — The British Experience, *Irish Banking Review* (Autumn): 55–65.

Lord Chancellor's Department (1989): *Report on The Work and Organisation of the Legal Profession,* CM 570, London: HMSO.

Lynk, E.L. (1993): *Evaluating Prices and Profitability Under Price-Cap Regulation: A Study of Telecommunications*, London: Chartered Institute of Public Finance and Accountancy.

McDowell, M (1995): "Effective Criminal Penalties Require More Amendments and Debate", *Competition* 4(10): 260–62.

McGowan, P. (1986a): "Competition in Irish Banking", *Irish Banking Review* (Autumn): 27–40.

McGowan, P. (1986b): "Innovation in Irish Banking", *Irish Banking Review* (Autumn): 41–54.

McGowan, P. (1988): "Money and Banking in Ireland: Origins, Development and Future", *Journal of the Statistical and Social Inquiry Society of Ireland*, 36(1), 1988/89: 45–132.

Magenheim, E.P. and Mueller, D.C. (1988): "Are Acquiring Firm Shareholders Better Off After an Acquisition", in Coffee, J. Lowenstein, L. and Rose-Ackerman, S. (eds.), *Knights, Raiders and Targets: The Impact of the Hostile Takeover,* New York: Oxford University Press.

Mason, E. (1939): "Prices and Production Policies of Large-Scale Enterprise", *American Economic Review,* Supp. 29: 61–74.

Massey, P. (1984): "The Role of Building Societies in Irish Financial Markets", *Irish Banking Review*, March: 6–17.

Massey, P. (1994): "Should Irish Taxis Compete?" in McNutt, P. (ed.), *Perspectives on Competition Policy Issues: Ireland and the European Community*, Belfast: Centre in Economics and Law, University of Ulster.

Massey, P. (1995): *New Zealand: Market Liberalization in a Developed Economy*, Macmillan: London.

Massey, P. and O'Hare, P. (1996): "Competition and Regulatory Reform in Energy and Telecommunications", *Journal of the Statistical and Social Inquiry Society of Ireland,* 1995/96, forthcoming.

Meeks, G. (1977): *Disappointing Marriage: A Study of the Gains from Merger,* Cambridge: Cambridge University Press.

Meenan, J. (1970): *The Irish Economy since 1922,* Liverpool: Liverpool University Press.

Milbourne, R. and Cumberworth, M. (1990): *Australian Banking Performance in an Era of De-regulation: An Untold Story,* School of Economics, University of New South Wales, *mimeo.*

Milgrom, P. and Roberts, J. (1982): "Limit Pricing and Entry with Incomplete Information: An Equilibrium Analysis", *Econometrica*, 50: 443–60.

Mill, J.S. (1848): *Principles of Political Economy: Books IV and V,* London: Penguin 1985 paperback edition.

Ministry of Transport (1991): *Taxi Industry — Progress Report,* Wellington: Ministry of Transport.

Monopolies and Mergers Commission (1973): *A Report on the General Effect on the Public Interest of the Practice of Parallel Pricing*, London: HMSO.

Moore, T. (1961): "The Purpose of Licensing", *Journal of Law and Economics,* 93: 103–117.

Mulgan, G. and Briscoe, I. (1995): *The Society of Networks: A new model for the information superhighway and the communications supermarket,* London: Demos.

Murphy, K. (1994): *Mergers and Acquisitions and Irish Competition Law — A Practical Guide through the Maze,* Irish Centre for Commercial Law, *mimeo.*

Murray, B. (1993): "The Right to Silence and Corporate Crime" in Whelan, A. (ed.), *Law and Liberty in Ireland,* Dublin: Oak Tree Press.

Murray, C. (1980): "Monetary Policy", *Central Bank of Ireland Annual Report*: 110–117.

Nathan, A. and Neave, E. (1989) "Competition and Contestability in Canada's Financial System: Empirical Results", *Canadian Journal of Economics*, 22(3): 576–94.

National Economic and Social Forum (1995): *Jobs Potential of the Services Sector,* Forum Report No. 7, Dublin: National Economic and Social Forum.

National Planning Board (1984): *Proposals for a Plan,* Dublin: Stationery Office.

National Prices Commission (1972a): *Bus Services in Ireland,* NPC, Occasional Paper No. 10.

National Prices Commission (1972b): *The Price of Drink,* NPC, Occasional Paper No. 3.

National Utility Services (1995): *International Telecommunications Price Survey*, London: NUS.

Neumark, D. and Sharpe, S. (1992): "Market Structure and the Nature of Price Rigidity: Evidence from the Market for Consumer Deposits", *Quarterly Journal of Economics*, 57(2) (May): 657–80.

Noether, M. (1986): "The Effect of Government Policy Changes on the Supply of Physicians: Expansion of a Competitive Fringe, *Journal of Law and Economics*, 29: 231–62.

OECD (1992): *Regulatory Reform, Privatisation and Competition Policy*, Paris: OECD.

OECD (1993a): *Economic Survey Ireland*, Paris: OECD.

OECD (1993b): *Communications Outlook*, Paris: OECD.

OECD (1995): *Telecommunications Infrastructure: The Benefits of Competition*, Paris: OECD.

OFFER (1995): *The Transmission Price Control Review of the National Grid Company*, London: Office of Electricity Regulation.

OFTEL (1994): *A Framework for Effective Competition*, London: OFTEL.

OFTEL (1995): *Effective Competition: Framework for Action*, London: OFTEL.

OG/CC (1946): *Official Gazette, Control Council for Germany*, Supplement No. 1, 30 April.

Ordover, J. and Baumol, W.J. (1988): "Antitrust Policy and High Technology Industries", *Oxford Review of Economic Policy*, 4(4) (Winter): 13–34.

Peltzman, S. (1989): "The Economic Theory of Regulation after a Decade of Deregulation", *Brookings Papers on Economic Activity*, 1989: 1–55.

Pigou, A.C. (1924): *The Economics of Welfare*, London: Macmillan.

Porter, M.E. (1990): *The Competitive Advantage of Nations*, London: Macmillan.

Posner, R.A. (1970): "A Statistical Study of Antitrust Enforcement", *Journal of Law and Economics*, 13: 365–419.

Posner, R.A. (1975): "The Social Costs of Monopoly and Regulation", *Journal of Political Economy*, 83: 807–27.

Posner, R.A. (1977): *Economic Analysis of Law*, 2nd edition, Boston: Little Brown.

Posner, R.A. (1979): "The Chicago School of Antitrust Analysis", *University of Pennsylvania Law Review*, 127:

Ravenscraft, D.J. and Scherer, F.M. (1987): *Mergers, Sell-Offs and Economic Efficiency*, Washington: Brookings Institute.

Rees, R. (1993): "Collusive Equilibrium in the Great Salt Duopoly", *Economic Journal,* 103: 838–48.

Report of the Committee of Enquiry into the Road Haulage Industry (1965): London: HMSO.

Report of the Interdepartmental Committee to Review the Operation of Small Public Service Vehicles (1991): Dublin: Stationery Office.

Report of Posts and Telegraphs Review Group 1978–1979 (1979): Prl. 7883, Dublin: Stationery Office.

Reserve Bank of New Zealand (1986): *Financial Policy Reform,* Wellington: Reserve Bank.

Restrictive Practices (Amendment) Act, Dublin, Stationery Office.

Restrictive Practices Commission (RPC) (1965): *Report of Enquiry into the Licensed Drinks Trade,* Dublin: Stationery Office.

Restrictive Practices Commission (RPC) (1977): *Report of Study of Competition in the Licensed Drinks Trade,* Dublin: Stationery Office.

Restrictive Practices Commission (RPC) (1980): *Report of Enquiry into the Retail Sale of Grocery Goods Below Cost,* Prl. 9428, Dublin: Stationery Office.

Restrictive Practices Commission (RPC) (1982): *Report of Enquiry into the Effects on Competition of the Restrictions on Conveyancing and the Restrictions on Advertising by Solicitors,* Pl. 902, Dublin: Stationery Office.

Restrictive Practices Commission (RPC) (1987a): *Report of Study into Concerted Fixing of Fees and Restrictions on Advertising in the Accountancy Profession,* Dublin: Stationery Office.

Restrictive Practices Commission (RPC) (1987b): *Report of Study into Concerted Fixing of Fees and Restrictions on Advertising in the Engineering Profession,* Dublin: Stationery Office.

Restrictive Practices Commission (RPC) (1987c): *Report of Review of Restrictive Practices (Groceries) Order, 1981,* Pl. 4678, Dublin: Stationery Office.

Rey, L. (1995): "Competition Comes to Mexican Telecoms", *OECD Observer,* 194 (June/July): 26–29.

Road Transport Act, 1932, Dublin: Stationery Office.

Road Transport Act, 1933, Dublin: Stationery Office.

Robinson, J. (1934): *The Economics of Imperfect Competition,* London: Macmillan.

Ross, T.W. (1991): Proposals For a New Canadian Competition Law on Conspiracy, *Antitrust Bulletin*, 36: 851–82.

Rothnie, W.A. (1993): *Parallel Imports*, London: Sweet and Maxwell.

Ruane, J. (1987): "Changes in the Financial Services Marketplace", *Irish Banking Review*, (Spring): 15–28.

Schaub, A. (1996): "Competition Policy in the Telecoms Sector", *EU Commission Competition Policy Newsletter*, 2(1) (Spring): 1–7.

Scherer, F.M. (1981): "Comments on Patents, Sleeping Patents and Entry Deference" in Salop, S. (ed.) *Strategy, Predation and Antitrust Analysis*, Washington: FTC.

Scherer, F.M. and Ross, D. (1990): *Industrial Market Structure and Economic Performance*, New York: Houghton-Mifflin, 3rd edition.

Schick, M. (1993): "Nationalization and the Background to Recent Regulatory Issues" in Sugden, R. (ed.), *Industrial Economic Regulation: A Framework and Exploration*, London: Routledge.

Schmalensee, R. (1978): "Entry Deterrence in the Ready-to-Eat Breakfast Cereal Industry, *Bell Journal of Economics*, 9: 305–27.

Schmalensee, R. (1982): "Product Differentiation: Advantages of Pioneering Brands", *American Economic Review*, 72: 349–65.

Schrank, W. and Roy, N. (1991): "Market Delineation in the Analysis of United States Groundfish Market", *The Antitrust Bulletin*, 36(1) (Spring): 91–154.

Schumpeter, J.A. (1942): *Capitalism, Socialism and Democracy*, New York: Harper.

Schwartz, M. (1986): "The Nature and Scope of Contestability Theory" in Morris, D.J., Sinclair, P.J.N., Slater, M.D.E. and Vickers, J.S. (eds.); *Strategic Behaviour and Industrial Competition*, Oxford: Clarendon Press.

Scott, S. and Convery, F. (1990): "Energy and Privatisation in Ireland in Convery, F. and McDowell, M. (eds.), *Privatisation: Issues of Principle and Implementation in Ireland*, Dublin: Gill and Macmillan.

Shenefield, J.H. and Stelzer, I.M. (1993): *The Antitrust Laws: A Primer*, Washington: AEI Press.

Shepherd, W.G. (1982): "Causes of Increased Competition in the US Economy, 1939–80", *Review of Economics and Statistics*, 64 (November): 613–26.

Shepherd, W.G. (1990): "Section 2 and the Problem of Market Dominance", *Antitrust Bulletin,* 35(4) (Winter): 833–78.

Shepherd, W.G. (1994): "Antitrust Repelled, Inefficiency Endured: Lessons of IBM and General Motors for Future Antitrust Policies", *Antitrust Bulletin,* 39(1) (Spring): 203–34.

Shinnick, E. (1996): "A Survey of Solicitors' Conveyancing Fees", UCC Department of Economics, Working Paper No. 96/1.

Short, J. (1985): *Aspects of Freight Transport in Ireland,* Dublin: Economic and Social Research Institute.

Siegfried, J.J. and Mahoney, M. (1990): "The First Sherman Act Case: *Jellico Mountain Coal, 1891",* *Antitrust Bulletin,* 35(4) (Winter): 801–32.

Singh, A. (1993): "Regulation of Mergers: A New Agenda", in Sugden, R. (ed.), *Industrial Economic Regulation: A Framework and Exploration,* London: Routledge.

Smith, A. (1776): *The Wealth of Nations,* London: Penguin 1985 paperback edition.

Spencer, G. and Carey, D. (1988): "Financial Policy Reform — The New Zealand Experience, 1984–87", Wellington: Reserve Bank of New Zealand, Discussion Paper, G88/1.

Spicer, B., Bowman, R., Emmanuel, D. and Hunt, A. (1991): *The Power to Manage: Restructuring the New Zealand Electricity Department as a State Owned Enterprise — The Electicorp Experience,* Oxford: Oxford University Press.

Spring, P. (1992): *An Investigation of RPI-X Price Cap Regulation Using British Gas as a Case Study,* London: Chartered Institute of Public Finance and Accountancy.

Steiner, R.L. (1991): "Intrabrand Competition — Stepchild of Antitrust", *Antitrust Bulletin,* 36(1) (Spring): 155–200.

Stern, J (1992): *Third Party Access in European Gas Industries,* London: Royal Institute of International Affairs.

Stigler, G.J. (1952): "The Case Against Big Business", *Fortune,* May.

Stigler, G.J. (1975): *The Citizen and the State: Essays on Regulation,* Chicago: Chicago University Press.

Stigler, G.J. and Friedland, C. (1962): "What Can Regulators Regulate? The Case of Electricity", *Journal of Law and Economics,* 5: 1–19.

Stiglitz, J. (1990): *Economics of the Public Sector,* New York: Norton.

Stockmann, K. and Strauch, V. (1984): *World Law of Competition, Vol. 5 Federal Republic of Germany,* New York: Mathew Bender.

Swedish Competition Authority (1995): *Annual Report 1994.*

Swedish Competition Authority, *Deregulation of the Taxi Industry in Sweden, mimeo.*

Telecom Éireann, various years, *Annual Reports.*

Tellis, G. and Golder, P. (1996): "First to Market First to Fail? Real Causes of Enduring Market Leadership", *Sloane Management Review*, 37(2).

Temple Lang, J. (1991): *Effects of European Competition Law on National Competition Cases,* Irish Centre for European Law, Trinity College, Dublin, *mimeo.*

Third Programme for Economic and Social Development 1969–1972 (1969): Dublin: Stationery Office, Prl. 431.

Thom, R. (1984): *Financial Deregulation and the Building Societies,* Dublin Economics Workshop, *mimeo.*

Tirole, J. (1988): *The Theory of Industrial Organisation,* Cambridge, MA: MIT Press.

Trans Power Establishment Board (1991): *The Separation of Trans power: A Report to the Minister for State-Owned Enterprises,* Wellington: Trans Power Establishment Board.

Treasury and Ministry of Commerce (1995): *Regulation of Access to Vertically-Integrated Natural Monopolies,* Wellington: Treasury/ Ministry of Commerce.

Treitel, G.H. (1988): *The Law of Contract,* London: Stevens.

Turner, K. (1989); "The Electricorp Experience", *Public Sector,* 12(2): 3–5.

United States Army (1949): *Special Committee to Study Decartelization and Deconcentration in Germany, Report to the Honourable Secretary to the Army.*

United States Department of Justice (1985): *Vertical Restraints Guidelines,* Washington: US Department of Justice.

United States Department of Justice (1994): *Antitrust Division Annual Report for Fiscal Year 1994,* Washington: US Department of Justice.

United States Department of Transportation (1984): *Regulatory Impediments to Private Sector Urban Transit*, Washington: US Department of Transportation.

United States Federal Trade Commission (1989): *Submission to Hearing Examiner*, Boston: Department of Public Utilities, *mimeo*.

Walsh, J. (1974): "Restrictive Business Practices in Ireland: Legislation and Administration", *Antitrust Bulletin*, 19(4) (Winter): 803–50.

Walsh, M. (1987): *Building Societies. Their Future Role*, Dublin Economics Workshop, *mimeo*.

Walsh, M. (1988): "Perspectives on Irish Financial Markets", *Irish Banking Review*, (Spring): 22–37.

Walsh, P. and Whelan, C. (1996): *The Optimality of Loss Leading in Multi-Product Retail Pricing — A Rationale for Repealing the 1987 Groceries Order in Ireland*, Trinity Economic Papers No. 96/1, Dublin: Trinity College.

Werden, G.J. and Simon, M (1987): "Why Price-Fixers Should Go To Jail", *Antitrust Bulletin,* 24(4) (Winter): 917–37.

Whelan, C. (1995): *Competition Policy and the Groceries Order*, TCD, Department of Economics, *mimeo*.

Whish, R. (1993): *Competition Law*, 3rd edition London: Butterworths.

Whish, R. and Wood, D. (1994): *Merger Cases in the Real World: A Study of Merger Control Procedures*, Paris: OECD.

White, L.J. (1993): "Competition Policy in the United States: An Overview", *Oxford Review of Economic Policy*, 9(2): 133

Wholesale Electricity Market Development Group (1994): *New Zealand Wholesale Electricity Market*, Wellington: Government Printer.

Wiedenfeld, K. (1927): *Cartels and Combines*, Geneva: League of Nations.

Williamson, O.E. (1968): "Economies as an Anti-trust Defence: The Welfare Trade-offs", *American Economic Review,* 58: 18–36.

Willig, R.D. (1979): "The Theory of Network Access Pricing" in Trebing, H.M. (ed.), *Issues in Public Utility Regulation,* Michigan State University Public Utility Papers.

Ysewyn, S. (1995): "Uncertainty Relating to Merger Notification Requirements under Belgian Competition Law, *European Competition Law Review,* 16(2): 323–7

INDEX